Horses

3rd Edition

by Audrey Pavia
with Janice Posnikoff, DVM

for
dummies®
A Wiley Brand

Horses For Dummies®, 3rd Edition

Published by: **John Wiley & Sons, Inc.**, 111 River Street, Hoboken, NJ 07030-5774, www.wiley.com

Copyright © 2020 by John Wiley & Sons, Inc., Hoboken, New Jersey

Published simultaneously in Canada

For general information on our other products and services, please contact our Customer Care Department within the U.S. at 877-762-2974, outside the U.S. at 317-572-3993, or fax 317-572-4002. For technical support, please visit https://hub.wiley.com/community/support/dummies.

Wiley publishes in a variety of print and electronic formats and by print-on-demand. Some material included with standard print versions of this book may not be included in e-books or in print-on-demand. If this book refers to media such as a CD or DVD that is not included in the version you purchased, you may download this material at http://booksupport.wiley.com. For more information about Wiley products, visit www.wiley.com.

Library of Congress Control Number: 2019952062

ISBN 978-1-119-58940-2 (pbk); ISBN 978-1-119-58955-6 (ebk); ISBN 978-1-119-58950-1 (ebk)

Manufactured in the United States of America

C10014669_101419

Contents at a Glance

Table of Contents

Introduction

Welcome to the third edition of *Horses For Dummies*, the one and only book you need to get started in the hobby of horses.

Why do you need a book on horses? If you want to ride, can't you just climb up on a horse and hit the trail? What's so complicated about letting a horse carry you around on his back, anyway?

The truth of the matter is that as simple as riding may seem, it's anything but. Here's why: With most other hobbies, your main component is something rather undynamic. For example, the racket and ball you use to play tennis, or the clubs and balls you require for golf. Without human energy to put these pieces into motion, they're nothing but unfeeling, unmoving, inanimate objects.

Horseback riding, on the other hand, relies crucially on something that is hardly passive in the process: the horse. Horses have the ability to operate on their own — they don't need a human to set them in motion. This fact is not only true of the equine body, but it's especially true of the equine mind.

So why *do* you need this book? Because we can help you understand the horse and how it functions, both physically and mentally. Because we can show you how to communicate what you want to a horse so he'll do your bidding. And because we can show you how to care for this amazing creature, which, by the way, needs much more maintenance than your average set of golf clubs!

After you're comfortable with the basics of horsemanship, you'll likely be hooked on horses for good. Then you'll be hungry to explore the world of horses in even greater depth. But to get acquainted with things equine, you've come to the right place. Whether you're contemplating riding a horse for the first time in your life, thinking about adding riding to your list of hobbies, or wondering how to care for your first horse, we're certain this book will be a great help you.

About This Book

We've designed the third edition of *Horses For Dummies* to be a useful reference for beginning horse people. You can turn to any section of the book that interests you and begin reading at that point — and not feel lost. You don't have to remember what you read yesterday, and you don't have to read chapters or sections in order. Just find something that interests you, read it, do it, and put the book back on your shelf. We don't expect you to read it from cover to cover.

If *Horses For Dummies* were a building, it would be a department store that you can enter on whatever floor you like. You don't have to walk past that smelly perfume counter to get to the housewares section on the third floor. You just walk into the housewares section.

Of course, you can feel free to read this book from cover to cover to avoid missing one pearl of horse wisdom (or horse sense) that we've painstakingly compiled for you. You won't hear us say nay to that!

We've worked long and hard to bring you what we think is the consummate beginner's reference book on horses, and we hope that you find it as fun to read as we found it to write. We also hope that you take all of our advice and thank us for the rest of eternity for all the equine wisdom we've brought you.

Seriously, though, we've found great joy, comfort, and fulfillment in our personal involvement with horses, and we hope for you the same kind of experience. We're certain that once you dive deep into the ocean of horseness, you'll never try to make it to shore.

By the way, in this book, we refer to horses with the male pronoun (he, his, and him). We understand that horses aren't all male, and we don't prefer male horses to female horses particularly (coauthor Audrey Pavia is actually partial to mares). This convention is merely for readability's sake. We don't call horses "it" (not *our* horses!), and using both sexes ("his or her," "he or she," and so on) makes the text hard to read. So we flipped a coin: It came up heads he.

From time to time in this book, we tell you stuff that may be nice to know, but isn't essential to understanding the topic. In these cases, we place the text in a gray box that we call a sidebar. Don't feel like you have to read these, but they're usually kind of interesting, nonetheless.

Foolish Assumptions

In this book, we assume that you know a horse when you see one. That's really about all we assume. Well, we do assume that you're interested in these magnificent creatures and that you want to treat them kindly. You may be considering buying a horse or learning how to ride one, or perhaps you're currently a horse owner and/or rider and would like to find out more about these wonderful animals.

We also assume that you're no dummy. You may not be an expert in the horse field, but you're not one to go around pretending that you are. You know that the best way to find out about things is to read up, ask questions of those who've been around the block, and keep your eyes open. We think you're pretty smart; after all, you bought this book, didn't you?

Icons Used in This Book

As with all the other books in the *For Dummies* series, this book has little icons in the margins that call your attention to specific types of information. Here's an explanation of what each of those icons means:

REMEMBER

This icon appears frequently throughout this book. That's because when it comes to horses, you need to do plenty of remembering. We've placed this icon next to information that we think is important and shouldn't be missed or forgotten.

TIP

This icon alerts you to helpful hints regarding horses, pertaining to their care and handling. If you read the information so highlighted in this book, you'll find your life around horses much easier.

WARNING

When you see this symbol, beware! It indicates something serious to watch out for.

Beyond the Book

This book comes with a free online Cheat Sheet with lots of useful information that you can access with your smart phone, tablet, or computer. Included on this Cheat Sheet is a huge listing of online equine resources, including breed registries, educational organizations, rescue groups, pet loss hotlines, equine activity organizations, and more. To get the Cheat Sheet, simply go to www.dummies.com and type "Horses For Dummies Cheat Sheet" in the Search box.

Where to Go from Here

Go wherever you want. You can start at Chapter 1 and read all the way through to the end. Or you can skip here and skip there. Or you can go for a ride.

If you're going to do the skipping around thing, though, can we at least ask you to do us a favor? Before you start jumping from place to place, take a few moments to read through Chapter 2, which gives you insights into the equine mind. These issues are what *every* potential horseperson should know.

Go ahead! Start hoofin' it!

1
Beginning with Horse Basics

Discovering the basic information you need to know about horses

Understanding how the equine mind works and getting pointers on how to communicate effectively with horses

Getting to know a variety of popular horse breeds and figuring out how to pick the best one for you

Chapter **1**

Welcome to the World of Horses

I t's hard to find a person alive and breathing who doesn't have a strong reaction to horses. Most people love their power and grace; some find them soulful and irresistible; others find them scary and intimidating. Regardless of whether their response to horses is positive or negative, most people can't help but have an opinion about these dramatic creatures.

What is it about horses that elicits such intense reactions in people? The more thoughtful among equiphiles have pondered this for ages. Perhaps their combination of power and grace is what intrigues people. Or their sheer mass and speed may attract others. Some — such as Audrey Pavia, your humble, nonvet coauthor — believe the close connection between the human and equine races is an expression of genetic memory. After all, without the horse, many of our human ancestors would not have survived.

Although people no longer need horses to transport them from place to place, plow their fields, and carry them into war, they still need to understand them. Those of us who have chosen to live with these beautiful animals have an obligation to care for them properly and enjoy them for all they are worth. In this chapter, we introduce you to the wonderful world of horses.

Looking at a Horse's Build and Mind

You need to understand a horse's body and brain to appreciate what he is all about. In horses, the same as with other creatures, the two are closely linked. Horse people are obsessed with their horses' bodies because a horse's physical structure determines not only his appearance but also his ability to function with a rider.

Horse people have a lingo all their own when describing horses, and knowing this terminology is important for communicating effectively on the topic of horses. Each part of the horse's body has a name to describe it. Knowing the parts of the horse helps you understand and be understood by your horse's veterinarian, farrier (horseshoer), and horsy friends. People in the equine world also use specific language to describe a horse's measurements, colors, markings, and movements.

TIP

Chapter 2 has a diagram showing the parts of the horse. Before you embark on your new hobby, take a look at this diagram and memorize it. You'll be glad you did.

The horse's mind is just as important as his body because the brain controls everything the body does. When you're riding a horse, this reality becomes evident very quickly. Primitive ancestors of today's horses were seen as potential meals by a great many predators, and today's domestic horse has retained that information in his DNA. The consequence is that horses can be flighty, especially when they find themselves in unfamiliar surroundings or faced with an object or situation that makes them uncertain. The motto of just about every horse out there is "Run first, ask questions later." Knowing that motto is extremely important if you choose to sit on the back of one of these half-ton animals.

REMEMBER

Training and experience can override much of the horse's instincts to flee perceived danger, which is why it's so important to ride a horse that has had both — especially when you're a newcomer to horses. It's also imperative that you learn how to ride before you embark on any horseback sojourns, regardless of whether it's on a local trail or through the mountains of Mongolia. Knowing how to handle a horse can mean the difference between a wonderful, relaxing experience and one you'll spend your lifetime trying to forget.

To find out more about how the horse thinks, see Chapter 2.

Checking Out Various Horse Breeds

Horses, like dogs, come in a wide variety of breeds — more than 300 the world over, in fact. Some breeds have existed for centuries, while others were developed only during the last 20 years or so. Each breed has its own characteristics that make it unique, leaving horse people with a healthy selection of breeds to admire. Knowing a thing or two about the various breeds of horses helps you choose the right horse when the time comes for you to join the ranks of horse owners.

Although most horse breeds were developed in Europe and other parts of the world, a number of breeds are uniquely American. Among these is the world's most populous breed, the American Quarter Horse. In the nearly 70 years since this versatile breed officially was established in the U.S., it has spread to a number of other nations. The second most popular breed in the U.S. is the Paint Horse. A spinoff of the Quarter Horse, the colorful Paint's popularity has shot up to high numbers in the past 15 years.

Other breeds in the top 10 include the Appaloosa, Arabian, Miniature Horse, Morgan, Saddlebred, Standardbred, Tennessee Walking Horse, and Thoroughbred. Each breed has a distinct history and appearance and appeals to a vast number of horse lovers.

For more details on the top 10 breeds, see Chapter 3. That same chapter also provides information on some lesser-kept breeds such as the Peruvian Paso, the Friesian, the warmblood, and draft-horse and pony breeds.

Making a Match with the Perfect Horse

The choice you make in a horse to ride can make a huge difference in whether you come to love this hobby or dislike it. Choosing a horse is much like choosing a mate: If you pick the wrong one, you won't be happy.

Asking a few questions before you buy

Before you embark on the tremendous responsibility of horse ownership, make certain owning a horse is really what you want. Ask yourself some questions before you take the plunge:

>> Why do I want a horse?

>> Do I have the time and money for a horse?

>> How do I want to ride (English, Western, shows, on trail), and how do I want to learn the riding style of my choice?

>> Who will take care of the horse on a daily basis?

>> Might leasing be a better option than buying?

For more guidance on what to ask yourself and on other issues to consider before buying a horse, see Chapter 4.

Locating the right horse for you

REMEMBER

The single most crucial aspect to finding the right horse is getting the help of someone with experience. Without expert help, as a novice horse person, you're likely to make the wrong decisions about which horse is best suited for you.

Ideally, the person who helps you with your decision will be a *horse trainer*, someone who makes a living riding, training, and evaluating horses. If you can't find a horse trainer to help you, a riding instructor, an equine veterinarian, a farrier, or someone with years of horse experience under his or her belt is your best bet.

You'll find available horses in any number of outlets, including:

>> Classified ads from individuals in equine publications

>> On the Internet

>> Through trainers and breeders

>> At horse shows

>> Via horse adoption groups

For more details about shopping for a horse, see Chapter 5.

Purchasing horse supplies

After you purchase your own horse, you'll need all the accoutrements to go with him. There is no shortage of stuff out there that you can buy for your horse. For starters, you'll need these basics:

>> Saddle and pad

>> Bridle (the headgear used on a horse during riding)

- » Halter and lead rope (which provide control when you're working with your horse on the ground)
- » Grooming supplies

You'll also need some stuff for yourself:

- » Riding boots or shoes
- » Riding pants and shirt
- » A helmet (if you're smart and want to continue to be that way)

All these items can be purchased in your local tack and feed store, through mail-order catalogs or over the Internet, among other options. For more details on these and other items for you and your horse, see Chapter 6.

Housing your horse

Where to keep your horse is a primary concern. If you're like thousands of horse owners around the country who live in an urban or suburban community, a boarding stable is your only option. Choosing the right boarding stable for your horse is important because the place where he's kept will determine his health, his safety, and how much you enjoy of him.

When considering a boarding stable, look for the following:

- » Safe, sturdy accommodations
- » Clean, safe surroundings
- » Security
- » Water and quality feed
- » Good care
- » Health requirements
- » Riding facilities
- » Tack storage
- » Professional demeanor

But if you live on property zoned for horses and have or plan to build horse facilities, the answer is easy: You can keep your horse at home. You have the choice of housing your horse outdoors or indoors. In either case, you need to provide him with a safe enclosure and shelter from the elements. You're also responsible for feeding him every day and cleaning up after him.

TIP

If you don't have room on your property for a riding arena, you need access to a community arena or one belonging to a neighbor. Finding room to ride is especially important when you're new to horses because you need a place to ride where you feel safe and comfortable before you head out onto the trail.

For more details about boarding your horse or keeping him at home, see Chapter 7.

Taking Great Care of Your Horse

Cowboys in the movies make horse care look easy. After a long gallop, they jump off their horses and leave them standing in the street while they head to the saloon for some refreshments. In reality, horses need plenty of care to stay happy and healthy, and as a horse owner, you're the one to provide it.

Handling daily tasks

If you keep your horse at home, you'll be caring for him on a daily basis. Your most important duties include feeding, providing fresh water, and picking up manure.

TIP

If your horse is in a large pasture, he won't need to get out for exercise every day. But if he is confined to a stall or paddock, part of your job will be to ride him, walk him, or provide him with exercise in some other way, preferably on a daily basis.

Chapter 8 provides intricate details on caring for your horse's daily needs.

Grooming your horse

An important part of horse care is grooming. A well-groomed horse looks good and usually feels good too. Grooming gives you a chance to spend quality time with your horse and keep an eye on his body for any changes that can indicate disease.

Grooming involves both caring for your horse's body and managing his mane and tail. Hoof care is an essential part of grooming that requires you to clean out your horse's feet on a daily basis. In addition, it's a good idea to bathe your horse on a regular basis. You may also want to clip his hair during the winter if you live in a warm climate.

For details about how to groom your horse, see Chapter 9.

Treating your horse's illnesses

Despite their size and imposing presence, horses are fragile creatures that often become sick or injured. Preventive care is important for horses, and it includes:

>> Routine vaccinations against a variety of equine ailments

>> Deworming to get rid of harmful parasites

>> Regular dental care to ensure that teeth are in good health

>> Proper hoof care

>> Quality feed and fresh water

>> Regular exercise

As a horse owner, your job is being able to recognize signs of illness in your horse and calling a vet immediately whenever your horse is ill. Some signs that you need to call the vet include:

>> Diarrhea

>> Inability to stand

>> Indications of pain in your horse's abdomen, known as colic

>> Labored breathing

>> Limping (known as lameness)

>> Refusal to eat

>> Straining to urinate or defecate

>> Swollen, painful eyes

For more information on preventive care for your horse, see Chapter 10. For details on common equine ailments, see Chapter 11.

Knowing when to part with your horse

It may be hard to imagine now, but the time may come when you want or need to say goodbye to your horse. You may need to part ways because you've outgrown him and need a mount more suited to your current skill level, because your financial situation has changed and you can no longer afford him, or (worse yet) because he has a terminal illness that can't be cured.

REMEMBER

If you need to sell your horse, do it in a way that ensures he will have a good home, and won't end up in the slaughterhouse — a fate that befalls many unwanted horses. Some of your options for your horse include

>> Selling

>> Leasing

>> Donating to a program

>> Gifting to a family member

>> Retiring

If your horse is sick, in pain, and can no longer be helped by veterinary medicine, consider euthanasia. This humane way of ending a horse's life is the kindest thing you can do for your old friend.

For more details on giving up your horse, see Chapter 12.

Riding Your Horse Safely and Easily

Horse handling is a skill perfected with training and experience. Receiving the right kind of training and instruction from a qualified expert is important for getting the most from the time you spend with horses. After you have some knowledge under your belt, you can safely handle your horse in a variety of situations. Remember that horses are large animals, and it takes some know-how to deal with them.

Working with your horse from the ground

Before you can ride your horse, you need to handle him from the ground. Given that your horse outweighs you by something like 10 times, it's a good idea to know how to properly deal with him when you're standing at his side.

If you pay close attention to the info we provide about buying a horse in Chapter 5, you can acquire an animal that has what horse people call good ground manners. A horse with good ground manners maintains a proper distance from you — doesn't crowd your space — and respects you as the authority when you're leading him or working around him. In turn, you need to know how to handle your horse properly so you don't confuse him or inadvertently put yourself in harm's way. Make sure you know to succeed at:

>> Approaching your horse in a stall or pasture

>> Haltering your horse

>> Leading your horse

>> Tying your horse

>> Longeing your horse

Flip to Chapter 13 for full details on handling your horse on the ground.

Looking at riding basics

Getting up on a horse's back can be exciting. It can also be frustrating and scary if you don't know what you're doing. Learning to ride in a formal setting is crucial, because qualified instructors know how to properly teach you riding basics.

Your first decision is determining in which riding discipline you'd like to learn; Chapter 14 has complete information on different riding disciplines. English style riding is made up of several subtypes, including dressage, hunt seat, and saddle seat.

>> Hunt seat is used by people who want to jump their horses, although plenty of hunt-seat riders don't jump — they simply enjoy this style of riding.

>> Dressage is an ancient discipline that's growing in popularity among English riders in the U.S. It emphasizes grace and athleticism in the horse.

>> Saddle-seat riders tend to ride a certain type of horse, one that tends to have high leg action. Many saddle-seat riders show their horses.

TIP

>> Western riding, the most popular of all the disciplines, is often the style of choice for beginning riders, because Western saddles provide the most security. Western riding is popular with casual trail riders, as well as those working with cattle.

Part of your equine education will include learning to saddle and bridle your horse; see Chapter 15 for more details. When you have hoisted yourself into the saddle, you are ready to start riding. For most people, this is what being around horses is all about. Of course, doing it right takes education and practice. You can get an idea of the basics of mounting and riding in the different disciplines by reading Chapter 16.

Staying safe on your horse

Horseback riding has been deemed one of the most dangerous sports, and it results in a significant number of serious injuries to people every year. For this reason, safety when riding is crucial.

One way to ensure that you have a safe ride on your horse is wear the proper apparel. Footwear designed especially for riding is mandatory. Proper footwear can keep you from getting caught up in the stirrups and being dragged if your horse becomes out of control.

REMEMBER

A riding helmet is an important part of safety apparel. Most horse-related accidents involve head injuries, and more than one rider has ended up in a vegetative state as a result of a blow to the head when falling off a horse. Helmets designed specifically for riders can protect your valuable grey matter in the event of an accident.

Knowing the proper way to handle a horse — on the ground and in the saddle — also increases your odds of staying safe while participating in your new hobby. Don't skimp on getting a good education on how to ride and handle horses. You should find out how to do the following:

>> Care for a horse's hooves

>> Handle yourself when you're in close quarters with a horse

>> Lead a horse

>> Move around a tied horse

>> Check your tack

>> Ride safely by yourself and with others

You find details on all of these topics and more in Chapter 17.

Chapter **2**

Understanding Horses from Head to Hoof

For some reason, horses attract human beings like magnets attract steel. This human infatuation has been going on for thousands of years. The fascination began when primitive man saw horses as food. As cavemen became more civilized, horses became valuable as beasts of burden. Basically, for most of the horse's history with humans, he has helped humans survive in a hostile world.

Nowadays, however, humans have few practical reasons for keeping horses around. Whereas humans used to use horses to provide transportation and sustenance, we now have much speedier ways of getting to the grocery store.

So why do humans still want to keep big, unwieldy creatures that cost a lot to house, take a lot of time to care for, eat a great deal, and produce significant amounts of poop? What could horses possibly offer modern humans that would make keeping *equines* — that is, members of the horse family — worth all the trouble?

You get different answers to these questions depending on whom you ask. But because we're the ones writing this book, you're going to get ours:

> Horses are amazing, incredible creatures. They're as breathtakingly beautiful as they are powerful and fast. They're wild in their souls yet gladly give us their hearts. Horses offer us beauty, a connection to nature, and a quiet and dignified companionship that no other animal can provide in the same way. If you don't believe us, it's only because you really haven't gotten to know a horse yet. After you do, the equine mystique will reveal itself to you.

If you want to be around horses, you need to acquire some horse sense. By that, we mean that you need to understand some basics about horses, such as how they're put together physically and how to improve your relationship with your horse by getting into his head — doing a little horse psychology, if you will. This chapter covers these things and more.

Horse Talk: Describing Horses Correctly

If you hang around a stable for any length of time, you'll notice that horse people have a language all their own. This language — which sounds like a foreign tongue to the uninitiated — is what horse people use to describe the intricate details of the horse's body.

If you want to fit in with the horsy set, you need to know the lingo and the basic knowledge of horses that goes along with it. The horse's anatomy, and the horse's height measurements, colorations, markings, and movements all are essential details that real horse lovers know.

Checking out the horse's parts

Horses are really put together. Nature made them to be virtual running machines that can reach speeds of nearly 40 miles per hour. The equine body is an impeccably designed combination of muscle and bone in an elegant and graceful package.

People who spend time around horses not only begin to appreciate equine anatomy but also come to understand it. Horse people talk about their horses' bodies the way mechanics talk about cars. In the equine world, if you want to keep up with such conversations, you must know the lingo and the blueprint. Here are some parts of the horse you need to know (see Figure 2-1 for more):

» **Withers:** The area on the horse's back just after the neck but above the shoulders

» **Fetlock:** The horse's ankle

» **Forelock:** The hair between the horse's ears that falls onto the forehead

» **Hocks:** The elbow-like joint of the horse's back legs.

» **Muzzle:** The area of the horse's head includes the mouth and nostrils

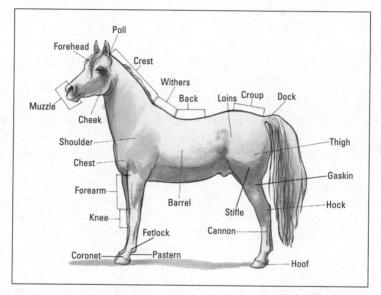

FIGURE 2-1:
The parts of the horse work together to build a virtual running machine.

TIP

Heard the expression, *No hoof, no horse?* Well, it's true. Without healthy hooves, horses can't function well. Becoming familiar with the parts of the horse's hoof gives you intimate knowledge of this most important part of the equine body. This knowledge helps you take better care of your horse's tootsies, too (see Figure 2-2).

Measuring a horse correctly

The average horse weighs anywhere from 1,000 to 1,200 pounds. But horse people rarely refer to a horse's weight when describing the animal's size. Instead, the horse's height, measured in something called *hands*, is the appraisal of choice.

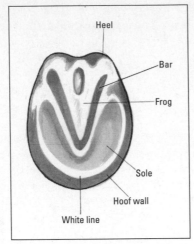

FIGURE 2-2:
Knowing the parts of the hoof is essential in caring for horses.

One hand equals four inches, and horses are measured from the ground to the top of the *withers* (see Figure 2-3), or the area of the back behind the neck and above the shoulder. So, if a horse stands 60 inches from the ground to its withers, the horse is 15 hands high (or 60 divided by 4). If the horse stands 63 inches from the ground, the horse is 15.3 hands (which is 60 divided by 4, and then 3 inches). Because a *hand* is an increment of 4 inches, a horse that is 64 inches from the ground to the withers would not be 15.4 hands high but instead is considered 16 hands. Height in hands is sometimes written as *h.h.,* which stands for *hands high.*

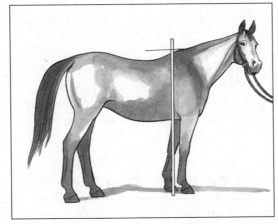

FIGURE 2-3:
Measure the horse from the ground to the top of the withers to determine its height in hands.

A horse's height is important mostly if you plan to ride it — which, of course, is what most people do. Generally speaking, an average-sized woman can comfortably ride a horse that is anywhere from 14.2 hands to 16.1 hands in height. If you're a rather tall woman, or are a man of average male height, you'll probably want to lean toward a horse on the taller side of the range.

All this is mostly aesthetics, of course. If you're a tall person, you look better on a taller horse. Of course, if you're above average in weight, a larger horse can carry you more comfortably. If you plan to show your horse or perform particular events with it, height may also be a consideration.

TIP

You can use a regular measuring tape to determine a horse's height, as long as you're good at division, because you need to divide the number of inches you come up with by four. If you'd rather not bring your calculator to the stable, you can buy a special horse measuring tape or a measuring stick (even more accurate) at your local tack store. These devices are labeled in hands, so you don't have to do any calculating of your own.

Horse measuring tapes also are useful in determining your horse's weight, because the tapes usually have pound increments on one side and hand measurements on the other. To determine your horse's weight, wrap the tape around the horse's girth, just behind the elbow, and up behind the withers.

Seeing horses of many colors

Nature made horses to blend in with their surroundings, so the colors you typically see in horses are meant to camouflage. Based on this definition, you may think that horse colors should be dull, but the exact opposite is true. The many different shades and variations of coat color that you find in the equine world is amazing, and knowing the different horse colors helps you describe and identify individual horses you may come across in your equine travels. Having this knowledge also permits you to converse intelligently with other horse lovers. You may even end up finding a favorite coloration that you'd like to see on your own future horse!

The best way to learn horse colors is to see them. In the color section of this book, you can find color photographs of 16 of the most common horse colorations, along with names and descriptions of each. Some of the colors you'll see in the horse world include bay (reddish brown with black mane, tail, and legs), black, chestnut (reddish body with red or blonde mane and tail), gray (anything from nearly white to dappled gray), and palomino (gold with lighter mane and tail).

Looking at different horse markings

Leg and facial markings are great for helping to identify individual horses. Each marking has a name, and each name is universal among equine aficionados.

Figure 2-4 shows the most common horse facial markings. Keep in mind that the following patterns often have subtle variations.

>> **Bald:** White that starts above the forehead, goes to the muzzle, and extends beyond the bridge of the nose to the side of the face

>> **Blaze:** Wide white area that runs along the bridge of the nose

>> **Snip:** White spot located on the muzzle, between or just below the nostrils

>> **Star:** White spot on the forehead

>> **Stripe:** Narrow white stripe down the center of the face, on the bridge of the nose

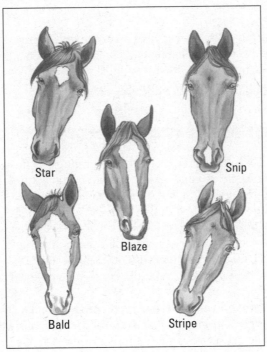

Star   Snip

Blaze

Bald   Stripe

© John Wiley & Sons, Inc.

Figure 2-5 shows typical white leg markings on horses. They include

>> **Coronet:** A small white band just above the hoof

>> **Half cannon:** A white marking that extends from the edge of the hoof halfway up the middle of the leg

>> **Half pastern:** A white marking that extends from the edge of the hoof halfway up the pastern

>> **Sock:** A white marking that extends from edge of the hoof two-thirds of the way up the leg

>> **Stocking:** A white marking that extends from edge of the hoof to the knee or hock

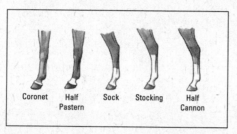

Coronet Half Pastern Sock Stocking Half Cannon

FIGURE 2-5: You can find a variety of white leg markings on horses.

© *John Wiley & Sons, Inc.*

Figuring out horse movements

If you've ever seen a Hollywood western, you know that horses gallop. In fact, in the movies, all horses seem to do is gallop. In real life, however, most horses have several other gaits besides the gallop.

The gaits are considerably different from one another. One difference is speed: The walk is the slowest of the three. The trot is faster than the walk, and the canter is faster than the trot. The gallop is the fastest gait of them all.

A big difference in the gaits is in the way the horse positions his legs while he's moving.

>> In the *walk,* the horse puts each foot down one at a time, creating a four-beat rhythm.

>> In the *trot,* one front foot and its opposite hind foot come down at the same time, making a two-beat rhythm.

>> In the *canter,* one hind leg strikes the ground first, and then the other hind leg and one foreleg come down together, then the other foreleg. This movement creates a three-beat rhythm.

>> In the *gallop,* the basic canter movement is sped up so that all four feet are off the ground for a suspended moment. Then, each hind foot hits the ground individually, followed by each front foot individually. To the rider, the gallop feels very much like the canter, only faster.

When you're riding a horse, you can feel each of these different rhythms. (See Figure 2-6 for a visual sense of how this all works.)

Walk

Trot

Canter

FIGURE 2-6:
The leg positions of the walk, trot, and canter (which is slower than a gallop).

© John Wiley & Sons, Inc.

Depending on the discipline or type of riding you're doing, you may hear other terms to describe these gaits. For example, western riders use the term *jog* to describe a slow trot and *lope* for a slow gallop.

Just to confuse matters, the horse world has something called *gaited horses,* which are horses that naturally possess one or more gaits in addition to or instead of one or more of the basic gaits. Only horses of particular *gaited breeds* have these peculiarities. Chapter 3 has info on various horse breeds, including gaited breeds.

Mind Games: Getting into the Horse Psyche

You need to comprehend the world that the horse lives in to be able to understand the horse. Think about it: The world of horses is not composed of fast-food joints, unbalanced checkbooks, and vacations to far away countries. Instead, horses live in a world made up of hay and grass, buzzing insects, and assorted horsy politics.

Looking at the world through a horse's eyes can open up all sorts of avenues for communication between you and the horse. When you finally connect with your horse, you'll find that suddenly, this huge, four-legged alien is very special.

Examining equine instincts

Horses have a way of thinking about and viewing things that is uniquely their own. The evolution of horses as prey animals gives them a special viewpoint that helps them survive.

The components of this perspective (such as viewing the world as a series of threats, finding safety in numbers, and looking to an authority figure for guidance) make up the essence of the horse's being. The human who understands and sympathizes with these sometimes unhumanlike ways of looking at the world is the person who becomes most adept at conversations with the horse.

Prey, not predator

The first thing you need to know about horses to really get into their heads is that horses are prey animals, not predators. (The one interesting exception to this fact is in Iceland, where Icelandic Horses have been seen catching and eating fish from the ocean.) In the wild, horses are at the top of most large predators' dinner menus. Dogs and cats, on the other hand, evolved to be hunters. Consequently, the horse looks at the world differently than the domesticated dog and cat.

Nowadays, horses live in domestic situations where their biggest worries are horsefly bites, but try telling that to a horse. Long before humans ever considered building barns, haylofts, paddocks, and arenas, bolting from a potential threat is what literally saved the horse's hide. This instinct to flee first and ask questions later is at the core of every equine personality.

You don't need to spend much time around horses to witness the equine instinct to flee: In a nutshell, horses scare easily. They often spook at what humans view as the most benign of things: a plastic bag blowing in the wind, a low-flying plane passing overhead, or a car backfiring nearby. To humans, these distractions are minor, but to the ever-watchful horse, they are potentially life-threatening hazards.

REMEMBER

The ease with which horses spook may seem ridiculous, but the instinct to flee from trouble is at the center of a horse's psyche. Although most domestic horses don't have predators chasing them, they nevertheless have a powerful instinct to be on guard. Their brains are telling them that horse-eating monsters are out there, so they need to be on the lookout. If a real predator can't be found, then, by golly, the horse will conjure up a hunter to run from.

Let's stay together

Closely associated with the get-the-heck-out-of-Dodge-now instinct is the herd instinct, which is represented by the horse's burning desire always to be with other horses. This need stems from the fact that in the wild, large numbers mean safety. It works like this: Pretend for a moment that you're a horse, and a huge, terrifying saber-toothed tiger has selected horsemeat for his next meal. When a big cat starts chasing your herd looking for prey to take down, the chances of *you* being the horse that gets nailed are less when a whole herd of other horses surrounds you.

In addition to decreasing your odds of being the unlucky item on the big cat's menu, being in a herd also means that you can find out about impending danger much sooner than you would if you were alone. After all, a herd of eyes is better than one measly pair.

Yet the horse's love for other horses is not completely mercenary, however. You only need to watch a group of horses out in a field to discover that they genuinely enjoy each other's company. Although each horse is an individual with his own distinct personality, horses nonetheless thrive on companionship and bond strongly with their herdmates. They groom each other with their teeth, take turns tail swishing flies from each other's faces, and even play horsy games together, such as tag and I-dare-you-to-try-and-bite-me.

Follow the leader

Horses are social creatures, and they even have their own societal rules. In any given herd of horses, some horses are dominant and others are submissive. Horses follow a precise pecking order, with one big kahuna at the top of the heap who lords over all the other horses. The individual personalities of various herd members, along with factors such as age and physical ability, determine which horses take on different roles within the herd. All in all, horse society doesn't operate that much differently than human society.

Human beings, on the other hand, have benefited greatly from the horse's intrinsic need for leadership. The horse's penchant for dutifully submitting to authority is what ultimately enabled humankind to domesticate the horse thousands of years ago. After a human earns a horse's respect (the same way a leader horse must earn the respect of his fellow horses), the horse views the human as an authority figure to be respected and followed in much the same way as he views the leader horse.

TIP

When a human fails to gain a horse's respect early on in their relationship, the horse automatically takes charge. From the horse's perspective, every herd — even one made up of only two members — must have a leader. Although first impressions are important to horses, overrun humans can make up lost ground by becoming more assertive and telling the horse (in so many words), "I'm the one in charge now."

REMEMBER

In the same way that horses test the leader horses in a herd, they also periodically test their human companions to make sure that the humans still are worthy of leadership. Horses that misbehave often do so to challenge the authority of whoever is handling them, and they're incredibly astute at determining the qualifications of those giving them orders. For a horse to feel secure, he must have strong leadership. If you don't measure up in this department, or if the horse has a history of dealing with humans that don't measure up as leaders, the horse will take the leadership position from you — and we promise you won't like the results!

For example, in horse/human relationships where the horse has taken charge, you often see horses leading humans around the stable instead of vice versa. Leader horses that are being ridden make the decisions about where and when to go, despite their riders' pleas.

Equine followers feel safest when they have a strong leader making decisions for them and helping them determine what is and isn't dangerous. Human leadership accounts for why many horses find comfort in their associations with human beings. If we humans do things right, they see us as leaders. And if we say things are okay, then they must *be* okay.

The role of leader places a great responsibility on human shoulders, of course. We must convince the horse that we are confident and knowledgeable and worthy of their invaluable equine trust.

Surveying equine senses

From the horse's perspective, you need to know — or literally see — how the horse takes in the world. Humans evolved to be hunters and gatherers, chasing down prey and finding appropriate plants to eat. Horses, on the other hand, are built to avoid hunters and eat nearly everything that grows around them. Given these fundamental distinctions, the horse's senses are bound to have nuances that are somewhat different from those of a human.

Sight

Sight is the most important equine sense. For a prey animal like the horse, in the wild, good eyesight means the difference between life and death. Literally seeing trouble coming is the best way the horse has to make it to safety before a predator gets too close.

Because horses have long, narrow heads with eyes on either side, they have the ability to take in more of the view than do humans. When their heads are facing forward, horses have a nearly 180-degree field of vision in each eye (as shown in Figure 2-7). They can see in front of and almost all the way around their bodies, although they do have some blind spots.

WARNING

One of a horse's blind spots is directly behind, so you should never approach a horse from the back unless the horse already knows you're there. If you're already next to the horse and move toward his blind spot, keep one hand on him at all times so he is aware of your presence.

No one knows for sure how far horses can see, mainly because horses have trouble pronouncing the letters on eye tests. Scientists who have done experiments in this field have made some educated guesses that horses can see pretty darn far, in the realm of at least hundreds of yards away. Horses can distinguish patterns, which means they're able to take in fine details. They also perceive depth well.

Horses also have much better night vision than humans. Many a rider has been out on a dark, moonless trail, dumbfounded by his or her horses' ability to see where the pair is going despite the incredibly dim light.

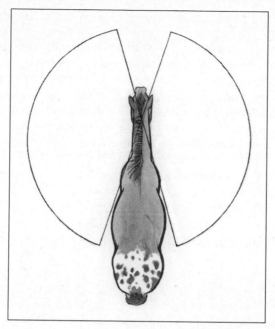

FIGURE 2-7:
A horse can see
this much when
facing straight
ahead.

Scientists know far less about horses' color vision than they do about other areas of equine sight, but they're certain that horses see many of the same colors that we see, with two exceptions: red and green. In fact, they believe that horses have the same color vision as humans who suffer from red-green color blindness. So red and green don't look the same to a horse as they do to a person with full color vision. That said, horses are still able to pick out the greenest grass in a field!

Hearing

A species that survives by getting a head start on marauding predators needs a pretty good sense of hearing. The fact that horses have survived all the way to modern times is testimony to their incredible hearing, which is considerably better than a human's.

If you look at the shape of the horse's ear, you can see that it's built sort of like a funnel. With this design, the ear can capture sound in its outer part and channel it down into the ear canal. The broad outer part of the horse's ear very adequately takes in the slightest sound in the horse's environment.

The horse's ear also has an amazing ability to swivel. Just watch a horse's ears sometime while the horse is busy eating or just hanging out. You'll see one ear turn forward, while the other swings to the back. Sometimes both ears go forward at the same time, while at other times, both are poised to the rear. The purpose of all this twisting is simple — to take in as much information as possible at one time.

Using their extremely mobile ears, horses constantly monitor the world around them. Just imagine trying to pay complete attention to different sounds coming in to either ear at the same time. Impossible for a human, yet the horse does this on a steady basis. A horse can take in the sounds of a car driving by, children playing, a bird chirping, and a human approaching, all at once, from different places in the environment. The horse then processes that information and makes split-second decisions about whether to react — all the while picking out the best blades of pasture grass or meandering down a rocky trail. The process really is mind-blowing.

TIP

Loud, unfamiliar noises can send a relaxed horse into a tizzy. On the other hand, a placid, reassuring sound can ease a horse's worries. It's amazing to see how a frightened horse can be comforted by a soft, gentle voice from a calm and confident human. Keep this fact in mind when handling your horse in a particularly noisy or frightening environment.

Smell

Like most nonhuman animals, horses have an acute sense of smell that they regularly employ to provide them with information on what is going on around them. Horses use their sense of smell in a number of different and important ways.

People talk about smelling danger, but when it comes to the horse, this metaphor is literally the case. Nature equipped the equine with a strong olfactory sense that can tell the animal whether a predator is near. All it takes is a strong upwind breeze to bring a dangerous scent to the attention of a wild herd. After getting a whiff of the predator, the herd literally high-tails — their tails stick way up in the air as they flee — it out of there in a flash.

Horses also use smell as part of their complicated social structure. Horses typically greet each other nose to nose, each taking in the odor of the other. Horses also come to recognize each other by scent and by sight. Mares and foals quickly memorize each other's scents and use this information to help locate each other in a crowd of horses.

TIP

Most horses also greet humans in the same way. When you introduce yourself to a horse for the first time, notice how the horse reaches out his muzzle to sniff you. Given this olfactory penchant, the most polite way to approach a horse is with the back of your hand extended so the horse may take in your personal scent. Letting a horse breathe in your scent tells the animal that you are a fellow herdmate (not a predator), and usually makes the horse more agreeable to being handled.

The equine sense of smell also comes in handy when it's time to eat. Although horses also use their eyes and muzzles to ferret out the tastiest morsels in a pasture, sense of smell plays a part as well. One plant may look just like another to you, but a horse can get a sense of whether foliage tastes good by first getting a whiff of it.

Touch

The equine sense of touch is an important (although often overlooked) element to the horse. Although many people think that horses have tough hides, they really don't. Their skin obviously is tougher than human epidermis, but it still is rich with nerve endings. If it weren't, how else could a horse possibly feel a tiny little fly landing on his body? Trust us, he can!

If you sit on a pasture fence and watch a herd of horses for a few hours, you'll see plenty of evidence of how horses use touch to communicate with each other. Mothers reassure their babies with a brush of the muzzle; comrades scratch each other's itches with their teeth. Whenever a message needs to be sent from one horse to another, visual cues and touch — or the threat of it — nearly always are used.

TIP

Humans also use touch to convey messages to the horse. A gentle rubdown, a pat on the shoulder, a vigorous massage in just the right place — these all are ways of saying, "I'm your friend," to a horse. Sometimes, if you're lucky, you get a similar tactile message in return.

Understanding equine language

Because horses are such highly social creatures, they do quite a bit of talking to one another. Of course the equine way of communicating is nothing like what Mr. Ed did. Horses have their own exclusive language, and traditional nouns and verbs aren't part of the picture.

Humans primarily use verbal language to express thoughts and emotions to one another. Horses do the same thing within their species, only they mostly use their bodies to get their points across. This clear way of expressing a variety of attitudes, intents, and emotions is universal among all members of the equine family.

REMEMBER

To truly understand horses, you absolutely have to know how to read equine body language. Trying to get by without this crucial skill is like trying to conduct business in a foreign country without comprehending the native tongue. You just can't do it.

Focusing on facial expressions

One of the most obvious ways that horses talk to each other — and to humans — is by using facial expressions. Horses send out at least four distinct messages by using their faces (as shown in Figure 2-8). Each message has a distinct look.

>> **I'm afraid, and I'm about to bolt.** Horses that are on the verge of panic often warn you with this expression before they take off (although they may act in a matter of seconds). The ears are pointed toward whatever is the source of

fear. The head is held high and the whites of the eye are showing. You sometimes can actually see the muscles in the neck tense up.

>> **I'm alert and wondering what's next.** This welcome expression indicates that the horse is content and curious about his surroundings. The ears are pricked forward; the eyes are focused on the object of wonder. The head is held at medium height.

>> **Get away or else!** This expression immediately precedes a bite or a kick. The horse usually directs the aggression at other horses, but occasionally, ill-tempered horses direct this aggression at humans. The ears are laid back flat against the head, the nostrils take on an oblong shape and the mouth is open with teeth exposed. (Don't confuse flattened ears with ears that are simply cocked back for listening.)

>> **I'm relaxed and secure.** The sign of a happy, healthy horse, you may see this expression while you're grooming, while your horse is dozing in the pasture, or even while you're riding together along a familiar trail. The ears are in a relaxed state, usually pointing backward. The eye has a calm look, and the head is at medium height.

Relaxed

Afraid

Threatening

Alert

FIGURE 2-8: Horses use these four basic facial expressions to communicate.

© John Wiley & Sons, Inc.

TIP

Individual horses exhibit these expressions with subtle variations, so getting to know the individual expressions of your particular horse helps you understand him even better.

Listening to the equine voice

Although body language is the primary means of equine communication, horses also use a range of sounds to talk to each other. The most prominent among these are the neigh, nicker, snort, and squeal. Each sound serves a particular purpose in a herd situation, and horses often use the sounds as a way of communicating with human beings, too. Although scientists aren't completely sure what each of these vocalizations means in a literal sense, each one seems to take place under certain circumstances, giving us a clue as to its intent.

>> **Neigh:** A neigh, or whinny, is the loud call that most people associate with the horse. You hear it as a sound effect in Hollywood westerns all the time (usually used incorrectly — see Chapter 20 for more details). The neigh seems to be used most often by horses that have been separated from their herd or from a very close companion. Neighs have a sense of urgency to them that seem to be saying, "Hey, I'm over here!"

>> **Nicker:** The nicker is a soft, gentle call that is usually heard when horses with a close bond greet one another. Mares nicker to their foals, and herdmates nicker to each other. Horses that are attached to their human caretakers sometimes nicker to them. You can also hear nickering at feeding time as the person delivering the food approaches.

>> **Snort:** The snort, made by a rapid blowing of air from the nostrils, is most often heard when a horse is alarmed in some way. If a horse comes upon something that scares him, he may bolt, then spin around and snort at the offending object. Horses sometimes snort at random when they are feeling frisky, too.

>> **Squeal:** One of the more amusing equine vocalizations is the squeal. The squeal is usually reserved for other horses, and seems to be a message of controlled aggression. Strange horses often approach one another with heads up and necks arched. After a short muzzle sniffing session, one horse squeals to show dominance. The other horse often reacts with an aggressive facial expression or a return squeal. The horses almost seem to be testing each other to see who backs down first. A mare that isn't quite ready to breed may squeal to tell a frisky stallion to back off.

Another type of squeal comes from horses that are really frightened. These *fear squeals* are higher pitched and shorter in length than their more assertive cousins.

THE PHENOMENON OF IMPRINTING

In 1991, a California veterinarian by the name of Robert M. Miller, DVM, authored a book called *Imprint Training of the Newborn Foal,* which highlighted a method for getting deep into the equine mind. Called *imprinting,* this procedure involves intense handling of newborn foals, even before they have bonded with their mothers.

The theory behind imprinting is that foals, as herd animals, will bond closely to whomever they make physical contact with shortly after birth. In the wild, this instinct to bond helps the foal stay close to its mother and the herd, and helps him understand that he is a horse.

By spending time ritualistically handling a newborn foal before it has even had a chance to rise to its feet, a human being can make an impression that will last the horse its entire lifetime.

Advocates of imprinting say it produces horses that have a strong connection to their human handlers, making them easy to train and willing to work. However, if not performed correctly, imprinting can result in a horse that has no respect for humans and can be difficult to deal with.

Regardless of any pitfalls in the technique, a great many horse breeders have incorporated imprinting into their foal management programs. The result: Any horse you meet born after 1991 may well have been imprinted.

Do You Trust Me? Developing Bonds Between Horses and Humans

The very instincts that have served the horse well in dealing with life as a prey animal often are in direct conflict with life in the human world. Domesticated horses need no longer fear ferocious carnivores because the horse's safety is guarded by his human companions, and his needs are (it is hoped) always met. This new way of being, however, conflicts with everything the horse has become throughout its long history.

Making things even odder for the horse is the fact that humankind itself was one of the very predators that preyed upon horses thousands of years ago. Scientists are certain that primitive man actively hunted horses for food. In fact, many believe that human overhunting may be partially to blame for the horse's extinction in North America some 10,000 years ago.

This reality creates a conundrum for both horse and human. The human creature that horses once feared is now the very same one asking the horse for trust and companionship. These same human beings have also placed the horse in a human world where much of its natural survival behaviors are unnecessary. This paradox creates a weird scenario for both the horse and human, no matter how you look at it.

The dilemma that humans and horses face boils down to a couple of questions:

>> How do humans deal with the horse's penchant for fear and flight?

>> How do horses deal with this strange world so alien to anything they would have ever encountered in the wild?

REMEMBER

Because of mankind's greater brain capacity, the burden of bridging the gap between the reality of the domesticated horse's world and what a horse's instincts tell it falls on the human. Communicating to the horse that everything's really okay, however, requires the human to understand the equine mind and to pay close attention to the horse's modes of communication.

Developing a trusting relationship between horse and human can achieve miraculous results. Many, many horses trust their human caretakers so much that they tolerate all kinds of bizarre situations with minimal fear. Go to any horse show and you can see what we mean. The constant commotion and chaos that is a regular part of many horse shows would otherwise make every horse at the show go nuts. But that rarely happens. Instead, you see scores of horses calmly lounging around, quietly munching their hay, and performing beautifully in the show ring when it's their time in the spotlight. These horses have grown accustomed to the human-dominated world in which they live and have developed a basic trust in the humans who guide their lives.

Other examples of how horse-loving humans have helped horses transcend the gap between primitive equine instinct and the modern human world can be seen everyday in stables and pastures around the globe. There you find horses that greet their caretakers with an obvious joy. Some horses become incredibly attached to just one special person. Even more horses truly love their jobs and are eager to come out of their stalls or pastures and do whatever work is asked of them.

TIP

If you want to achieve a profound bond with your horse, always put yourself in your horse's place and try to comprehend the equine experience. Not only will you come to understand and appreciate your horse, but your horse also will come to view you as a protector and ultimately will grow to trust you with his very life.

The sections that follow cover just a few of the tasks that humans can undertake to develop trust with their horses.

Providing companionship

Horses are herd animals, and you can't get around that fact (see "Let's stay together" earlier in this chapter for more details). Just like humans, horses need to have regular interaction with members of their own species to maintain a healthy sense of well-being. For a horse, being alone means being vulnerable — so vulnerable that it can be a matter of life or death.

REMEMBER

Depriving a horse of regular companionship is inhumane and tantamount to keeping a person in solitary confinement. Some horses can tolerate the situation better than others, depending on the individual personality of the horse. But none enjoy isolation. In fact, a horse deprived of companionship often becomes neurotic and develops stable vices, the equine equivalent to human nail-biting (see the section "Taking some stable vice advice" later in this chapter). Every horse needs to have some company, whether it's on two or four legs.

One or more horses for a friend is the best scenario, but many horses can also find solace in the companionship of a goat, sheep, donkey, or other hoofed animal. Human companionship also means a great deal to horses. Some horses — usually ones that were imprinted on humans at birth (see the sidebar on imprinting earlier in this chapter) — actually prefer human companionship to that of other horses. But with most horses, human companionship alone doesn't fit the bill. Human companionship is better than nothing, however, and needs to be provided often to a horse that has no other comrades.

Chowing down

Horses evolved on grassy plains, and in nature, horses spend most of their time grazing. The equine digestive system supports almost constant consumption of low-grade grasses.

The equine brain also is designed for plenty of foraging and chewing. Grazing for a horse is the human equivalent to working, reading, or watching TV. For a horse, grazing provides not only nutrition, but also mental stimulation.

The ideal situation for a horse is to be in a pasture, where he can munch on grass for nearly 18 hours a day. A horse that can do just that is going to be a happy, well-adjusted critter that can give in to the natural urge to chew, chew, chew.

Unfortunately, for a number of reasons, providing a horse with pasture isn't always possible. Many horses — especially those in more urban areas — live in small dirt paddocks or tidy box stalls, without access to grass. Sometimes, these grazing-deprived horses develop stable vices because they are bored and frustrated by their inability to express their natural urge to graze (see the section "Taking some stable vice advice" later in this chapter).

For horses that can't graze in a field of grass, the next best thing is frequent feeding of roughage, like hay. You must feed horses a minimum of twice a day for basic nutrition. More frequent feedings are even better for their brains and help keep their digestive tracts working properly. (See Chapter 8 for more details on feeding horses.)

Whatever you do, don't let your horse become overweight. Overweight horses are prone to serious health problems. If your horse is what those in the horse world call an "easy keeper," talk to your veterinarian about how to keep him at a good weight while still providing him with enough roughage to satisfy his need to chew and digest.

Stretching out

Just as Mother Nature designed the horse to eat on a nearly constant basis, she also built the horse for nearly constant movement.

If you watch a horse grazing out in a pasture, you'll see that with just about every bite of grass, the horse takes a step. In a 15-minute period, the horse moves quite a few feet from where he originally started nibbling.

This regular movement provides exercise for both the horse's body and mind. Energy is slowly released as the horse moves steadily around the pasture. Take this same horse and put him in a box stall or small paddock, and you have a horse that feels cooped up.

For the horse that must live in small quarters without the freedom to move about and graze, daily exercise is of vital importance (see Chapter 8 for the full scoop). Every day, your confined equine needs to be taken out of the stall and walked for at least half an hour, turned out into a larger paddock to run around, or be ridden at least 45 minutes. If the horse doesn't receive adequate exercise, not only will he be prone to developing leg problems, but he'll also have plenty of pent-up energy. The horse often expresses his overabundance of energy through stable vices (see the next section) or through misbehavior when he finally does get out of his stall.

Taking some stable vice advice

Horses that are kept by humans in a way that is very unnatural to how they evolved (cooped up, unable to eat with frequency, lacking mental stimulation) sometimes develop neurotic behaviors. These *stable vices*, as they are known, are the equine equivalent to nail-biting and hair-twisting. Horses with theses problems need more stimulation in the forms of more frequent feeding, more exercise, more companionship with other horses, and/or more room to move around (see the previous sections). After a horse develops one of these habits, it's hard to break, even with a change in environment, so prevention is key:

>> **Cribbing:** Cribbing is a bizarre but all-too-common habit, and seems to be the equine version of obsessive-compulsive disorder. The cribbing horse grabs a fence post or barn door in between his teeth, arches his neck, and sucks air into his stomach. This air sucking creates a head rush that becomes addictive. Cribbing is not only a sign of extreme boredom or stress, it can be harmful to the horse's teeth. Devices exist that are meant to curb this behavior, but in our opinion, you're better off addressing the source of the problem, which is a lack of stimulation. When it comes to cribbing, prevention is more effective than a cure. *Provide your horse with enough exercise and stimulation so that he doesn't get into the cribbing habit.*

>> **Wind-sucking:** Similar to cribbing, wind-sucking involves the horse taking hold of a horizontal surface between his teeth and sucking air into his stomach. Sometimes the horse doesn't take hold of anything but just sucks air into his windpipe. Usually the result of boredom, wind-sucking is a hard habit to break. *Providing a horse with plenty of roughage (hay or pasture) to eat and daily exercise can discourage the habit.*

>> **Weaving:** A horse that weaves stands in one place, shifting weight from one foot to the other in a rhythmic motion, back and forth, his head swaying from side to side. Weaving horses are pitiful to watch. Weaving is not only a sign of extreme boredom, but can also be a symptom of anxiety. *Weaving is almost always a stall problem that usually goes away when the horse is moved to a pasture or a bigger paddock.*

>> **Pacing:** A pacing horse walks endlessly around his stall. Horses that exhibit this behavior usually are showing discomfort with confinement. In most cases, horses that pace are the ones kept in box stalls. Horses in paddocks occasionally pace, too, especially if they have a neighboring horse they don't get along with. Pacing is a horse's way of saying "Get me out of here!" *Move the horse to a more open environment if possible.*

>> **Bolting feed:** *Bolting feed* means eating too quickly, something that horses sometimes do when they are feeling overly hungry, anxious about the security of their food, or simply anxious in general. This manner of eating usually happens with hay pellets or commercial feed because these feeds are easier to bolt than hay. That said, some horses are capable of bolting hay, too. It's not healthy for a horse to bolt his feed, because the food isn't thoroughly chewed or moistened. This situation can cause a blockage in the esophagus, or in the intestines, where it can lead to colic. *Feed the horse more often. Put medium-sized stones in the feeder along with the pellets or commercial feed to slow down his eating (as he'll have to pick around the stones). If your horse bolts his hay, use a slow-feeder to keep him from being able to take in too much hay at once. Be sure to also create a more secure environment for the horse so that he's less worried about another horse taking his food.*

Chapter **3**

Perusing Popular Horse Breeds

H orses have been domesticated for thousands of years, and in that time, scores of breeds have developed. Plenty of these breeds still exist today, giving newcomers to the equine world a swarm of choices to contemplate. Given this vast plethora of breeds, how in the world are you supposed to pick just one to ride or own? That's where we come in.

Figuring out which breed is for you is the main objective of this chapter. Feel free to turn to the color section, too, to take a peek at what some of these breeds look like.

Picking the Best Breed for You

You may not need to settle on just one breed. Many horse owners have absolutely no preference for a particular breed. Instead, they simply look for individual horses that possess the character traits they prefer. If that horse turns out to be a Quarter Horse, fine. If the horse turns out to be a Paint, that's fine, too. Basically, it doesn't matter. You can go this route if you choose. You sure won't be the only one out there who has.

In our humble opinion, however, one of the neatest things about the horse world is that you can choose from so many different breeds. We *like* the fact that the horse world is so diverse, and that each and every breed has a small subculture that surrounds it. That's why we encourage you to find a few breeds that really strike your fancy. You may not end up buying a horse of one of these breeds, but at least you'll have formed a strong opinion on the subject — and strong opinions are mandatory for all horse people!

REMEMBER

We can't tell you which breed is best for you because every person is an individual with different wants and needs. But we can give you some advice on how to go about making your decision:

>> **Research, research, research:** Do as much reading as you can about the different breeds. Narrow your likes down to a few breeds, based on the way the breed looks, its history — whatever strikes you. Then visit the breed association Web sites. Here, you'll find just about everything you need to know about the breed you are interested in.

>> **Meet the horses:** Find a horse show for the breeds you like, and spend the day watching real horses in action. Go backstage to visit with the horses and their owners. (Always ask permission before petting any horse, and never feed treats without a go-ahead from the owner.) This kind of close contact gives you a real sense of what the horses — and the people who care about them — are all about.

>> **Spend some time:** If you find yourself getting serious about a breed and are thinking about buying a horse to show, spend time with a few representatives of the breed, both equine and human. Lease a horse of the breed for a while, or ask a breeder whether you can come over and spend time riding and handling the horses so you can get to know the breed. Meanwhile, start hanging around at breed shows and becoming acquainted with people involved with the breed. Horse people love to talk about their horses, so all you have to do to get a conversation going is ask questions and let people know you're a fan of the breed. The purpose of all this socializing is to make sure that you really are in love with this breed *before* you make a commitment.

ALL TOGETHER NOW: BREED ASSOCIATIONS

Breeds of horses don't exist by themselves. Each and every one was created by human beings, and to this day, human beings continue to manage the breeds.

Working together in clubs known as *breed associations*, these groups serve as watchdogs for their breeds and perform a number of vital functions, the most vital of which is to *register* horses. When a horse is registered with a breed association, its name along with its parentage and other vital information are recorded with the group. If you buy a purebred horse, chances are the animal already is registered with a breed association. By registering every horse that's born in the breed — and thereby establishing each individual horse's genetic purity — the associations are ensuring the continuation of their breed.

Breed associations also work to promote the breeds they represent by offering information about the breed to the public, sponsoring shows that encourage people to own a specific breed, and performing other services that increase the breed's visibility.

Breed associations are valuable resources for information on specific horse breeds and can be a huge help to you when you want to find out even more about a breed than we tell you here. Visit the breed association Web site for more information.

If the horse you buy or lease is a purebred, consider getting involved with a local chapter of your breed association. You'll meet plenty of other people who own and love the same breed you do, and you'll have a chance to participate in a variety of activities with your horse. Most regional breed clubs give out year-end awards and stage shows, social events, and even educational clinics. Getting involved with a regional club is the best way to discover more about your breed of choice.

Meeting the Top Ten Horse Breeds

Hundreds of horse breeds exist in the world today, but only a handful of them are among the top ten most popular breeds in the United States. The reasons for the popularity of these breeds can be narrowed down to a couple of factors: Each breed has a strong registering organization that promotes it among the horse-owning public, and each breed has redeeming qualities that a large number of horse people have come to appreciate.

Owning or riding one of the top ten breeds has its benefits. Plenty of information and support is available on the animals that make up the breed. Horse shows for the breed also are common and so are an array of sources from which you can learn more about the breed. Additionally, if you want to buy a horse of one of these breeds, you won't have too much trouble locating one. Fans of lesser-known breeds of horses don't have these advantages and must fend for themselves in many respects.

As you read our breed descriptions, keep in mind that we speak in generalities when it comes to the personalities of different horse breeds. For example, we say that Arabians are friendly horses. However, you may meet one or two Arabians in your travels that are complete grouches. Remember that each horse is an individual, and as you get to know different horses, you'll find horses that simply don't match the personalities typically attributed to their breeds.

That said, we're going to take a look at the top ten most popular breeds in the United States. Their popularity is determined by the number of horses that are registered in the breed each year. We list them here in alphabetical order, and you can see photos of each breed in the color section in the middle of the book. (Flip to Chapter 2 if you want general info about horse parts, colors, markings, and movements, and check out Chapter 18 for details on equine competitions.)

Appaloosa

The Appaloosa horse first was kept by the Nez Percé Indians of northern Idaho during the 1700s and 1800s. When the Nez Percé were forced onto reservations, the Appaloosa breed nearly died out. However, in the 1930s, a concerned group of horsemen gathered together to start a registry to save the breed. Since then, the Appaloosa horse has grown to considerable popularity.

The Appaloosa horse's most distinguishing characteristic is its spotted coat, particularly the white rump with dark spots, which is characteristic to the breed. That said, the Appaloosa horse is represented in several different patterns, including:

>> *Leopard* — the popular white with dark spots over the body

>> *Blanket with spots* — a dark body color with white over the rump that's covered with dark spots

Other physical traits include white *sclera* — the tissue that surrounds the pupil and gives the eye an almost human appearance, striped hooves, and mottled skin. Some Appaloosas also have thin manes and tails. The height range for an Appaloosa is 14.3 to 16 hands.

Appaloosas are known for their quiet and willing temperaments. They excel in western events, three-day eventing, and trail riding, and are known for being athletic and versatile. Appaloosas make excellent and colorful companions.

Arabian

The Arabian is one of the oldest breeds of horse still in existence. Developed in the Middle East several hundred years ago, many experts consider the Arabian horse one of the finest and purest breeds alive. The Arabian also is the most influential: Throughout equine history, humans have used Arabians to improve the quality of other breeds. Some examples of half-Arabian breeds are the Anglo-Arab (half Thoroughbred, half Arabian), the Quarab (half Quarter Horse, half Arabian), the Morab (half Morgan, half Arabian) and the Ara-Appaloosa (half Appaloosa, half Arabian). The purpose of these matings is to create half-Arabians that possess the refinement of the Arabian breed with the traits of another breed.

Arabian horses are known for their elegant and graceful beauty. Arabians have small heads, and concave (or *dished*) faces, small ears that curve inward, and long and arched necks. Most Arabian horses have only five spinal vertebrae as opposed to the six vertebrae typically found in most other breeds. Having one less vertebra gives Arabians a shorter back than many other breeds. (Horses that are part Arabians can have either five or six vertebrae, depending on the horse.)

Arabians are small horses that rarely measure much more than 15 hands in height. You can find them in a number of different colors, particularly gray, chestnut, bay, and black. Arabians are friendly and inquisitive horses, but they can be high-spirited. They perform especially well in endurance competitions and are shown in western, hunt-seat, eventing, dressage, and saddle-seat classes. Half-Arabians usually make excellent pleasure and show horses.

Miniature Horse

Miniature Horses are the dwarfs of the equine world (smaller than ponies), and number one in the adorable category. They are becoming increasingly popular in the United States, even though they are too small to be ridden. The Miniature Horse has all the physical and psychological characteristics of a regular horse in a small package.

Miniature Horses were developed in the United States in the 1800s to pull carts in and out of coal mines. This job required a tiny horse because mine tunnels rarely accommodated normal-sized horses.

The Miniature Horse of today, which stands anywhere from 6 to 7 hands high, is kept primarily as a pet. Tiny tots can ride Miniature Horses, but anyone older than 4 years of age probably is too big to ride a Miniature Horse.

Despite their small size, Miniature Horses can easily pull a fully grown human in a light cart. Many Miniature Horses are used for pleasure driving, and you can see them at special Miniature Horse shows pulling light rigs in competition. They also are shown in halter classes and other special events. You can check out a Miniature Horse in the color section.

Morgan

The Morgan horse is a quintessential American breed that was developed in Vermont during the 1700s from one horse, a little stallion named Justin Morgan. Named after the man who owned him, Justin Morgan achieved considerable fame for his astounding strength and willing disposition. The Morgan breed was developed by breeding a variety of different mares to Justin Morgan. These mares produced foals that looked almost exactly like Justin Morgan, and so the breed was born.

Morgans today have small, elegant heads and strong, highly arched necks. Just like their founding sire, Morgans tend to be smaller horses and rarely reach more than 15.2 hands in height. They're typically seen mostly in bay, black, and chestnut, and like their founding sire, Morgans are eager to please and willing to do whatever is asked of them.

Most Morgans are ridden simply for pleasure and on the trail, although a good many are shown in saddle-seat, western, and hunt-seat classes. The breed also is popular as a light-carriage horse.

Paint Horse

The Paint Horse used to be considered an anomaly — a colorful but unwanted result of many Quarter Horse-to-Quarter Horse breedings. (See the following section for more about Quarter Horses.) Rejected by the Quarter Horse registry because of their coat markings, these patterned horses had no official recognition in the horse world. However, in the early 1960s, a group of horse lovers who appreciated the Paint for its unusual appearance created a registry for the breed that helped it survive and grow.

Paint Horse coats come in a variety of different patterns, most of which fall under the headings:

>> *Tobiano* — a white base with dark patches

>> *Overo* — a dark base with white patches

The breed's *conformation*, or the way its horses are put together, is identical to that of the Quarter Horse, with a height range of 15 to 16 hands. Its temperament is much like that of the Quarter Horse too — mellow, easygoing, and eager to please.

The Paint Horse has become wildly popular during the last two decades and can be readily seen in stables and show arenas throughout the country. Most Paint Horses are shown in western classes, although an occasional Paint is seen in dressage, hunt-seat, and other English events. Paints also make excellent companions and trail horses.

Quarter Horse

In the 1600s, American colonists bred horses kept by the Chickasaw Indian nation to horses they had imported from England. The result was the beginnings of the American Quarter Horse, a breed that later developed to its present state in the American West. Used to herd cattle and carry cowboys across the arid desert in the 1800s, the Quarter Horse has a rich and glamorous history. The breed earned its name as a result of its ability to run a quarter of a mile distance faster than any other breed, a feat it still accomplishes today.

The Quarter Horse is a sturdy horse with a small head and muscular neck. The breed's hindquarters are powerful, and its legs are straight and solid. Quarter Horses come in a number of different colors, including sorrel, chestnut, bay, black, dun, grulla, palomino, roan, and gray (see the color section for photos showing various horse colors). They have a big height range, standing anywhere from 14.3 to 16 hands tall.

One of the Quarter Horse's most outstanding features is its disposition. This quiet temperament is a big reason behind the Quarter Horse's huge popularity. Well-known for its steady, easygoing personality, the Quarter Horse makes a good mount for beginning riders who need a quiet and forgiving horse to help them learn.

In the show ring, Quarter Horses prevail in western events; you see them most often in cattle-working competitions, western-pleasure classes, and gymkhana events (see Chapter 18). The Quarter Horse is the most popular breed of horse in the world, and numbers in the millions.

Saddlebred

The American Saddlebred horse was developed in Kentucky in the early part of America's history, using Morgans (see the section earlier in this chapter), Canadian horses, Narragansett Pacers (now extinct), and horses of Spanish breeding. The goal of the people who created the Saddlebred breed was to develop a horse that could comfortably carry riders across Eastern terrain.

The Saddlebred is a *gaited horse,* capable of performing a four-beat gait called a *rack* and a *stepping pace* in which the legs on each side move nearly in unison with each other, in addition to an animated walk, trot, and canter. Saddlebreds with these two extra gaits are called five-gaited Saddlebreds; they're used in the show ring. Not all Saddlebreds are born with the ability to move at the rack-and-stepping pace. The ones that move only in the breed's high-stepping walk, trot, and canter are referred to as three-gaited. Five-gaited Saddlebreds, while bred to have the ability to do the rack and stepping pace, have been trained to perform these gaits.

Saddlebreds typically have long, arched necks and fine heads that they carry rather high. The Saddlebred's body is lithe and lean, almost like that of a human ballet dancer. Saddlebreds range in height from 15 hands to 17 hands high. The most common colors for this breed are bay, black, brown, chestnut, sorrel, and gray. Known for having spirited, but willing temperaments, Saddlebreds are easily trained, according to the people who ride them.

In the breed show ring, Saddlebreds are exhibited as either five-gaited or three-gaited and usually in saddle seat. Driving classes also are popular for this breed. Despite their innate penchant for being flashy, Saddlebreds also make good pleasure horses and are shown even in open-breed events like dressage and gymkhana.

Standardbred

If you've ever seen harness racing, then you've seen a Standardbred horse. Standardbreds originated during the early part of American history and were created specifically to race under harness at either the trot or the pace.

Standardbreds have an inborn ability to move at great speeds without galloping. Some members of the breed are natural born trotters and can trot at nearly 30 miles per hour. Others are bred and trained as *pacers* (where the legs on one side move in unison) and can attain the same speeds. The early training of prospective Standardbred racehorses fine-tunes these innate skills while discouraging the urge to gallop. However, Standardbreds *are* physically capable of galloping, as is evidenced by the many Standardbred pleasure horses that do so every day.

The Standardbred is closely related to the Thoroughbred (which we cover later in this chapter), although the Standardbred is considerably more muscular. Standardbreds have rather large heads and powerful legs. They usually measure anywhere from 15 to 16 hands, and come in bay, chestnut, brown, gray, and black. The Standardbred's disposition typically is gentle and trainable.

Although the majority of Standardbreds are used for harness racing, many retired racehorses are used as show horses and pleasure mounts. You can see them competing in a variety of different events including western classes and even dressage.

Tennessee Walking Horse

A group of American breeds was used to create the Tennessee Walking Horse in the early part of the 18th century. Southern plantation owners needed a mount that was capable of covering quite a bit of ground and doing so comfortably. Early Tennessee Walking Horses worked in the fields, carried their owners long distances, and pulled the family wagon on weekends.

The Tennessee Walking Horse is a *gaited* horse that can perform the walk, trot, and canter, in addition to the four-beat running walk for which it is famous. A well-gaited Tennessee Walking Horse gives its rider the impression of floating on air.

Tennessee Walking Horses have a straight head with larger-than-usual ears. The breed has a gracefully arched neck, prominent withers (or front shoulders), and large hooves. They come in just about any horse color. Ranging in height from 15 to 16 hands, Tennessee Walking Horses tend to be easygoing in personality.

Shows featuring the Tennessee Walking Horse emphasize the breed's gaited aspects. However, in open shows where many breeds compete together, you find Tennessee Walking Horses in all kinds of varied events. Many Tennessee Walking Horses are used as trail horses, too.

Thoroughbred

The Thoroughbred was developed in England in the 1700s strictly for the purpose of racing. The breed later was imported to the American colonies, where it ultimately influenced other breeds such as the Standardbred and Quarter Horse (see the sections about these breeds earlier in this chapter).

Thoroughbreds are the fastest horses in the world, and can reach speeds of 40 miles per hour on the racetrack. But racing isn't their only talent. You typically see Thoroughbreds in the show ring, where they make terrific jumpers and dressage mounts.

The typical Thoroughbred has a straight head, high withers, and long, fine legs. Standing anywhere from 15 to 17 hands high, Thoroughbreds have a lean, lanky appearance that sets them apart from other breeds. The colors you most often see in this breed are bay, chestnut, black, brown, and gray.

WARNING

Although Thoroughbreds are willing horses, they can be somewhat complicated in temperament, meaning they can be hard for some people to figure out. Beginning riders sometimes have trouble handling Thoroughbreds because of their spunky personalities.

The Thoroughbreds you most commonly see in stables and backyard pastures are retired racehorses and horses bred specifically for the show world. Most of the horses shown in hunt-seat competitions are Thoroughbreds, although this breed also does well in other English events, such as dressage, three-day eventing, and show jumping.

MAKING THE GRADE HORSE

Oh sure, everyone wants a purebred. But what about *grade horses*, those mutts of the equine world whose parentage is unknown? Does horseland hold a place for them?

You'd better believe it. Although everyone makes a fuss about purebred horses, the fact of the matter is that most companion horses are grade horses. These horses make wonderful, loyal, and loving equine companions despite the fact their individual heritages are one of life's great mysteries.

Experienced horse people can usually spot a breed type in any grade horse, and can tell you whether a particular grade is a Quarter Horse, Thoroughbred, Arabian, or Morgan horse type. But regardless of the breed type evident in any grade horse, what's most important is the horse's health and personality.

Although the purebred world sometimes looks down on grade horses, grade horses perform the role of companion just as well or better than any purebred. Some of the best trail and pleasure horses in the world are grade horses. People who love these special horses don't mind living with the mystery of the horse's parentage.

Going Beyond the Top Ten

Not all breeds have substantial numbers of horses in their ranks. Plenty of smaller, lesser-known breeds exist and are popular among certain factions of the horse world. These types of horses have characteristics that set them apart and make them attractive to people who want something specific from their horses.

We cover several types of smaller breeds in the following sections. Check out Chapter 2 if you want general information about horse parts, colors, markings, and movements, and see Chapter 18 for the scoop on equine competitions.

Crossbreds

Although purebreds are the name of the game for many people, some prefer crossbred horses. Crossbred horses possess characteristics from both of the breeds in their parentage, which is why some people prefer them to purebreds. They believe they're getting the best of two breeds instead of one.

Some crossbreds have their own registries, such as the Morab (Morgan/Arabian), Azteca (Andalusian/Quarter Horse), and National Show Horse (Standardbred/Arabian). Others are recognized by the registry of one of the parent breeds, such as the Appaloosa (may have one Quarter Horse, Arabian or Thoroughbred parent), Quarter Horse (may have one Thoroughbred parent) and Paint (may have one or two Quarter Horse parents).

Other crossbreds can be the result of experiments conducted by individual breeders and can feature any two breeds that someone decided to put together. Crossbreeding has been a staple of the equine industry for centuries and has resulted in the development of a number of pure breeds. It also results in grade horses, which are the well-loved mutts of the equine world (see the nearby "Making the grade horse" sidebar).

Draft breeds

Draft horses are living relics of humanity's agricultural past. Originally bred for hundreds of years to pull heavy loads, draft breeds were used only until recently to work farms around the globe. When motorized tractors replaced draft horses in agricultural society, these magnificent creatures nearly died out. The work and dedication of people who love these horses saved draft horses from sure extinction.

Today, draft horses are used mostly for showing and exhibition, although some still are used to work small farms and perform other hauling jobs not suited to trucks and tractors. Draft horses are also ridden, and because of their docile temperaments, make wonderful — if not rather large — companions.

Although draft horses still are considered rare, you can find several breeds of them in North America. Each of the breeds in the following sections has an American registry and a good number of devotees in various countries.

Belgian

American Belgians differ somewhat from their European counterparts. Belgians in the United States are larger, heavier horses than those seen in the breed's native country. American Belgians stand around 18 hands and are mostly seen in one coloration: sorrel with a flaxen (blond) mane and tail.

These days, Belgians are used primarily in the show ring and for pulling contests. Some Midwestern American farmers still use Belgian teams to work their fields, as do many of the Amish in the United States. You can see a Belgian in the color section.

Clydesdale

The Clydesdale probably is the most well-known of all the draft breeds, thanks to Anheuser-Busch. Clydesdale horses have been pulling the Budweiser beer wagon for decades, and are regularly seen in the company's TV commercials and in exhibitions around the country.

Clydesdales usually come in a bay coloration, although they can also be seen in chestnut, black, brown, and roan. These horses can be anywhere from 16.1 to 18 hands in height. They have wonderful dispositions and are often used for riding as well as pulling.

Gypsy Horse

The Gypsy Horse is also known as the Gypsy Vanner and the Gypsy Cob, depending on which registry you look at. This stunning, small draft horse traces its roots to the Traveler people of the United Kingdom, who used this horse to pull their colorful wagons from town to town in the 1800s. The breed became known in the U.S. in the 1990s and has become well known for it's striking markings, long mane and tail, and feathered — that is, hairy — legs.

Gypsy Horses make good riding horses because of their smaller size, and they are often used for trail riding, parades, and horse shows. They are most often seen in black and white, but they actually come in a variety of horse colors.

Percheron

Percherons are seen only in gray or black, and average around 16 hands in height — a little on the short side for a draft horse. What they lack in height, they make up for in bulk. They are strong and stocky horses.

You can ride Percherons or use them to pull carts and wagons; this breed is shown extensively in the United States. They're known for having calm personalities and being trainable.

Shire

Shires are attractive horses with heavy feathering around their fetlocks (ankles) see Chapter 2 for a diagram on parts of the horse) and long fuzzy beards on their jaws. They are medium height for a draft breed, measuring anywhere from 16 to 17.2 hands.

Shires are shown in harness and at halter in the United States and in other countries. The breed is often seen pulling beer wagons at events in Great Britain, and some people still use Shires to haul goods in other parts of the world.

Suffolk Punch

The Suffolk Punch, or simply Suffolk, is a smaller draft horse, measuring in at around 16 hands. An unusual aspect to the breed is its single color; Suffolks only come in chestnut (which devotees of the breed spell *chesnut* in the archaic way).

Suffolks are still used to do field work and pull wagons for exhibitions, but they're also shown and ridden.

Gaited horses

Gaited horses are those breeds possessing one or more additional gaits in addition to or instead of the usual walk, trot, and gallop found in so-called nongaited horses (see Chapter 2 for more about these movements). These unusual gaits were developed in these breeds by humans to make long-distance riding more comfortable. Equestrians who love gaited horses claim these horses are the most enjoyable mounts to ride.

Gaited breeds are among the most popular horses in the United States: the Tennessee Walking Horse and the American Saddlebred (covered in earlier sections of this chapter). Other, lesser-known gaited breeds are found in the United States, each with its own fascinating history and characteristics. Although the breeds highlighted in the following sections aren't as common as the ones that made it to the top ten, they are nonetheless available in many parts of the country.

Icelandic Horse

The Icelandic Horse is a small but sturdy creature with its roots in Viking history. The breed developed in complete isolation for more than 1,000 years and is believed to be the horse the Vikings used in their mounted exploits.

The Icelandic Horse is known for having either four or five gaits. In addition to the walk, trot, and gallop, all Icelandic Horses possess a gait called the *tolt*, which is similar to the Tennessee Walker's running walk. Some Icelandics also have a gait called the *flying pace*, where the legs on each side of the horse move in unison.

The Icelandic looks somewhat like a pony and measures only 12.3 to 14 hands in height. However, despite its small size, the Icelandic is considered a horse breed and not a pony breed. Full-grown men can easily ride this rugged little animal. (See the section on pony breeds later in this chapter for more about ponies.) These horses are ridden for pleasure and are good in the show ring.

Missouri Fox Trotter

The Missouri Fox Trotter was created by Missouri cattlemen in the 1800s to carry riders across long distances of rough terrain and to work cattle. Because the Missouri Fox Trotter was intended to be ridden for long periods of time, a comfortable gaited aspect was bred into this willing horse. As a result, the Missouri Fox Trotter has a special trot exemplified by a four-beat gait instead of the usual two beats found in a typical trot.

Missouri Fox Trotters are handsome horses, measuring between 14 and 16 hands. They have easygoing personalities and generally are considered a good horse for beginners to ride and to show.

National Show Horse

The National Show Horse is a relatively new breed created in the 1980s by crossing Arabians to American Saddlebreds. The resulting horse turned out to be a flashy and refined animal perfect for the show ring.

As a result of its Saddlebred heritage, the National Show Horse is trained in two other gaits besides the walk, trot, and gallop. National Show Horses are capable of performing the *slow gait* and the *rack*, both four-beat gaits that are comfortable to ride.

National Show Horses are on the taller side, standing 15 to 16 hands in height. They come in a variety of horse colors, and tend to be spirited. Their primary use is in the show ring (hence the name), where they can show off their high-stepping gaits.

Paso Fino

You most often see the Paso Fino breed in Cuba, Puerto Rico, and Colombia, although it has quite a few fans in the United States, too. Paso Finos originally were created by crossing Spanish Andalusians (see "Rare Breeds" section later in this chapter) with the now extinct Spanish Jennets a couple of centuries ago.

The Paso Fino gaits include the *paso fino, paso corto,* and the *paso largo.* Each gait varies in speed and is a four-beat lateral gait (each foot hits the ground separately, and the legs on each side move in unison) that is extremely comfortable to ride, and covers considerable ground. Some Paso Finos can also canter.

Paso Finos typically measure around 14 to 15 hands in height and have a pleasing and distinctive conformation. Paso Finos possess a personality trait known as *brio,* which means controlled spirit. Horses with *brio* are full of energy but are completely under the rider's control. Superb on the trail, Paso Finos also are shown extensively in their special gaits.

Peruvians

Peruvians (once called Peruvian Pasos) have found a devoted following in the United States. Developed in Peru in the 1800s to carry landowners across vast areas of the country, the breed contains the blood of Spanish Andalusians, Arabians, and Thoroughbreds.

Peruvians possess three gaits: the *paso llano,* the *sobreandando,* and the *huachano.* Each of these gaits is a four-beat lateral gait and is designed to be comfortable while covering considerable ground. Peruvian horses that are in top condition can maintain these gaits for hours on end.

Peruvians are on the small to medium side, measuring 14.1 to 15.1 hands in height. They have well-muscled necks and long, thick manes and tails. They make excellent trail horses, and are shown under saddle in their natural gaits. You can see a Peruvian horse in the color section.

Racking Horse

The Racking Horse is not as easy to define as most other breeds of horses. Racking Horses shared a history with the Tennessee Walking Horse (covered earlier in this chapter) until 1971, when a group of Alabama horsemen broke off from the Tennessee Walking Horse breed for political and economic reasons, and started a registry for what they dubbed the Racking Horse. A few years later, in 1975, the House and Senate of the Alabama Legislature named the Racking Horse the official state horse of Alabama.

What makes the Racking Horse so special is that it is a *gaited* breed, able to perform a four-beat racking gait, in addition to a walk and a canter.

Racking Horses have graceful builds, with long, sloping necks. Their legs are smooth and their hair finely textured. The typical Racking Horse averages around 15.2 hands, and comes in a number of colors including sorrel, chestnut, black, roan, white, bay, brown, gray, yellow, dun, and palomino. You may also see a pinto coloration, known within the breed as *spotted*. These horses are willing to work and eager to please their handlers.

Riders exhibit Racking Horses in saddle-seat and driving classes that are meant to show off their racking gait, but they also show less flashy individuals in more traditional pleasure classes. Racking horses make good trail horses and are popular for simple pleasure riding.

Pony breeds

By definition, a *pony* is a small type of horse standing less than 14.2 hands at the withers. However, a distinction exists between a true pony and a horse that is simply on the short side. Not every horse under 14.2 hands is considered a pony, and not every pony over 14.1 hands is considered a horse. Ponies are members of distinctive pony breeds. In other words, you can't breed two Thoroughbreds or two Arabians and get a pony. Breeders produce a pony by breeding two ponies, or by breeding a pony to a small horse.

Ponies tend to be hardy little creatures. Most pony breeds developed in harsh European climates with rugged terrain; they had to become durable and level-headed to survive.

Most adults are too big to comfortably ride a small pony (neither the pony nor the adult will be happy), although a smaller adult can do fine with a larger pony. If you want a mount for your child, however, a pony can certainly do the job.

The following pony breeds are popular in North America:

>> **Shetland**: The Shetland pony is the creature people most often think about when they hear the word *pony*. This breed is one of the smaller ponies around. Shetlands make excellent mounts for young children as long as the ponies — and the kids — are properly trained. American Shetlands are usually around 11 hands high and come in a wide variety of horse colors.

>> **Welsh Ponies:** These ponies come in four different types: the Welsh Mountain Pony, the Welsh Pony, the Welsh Pony of Cob Type, and the Welsh Cob. Each of these four names represents different heights and conformation types

within the Welsh breed. Okay, we know it's confusing, but stay with us. If you think of each type in terms of its height, it gets a little better: The Welsh Mountain is 12.2 hands or shorter; the Welsh Pony 12.2 to 13.2 hands high; the Welsh Pony of Cob Type is 13.2 hands high or less; and the Cob Type is actually horse-sized at 14 to 15.1 hands tall. All versions of Welsh Ponies make excellent equine companions for children. The taller ones are big enough for some adults. Check out a Welsh Pony in the color section.

>> **Connemara:** The Connemara is a refined-looking pony that excels in jumping. Measuring on the tall side (13 to 14.2 hands), Connemaras make suitable mounts for some adults and for children.

>> **Pony of the Americas:** The Pony of the Americas, or POA as it is commonly called, originated from crossings with the Appaloosa horse and the Shetland pony. POAs typically have Appaloosa markings, and are good ponies for kids. In fact, the American POA breed association has one of the most extensive youth show programs in the country. POAs typically stand anywhere from 11.2 to 14 hands high.

>> **Highland Pony:** The Highland Pony is a rugged Scottish breed with roots that go back to the 8th century BCE. Although popular in the U.K., only a handful of Highland Ponies can be found in America. They measure from 13 to 14 hands, and are shown in dressage, eventing and driving, and used for trail riding.

Warmbloods

In the 1980s, a European type of horse called the warmblood became popular in the United States. Seen for years in international jumping and dressage competitions, the warmblood suddenly became the horse of choice for Americans who wanted to compete in the upper levels of Olympic disciplines like dressage, jumping, combined training (or three-day eventing), and driving.

Several different warmblood breeds exist, each named for the region it comes from, with its own distinct characteristics. What they all have in common is a large stature, profound athletic ability, and a high price tag. Some of these breeds are common in the United States and Canada, while others are only available in Europe.

Here's a list of the warmblood breeds you see most often in North America:

>> **Belgian Warmblood:** Averages around 16 hands; good in show jumping, eventing, and dressage

>> **Dutch Warmblood (check out one of these horses in the color section):** Average around 16.2 hands; known for talent in dressage and jumping

- » **Hanoverian:** German breed known for abilities in dressage, eventing, and jumping; averages 16 to 17 hands

- » **Holsteiner:** Developed in Germany; averages 16 to 17 hands; excels in driving, eventing, jumping, and dressage

- » **Oldenberg:** Hails from Germany; averages 16 hands high; talented jumping, dressage, and eventing horse

- » **Swedish Warmblood:** Averages 16 hands; used for show jumping, dressage, and eventing

- » **Trakehner:** German breed used for jumping, dressage, and eventing; averages 16 to 17 hands

Rare breeds

The world is full of horse breeds, many of them rather rare. Despite their small numbers, a handful of these breeds have managed to capture the hearts of horse lovers everywhere. You frequently see horses of these breeds in motion pictures or at equine fairs and exhibitions around the world. Though their numbers are scarce, they're important members of the horse community and worth taking a look at.

Andalusian

The Andalusian horse, also known as the Pure Spanish Horse, is one of the most spectacular studies in horseflesh on the planet. You see this horse in museum pieces and paintings from the Middle Ages: Leonardo da Vinci sculpted this horse, and the winged Pegasus was based on this breed. Because Andalusians have been around for so long, they have been instrumental in the development of other breeds such as the Peruvian, Spanish Mustang, and Lipizzaner.

Andalusians have a distinctive look. Their necks are heavy and arched; their manes and tails are long and wavy. With a regalness about them that's hard to equal, even a relatively untrained eye can easily spot this breed.

Andalusians are spirited horses used for showing and pleasure riding. The majority of individual Andalusians in the United States are located in California, although a number of other states have small populations of this beautiful horse. Flip to the color section to see a photo of an Andalusian.

Friesian

The Friesian horse is hard to miss in a crowd. This regal, all-black equine has been around for centuries, developed first in Holland. The Friesian has had a great influence in the horse world, having been used to create a number of European breeds.

Friesians usually stand around 15 to 16 hands in height, although their proud carriage gives the impression that they are taller. Their manes and tails are long and flowing, and they have heavy feathering on their fetlocks. The high-stepping movement of the Friesian is a sight to behold.

During the last several years, the Friesian's numbers have grown in the United States, where the breed now sports around 8,000 individuals. Friesians are being used successfully in dressage and in carriage work.

Kiger Mustang

The U.S. Bureau of Land Management (BLM) has been rounding up wild horses since 1971 and placing them up for adoption. In 1977, during one of these round-ups in remote Beatty's Butte, Oregon, a BLM official noticed that a number of horses were very similar in color and conformation. The horses were separated from the herd and determined to be of Colonial Spanish origin.

In an effort to preserve these horses, Herd Management Areas were set up in southeastern Oregon, where the horses were re-released. This was the beginning of the Kiger Mustang breed. Today, most Kigers are bred in captivity.

Kigers are used for a variety of purposes, with trail riding being most common. They are often seen in dun colorations, although all horse colors are possible in the breed. They typically stand between 13.2 and 15.2 hands.

Lipizzaner

Lipizzaners are among the most well-known of all breeds, thanks to the famous Lipizzaner stallions of Vienna. These highly trained stallions have gained notoriety the world over for their skill at performing classical dressage movements also known as *airs above the ground.*

Lipizzaners originated in Austria as war horses and are now seen mostly in Europe. A handful of Lipizzaners exist in the United States where they are shown and used for exhibitions.

Lipizzaner foals are born dark brown or black and mature to a light gray (nearly white). Adult Lipizzaners typically have thick, wavy manes and tails and heavy, arched necks.

Lusitano

The Lusitano, a Portuguese breed, is closely related to the Andalusian horse (covered earlier in this chapter). The two breeds had identical histories until modern times, when Portuguese breeders developed the Lusitano into a separate horse from the Andalusian.

Although Andalusians typically are seen in a grey coloration, Lusitanos often come in palomino, buckskin, dun, bay, chestnut, and other colors. Lusitanos have a rounder head and body than the Andalusian and are more compact and agile.

Lusitanos are seen in shows and exhibitions and are used for dressage and pleasure riding.

Spanish Mustang

In the 1500s, Spaniards entered what is now the United States through New Mexico, bringing with them a number of their horses to populate the New World. The descendants of these original Spanish mounts are believed to be a breed now known as the Spanish Mustang.

Spanish Mustangs once roamed wild in the American West and have come to be exceptionally hardy and intelligent. They tend to be on the small side, measuring around 14 to 15 hands. Known for their endurance, Spanish Mustangs make great trail horses and companions.

Wild horse

One of the most romantic histories in horsedom belongs to the American wild horse, a creature that still inhabits certain parts of the United States. Believed by many to be escaped descendants of those horses used to build the American West, wild horses are protected by federal law. Consequently, horse wranglers can no longer capture the wild ones and sell them for pet food, a deplorable action that was rampant until the early 1970s, when the Wild Horse Protection Act was passed.

Despite official protection, wild horses still are at the center of political controversy. Ranchers who use public lands to graze livestock want wild-horse herds kept to a minimum to allow more cattle to be graze there, but many horse lovers believe the wild horse has first rights to the land. Ranching interests usually win out of late, and the Bureau of Land Management regularly reduces the number of horses present on the land by rounding them up and putting them up for public adoption. Anyone who can prove they have access to proper horsekeeping facilities can pay a small fee to adopt a wild horse. (See Chapter 5 for more about wild horse adoptions.)

WARNING

Although young wild horses can be trained in much the same way as domestically born horses, adult wild horses need special handling to adapt to captivity. For that reason, full-grown wild horses that are fresh off the range are not recommended for beginning equestrians.

2

Selecting a Horse and the Stuff that Goes with Him

Chapter **4**

Preparing to Make Your Purchase

B ecoming a horse owner is a serious decision; it's serious business. Unlike skiing, golf, or tennis, horseback riding is a hobby that involves *a living, breathing creature.* When you don't feel like playing golf or aren't in the mood to ski, you can just toss your equipment into the garage and forget about it until the urge strikes again. But owning a horse is different ballgame.

When you own a horse, you're taking responsibility for another living being that you must feed, groom, and even ride on days when you don't feel like it. A horse can't sit in a corner while you decide to do something that better suits your mood. Horses need regular care and attention, and they need TLC.

For these reasons, you need to consider some serious points before embarking on the journey of horse ownership. In this chapter, we take a look at these important considerations and give you some advice about preparing for the day when a horse ultimately calls you "Mom" or "Dad."

Finding Out Why You Want a Horse

When you find yourself developing the urge to own a horse, you need to do some soul searching. We want you to ask yourself some profound and difficult questions. Not only does your happiness and enjoyment depend on the answers you give, but so does a horse's well-being.

We've heard too many stories of people coming into the horse world on a whim, casually entering into horse ownership without realizing the commitment involved. The final result: The newcomer grows unhappy, and the horse ends up paying the price for it. The owner loses interest, and the horse winds up standing in his stall for weeks or months at a time with little or no attention other than a minimal amount of care. Or the animal ends up being sold for a quick buck and is marked for the slaughterhouse. In extreme cases, the owner abandons the horse, leaving it to slowly starve to death in a grassless pasture because no one cares anymore.

Although these scenarios sound dramatic, they do occur. We know that you don't want to be guilty of inflicting any such unfair treatment on a horse, the most noble and beautiful of all domestic creatures. That's why you need to probe deeply into your psyche to make sure that owning a horse is really something you want to do. And we're going to help you do just that.

Rating your reasons for wanting a horse

People are drawn to horse ownership for a number of reasons. Some of them are good, and others are not so good reasons.

Maybe you've wanted a horse your entire life, but couldn't afford one until now. If so, you're part of a fascinating, primarily female trend in the horse world. As little girls, many women longed to have a horse of their own. In fact, a horse obsession is almost a prerequisite to *being* a little girl, it seems. This little-girl passion for horses apparently reached an all-time high in the 1950s and 1960s. And now these once-obsessed little girls are all grown up and have the disposable income to fulfill their dreams.

Men are not exempt from this phenomenon. More than one little boy grew up wanting to be a cowboy riding on a swift steed and galloping off into the sunset. For many men, that John Wayne fantasy never went away, and horse ownership makes that fantasy a reality — well, sort of.

Wanting a horse to fulfill a dream is fine as long as you realize all the real-life responsibilities that come with horse ownership. Here's a list of the not-so-glamorous things you'll be dealing with after taking the ownership plunge:

>> **Unappealing jobs:** You won't only be riding your horse, you'll also be feeding him, grooming him, and cleaning up after him. The feeding and cleaning part is especially true if you're keeping the horse on your own property. Mucking stalls is hardly one of the more romantic aspects of horse ownership, yet the task is inevitable and just about every horse owner does it at some point in his or her life. Although horse manure doesn't smell anywhere near as bad as dog doo, you still won't relish the job. (Check out Chapters 8 and 9 for feeding and grooming details.)

>> **Assuming total responsibility:** The horse is completely dependent on you for food, water, exercise, and attention, so you must be willing to make the horse's needs a priority in your life. That means no going out to the karaoke bar with your friends after a hard day at the office until *after* you feed your horse. It also means braving any kind of weather Mother Nature throws at you — and she can have a pretty wicked aim — to get your horse out for grooming and exercise — whether you feel like doing it or not. The horse stands there waiting for you to show up and give it the care it needs, and doing so is your responsibility. Period.

>> **Enslaving financial obligations:** Owning a horse is downright expensive. Some horse people sport a bumper sticker on their cars that reads, "Poverty is owning a horse," which is not that much of an exaggeration.

  If you get lucky and end up with a horse that never gets sick or injured and doesn't need shoes or supplements, that bumper sticker may not be for you. However, we've yet to meet anyone who owns such a creature, so odds are that you'll be regularly coughing up cold hard cash to tend to your horse's special needs.

Fulfilling a dream isn't the reason that everyone is drawn to horse ownership. Some people just love animals and find the idea of spending time and bonding with a horse appealing. Others see people riding and think it looks like great fun. Both are legitimate reasons for delving into horse ownership as long as you understand the responsibilities and drawbacks of horse ownership that we outlined in the preceding bulleted list.

Don't fall prey to some of the not-so-good reasons for wanting a horse:

>> **Zoning ordinances:** You just bought a house in the country that happens to be zoned for horses, and even though you've never had an interest in horses before and aren't terribly interested in them now, you feel like you need to have one, well, because you can.

>> **Lawn ornaments:** You think that horses are attractive creatures, and even though you don't have any great urge to care for or ride one, having a horse on your property would make your yard look nicer.

>> **Junior wants one:** You don't have much interest in horses, but your child wants one. Your child has never ridden a horse before, but rather than giving him lessons first, you'd rather just buy a horse right away.

>> **Romance:** You have absolutely no experience with horses but think that the whole notion of riding is romantic. Rather than take lessons first to see whether you actually enjoy riding, you decide to buy a horse instead.

>> **Spare change:** You just inherited a little bit of money and want to spend it all on buying a horse. You think that the biggest expense in horse ownership is the purchase price, so you aren't worried about maintenance costs.

WARNING

If any of these scenarios sound like you, stop before you buy a horse and *think*. None of the reasons in this list is adequate for taking on the huge commitment and responsibility of horse ownership. You first need to do much more research into what owning a horse is all about. Most important, you have to develop a genuine interest in horses before taking the plunge into owning one. Horses require a huge commitment of time, money, and energy, and if you aren't sincerely dedicated to your equine charge, the responsibility soon feels more like a burden, and ultimately, you and the horse will suffer.

Determining whether you're ready

Before you accept the challenge of horse ownership, you must prepare yourself for the experience by developing a basic knowledge of horses and what owning one is all about.

Forfeiting the green: The money factor

Money — and how much of it you have — is a big thing to consider when you're debating whether to buy a horse. Horses are expensive animals to have around, and knowing exactly *how* expensive before you go out and buy one is imperative.

Find out the costs of various aspects of horse ownership in your area and make sure that the total amount fits in your budget. Following is a rundown of what costs you can expect to incur.

STARTING UP: INITIAL COSTS

Buying a decent horse means shelling out some decent money. The cost of horses varies considerably from one place to another, but expect to spend at least $1,500 (usually more) for a trained riding horse and much more for an animal you want to show.

In addition to the expense of getting the horse, you need to buy equipment and supplies, including a saddle, saddle pad, bridle, halter, grooming tools, and so on. Plus, you need riding apparel for yourself and possibly your family (see Chapter 6 for details on horse equipment). All these things can really add up. Depending on whether you buy these items new or used, you can spend anywhere from $800 to $3,000 for all this gear.

If you plan to keep your horse on your own property, you also need enough money to create the appropriate housing for the animal. This sum can be substantial, depending on the amount of work you have to do (see Chapter 7 for details about housing a horse).

KEEPING YOUR HORSE: MAINTENANCE COSTS

One big mistake that newcomers to the horse world make is underestimating the cost of maintaining a horse. In most cases, the purchase sum is minimal compared with the amount of money that keeping the horse requires.

REMEMBER

Here is a list of the regular expenses you can expect with horse ownership. The costs of each item or service vary considerably depending on where you live, so we advise calling commercial stables, veterinarians, *farriers* (the people who trim and put shoes on the horse's feet), and tack and feed stores in your area to get a sense of how much each of these items runs:

>> **Boarding:** If you plan to keep your horse at a commercial boarding facility rather than on your own property, you pay a monthly fee for a stall, pasture, or *paddock* (a fenced enclosure). This fee usually includes food and stall maintenance; it may or may not include bedding.

>> **Bedding:** If your horse is kept in a stall that you're responsible for maintaining, you have to provide shavings or another type of bedding, which you must clean and freshen daily.

>> **Feed:** If you're keeping the horse on your own property, feed includes hay and/or pasture maintenance. If you plan to give grain or other special-diet foods to your horse, figure in that cost as well. See Chapter 8 for more about horse feed.

>> **Supplements:** Many horses benefit from including feed supplements in their diets. If your horse needs these supplements, add this cost to your monthly expenses.

- » **Shoes:** Most horses require new shoes every 6 to 8 weeks. A farrier still needs to trim the hooves of horses that don't need shoes — because they're either not doing much work or have tough feet — every 6 to 8 weeks. (Chapter 10 has more info about shoeing and hoof care.)

- » **Preventative veterinary care:** Regular health maintenance for most adult horses includes vaccinations, deworming (or checking for worms) several times a year, and teeth floating once or twice a year. Teeth floating doesn't mean your horse's teeth will be set adrift in a bucket of Efferdent. *Floating* is another term for filing them down. See Chapter 10 for details.

- » **Veterinary treatment:** When a horse gets sick, the problem can be anything from a minor illness to a situation that requires major surgery. As an owner, you must be prepared to spend money on veterinary treatment whenever your horse becomes ill.

- » **Insurance:** If you insure your horse for major medical, mortality, loss of use, and/or liability, add the premiums to your list of expenses. (See "Investigating Horse Insurance" later in this chapter for more info.)

- » **Training/lessons:** New horse owners with little riding experience need to continue their own and their horse's educations with a trainer or riding instructor. Training is a must if you intend to show your horse, and weekly training or lessons for horse and/or rider are an expense.

- » **Show expenses:** If you plan to show your horse, you'll spend money on show clothes and tack, entry fees, and transportation. (See Chapter 18 for details on showing.)

- » **Transportation:** If you're like most horse owners, you'll want a horse trailer so that you can take your horse places. Depending on the type you buy, you can spend a few thousand dollars for a small used trailer or tens of thousands for a brand-new trailer with all kinds of amenities. Remember too that you'll need a heavy-duty vehicle to haul the trailer as most occupied horse trailers are much too heavy for a car or small truck to pull.

Watching the clock: Time issues

Owning a horse is much more time consuming than people usually think. The daily care of a 1,000-pound animal that can't be housebroken is involved.

If you're keeping the horse at home, and the horse is going to be in a stall or "dry" (without grass) paddock, you must find time to feed it two to three times a day and make time to clean the enclosure (remove the manure and soiled bedding) at least once a day. Add the time to do these chores to the amount of time you need to spend grooming and exercising the horse, and you're going to spend a noteworthy chunk of your day on horse care.

WARNING

Although a horse can be an ideal family companion, don't expect your kids to take on too much of the time responsibility. Sure, they can help out, but as the adult, you're the one ultimately responsible for the horse's care and well-being. And considering how most kids are about such things, you'll probably end up having to make time to do the work yourself.

Staying loyal: Commitment issues

You have to be willing to be there for your horse every day, rain or shine, time or no time. You can ask yourself the following questions to help determine whether you're ready and willing to make this commitment:

» Am I willing to give up some of my other activities to spend time caring for my horse?

» Am I willing to drop everything and run to my horse's side should he get sick?

» Am I willing to spend time giving my horse medicine or treatment if he becomes ill?

» Am I willing to take time out of my busy week, each and every week, to groom and exercise my horse?

» Am I willing to work with my horse to solve any problems the two of us may encounter?

» Am I willing to perform (or pay someone else to perform) the sometimes hard physical labor that horse care calls for?

» Am I willing to think of my horse as a partner, one who deserves the best care and treatment, regardless of the inconvenience I may experience?

» If I am buying this horse primarily for my children, am I willing to continue to care for him even if my children lose interest?

If you answered yes to all of these questions, then you're ready to make the commitment to horse ownership.

Exploring which way you want to ride (and how you want to learn)

If you haven't yet figured out how you want to ride, flip to Chapter 14 to decide which discipline interests you most. Four popular styles are hunt seat, dressage, saddle seat, and western. Figuring out in which discipline you want to ride is one of the first decisions you need to make, because the way you ride determines what kind of horse you buy.

Most horses are trained in only one or two of the disciplines. You may want to get some riding experience in the discipline you've chosen to make sure that you really like it before you commit to buying a horse and tack that you can ride only in that style.

Learning to ride is one of the smartest things you can do before you go out and buy a horse. Although this statement sounds obvious, if you don't know much about riding, you may not realize how hard it is and how much work proper riding takes. After all, you need to know much more about riding than just hopping up on the critter's back — which isn't that easy, either!

REMEMBER

Some of the benefits of learning to ride *before* you get your own horse are:

>> Knowing for certain that riding is something you truly enjoy because you've already been doing it.

>> Having a good sense of what type of horse is best for you, based on your riding style and skill level.

>> Evaluating horses for purchase with better insight from being able to ride them competently.

>> Avoiding the risk of *ruining* a new horse with poor riding skills that can disrupt its previous training.

>> Enjoying your new horse right away, instead of spending precious bonding time just trying to learn the basics of riding.

We cover a few ways to get some riding experience in the following sections.

Taking regular lessons

Formal riding lessons are the best way to learn how to ride a horse. In most areas of the civilized world, riding lessons are relatively easy to come by. Nearly every commercial boarding facility has trainers and instructors on staff who give lessons by the hour. In the United States, both western and English lessons are staples at commercial riding facilities.

You can look for riding lessons by searching the Internet for "Riding Academies" in your area. If several riding facilities are accessible to you, contact an equine veterinarian in your area for help choosing a good one. (You can find an equine vet in your area via the Internet too.) Tell members of the veterinarian's staff that you're looking for beginning riding lessons and ask whether they can recommend a good facility in the area.

After locating a facility, we recommend that you take an initial riding lesson in the discipline of your choice, and if you like the instructor and the quality of the experience, sign up for a series of lessons. Most facilities offer discount packages of four or more lessons.

If you're arranging riding lessons for your child, make sure that the facility you contact offers lessons for young riders in your child's age group.

The number and type of lessons you ultimately take depends on what you can afford and how much you still need to learn. We suggest that you take as many lessons as fit your budget. Group lessons are less expensive and can be a fun way to learn from watching others. Individual lessons cost more, but you'll get more personalized attention from the instructor.

Some people continue to take lessons for years, gradually moving up in their individual training level just as any athlete does. You can never educate yourself enough about riding. In fact, Olympic equestrian team members continue to take lessons even after they've won gold medals!

Attending horse camps

A horse camp is another way that you can start riding. By attending a horse camp, you can combine a vacation with an intensive riding experience.

Horse camps are resorts that specialize in equine activities. Most offer lessons for beginners and enable you to spend a concentrated amount of time with and around horses. The camps provide access to other activities — tennis and hiking, typically — but you have the option of spending all your time checking out horses. (See Chapter 19 for details on horse camps.)

Horse camps are a great way for beginners to start riding. However, plan to continue your riding education when you return home from your vacation. True, you'll get a good foundation in the week or two that you spend at horse camp, but this short amount of time isn't enough for you to completely develop your riding skills. Sign up for ongoing lessons at a local riding academy to give yourself more time learning in the saddle.

Participating in adult education programs

More and more community colleges and private learning centers are offering introductory courses in riding for adults. These classes can be a great way to have a first experience on a horse because they almost always include riding lessons. Basic information on equine anatomy, care and feeding, grooming, and other aspects of horsemanship often are often a part of these courses.

You can use the Internet to browse the curriculum of the community colleges and private learning centers in your area.

Using breed club programs

A number of national breed clubs sponsor programs that introduce people to the world of horses, particularly that association's breed. These programs match up beginning riders and experienced professionals within the given breed. The goal is to give new riders more information about horses and to assist them when they're ready to purchase that breed of horse.

Avoiding rental stables

WARNING

Rental stables are places where you can rent a horse in increments of typically one hour and take the horse out on a trail ride, usually with a group. Instead of offering riding lessons, these facilities stick you up on a horse and send you on your way. Most rental stables offer nothing in the way of instruction and plenty in the way of potential disaster. Stay away from them while trying to acquire basic horsemanship skills.

Although you can find a few good rental stables, they are not common. At most rental stables, the horses are poorly treated and make terrible mounts. Because they're ridden day in and day out by people who don't even know the basics of riding, they lose whatever training they may have had when they first came to the place. Horses that are uncooperative and sometimes even dangerous are the end result.

The sad truth is that most first riding experiences occur at these kinds of stables. Consequently, most first riding experiences are unpleasant ones. Ask your non-horsy friends about the first time they ever rode a horse, and you'll see what we mean. Tales of horses trying to rub riders off on trees, horses rolling on the ground with the riders still in the saddle, horses running back to barn while the riders hold on for dear life — these all are common rental stable stories.

Establishing responsibility for your horse

Before you go out and start looking for a horse, figure out exactly who is going to ride it. Is the horse just for you, or will your spouse or children also be riding the animal?

REMEMBER

When more than one person in your family is going to ride the horse, you must consider those individuals as you're figuring out which horse to buy. The horse needs to be suitable for the family member with the least amount of riding experience. If you've been riding for years, but your spouse has never been on a horse before, get a horse that can take care of a rank beginner (sorry, dear). Meanwhile, sign your spouse up for riding lessons.

If your children are the only ones who plan to ride the horse, then you'd better be absolutely certain that they're committed to riding (as committed as a child can be anyway). After all, if your kids can't even sit relatively still through *The Incredibles*, they may not be ready for the amount of concentration that's required in horseback riding. Make them take riding lessons for at least a year before you actually buy a horse. If they're still enthusiastic about riding after taking instruction for that long, then they'll probably stick with it after you purchase a horse.

Deciding between leasing or buying

Most people who want a horse have the impulse to buy one. Many horse lovers have dreamed of having their own horse since childhood, and as adults, are in the position to make it happen. However, owning a horse requires a huge commitment in time and money. So, we heartily recommend another option: leasing one.

Leasing a horse instead of or before you buy one gives you a great opportunity to find out what horse ownership is all about before you commit to it. When you lease, you function pretty much as a horse owner but without the same financial or long-term pledges.

Shortages of horses that are available for lease never seem to occur. On the contrary, leasing is a perfect arrangement for an owner who doesn't have time to ride the horse, doesn't have the money to care for him, or no longer has the desire or ability to ride. Why don't people in these situations just sell their horses? Because leasing enables them to stay in control of the horse's fate while eliminating some or all of the ownership responsibilities.

Although leasing can be a great way to test out your commitment to horse ownership, the one pitfall is that you can find yourself growing attached to the horse you're leasing, only to discover that the owner refuses to sell the animal or wants to sell but you can't afford to buy.

We give you the scoop on leases in the sections that follow.

Deciphering different types of leases

Leases, which often are flexible, can work in a number of different ways. The one you ultimately choose needs to be the one best suited to your own needs and wants. Some examples of common lease arrangements include:

>> **Full leases:** The owner leases the horse out completely, letting the lessee keep the horse in the facility of his or her choice. The lessee pays a flat fee upfront on the lease for a given amount of time (usually a year) and assumes all of the horse's maintenance costs, including food, shoes, and routine

veterinary care. In most cases, if the horse becomes seriously ill or is injured, the owner is responsible for the horse's medical bills. These leases sometimes come with an option to buy the horse at the end of the lease term. Consider this option if you want to get a realistic taste of horse ownership before you commit to buying one or if you don't have the cash upfront to actually purchase a horse.

» **Full leases with stipulations:** The owner leases the horse to you but requires that the horse be kept at the owner's or another approved facility. The lessee can ride the horse each and every day, but must request permission to trailer the horse off the property or do anything out of the ordinary with the animal. Payment arrangements tend to vary considerably with this type of lease. Owners sometimes charge a monthly fee for the lease, which may or may not include the horse's vet care and shoeing. This lease arrangement is good whenever you want to get a sense of horse ownership without the total commitment of buying. Because of the stipulations, these kinds of leases often are cheaper than straightforward, full leases.

» **Feed lease:** The owner allows you to lease the horse full time in exchange for you providing complete care to the horse. With a feed lease, there is no leasing fee. The only money you spend is whatever is required to care for the horse. Owners often choose this method of leasing when they just don't have the time or money to take care of a horse but want to keep ownership. This type of arrangement is often used among people who know each other, and it is appealing to owners when they know that their horse will receive very good care.

» **Partial leases:** With a partial lease, or half-lease, the owner leases the horse to a lessee for riding only a few days a week. Oftentimes, the owner rides the horse on the other days. Sometimes, the owner gives two half-leases to two different people, who end up sharing the horse. In a partial lease situation, the lessee rarely pays for any costs other than the leasing fee. This option is great if time and/or money are limited.

Finding and choosing a horse to lease

Locating a good horse to lease is much easier than finding a good horse to buy, in most cases. Here are some methods:

» **Word of mouth:** Asking around at boarding stables is one way to find horses for lease. This method seems to work particularly well — undoubtedly because of the strength of the horse-owner grapevine.

» **Trainers:** Horse trainers often have clients looking to lease out their horses. Asking trainers in your area may turn up several options.

>> **Advertisements:** If your area has a horse-oriented publication, check the classified section for "for lease" ads. Tack and feed stores almost always have bulletin boards with notices featuring horses for lease.

REMEMBER

When you consider leasing a horse, evaluate the animal as though you were buying it. Because your commitment is limited in a leasing situation, you don't need to be quite as certain of your choice, but you still want to make sure that the horse you choose is good for you. For more about characteristics to consider when choosing a horse, see "Considering a Horse's Traits" later in this chapter.

TIP

If you're going for a full lease, where you're be responsible for all the horse's veterinary care, you may want to pay for a basic veterinary pre-purchase exam to ensure that the horse is healthy. People often don't take this step because of the costs involved, but you may want to consider it. Check out Chapter 5 for more info about pre-purchase exams.

Securing a written agreement

TIP

A lease is a business transaction, so put the details of the arrangement in writing and have both parties sign the agreement. Having the agreement looked over by an attorney before signing and then notarized upon signing also is a good idea.

REMEMBER

If the owner doesn't offer a contract, draw one up yourself or have an attorney do it for you. If the horse's owner provides a contract, make sure that the document includes these details:

>> **Names:** Your name, address, and telephone number, and that of the horse's owner.

>> **Description:** The name and a description of the horse, including age, color, height, and registration number, if any.

>> **Purpose or intent:** How you intend to use the horse — trail riding only, showing in hunter classes, and so on. Write out all intended uses you have for the horse (after discussing them with the owner).

>> **Equipment:** Whether the lease includes use of the horse's tack.

>> **Restrictions:** What you *won't* be doing with the horse. If the owner doesn't want you to trailer the horse off the property, for example, the owner needs to stipulate that information in the lease.

>> **Care requirements:** Any physical care the horse needs, including grooming, exercise, feeding, and so on. Don't forget to include any regular medications or treatments the horse is receiving.

>> **Riders:** Who is permitted to ride the horse.

>> **Lease terms:** How long the lease is for, and whether it's renewable.

>> **Options:** If you hope to buy the horse at the end of the lease, make sure that the contract includes an option to buy.

>> **Price:** The price you're paying for the lease and how you're going to make payments.

>> **Insurance coverage:** Details on what kind of insurance covers the horse, particularly who is responsible for maintaining the premiums. If no insurance covers the horse, indicate who is responsible if the horse is injured, becomes ill, or dies. See "Investigating Horse Insurance" later in this chapter for more about insurance.

>> **Medical care:** State who is responsible for paying the horse's medical bills.

>> **Cancellation policy:** Indicate whether the lease can be canceled, by whom, and under what circumstances.

>> **Availability:** If you're signing a partial lease, spell out which days you can ride and which days the owner or other lessee is using the horse.

Getting some equine exposure

While you are considering buying or leasing a horse, it's a good idea to spend some time around horses in general. If you don't know anyone with a horse, here are some suggestions on how to do that:

>> **Rescues and riding centers:** Most horse rescues and therapeutic riding centers welcome volunteers to help with daily chores and caring for horses. Look online for a rescue or therapeutic riding facility in your area.

>> **Horse shows:** You may already know a venue near your home or work where horse shows are held. Going to a show and watching the horses can be fun and educational. You can even get to know fellow horse people by visiting with exhibitors after they are finished with their classes.

Considering a Horse's Traits

Okay, you're certain that you want a horse, can afford it, have the time for it, and you're ready for the commitment. Now you need to start thinking about what kind of horse you need. In the sections that follow, we provide you with a few important characteristics to consider when thinking about what you'd like in a horse. In Chapter 5, we get into deeper details on horse selection.

Thinking about a horse's age

Age is an important factor when selecting a horse, for reasons we'll explain in the sections that follow.

Why age matters

WARNING

The idea of getting a young horse may be appealing because of the potential for the animal to live longer than an older horse. However, you can't go in a worse direction when purchasing a first horse. Young horses typically are inexperienced and full of bugs. They don't have much confidence or knowledge, and their training usually is only cursory. Combine these elements with an inexperienced horse owner or rider, and you have a recipe for disaster.

The notion that a young, untrained horse and an inexperienced rider can learn together is a romantic one that doesn't cut it in the real world. In these situations, the horse generally becomes unmanageable, the rider becomes miserable, and the relationship dissolves into disaster.

REMEMBER

When you're learning to ride and care for a horse, your best teacher is an older, wizened horse that forgives your mistakes and helps show you the right way to do things. Horses older than 6 years are adults and capable of the kind of equine maturity and experience that you need in a first horse.

For example, coauthor Audrey Pavia got her first horse at the age of 13. She'd been riding for a couple of years but definitely was a neophyte when it came to horse ownership and serious riding. The horse her parents chose for her was a quiet, affectionate, older mare named Peggy, who was about 15 years old. Peggy had seen it all — including little kids who didn't really know how to ride — and she patiently taught Audrey much of what she, your humble author, now knows about horses.

Age differences

The horse world has standardized ways of evaluating horses by their age. In humans, we think of youngsters, teenagers, adults, and senior citizens. Well, equine equivalents of these stages of life exist, too. You may be surprised to see how horse age groups are similar to human age groups.

Although horses tend to age somewhat differently based on breed (larger draft and warmblood breeds take longer to mature than smaller, lighter breeds), what follows is a generalization about how you can categorize horses by age. Looking at horses' ages in this way helps you get a sense of who they are at any given point in their lives:

>> **Foals:** Foals are baby horses, anywhere from newborn to the age when they are weaned from their mothers (4 to 6 months, usually). Foals are physically awkward and curious about their surroundings, not unlike human infants and toddlers.

>> **Weanlings:** Weanlings usually are anywhere from 4 to 6 months in age. As the term suggests, they are babies who have been removed from their mothers. In human terms, weanlings are equivalent to preteens.

>> **Yearlings:** Yearlings are young horses that have reached their first year of life. They are the equine version of a teenybopper.

>> **Young horses:** Horses in this category are 2 to 3 years old and are just starting to be trained for riding. These are formative years for a horse, and equivalent to the older teenage years for a human. These horses tend to be harder to work with because they're not yet mentally mature. Physically, they're pretty much grown up, but they still have plenty of mental growth to go. Horses in this age range are not usually suitable for beginning riders because of their lack of training, experience and maturity.

>> **Young adult horses:** Horses in the range of 3 to 6 years old are in their peak learning phase. The majority of a horse's basic training takes place during this stage of life. As the horse slowly matures physically and mentally, he becomes ready to take on the role of serious worker and companion. The human equivalent to this age group is the late teens to early 20s. Most horses in this age group still are learning and so often are not right for beginning riders. Exceptions to this rule do exist, and mellow horses in this age bracket can be found.

>> **Adult horses:** This category is for horses between 6 and 14 years of age. Horses in this age group have matured physically and mentally, and most of their training is complete, so they're ready to happily do their jobs. Adult horses are similar to humans in their late 20s to late 40s. Horses at these ages can make good companions for novice riders, provided their training has been good and they aren't too full of energy.

>> **Senior horses:** Horses 15 years old and older are seniors. Just like humans in their senior years, 15-year-old horses may start to become arthritic and may have other health problems. When a horse reaches the age of 20, it moves into the upper reaches of the senior range (the human equivalent of the mid-60s and 70s age bracket). Horses at this age usually make good mounts for beginners. They have seen it all and done it all, and not too much fazes them. They tend to be mature, mellow, and forgiving of beginning riders.

Studying horse bodies

A horse that has a better build, or *conformation,* is the one most capable of doing the work humans ask of them. If you take time to study a horse's structure and anatomy, you develop an eye for what horse people call *good conformation.* Horses with good conformation are the ideal for most horse people. The following sections tell you how to spot both good and bad conformation. (See Chapter 2 for additional general info on horse parts.)

Recognizing normal conformation

Before you can spot the abnormal (covered in the following section), you need an idea of how a horse with normal conformation looks. When viewing a horse's legs from the front, drop imaginary line from the top center of the leg (at chest level) down to the ground. The centerlines on the legs of a horse with good conformation essentially split each leg in half all the way to the ground and appear to be parallel with each other.

Do the same thing when looking at the foreleg from the side. In your mind, draw a line from the top center of the leg all the way to the ground. A horse with good conformation has a centerline that splits the leg to the level of the fetlock (the horse's ankle), and then falls to the ground just behind the heel. (See Figure 4-1 for front and side views of straight legs.)

When you view the hind leg from the side, imagine a line from the back of the hindquarters to the ground. In a horse with good conformation, this line runs along the back of the cannon bone to the bulbs of the heels. (See Figure 4-2 to see correct hock angles. The hocks are the elbows of the back legs).

REMEMBER

Although these lines and angles may sound like a lesson from geometry class, they're important indicators of the effects of *concussion,* the impact of weight on the ground as it's felt through the horse's legs and hooves when it moves. A horse with proper leg angles is able to absorb the concussion more effectively and efficiently, thus placing less stress on its joints than a horse with the wrong angles. A horse with good angles is more likely to stay sound and healthy into old age than a horse with poor angles.

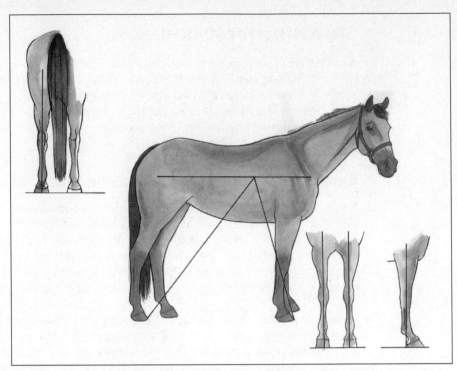

FIGURE 4-1:
A horse
with good
conformation has
a well-balanced
appearance.

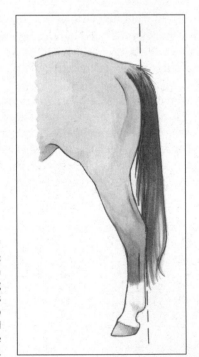

FIGURE 4-2:
A horse with
good hind-leg
conformation is
more likely to
stay sound
through the
years.

Detecting conformation faults

No horse is perfect. Every horse — just like every human — has some physical characteristic that is less than pleasing to the eye. In horses, these *conformation faults* may not only affect the appearance of the horse, but also the horse's ability to function properly in its work.

REMEMBER

Just because a horse has some conformation faults doesn't necessarily make it a bad horse; however, being aware of those faults can help you know your horse's limitations. Ask a vet, trainer, or wise horsy friend to help you learn to spot these faults.

Leg faults are a common problem for horses and can cause performance and health troubles. Spotting conformation faults in horses helps you anticipate a horse's potential troubles. Here's a list of some typical leg conformation faults that can affect a horse's health or ability. You can learn to recognize them by sight. To spot these, view the horse when it's standing still and alert:

>> **Base narrow:** *Base narrow* is the exact opposite of base wide (see next item). When viewed from the front, the distance between the imaginary centerlines of the legs is narrower at hooves than it is at the chest, meaning they tend to point inward from top to bottom. This construction occurs in wide-chested horses and tends to go with toed-in or toed-out hoof conformations. Horses with base narrow legs carry more weight on the outsides of their legs, which means that bruising, sidebone (where cartilage in parts of the foot become bony and hard), and arthritis commonly occur in these horses, affecting the outside of the leg regardless of whether the horse is toed-in or toed-out.

>> **Base wide:** When viewed from the front, the centerlines of the legs of horses with base-wide conformations are wider at the hooves than they are at the chest, meaning they tend to point outward from top to bottom. This fault tends to show up in narrow-chested horses and usually goes hand-in-hand with toed-out hooves. As a result of this construction, the horse carries more weight on the inside of the leg, so the hooves tend to land on the inside first, creating more strain on the inside of the leg. Horses with this conformation are more prone to problems on the inside of the leg such as bruising, sidebone, and arthritis.

>> **Bowlegged:** The centerlines of the legs of bowlegged horses, when viewed from the front, arc outward at the knees. If the bow in the legs is severe, the horse may be more prone to developing arthritis in the knees.

>> **Calf knee:** The forelegs of calf-kneed horses appear to bend backward at the knee, when viewed from the side. When asked to work hard, horses with this problem may suffer from chip fractures of the knee.

- » **Knee-sprung:** Knee-sprung horses, which also are described as being over at the knee, have forelegs that appear to bend forward, when viewed from the side. If the problem is severe, the horse is prone to developing issues with the sesamoid bone, with resulting lameness.

- » **Knock-kneed:** The legs of horses that are knock-kneed, when viewed from the front, have knees that appear to come together. If this construction is severe enough, it can cause arthritis in the knees.

- » **Sickle hocks:** With sickle-hock construction, the horse has too much angulation of the hock and stifle. Sickle hocks are the opposite of being straight behind, and can result in arthritis of the hock if severe enough.

- » **Straight behind:** The straight-behind build means the horse has very little angle to its hock and stifle. Horses that are straight behind are much more prone to hock arthritis and locking kneecaps.

- » **Toed-in:** Also called *pigeon-toed,* this conformation fault results in hooves that point toward each other. The legs usually start to turn inward at the level of the fetlock but may start as high as the point where the leg meets the chest. This conformation causes the hooves to paddle, or swing outward while moving, creating interference between the legs and possible injury.

- » **Toed-out:** Also known as *splayfooted,* toed-out hooves point away from each other. Similar to toed-in conformation, the toeing out may start at the fetlock or higher up the leg. Horses with this problem tend to *wing,* or swing inward while they're moving. Sometimes the hooves can wing in to the point where they hit each other.

Looking at gender differences

Among humans are boys and girls and men and women. Horses, however, have a whole slew of genders that we show you in the following list:

- » **Colts:** Intact male horses younger than 4 years old, *colts* typically are full of energy. The older ones are looking for females under every rock.

- » **Fillies**: Females younger than 4 years old, *fillies* are the female horses that hormone-enraged colts most eagerly seek. Like colts, fillies also have considerable energy, but they aren't as hormone driven as their male counterparts, and they don't hide under rocks.

- » **Geldings:** Geldings are castrated males. Many horse people think geldings make the best mounts because they aren't plagued by hormones and the distractions that often accompany surges of these chemicals.

>> **Mares:** Mares are female horses ages 4 or older. We think that mares make wonderful companions, although many people find some mares difficult to handle whenever the mare comes into season (heat). Hormones, you see.

>> **Stallions:** Colts that are 4 years or older with their reproductive organs intact are called *stallions.* They have a strong interest in breeding that can drive them to distraction, so they aren't recommended for beginning riders. In fact, many boarding stables don't permit them on the premises because they sometimes are unruly. Only experienced horse handlers have what it takes to train and manage most stallions.

WARNING

Realistically, your choice of horse is limited to either mares or geldings. If you're thinking about a stallion, forget it. Few stallions are suitable for beginners, no matter how romantic the notion of riding one is. And all stallions come with logistical problems. For instance, most boarding stables won't allow stallions on the premises. If a stallion gets out of a pasture and impregnates a neighbor's mare, the situation is ripe for a lawsuit.

REMEMBER

The question of whether to get a mare or a gelding is a big one to some horse people and not something that everyone agrees upon. Many people own only geldings, while others swear by mares. Some people don't have a preference one way or the other. The decision on whether to get a mare or a gelding ultimately rests with you. If you don't have a preference — most people don't — then just look for the best horse regardless of gender.

Investigating Horse Insurance

Before buying a horse, think about the possibility of getting insurance coverage on the animal. Your horse represents an investment in money, time, and emotion, making insurance a good idea. Companies that specialize in insuring horses offer many different kinds of equine insurance. Explore all the types of insurance to see which ones you want to buy for your new horse:

>> **Major medical:** Major medical policies for horses are similar to the ones humans buy. The policy covers medical costs like diagnostic procedures, surgery, medication, and visits by a vet associated with an illness or injury. Preventative care is rarely covered. A deductible for each incident is common with major medical policies. You must supply a veterinary health certificate to assure that your horse has no preexisting conditions at the time you take out the policy. Age restrictions often apply to older horses; it's rare to find a policy covering horses aged 15 or older. Most companies require you to cover the horse for full mortality if you want to insure for major medical.

TIP

We highly recommend major medical insurance. If your horse develops a serious illness, veterinary bills can mount quickly.

>> **Surgical:** Surgical coverage is a medical policy that applies only to situations where surgery is required. You must also carry a full mortality policy on the horse. If you can't get or can't afford major medical insurance, surgical is the next best thing. It protects you and your horse if the animal requires colic surgery or another operation.

>> **Full mortality:** Full mortality insurance covers the horse if it dies because of illness or accident and usually pays the estimated or declared value of the horse. Full mortality coverage is effective if the horse is stolen and not recovered. The insurance company requires a veterinary health certificate indicating that the horse is healthy. If your horse is older than 14, you may have trouble finding coverage.

If you paid a substantial sum of money for your horse, full mortality insurance is a must. Even if your horse didn't cost that much, realize that without this insurance, your horse's unexpected death can result in a loss of your investment.

>> **Limited mortality:** Limited mortality usually only covers death as a result of accident or other specified causes. Because the policy doesn't cover illness, the insurance company doesn't require a health certificate.

WARNING

You're unlikely to need this insurance on your horse unless you have special circumstances that place your horse at risk of an accident. A typical example of special circumstances is shipping your horse cross-country. If you insure your horse with a limited mortality policy, and your horse dies in a trailer accident during the trip, the insurance company will pay out the value of the horse.

>> **Loss of use:** If the horse is injured or ill to the point where it can no longer be ridden, loss of use insurance compensates you. You'll be paid a predetermined sum, which is based on an amount of money agreed to by you and the insurance company. Loss-of-use policies require that you also carry some type of medical coverage.

Some horse owners like to have this option. Some policies allow the owner to euthanize the horse and still collect loss of use, while others allow the owner to keep the horse even though he can't be used for the specific purpose that the policy indicates.

WARNING

The downside of loss of use coverage is that it is difficult to collect on and many companies don't allow the owner to keep the horse, which means the horse is turned over to the insurance company, which likely will sell it for slaughter.

>> **Personal liability:** This type of insurance protects you if your horse injures someone or damages property. Your homeowner's insurance may already provide you with this coverage. Carrying personal liability on your horse is always a good idea, if you can afford it. You never know when your horse could accidentally hurt someone or cause damage to another person's possessions.

The cost of insurance depends on where you live and the type of insurance you purchase. If you plan to cover your horse for major medical and full mortality — the most common insurance coverages used by the average recreational horse owner — expect to spend several hundred dollars per year.

TIP

To find an equine insurer, ask your veterinarian for a reference. You can also peruse the advertisements of most any equine publication. Most insurers take out ads regularly, both large ads and classified listings. Locate an insurance plan that you want to use and be prepared to insure your horse the same day you buy it. Doing so affords you maximum protection for your investment.

Finding Expert Help

You can never educate yourself enough when it comes to horses. Even the most experienced, savvy horse people strive to gain more equine knowledge.

As a first-time horse owner, a whole world of information and experience awaits you. And the best place to garner that knowledge is from the professionals who deal with horses: your trainer (or other equine expert), your veterinarian, and your farrier. These people can guide you and help you with your new horse, so selecting them carefully is important. Take the time to get to know how each of these individuals relates to you and your horse.

Before you go out and start horse shopping, line up some solid people to help you with the task. Finding the right horse isn't easy, but you have better chance of making it happen when you have a decent trainer (someone who teaches horses and humans) or riding instructor (someone who teaches humans), veterinarian, and farrier to hold your hand through the process.

A trainer or riding instructor

REMEMBER

For beginning horse people, we can't stress enough the importance of getting help from someone more experienced and knowledgeable about horses, both before you buy your horse and afterward. Owning a horse for the first time can be challenging, and few things are more terrible than the feeling you'll have if something goes wrong and you have no one to turn to for help. Having someone to call when you have a question, someone to show you the ropes and actually teach you, hands on, how to handle, ride, and care for your horse can make all the difference in the world.

A good horse trainer is the best person to help you with your search for a horse. Horse trainers are able to evaluate a horse on the ground and from the saddle. They can ride any horse you're considering to make sure the animal is safe and well suited to you.

Assuming you can't find a qualified trainer, a riding instructor can assist you with finding a horse, if he or she provides this service to clients. However, an instructor may not to be willing to ride the horse for you to determine its suitability, because many instructors do not provide this service.

How to find a trainer or riding instructor

TIP

You have a number of options when looking for a good trainer, or at the very least a riding instructor, if no trainer is available in your area:

>> **Contacting an organization that certifies riding instructors:** These organizations may be able to provide you with the names of certified instructors in your area.

>> **Attending a few horse shows in your area:** As you watch the classes, you'll notice trainers and riding instructors working with their students on the sidelines. The trainer or instructor is the one functioning as a coach of sorts, giving advice before the student enters the ring, and constructive criticism or congratulations after the class is over.

Find a good moment and approach a trainer or instructor who seems to be working with students who are in your age range. Tell the trainer or instructor that you're a new rider, ask for a card, and get basic information about that person's program to make sure that he or she works with beginners. The person you contact may not have time to talk to you at length during the show but should be happy to discuss his or her program with you over the phone at a later date.

>> **Looking online:** Do a search for "Riding Academies." Contact a few trainers or instructors and talk to them about their riding programs. Let them know you're a beginning rider who's interested in learning horsemanship so you can eventually purchase your own horse. Take note of the person's personality, and get a sense of whether you think you'll work well with that person.

>> **Asking around for a referral:** Call a tack and feed store, a local equine veterinarian, or just talk to some horse owners in the area. Ask for the name of a trainer or instructor who works with beginning riders.

After you meet an expert or two with whom you're interested in working, take a few private riding lessons from that person (as opposed to group lessons). The trainer or instructor should begin and end your lesson on time and should pay complete attention to you during the session. You need to be comfortable and compatible with the trainer's teaching style.

REMEMBER

Be sure to choose a trainer or instructor who incorporates different aspects of horsemanship in his or her program. You should not only learn to ride a horse but also to groom it, put on its tack, lead it, and care for it after riding.

What to do if you can't find a trainer or instructor

If you live in a small town or rural area, you won't have many choices when it comes to picking a trainer or riding instructor. In fact, you may not be able to find one you like, or any at all, for that matter. If that's the case, the next best thing is another equine expert of some kind. The expert you find may be an equine veterinarian, a horse breeder, a shoer, or even just another horse owner who's been working with horses for a long time and really knows his or her way around a stable.

REMEMBER

When you don't have access to a professional horse trainer or riding instructor, you have to be creative in finding someone to help you with your horse. Go to a local horse show and introduce yourself to the competitors. Locate a local vet or farrier online. Do whatever is necessary to make contact with people experienced with horses and willing to lend you a hand.

If the expert you come up with is an equine professional, you may have to pay that person a fee to help you buy a horse, give you lessons, or teach you other aspects of horsemanship. If the person is a stranger to you, you need to at least offer to pay. Many horse people are more than willing to help a new horse owner, and some will provide you with free guidance out of the kindness of their hearts.

TIP

Several breed associations now offer mentor programs to help beginning riders hook up with experienced horse professionals.

A veterinarian

An important person in the lives of you and your horse is your veterinarian. The vet you choose ultimately provides your horse with regular preventative care and is the one who shows up in the middle of the night when your horse is colicking or has seriously injured itself. In emergency situations like these, your veterinarian appears as a guardian angel coming to Earth to rescue you from whatever trouble you and your horse have gotten into.

You won't need a regular veterinarian until after you purchase your horse. But you need to start searching now, because you need one for your pre-purchase examination (see Chapter 5 for details).

TIP

Before you actually start shopping for a horse, locate the veterinarian you want to hire to do the examination. Begin your homework on this subject long before you find a horse for the vet to look at. The night before you want someone to conduct the exam is not the time to start shopping for a vet!

If you like the pre-purchase veterinarian, you may want to consider keeping that person as your regular vet after you purchase a horse. If that's your plan, make sure that you evaluate the veterinarian per our advice in Chapter 10.

A farrier

Before you buy your horse, you'd be wise to start looking around for a qualified farrier. The *farrier* is the person who trims and shoes your new horse's hooves.

REMEMBER

Finding a really good farrier is incredibly important. A good farrier helps keep your horse's legs and feet healthy and sound. A poor farrier can make your horse lame and even permanently destroy his soundness.

Obviously, given the effect that your farrier has on your horse's well-being, the selection you make regarding this equine professional is rather important. The best person to ask for a farrier referral is an equine veterinarian. For more details on how to make the best possible choice in farriers, see Chapter 10.

IN THIS CHAPTER

» **Asking an expert to help you shop**

» **Looking for places to buy a horse**

» **Selecting important traits in a horse**

» **Evaluating your equine prospects**

» **Taking your new horse home**

Chapter **5**

Making the Big Buy

Before making the big decision to buy a horse, you need to do some soul-searching about horse ownership so that you're sure that buying a horse is what you really want. You also need to have a good idea of which riding discipline you and your family want to choose, what you want to do with your horse, and how you're going to house and care for your horse. (Chapter 4 gives you the background information you need to know before you go horse shopping.)

After you're sure that you want to progress into the realm of horse ownership, your next step is finding the right horse; however, doing so may not be as easy as you think. Finding a horse can be downright difficult; moreover, getting a horse with the disposition and physical capabilities to suit *your* needs and personality is almost as challenging as trying to find the right spouse — although much less stressful.

No need to fret, though! We're going to walk you through the horse-buying process in this chapter, and if you follow our advice, you should end up with a wonderful equine companion that is just right for you.

Enlisting an Expert to Help You Shop

If you're like most people, the first time you go out to a stable to look at a horse that you think you might buy, you're going to be nervous. As the seller shows you the horse, you'll be wracked with indecision and possibly a great deal of angst. Among the legitimate and important questions you need to ask yourself while shopping for a horse are:

>> How do I know whether this horse is the right one?

>> Will the horse and I get along?

Don't panic — you don't have to search for the answers to these questions alone or by the seat of your pants. You can get help with your decision and take your time making it. You can ask a trainer or an experienced horse person to help you decide whether the horse has the right disposition. Horse trainers are horse experts, and as such, a big part of their job is evaluating horses and matching them with the right riders.

Enlisting the services of a knowledgeable, experienced, and reliable horse trainer is imperative as you begin your horse-buying quest. Without the help of someone who has this kind of expertise, you're not likely to find the best animal for you. (For details about finding the right trainer, see Chapter 4.)

TIP

If you live in a rural area, finding a professional trainer to help you with your search may be next to impossible, but you still can get the kind of help you need for your search from an experienced horse person. A local breeder or show competitor may be happy to provide you with assistance. (Chapter 4 contains information on finding an alternative equine expert.)

REMEMBER

The best person to take with you when shopping for a horse is the trainer from whom you've been taking riding lessons or the one who's going to give you lessons on your new horse. This person has a relationship with you and is more motivated to help you find the best horse. Trainers also have a network of equestrians that they can tap into to help you find the right horse. If you've been taking lessons with a riding instructor rather than a trainer, talk to the instructor about his or her experiences purchasing horses. If your instructor lacks experience in this area, try to find a horse trainer to help you instead. (See Chapter 4 for tips on finding a good trainer.)

The trainer/expert you hire goes with you to see horses for sale, watches the seller ride and handle the horse, and takes the horse for a test ride, too. Then it's your turn to ride. The trainer/expert then gives you an opinion about whether the horse is a good match for you. Sometimes, a potential buyer falls in love with a horse, but the trainer/expert advises against buying him. The decision ultimately is up to you, but we advise you to weigh heavily on the recommendation of your trainer/expert. Trainers and experts sometimes are wrong — but usually not. If your trainer/expert doesn't like the horse, he or she probably sees something that your untrained eye doesn't, and you'd be wise to move on to the next prospect.

Knowing Where to Find a Horse

Unfortunately, buying a horse is more complicated than going to the mall to pick out a new china pattern. The process is complicated by the fact that you can shop in more than one type of place.

The best sources of horses for sale are individual sellers, horse dealers, and breeding and training operations. If you'd prefer adopting rather than buying a horse, rescue groups usually have them available and so does the occasional private individual. In the end, although your horse comes from just one of these sources, you don't have to limit your search to only one. Check out each of the following horse sources as you conduct your quest, and then settle on the ones that feel right for you.

Individual sellers

Individual horse owners put horses up for sale for any number of reasons. Some of the better reasons (for you, the buyer) include:

>> A teenage daughter who's gone off to college and left no one to ride the horse

>> A change in financial situation such that the seller can no longer afford to keep the horse

>> The desire to replace a beginner horse with a seasoned show animal

>> A loss of interest in the hobby

If you purchase a horse made available by one of these situations, you can end up with a wonderful animal at a reasonable price.

WARNING

Unfortunately, individuals also sell horses for less positive reasons. Some examples include horses that:

>> Are difficult or dangerous to ride

>> Won't load into a trailer

>> Are sick or have other medical problems

>> Are mean and dislike people

Buying a horse from an individual seller rather than from a trainer, breeder, or horse dealer can be a good way to save money, but you need to exercise caution. Individual sellers often advertise online, in local horse publications, and on the bulletin board at your area tack and feed store. Your trainer may also know of someone selling a horse that is a good match for you.

Some of the potential advantages of buying a horse directly from an individual are:

>> **Getting a bargain:** Under the right circumstances, you can get a really good horse for a really good price. For example, if the seller is attached to the horse yet desperate to sell him, she may charge you much less than the horse is worth if she knows you're going to provide the animal with a good home.

>> **Avoiding the middleman:** You'll probably already be paying a fee to a trainer or other expert to help you find the right horse (see "Enlisting an Expert to Help You Shop" earlier in this chapter). However, when you buy from an individual, you also avoid paying a middleman — that is, a trainer who is selling a horse on behalf of a client — which ultimately cuts down on the cost of the horse.

>> **Obtaining a history:** Horses that come from individual sellers often come with a known history. The seller probably can tell you who owned the horse before, what type of work the horse did, whether a mare produced any foals, and more. This information is important, because it helps you get a feeling for what the horse is all about, and if you end up buying the horse, you'll know something about your new charge. When you know absolutely nothing about your horse's background, any problems that come up can be frustrating.

Conversely, buying from an individual isn't always the best way to go. Some of the potential disadvantages of buying a horse directly from an individual are:

>> **Time-consuming searches:** Calling around and visiting horses for sale one at a time can take a great deal of time.

>> **Unappealing personalities:** If you deal directly with individuals, you may find yourself face-to-face with personalities that are less than appealing to you. You may even run across people who are downright dishonest and try to pull the wool over your eyes, an uncertainty that can add to the frustration of horse shopping.

>> **Burgeoning prices:** Although you may find a great bargain when looking to buy from an individual, you also stand to pay more for a horse from an individual than you would through a horse dealer, especially if the individual is in no hurry to sell the horse.

When you're thinking about buying a horse from an individual, be sure to bring an experienced horse person with you to see the animal. A person with experience can ascertain any obvious behavioral problems the horse may have. If the horse passes muster in terms of its behavior, a veterinarian can determine any medical problems during a checkup (see "Hiring a vet to check the horse" later in this chapter).

USING CAUTION WHEN E-BUYING A HORSE

The Internet has changed the way many things are accomplished and that includes horse shopping. Whereas horse shoppers used to be limited to whatever horses were available locally, the Internet has broadened the horizon of the market for horses to include animals all across the country and even around the world.

Web sites dedicated to buying and selling horses are plentiful on the Internet, leaving horse shoppers with the new dilemma of whether to buy a horse that is outside of their immediate vicinities.

Plenty of horse people make long-distance purchases, using videotapes and a trip out to where the horse is located to check out the animal. First-time horse buyers probably are better off buying a horse locally, because of all the complications of purchasing online and via long distance. A vet conducting a pre-purchase exam and simply spending time with the horse are two important issues that buying long-distance makes more difficult. Add to that the expense of shipping the horse to its new home and you may end up breaking your budget, because shipping responsibilities fall on the buyer and can run in the thousands, depending on how far the horse is going to be shipped.

Horses that are suitable for novices can readily be found in most areas where horses are common, so newbies to the horse world really don't need to shop long distance. If, however, you decide to take this route, be sure to:

- Use an independent veterinarian for the pre-purchase exam; don't rely on the seller's vet.

- Hop on a plane or drive to where the horse is located and spend some time getting to know the animal before you make a commitment to buy.

- Bring along your expert.

Just because a horse is located far away doesn't mean you need to skip the vital steps needed to make the right horse-buying decision.

Horse dealers

You can find horse dealers in most areas that have an active horse industry. Horse dealers typically purchase horses at auctions or from individuals and then sell those horses to others at higher prices. In essence, they're the middlemen of the horse-buying world.

You can get a good horse from an honest horse dealer. Most horse dealers are experienced horse people who know how to judge a horse's disposition, quality of training, and athletic ability.

TIP

If a trainer or horse expert is helping you with your search, ask whether he or she can recommend a reputable horse dealer. Don't approach a horse dealer without a recommendation from someone you know well and trust. Horse dealers are much like used car dealers: Some are ethical; others aren't.

WARNING

Some horse dealers will sell a horse with a guarantee that states you can return the horse within one year for another one if the horse develops medical or behavioral problems. The trouble with this type of guarantee is that, most people understandably become attached to the horse and don't want to return him to the dealer for fear the horse will end up going to the slaughterhouse (see Chapter 12 for more information about horse slaughter).

Breeding and training operations

Horse breeders and trainers routinely sell horses to individual buyers. In fact, selling horses usually is a large part of their business.

Breeders typically deal in purebred horses and sell young stock. The weanlings (horses between 4 and 6 months old) and yearlings (1-year-old horses) most often available from breeders aren't suitable for a first-time horse owner because they're so young. However, breeders occasionally offer older horses for sale, possibly a retired show horse or a broodmare that has been trained for riding.

Trainers are often good sources for older, trained horses — the kind you need to be looking for (see Chapter 4 for more about age considerations). The horse that's for sale may be one with only basic training that the trainer purchased and then schooled to a higher level. The horse may even belong to a trainer's client, and the client has outgrown the horse, so the trainer has taken on the task of selling the animal. Sometimes, a trainer wants to sell off a lesson horse to a private owner.

When healthy and sound (free from lameness), former lesson horses can make good mounts for beginning riders, and for that reason, you need to consider them when you shop.

TIP

If you've taken lessons from and intend to continue working with a particular trainer after you have your own horse, consider buying a horse directly from your trainer. After all, you've been working with the trainer, and he or she knows your skill level and personality and may have a horse for sale that is perfectly suited to you. Your trainer can also network with other trainers to help you find the best horse.

REMEMBER

As with anything else that you buy, the seller's reputation is important — especially when dealing with breeders and trainers. If you don't know the breeder or trainer, ask for referrals and find out what other horse people in the area know about them. Make sure that the business or individual has a good reputation before you get involved in any business dealings. You want to make certain you're dealing with someone who is honest about the horse you're buying and won't stick you with a lemon.

Horse shows

If you are working with a trainer who is helping you find a horse to buy, a trip to a horse show might be in order. If your trainer knows other trainers who are showing at a local event, you can go with your trainer to take a look at one or more horses that may be available. Your trainer will do most of the talking in a situation like this, but you can learn a lot about a horse from watching him at a show. All the commotion of a horse show is a real test of a horse's disposition. Plus, if you are looking to buy a horse you will compete on, getting to see how the horse looks and acts in the show ring is invaluable.

EXERCISING CAUTION AT HORSE AUCTIONS

Although many people buy horses from public auctions because they find good bargains, we don't recommend this route for first-time horse owners. At an auction, you won't have the opportunity to spend much — if any — time with the horse you're considering. In many cases, you won't have opportunities to ride the horse or have a veterinarian examine the horse. Because many public horse auctions sell horses without any kind of guarantee, you may be setting yourself up for a fall whenever you buy a horse this way.

Adoptions

You don't necessarily have to purchase a horse to acquire one. You can adopt a horse for nothing or for a minimal fee through several avenues.

WARNING

Although we like the idea of horse adoption, we want to caution you that it isn't always the best way to go when you're a first-time horse owner looking for a horse to ride. Some horses that are available for adoption make great riding horses for beginners, but others are not suited for inexperienced riders. If you want to pursue this option, do so with your horse-shopping expert in tow. Be honest with the rescue about your limited horse experience. Also remember to be rational and critical, the same way you would if you were buying. Don't take a horse home that isn't right for you just because he's free or because you feel sorry for him. If the relationship doesn't work out (and chances are that it won't), the results can be disastrous not only for you but also for the horse you're trying to help.

The following sections take you through different kinds of horse adoptions that are available.

Rescue groups

Horses are beautiful, noble creatures, but sadly, life sometimes deals them a bad hand. Neglect, abuse, and death at the slaughterhouse are problems that plague horses in today's society.

Many people around the world are sensitive to the suffering of horses and have banded together to help remedy the plight of these horses. The result is a bevy of private rescue and adoption groups that save horses from unfortunate situations. Many of these groups rehabilitate horses and then place them up for adoption. Some rescue groups simply give the horse a quiet place to live out his life.

Rescue groups that rehabilitate horses and place them for adoption are the ones you need to explore when you want to adopt a horse. Some of these groups take former racehorses (usually Thoroughbreds and Standardbreds — see Chapter 3 for details on different breeds), retrain them for riding, and then adopt them out or sell them at reduced fees. Others simply rehabilitate rescued saddle horses and try to find new homes for them.

REMEMBER

Before you consider adopting a horse from a rescue group, research the organization. Visit its facilities to find out as much as you can about the group's work. If the people who run the organization seem responsible, organized, and professional, then pursue the adoption process in the same way that you would when buying a horse. And as always, be sure to have an equine trainer or other horse expert with you when deciding to take on a horse — whether you're buying or adopting the horse — and have a vet check the horse's health.

You can also ask to take the rescue horse on a trial basis, because most responsible rescue groups have an open return policy on any horse they adopt out. In fact, many rescue groups insist that you take the horse for a trial period while they retain ownership. Some groups even send out inspectors to spot-check your property to make sure that you're properly caring for the horse. In many cases, the rescue group asks you to sign a contract stating that you must return the horse to the group if and when you decide you no longer want the animal. See "Signing up for a trial period" later in this chapter for details on trial periods.

Wild horse adoption

The U.S. Bureau of Land Management (BLM) regularly rounds up wild horses living in undeveloped regions of the country (mostly in the western U.S.) and places them in holding pens. These horses are put up for adoption at BLM facilities in several states; just about anyone can take one of these horses home for a nominal fee.

On the East Coast of the United States, wild ponies rounded up from the Chincoteague and Assateague Islands off the coast of Virginia are also available for adoption in the spring. Only young foals are adopted out, and they are sold by auction.

Wild horses are beautiful animals with a wonderful, historical past; however, because these animals have lived their lives with virtually no human contact, they're generally not suitable for first-time horse owners. Adult wild horses need extensive training before you can even handle them. Young foals are easier to work with, but they're years away from being ridden and usually too much for a beginning horse person to handle.

If your dream is to adopt a wild horse, don't fret. After you gain considerable experience riding and handling horses, you can always pursue that goal. When that time comes and you want to adopt a wild horse through the BLM, you need to meet certain government-established criteria before you're allowed to take ownership. You must

>> Provide a minimum 400 square feet (20-feet by 20 feet) enclosure per horse

>> Be at least 18 years of age or older (or have your parents' cooperation)

>> Prove that you can provide adequate feed, water, facilities, and humane care for the horse

The government has specific rules about the types of facilities in which these horses can be kept and charges an adoption fee of less than $200 per horse. (See Chapter 3 for more information about wild horses.)

Free horses

Once in a while, people find themselves in a situation in which someone wants to give them a free horse. Horse giveaways occur for a few common reasons:

>> An owner doesn't want the hassle of selling the horse.

>> An owner is primarily interested in the horse going to a good home.

>> A horse is such a big pain in the neck that no one will buy him.

Unfortunately, the last reason is most common when it comes to free horses. Any beginning rider who takes on a horse that is so difficult or so unsound that no one will buy him is looking for serious trouble.

WARNING

Just because a horse is free doesn't mean that he doesn't need to fit all the same qualifications as a horse that you'd buy. If someone offers you a free horse, and you want to consider him, jump through all the hoops you would if you were buying: Bring a trainer/expert with you to help evaluate the horse, have a veterinarian examine the horse, and take the horse out on trial basis.

You may be wondering why you need to go to all this trouble when the horse is free. It seems as though you have nothing to lose because you aren't paying anything for him, right? No, wrong! After you take possession, all of the horse's problems become your problems. And if you're like most people, you'll become emotionally attached to the animal and suddenly face some difficult decisions if the horse turns out to have serious behavioral or medical problems.

REMEMBER

If you're hoping to save a few bucks by taking any old free horse that someone offers, you are being penny-wise and pound-foolish, as the saying goes. Don't forget that the initial cost of purchase is *not* what creates the greatest expense in horse ownership; the training, housing, and veterinary bills make up the larger part of those costs. If you end up with a problem horse, those prices you pay become even greater.

Deciding On the Perfect Horse for You

REMEMBER

If your horse-owning experience is to be a successful one, you must find the right horse for you. We can't stress this point enough. If you get the wrong horse, you'll be miserable, the horse will be unhappy, and your venture into horse ownership will be disastrous. That's why heeding the advice that we give you in the following sections is so important.

In Chapter 4, you thought about the age, conformation, and gender of the horse you're purchasing. Now, it's time to get even deeper into the process.

Considering your riding style

You can't know what kind of horse to buy until you know how you want to ride. If you haven't already looked at Chapter 14, you need to do so before making any buying decisions.

Perhaps western riding is the discipline that appeals to you the most, or maybe you like the idea of riding hunt seat. Maybe you want a horse with which you can do both, or maybe you want a horse that you can ride English, and your spouse and the kids can ride western.

REMEMBER

Regardless of what discipline you choose, make sure that the horse you buy has been trained in that discipline. The only exception is when you want to have the horse trained in a new discipline after you buy him. However, don't make this judgment call on your own. Ask your trainer/expert to evaluate whether the horse is suited to and can be trained in your chosen discipline.

You can't ride every horse in every discipline, nor should you try. Specialization in the horse world dictates that you ride some horses western, some hunt seat, and some saddle seat. Some horses are versatile and can do two or more disciplines, but they still need to be trained in each one. If your only plan is to tool around the trail, then it probably doesn't matter too much whether you put a western saddle on a big, rangy Thoroughbred — if you don't care how odd it may look. But if you plan to show your horse at all, having the right horse for your discipline of choice is a big issue.

Choosing a purebred, cross-bred, or a non-purebred

Whether to buy a purebred horse, a cross-bred horse (two breeds combined), or a *grade horse* (a horse of unknown parentage) depends on several factors. Each has its advantages and disadvantages. Personal taste also comes into play. Some people couldn't care less about their horse's genetic background, but others are fanatical about it. Read on to discover which camp *you* are in.

Purebreds

In our opinion, purebred horses are really wonderful. Each and every breed has a fascinating and unique history, and every horse of that breed is a living, breathing relic of that amazing past (see Chapter 3 for a rundown of some of the more well-known horse breeds).

Purebred horses have been bred over time to fit into certain niches, each breed with its own specialties. Quarter Horses, for instance, are renowned for their abilities in western sports, just as Paso Finos are famous the world over for their *paso* gait. Clydesdales are known for their massive size and strength, while Shetland Ponies have found acclaim as durable and reliable children's mounts.

If you're planning to show your horse, and a particular breed dominates the sport you choose, then you need to seriously consider buying a purebred horse. If you want to show in open western pleasure shows at your local stable, for example, you'd do best purchasing a Quarter Horse or Paint. These are the breeds you see winning in these events most often.

Owning a purebred also provides you with an opportunity to show in breed-specific events, too. Nearly every popular breed has regional shows where owners can present their animals in a variety of classes.

TIP

Getting involved in breed showing is a good way to meet other horse people, too. By making contact with your local breed club, you have a whole slew of opportunities to meet horse owners with the same goals and interests.

For some people, owning a purebred horse is a status thing. Purebred horses typically cost more than non-purebreds, have a pedigree behind them, and are recognizable to most horse people as purebreds. If you care about that kind of stuff, then you'll probably want to own a purebred horse.

For other people, purebreds simply are more beautiful and more interesting than non-purebreds. These individuals are willing to spend more money on a purebred horse just so they can have a magnificent horse in their stable.

WARNING

The one distinct disadvantage to purebred horses is their tendency toward inherited diseases or weakness. Some Quarter Horses carry a gene for *hyperkalemic periodic paralysis (HYPP)*, a severe muscle disorder; Appaloosas are inclined toward *uveitis*, a serious eye condition; Arabians have a tendency to develop *enteroliths,* or stones in the intestines; Thoroughbreds are known for having poor hooves, and the list goes on.

You can screen horses for HYPP, but not for most other breed-associated diseases. Buying a purebred comes with the risk that your horse can develop one of the conditions associated with his breed.

Non-purebreds

A non-purebred can be a horse that is the result of the crossing of two breeds (called a *crossbreed*), or a horse whose parentage is simply unknown (called a *grade horse*). Many breed crosses have names for the cross and associations that register them. The Morab, which is a breeding between a Morgan and an Arabian, is one. The Anglo-Arab, a cross between a Thoroughbred and an Arabian, is another.

Cross-bred horses usually are the result of a deliberate breeding between horses of differing breeds, orchestrated by people who are looking to combine the qualities found in each breed.

Grade horses, on the other hand, are the mutts of the horse world. In most cases, little thought goes into their breeding. They're simply the product of a stallion and a mare, put together for the purpose of creating a generic horse. Some grade horses may actually be purebreds, but because of circumstances, their registration papers and pedigrees are lost somewhere along the way.

REMEMBER

The reality of the horse world is that non-purebreds are more plentiful than purebreds, which is just fine. Non-purebreds can make wonderful mounts and excellent companions, the same way purebreds can. The horse world differs from the dog world in that sense: Pedigree just isn't that important to the average horse person. For them, good behavior and a sound body have much more value than pure breeding.

Several differences exist between purebreds and non-purebreds, however. For one thing, non-purebreds typically are less expensive than purebreds and they're easier to come by. If you open your equine search to non-purebreds, you have many more horses to choose from. You're also less at risk of purchasing a horse with an inherited disease if you get a grade horse, which comes from a larger gene pool.

WARNING

The disadvantages to owning a non-purebred primarily are show related. In many show rings, you compete against purebreds that are carefully bred to perform in the discipline in which you're showing. Your non-purebred may be at a disadvantage. Some of the more performance-oriented sports like endurance riding and show jumping are exceptions, because more emphasis is placed on athletic ability than form and general appearance. You commonly see crossbreeds and even grade horses in such events.

If all you want in your first horse is an equine friend to take you out on the trail and spend time with you around the barn, then a non-purebred is more than qualified for the job. Coauthor Audrey Pavia's first horse, a little bay mare named Peggy, was a non-purebred and an excellent child's mount and companion. No one knew a thing about Peggy's ancestry, but it didn't matter. She was simply a wonderful horse.

Balancing emotions and rationality

Successful horse selection requires you to compartmentalize your brain. On the one hand, you want a horse that is emotionally appealing, but on the other hand, you need a horse that also makes sense for you from an unemotional standpoint. You find a particular horse attractive, friendly, and interested in you, and you can hardly wait to ride such a beautiful creature. These are matters of the heart, so they're important factors to consider in your decision. But you can't base your decision entirely on how you *feel* about the horse.

You need to balance your heart's reaction with your rational side. Is the horse well-trained and suitable for a beginning rider? Is the horse suitable for children to ride (if your kids are going to ride him)? Is the horse easy to handle from the ground and from the saddle? Is the animal free of any health problems? Truly *liking* the horse you're going to buy is important and so is having a good feeling about the animal, but the practical answers to these and other questions must take precedence over things like how good you think you look riding the horse.

REMEMBER

The decision to buy a particular horse needs to be a combination of intellectual and emotional thinking. Your intellect needs to stoically compute the practical information about any horse you're considering, while your emotional side needs to provide you with that all-important gut feeling that's so necessary when trying to decide such important matters. Using a good measure of intellect and a good measure of emotion is key to establishing a balance between the two debating sides of this decision.

Embarking on Your Horse-Shopping Journey

Okay, you're ready to roll up your sleeves and start really looking for that horse. This part of the process can be both fun and scary. But if you take our advice and have someone with you who is experienced in horse shopping and knows her way around a barn, the process is much less stressful.

Getting some initial information

Before you go look at a horse that is for sale, you need to get some basic information about the animal. Start by contacting the seller and asking the following questions (if the advertisement doesn't already give you the answers):

- » How much are you asking for the horse? Is this price negotiable?
- » How old is the horse?
- » How big is the horse (in hands)?
- » What is the horse's gender?
- » In which discipline is the horse ridden?
- » Has the horse ever had professional training?
- » Is the horse suitable for a beginning rider?
- » Is the horse suitable for children (if you have kids who will ride the horse)?
- » Does the horse load into a trailer?
- » Does the horse have any bad habits such as cribbing, weaving, or pulling back when tied? (See Chapter 2 for information on these vices.)
- » Does the horse have any medical problems or a history of medical problems like colic, lameness, or allergies?
- » Why are you selling the horse?

REMEMBER

The answers to these questions help you determine whether the horse meets your basic requirements of price range, age, gender, size, discipline, disposition, and health. If you sense a problem or incompatibility at this stage of the game, don't waste your time going to see the animal. Say "No, thanks," and go on to the next prospect. If the horse sounds great, set up a mutually acceptable time for you to see the horse, but make sure that your trainer/expert is available at that time, too.

Paying a visit

REMEMBER

Bringing your trainer or equine expert with you the first time you see a horse is important. You need that person's opinion about the horse immediately. If your trainer/expert gives the horse a thumbs up, then you can pursue a pre-purchase veterinary exam and possible trial period (we cover both processes in the sections on "Hiring a vet to check the horse" and "Signing up for a trial period" later in this chapter). If your trainer/expert gives the horse a thumbs down, then you shouldn't waste any more of your or the seller's time.

REMEMBER

In most cases, you ride the horse on that first visit, so be sure to wear your riding clothes when you go — and don't forget your helmet!

Start the evaluation process when you drive out to see the horse. Your trainer/expert can guide you through this process.

Follow these steps as you evaluate any horse:

1. **Take in the entire horse.** Take a long, hard look at the horse. The horse should be wearing only a halter so you can see his conformation, or the way he's put together. Your trainer/expert helps you evaluate the horse's conformation visually and with a hands-on exam, where you feel the horse's legs and pick up his feet to look at the underside of his hooves (see Chapter 4 to find out more about recognizing good and bad conformation). The two of you are looking for overall balance, blemishes, and conformation pluses and minuses in the horse. If the horse already has been tacked up (saddled) in anticipation of your arrival, ask to see the horse without tack after you ride him.

2. **Watch the horse move.** Ask the seller to walk and trot the horse away from and toward you on a loose lead, from the ground. The seller also needs to walk and trot the horse so that you can view him from the side and have the horse *longe,* which is to move in a circle with a long rope attached at the halter or bridle, on hard and soft ground. (See Chapter 13 for more information on longeing.) Your trainer/expert watches the horse's movement to judge whether the horse is sound.

3. **Watch the horse as someone else rides him.** Ask the seller to ride (or have someone else ride) the horse so you and your trainer/expert can watch the horse work under saddle. The rider needs to ask the horse to walk, trot, and canter. If you're buying a horse that is intended for jumping, ask the rider to take the horse over a few jumps; if the horse is for barrel racing, ask the rider to negotiate a few barrels, and so on. Observe the horse during this time to get a sense of what he's like when someone is riding him.

4. **Have your trainer/expert ride the horse.** This crucial step allows your trainer/expert to get a real feel for the horse's disposition under saddle and his suitability as a beginner's horse.

5. **Ride the horse yourself.** If your trainer/expert likes the horse, he or she will suggest that you ride him. Work the horse in a walk, trot, and canter. Pay attention to the way the horse feels as you ride, and ask yourself whether you're comfortable on the horse and whether you like the way horse responds to you.

   During this part of the process, you can rely heavily on gut feeling. Tune into yourself and see whether the horse *feels* right. If the horse is meant for your child to ride, have your child get up on the horse, too, assuming you and your trainer/expert consider the animal safe.

6. **Observe the horse.** If you and your trainer/expert like the horse, ask the seller whether you can spend some time handling the horse from the ground and observing him in his stall or pasture. Lead him around, groom him, and pick up his feet. Get a sense of what the horse's personality is like.

WARNING

The horse needs to exhibit gentle, easygoing behavior. If he's difficult to handle or tries to bite or kick, this horse isn't for you.

When in a stall or pasture, notice whether the horse has any stable vices like cribbing or weaving (see Chapter 2 for more information).

7. **Find out whether the horse loads into a trailer.** Ask the seller whether the horse willingly loads into a trailer. If the answer is yes, ask for a demonstration. Any horse that won't load into a trailer is not a good choice as a purchase. Even if you don't plan to trailer the horse on a regular basis, you may someday need to take him to the hospital or transport him from one area to another. In these and other situations, horses that won't load cause enormous problems for their owners.

TIP

Just because you have a trainer/expert with you when you evaluate a horse for purchase doesn't mean that you sit back and let your expert do all the work! Take this opportunity to learn about horses and how to look at them. Be involved, and after the evaluation, when the two of you are alone, ask plenty of questions.

Moving forward after the visit

After you evaluate the horse, thank the seller and tell him or her that you're interested in the horse (if you are) but need some time to think about what you just saw and experienced. After you leave the premises, discuss the horse with your trainer/expert. If the two of you agree that the horse is a good match for you, pay another visit to the horse and ride him again (you may have to do so as early as the next day if other people also are interested in buying the horse). If you are buying a horse for trail riding, talk to the seller about taking the horse on a short trail ride so you can see how the horse handles on the trail. Be sure to bring another rider with you; you shouldn't ride a strange horse alone on the trail.

If you still like the horse after the second ride, contact a veterinarian and arrange for a pre-purchase exam (see the following section).

REMEMBER

Whatever you do, don't purchase a horse without completing the entire evaluation process outlined here. You may be tempted to do so simply because you're afraid someone else may buy the horse first. Resist that temptation, because you're better off letting the horse go than you are buying him without knowing what you're getting. You'll soon find another horse that you like just as much.

TIP

If you and your trainer/expert feel positive about the horse, you may want to give the seller a small deposit (usually around 10 percent of the purchase price) to hold the animal while you make your final evaluation. If you decide not to buy the horse, and the seller turns down another offer while you're still in the evaluation process, be prepared to lose your deposit. Some sellers keep the deposit even if they receive no other offers on the horse. Stipulate the terms of your deposit up front and in writing.

Hiring a vet to check the horse

After you find a horse that you and your trainer/expert agree upon, you need to call in a veterinarian who specializes in horses. Most equine veterinarians offer a service known as a pre-purchase exam, or a *vet check* in casual terms. If you hire a vet to perform such an exam, the doctor comes out to where the horse resides and thoroughly examines the animal.

TIP

If you're working with a reputable trainer to find a horse, your veterinarian may recommend that you take the horse you're considering to a training facility and keep him there for a one-week trial period before conducting the pre-purchase exam. Doing so gives you a chance to spend time with the horse and ensures that the horse is drug-free before the exam. (Make sure the horse is up-to-date on shots, deworming, and shoeing before you take him, and discuss a contract with the seller to protect both of you during the trial period.) *Note:* Trainers and breeders usually extend this courtesy to other trainers and breeders, but not usually to individuals looking to a buy a horse on their own — another good reason to have a trainer help you with your purchase.

TIP

Make sure that you select an independent veterinarian to perform the pre-purchase exam — not one who the seller suggests or who considers the seller a client. (We give you great tips on finding the right vet in Chapter 4.) If you're unable to locate an independent veterinarian on your own, contact the American Association of Equine Practitioners for a referral (see the Appendix for this organization's web address).

Some aspects of the pre-purchase exam are included in the basic price, but other services cost you extra. The more tests you can have the vet perform, the more you'll learn about your prospective horse and the more you'll pay for the exam.

REMEMBER

The results of the examination give you a good idea about any health problems the horse may have. Keep in mind, however, that the pre-purchase exam is not foolproof. A disease or condition can evade discovery during a vet check.

The following are just a few of the things the vet examines:

>> **Vital signs:** The vet checks the horse for normal temperature, respiration, and pulse while at rest. After some light exercise, the vet checks these vital signs again. Abnormal readings sometimes are a way to detect illness.

>> **Heart and lungs:** The vet listens to the horse's heart and lungs with a stethoscope to determine whether any problems are present.

>> **Gut sounds:** Using a stethoscope, the vet listens to the sounds coming from the horse's gastrointestinal system. Normal gut sounds indicate a healthy digestive system.

- » **Teeth:** The vet examines the horse's mouth for problems with missing teeth, overgrown molars, poor alignment, and wear from the habit of cribbing (see Chapter 2 for information on cribbing).

- » **Eyes:** Using a light source, the vet checks the health of the horse's eyes, looking for corneal scarring, cataracts, inflammation, and other signs of disease.

- » **Lameness:** The veterinarian evaluates the horse's conformation for any faults that may affect the animal's ability to perform in the job you intend for him (see Chapter 2 for more information on conformation). The horse then undergoes something called a *flexion test,* where he is gaited in front of the veterinarian on hard and soft ground and in circles so the doctor can determine any problems in movement. During the lameness part of the examination, the vet also palpates the lower limbs in search of abnormalities and examines the hooves visually and with a device called a *hoof tester.*

- » **Blood:** At your request, the vet will draw blood from the horse and have it tested for equine infectious anemia (called a Coggins test), thyroid function, and other possible problems.

- » **X-ray and ultrasound:** At your request, the veterinarian may take X-rays or an ultrasound to further evaluate the horse's soundness and health.

WARNING

You also need to ask your veterinarian to do a blood or urine test for drug detection. We've heard stories of sellers tranquilizing or otherwise drugging horses before selling them, leaving the unfortunate buyers to discover the truth after the drug wears off and the horse's true personality comes out.

A veterinarian conducting a pre-purchase exam needs to ask the seller about the horse's medical history and current use. The vet also asks you about what you intend to do with the horse if you buy him. The reason for these questions is so the veterinarian can determine whether the horse is physically capable of performing the job you want him to do.

The veterinarian doesn't give the horse a pass or fail on the exam: He or she simply alerts you to the horse's condition at the time of the exam. The vet may tell you whether the horse seems suitable for certain disciplines or sports depending on the correctness of his conformation, although most veterinarians aren't willing to give an opinion on this subject for liability reasons. If the horse is suffering from a serious illness, the vet indicates the abnormal finding on the horse's report.

You can discuss the results of the pre-purchase exam with your trainer/expert to get his or her input, but the decision whether to purchase the animal ultimately is yours.

Remember that no horse is perfect. Whatever issues your trainer or veterinarian discover about the horse may or may not be a deal-breaker for you. Some training or health issues are minor, and you may choose to live with them. Just be sure you know exactly what you are getting into before you take on the responsibility.

If the horse's health is acceptable based on the pre-purchase exam, ask your trainer/expert for advice on how to proceed. We strongly recommend taking the horse for a trial period (see the following section); however, if doing so is not possible, your trainer/expert may recommend that you contact the seller to discuss another visit or the possible purchase of the horse.

Signing up for a trial period

REMEMBER

If a horse you're interested in has passed muster with your trainer/expert and turned up healthy in the pre-purchase exam, you can move forward to the trial period. Many sellers will allow you to take the horse for a trial period. We recommend negotiating for a 30-day trial period, which gives you the greatest amount of time to get to know the horse. A week or two is better than nothing, if that's all the time the seller will allow.

When negotiating for the trial period, put all the terms of the trial in writing and make sure both parties sign the agreement. As the potential buyer, you customarily pay for the horse's board and feed during the time he's in your care and possession; the seller usually pays any medical costs that come up. Or the seller may want to keep the horse at his property during the trial period.

If the seller doesn't agree to a trial period, suggest a lease agreement instead. You can opt to lease the horse for several months at an agreed fee with the goal of getting to know the animal. At the end of your lease, you can purchase the horse or return him to the seller (see Chapter 4 for more about leasing a horse). The seller may agree to this arrangement because it generates monthly income — with a good chance that you'll buy the animal as a result of the lease.

REMEMBER

Before you take a horse for a trial period, make sure that seller has insured the horse to cover any accidents or death that may result while the horse is in your possession. If the horse isn't insured, take out a temporary policy on the animal yourself (the cost is minimal) and make sure that you stipulate the terms of your liability in writing (like who is responsible for the horse's medical care during the trial and who is liable if the horse suddenly dies — whatever your insurance stipulates). Before you agree to be personally responsible for medical care when the horse is in your possession, be aware that equine medical bills can be high. In most cases, the seller is willing to assume this responsibility.

If a trial period or lease is out of the question (some sellers don't feel comfortable allowing the horse off their property or want to sell the horse quickly), try spending as much time with the horse as you possibly can before you decide to buy him. Ask the seller whether you can come and see the horse more than once, and when you're with the animal, tie him, lead, and groom him, and by all means ride him to get a sense of what the horse is really like.

If the seller refuses any kind of trial or lease agreement, and you can't spend more time with the horse, think hard about whether you really want to buy this animal. You'll be making a big commitment without really knowing if the horse is right for you. It's like getting married after only two dates! Rarely a good idea.

REMEMBER

During your trial period or lease, spend plenty of time with the horse so the two of you get acquainted. Perform the same tasks with the horse that you plan to do after you buy him — or at least as much as you can. If you want to trail ride, take the trial horse out on the trail, preferably with another rider for safety reasons. If you plan to jump, do some jumping with the horse. If your children or spouse are going to be involved with the horse after you buy him, have them spend time with the horse now so they can see how they feel about him. In addition, the horse's ground manners are extremely important yet often overlooked when people are evaluating a horse for purchase. Use this time to see what kind of ground manners the horse has by spending time tying the horse, grooming him, and leading him around the barn.

The point of all this evaluation is to make sure that you and your family are truly compatible with the horse. If the horse hates being on the trail, constantly refuses jumps, or is so ill-mannered that he drags you around when you lead him, you're better off finding out now as opposed to after you actually buy him.

Closing the deal

You've consulted with your trainer/expert, spoken to your veterinarian, asked yourself some important questions, and made a decision that you want to buy a particular horse. Now comes the business part of the deal.

Julie I. Fershtman, an attorney practicing equine law in Bingham Farms, Michigan, and author of the book *Equine Law & Horse Sense* (Horses & the Law Publishing, Franklin, Michigan) recommends that you draft a contract and present it to the seller to sign before the purchase. Such a contract needs to spell out all the terms of the sale for you and for the seller and significantly reduces the likelihood of any misunderstandings later on.

Fershtman suggests that the contract contain the following information:

>> **Names and pertinent information:** Include the names of the buyer and seller, along with their respective addresses and telephone numbers.

>> **Legal rights:** Ask for a guarantee that the seller is indeed the horse's legal owner and has the right to sell the animal.

>> **Description:** Include a description of the horse, including size, color, breed, and registration number, if any.

>> **The price that you and the seller agree upon:** Indicate whether the seller has received full payment or whether you're paying the price in installments. Be sure to indicate how much all installments are and the dates when they're due. Also list where you are to send the installments and how you will be making the payments. Include information on the recourses for you and the seller have if you are unable to make the payments.

>> **The date the horse becomes yours:** If registration papers and pedigrees are involved, give the dates by which you can expect to receive each of these records.

>> **The terms of the warranty on the horse, if any:** If you want the seller to guarantee the horse in any way, you must spell it out on the contract. The seller must agree to the warranty, of course. You can include express conditions, such as "does not rear," "is free of any lameness," or whatever you determine is most important to you, and whatever the seller will agree upon.

>> **Signatures of both parties.**

If you want even greater protection than this brief contract can afford, consult an attorney who's experienced in equine law and ask him or her to draw up a detailed contract.

Bringing Your Horse Home

Okay, you've bought yourself a horse. Do you now just hop on his back and ride away?

No! You need to get the horse home first. The seller may be willing to deliver the horse to your stable. If not, you can hire someone with a trailer to pick up your horse up and bring him to his new home.

WARNING

If you've never hitched up a trailer, loaded a horse, or driven a horse trailer before, we don't suggest that you buy or rent a trailer and do the job yourself just yet — unless you have an expert on hand to help you with these tasks. Your horse must have a good experience (as opposed to a traumatic one) traveling to his new home. Right now, concentrate on getting your horse to wherever you plan to keep him. You can always work on your trailering skills later.

REMEMBER

When your horse arrives at a new home, make him feel welcome by following these steps:

>> **Feed your horse:** If plan to keep your horse in a stall or paddock, have food waiting for him and make sure that you give him the same food he's been eating at his previous home so he doesn't develop colic. (See Chapter 8 for information on what to feed your horse.)

>> **Change food sources gradually:** If you're going to keep your horse in a pasture where grass is his primary food source, make sure that you gradually introduce him to the grass over a period of at least two weeks. By gradually, we mean keep him in a stall or paddock and feed him what his previous owner fed him, while letting him graze for only an hour the first couple of days, two hours the next couple of days, three hours the next two days, and so on, until his system acclimates to his new diet.

>> **Water your horse:** Have clean, fresh water available in his enclosure.

>> **Stay with your horse for a while:** Horses often are nervous and uncertain when they move from familiar surroundings to a strange new place. Your company helps soothe his worries and allows you to keep an eye on him as he takes in his new environment.

>> **Give your horse some adjustment time:** Don't ride him right away, and don't take him to a horse show two days after he's been in your possession! From the horse's perspective, he's just lost all that is familiar to him: his home, his routine, and most likely the person with whom he bonded. He needs time to adjust to his new life, and the two of you need time get to know one another.

>> **Give your horse attention:** Spend time grooming him, talking to him, and just hanging out with him. Deliver his food yourself, and stand by him as he eats. Let him graze on some grass outside his stall while you hold his lead rope. All these things help foster a bond between the two of you.

IN THIS CHAPTER

» **Determining where to shop for supplies**

» **Knowing saddle styles**

» **Understanding bits, bridles, and other riding equipment**

» **Examining different tools for horse care**

» **Dressing your horse (and yourself) properly for riding**

» **Transporting your horse**

Chapter **6**

Getting into Gear with Horse Equipment

I f you like to shop, horsemanship is the right hobby! All kinds of horsy stuff is available in the retail world. Some of it is necessary to every horse owner; some of it you need only if you plan to spoil your horse.

Either way, if you're going to be a part of the horse world, you must have a handle on all this stuff. We don't want you to share the fate of coauthor Audrey Pavia's non-horsy husband, who after walking through a tack store in a foiled attempt to buy his wife a gift, exclaimed, "Everything just looks like belts!" All that leather has a purpose. And we explain it all to you in this chapter.

Where to Buy Equine Equipment

If you're new to horses, you probably aren't sure where to buy the equine equipment and riding apparel you need. Here's a list of the places we recommend for buying tack and other horse supplies.

>> **Tack and feed stores:** Most communities that have horses also have at least one tack and feed store. These places not only sell food for horses, but equipment, too. If you have more than one tack and feed store in your area, be sure to comparison shop. Sometimes pricing differences are huge from one store to the next in the same area. Likewise, keep an eye out for used equipment in these places. Many tack and feed stores sell used saddles and other items on consignment.

>> **Mail-order catalogs:** The horse world has a number of quality mail-order companies that deal exclusively in equine equipment. You can buy everything from saddles to show apparel from these catalogs, often at big discounts from retail prices. The downside of buying from a catalog is that you can't try on the clothes or sit in the saddle before you make a purchase. These drawbacks shouldn't stop you from buying a catalog, however, because all good catalogs have a return policy enabling customers to send back whatever doesn't fit.

>> **The Internet:** A whole slew of equine retailers have popped up on the Internet, and many of them also have mail-order catalogs. You can get great deals shopping for horse equipment online, either through Internet stores or on auction sites. Make sure any items you purchase while cybershopping are backed up by a return policy.

>> **Consignment shops:** Less common than regular tack and feed stores, equine consignment shops deal almost exclusively in used tack. They are great places to shop if you have a limited budget (and who doesn't unless you're rich and famous), and the reputable ones have return policies on saddles and other items that require a good fit. Keep these shops in mind when you're ready to upgrade and sell off your old tack, too.

>> **Other horse owners:** Buying your equine equipment from another horse owner is a good way to get a good deal on tack. People who are getting out of horses, or simply have too much stuff (horse equipment is easy to accumulate, as you may soon find out) often are anxious to get rid of their horsy things and willing to sell the items at low prices. You can find these people by checking out bulletin boards at riding stables and the classified section of your daily newspaper under "horse."

If you buy a saddle from a private seller, take the saddle on a trial basis so you can make sure that it fits you *and* your horse. If the seller is a total stranger and doesn't like the idea of you taking the saddle off site, ask the seller to be present when you try the saddle on the horse. If the seller won't cooperate and expects you to buy the saddle outright without trying it on your horse, politely refuse to buy it.

Saddles and Related Accessories

There's more than one way to ride a horse.

Okay, that's not the original saying, but we're cat lovers and prefer it this way. Anyway, the modified statement is true: Riders have options in the particular style they choose.

Each riding discipline not only has its own associated style of riding, but also its own equipment. To function properly in the horse world — and to eventually shop intelligently for your own stuff — you need to know the differences. In the following sections, we get you started with the most important piece of equipment: saddles.

Surveying different types of saddles

REMEMBER

Most people know that a saddle is a big piece of wood or fiberglass covered with leather that goes on a horse's back. But there's more to it than that. Saddles come in different styles. The one you buy depends on the type of riding you plan to do. Pay close attention here; the saddle represents one of your biggest investment in your new hobby.

Knowing the parts of the saddle that are common to all disciplines helps when you're shopping for a saddle. They include:

>> **Pommel:** The front rise of the saddle

>> **Cantle:** The rear rise of the saddle

>> **Seat:** The center of the saddle where the rider sits

Hunt-seat saddle

The hunt-seat saddle (a type of English saddle) was originally designed for fox hunters, those members of the British aristocracy who found pleasure in chasing foxes through the countryside, leaping over fences, logs, and other obstacles in the process.

If you plan to ride your horse in the hunt-seat discipline — eventually learning to jump — you need this saddle, because it's designed to make going over jumps comfortable and secure for the rider. A *saddletree*, the wooden or fiberglass frame on which the saddle is constructed, determines the fit of the saddle on the horse's back.

A hunt-seat saddle and its parts are shown in Figure 6-1. These same parts also apply to other English saddles.

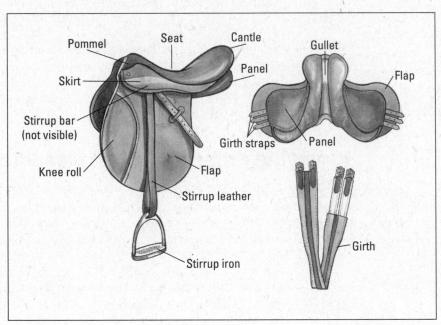

FIGURE 6-1:
The hunt-seat saddle makes jumping comfortable.

© *John Wiley & Sons, Inc.*

Dressage saddle

The *dressage saddle* is a type of English saddle that is specifically designed for use in the discipline of dressage. It differs from a hunt-seat saddle in that the cantle and pommel are a bit higher, the seat is deeper, and the stirrup irons are longer. Dressage saddles are constructed to put the rider in more of an upright position than you see in a hunt-seat saddle. The rider sits deep in the saddle with her legs underneath her body, providing more contact with the horse.

TIP

If you want to learn to ride in the dressage discipline, you need a dressage saddle. You can learn dressage in an all-purpose hunt-seat saddle, but this difficult discipline is made easier by using a saddle that's specifically designed for it.

A drawing of a dressage saddle appears in Figure 6-2. The parts of the dressage saddle are identical to the parts of a hunt-seat saddle. The only differences are the nuances of the design of those parts (refer to Figure 6-1 for the parts of the hunt-seat saddle).

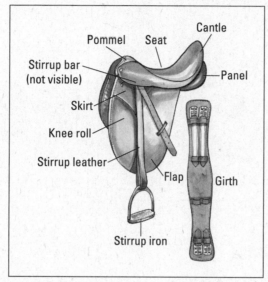

FIGURE 6-2:
The dressage saddle is similar to a hunt-seat saddle.

© John Wiley & Sons, Inc.

Show saddle

The *show saddle* is primarily used in American saddle-seat riding to show off flashy, high-stepping horses. Show saddles are designed to keep the rider's weight off the horse's front end, so the animal can produce a lot of action in his forelegs. Consequently, the rider sits farther back on the horse with his or her legs farther out in front than with a hunt-seat or dressage saddle.

If you ride an American-bred gaited horse, such as an American Saddlebred, Tennessee Walking Horse, or Racking Horse, and if you plan to show in gaited classes, you need a show saddle. You can also ride on the trail with a show saddle, although this activity is not the show saddle's primary purpose.

To get an idea of what a show saddle looks like and how it differs from other English saddles, see Figure 6-3. The parts of the show saddle are the same as those of a hunt-seat and dressage saddles, except that the show saddle doesn't have a knee roll (refer to Figure 6-1 for the hunt-seat saddle). The knee roll is the section at the front of the flap that supports the rider's knee.

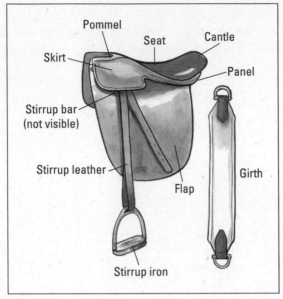

FIGURE 6-3:
The show saddle is similar to a hunt-seat saddle but lacks a knee roll.

© John Wiley & Sons, Inc.

Western saddle

The western saddle was created out of sheer necessity in the old American West. This quintessential working saddle hasn't changed very much in design during the past 100 years.

If you plan to compete in western events with your horse, or if you're simply attracted to western riding and want to participate in this discipline strictly for enjoyment, a western saddle is what you need.

The western saddle is designed to give you a secure, comfortable ride. The deep seat, high pommel, and high cantle help keep the rider in the saddle when the horse makes sudden maneuvers, making it the saddle of choice for calf roping, reining, cutting, and other western working sports. The long stirrups are meant for greater comfort during long hours in the saddle (see Figure 6-4 for parts of the western saddle).

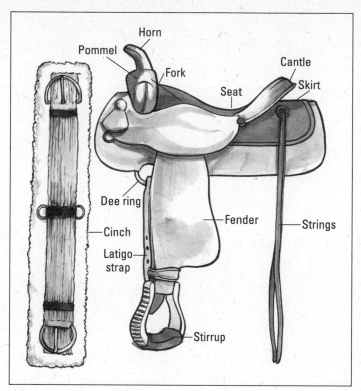

FIGURE 6-4: A western saddle provides a safe, comfortable ride.

© John Wiley & Sons, Inc.

Endurance saddle

If you plan to spend long hours on the trail, consider an endurance saddle. A cross between an English saddle and a western saddle, endurance saddles combine the best of both worlds. They are light and easy to lift like an English saddle, and thus give the horse less weight to carry around. The seat is deep and comfortable like a western saddle, and some have high pommels and even saddle horns for extra security. These saddles also have more D-rings to secure the kinds of items you need on a long trail ride, such as a water bottle, saddle pack, and lead rope.

Endurance saddles come in a variety of designs for a variety of tastes. Figure 6-5 shows a typical endurance saddle.

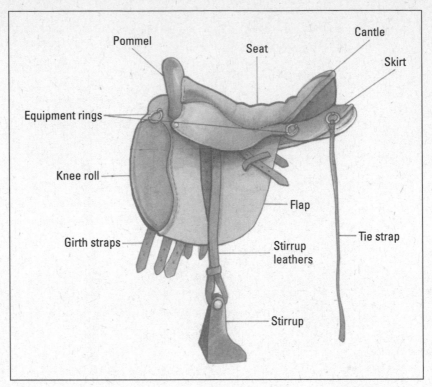

FIGURE 6-5:
The endurance
saddle combines
the best features
of an English
saddle and a
western saddle.

Picking out saddle pads

Saddle pads protect the horse's back from rubbing and chafing, and they protect the saddle from sweat. Regardless of whether you're riding English or western, you need to buy a good saddle pad or two to place underneath your saddle when you ride. Two popular types are:

>> **English pads:** The type of pad you need depends on the style of English riding you plan to do. Hunt-seat riders typically use white synthetic fleece pads underneath their saddles. Dressage riders usually use white square-quilted cotton pads called dressage pads, and saddle-seat riders typically use either no pad at all or a thin cotton pad.

>> **Western pads:** For a western saddle, you need a western pad. Most western pads are made from inch-thick (or thicker) synthetic fleece or felt. Many of these pads come in decorative designs. You can also get just a plain white-foam western pad and put a thin Navajo-style blanket on top of it.

Whatever type of pad you use, keep it clean by washing it regularly, either in a washing machine or by hand (don't put it in the dryer unless you want it to shrink). If not kept clean, a dirty pad not only starts to smell bad, but it also is likely to irritate your horse's back.

Buying a saddle the smart way

REMEMBER

A saddle is a big-ticket item — at least as far as horse equipment goes. That's why you need to do some homework before you buy. Here's our advice on buying a saddle:

>> Be certain that you're comfortable with the discipline you choose before you invest in a saddle. Take some lessons in that type of saddle first to be sure that you like how it feels.

>> Take an experienced horse person with you when you go saddle shopping. You need that person's expertise to help you make a good decision. (See Chapter 4 for tips on finding a horse expert.)

>> Buy your saddle only after you buy or lease your horse, because the saddle needs to fit the horse you're riding. (Chapter 5 has info on the horse-buying process.)

>> Buy the best saddle you can afford, because you're making a long-term investment. Spending money on a quality saddle now pays off later.

>> Research the brand names of saddles made for your discipline. Contact the manufacturers and ask them about the features of their products. Survey other riders in your discipline to see which brands they prefer.

>> Purchase a saddle with a return policy. You need time to try the saddle on your horse before you commit to keeping it (see the following section for more information on fitting a saddle). This practice goes for used saddles and new ones.

>> Have a trainer or independent saddlemaker inspect the saddletree during your trial period whenever you're buying a used saddle to make sure the frame is not broken.

>> Make sure the saddle fits your rear end. The seats of saddles come in different sizes, measured in inches (a woman of average size and weight typically fits in a 15- to 16-inch seat on a Western saddle, and a 17-inch seat on an English model). Try sitting in the saddle before you take it home (see the next section for more information).

>> Consider having a saddle custom-made whenever you can't find a saddle that fits both you and your horse. Although you'll spend more than if you buy a saddle off the rack, it's worth the money. Contact a local tack store for a referral to a saddlemaker in your area.

REMEMBER

English saddles do not include the stirrup leathers, stirrup irons, and girths. You need to purchase these items separately. The purchase of a western saddle always includes stirrups and usually includes cinches; however, you may want to upgrade to a better cinch if the one that comes with your saddle isn't of high quality.

Ensuring your saddle fits

Saddle shopping is more than just finding a nice-looking saddle in your price range. You have to make sure that the saddle fits you and your horse before you commit to buying it.

Fitting the horse

As far as the horse is concerned, a saddle that doesn't fit correctly can result in sore back muscles, and a corresponding bad attitude to go with it.

REMEMBER

Finding a saddle that fits your horse takes some work. Even though saddle manufacturers make saddletrees in different sizes (wide, medium, and narrow), each horse is an individual and may not fit into a saddle that corresponds to the apparent width of the horse's back.

For that reason, when you buy a saddle, take it on a trial basis so you can be sure that it fits. During that trial period, follow the steps outlined in the sections that follow to determine the saddle's fit and enlist an experienced horse person to help you determine the fit of the saddle. Saddle fitting can be tricky, even for the most experienced riders.

The true test of whether a saddle really fits your horse is time and usage. Ride the horse in the saddle over a period of time, and periodically check his back for soreness. You do this by using your fingertips to apply medium pressure along the horse's back as you move your hand along the muscles on either side of the spine. If your horse flinches under the pressure, he may have soreness from the saddle. If in doubt, ask your veterinarian or an equine chiropractor to check him out.

ENGLISH SADDLES

To determine whether an English saddle fits your horse, follow these steps:

1. **Put the saddle on the horse without using a saddle pad.** Tighten the girth so that the saddle is comfortably secure.

2. **Have someone sit in the saddle with his or her feet in the stirrups.**

3. **Using a flat hand, slide your fingers underneath the pommel, near the horse's withers (the rise as the base of neck, where it joins the back).** See Chapter 2 for a diagram showing the parts of the horse. Your fingers should fit

comfortably between the horse and saddle. Be certain that you can place at least three fingers between the horse's withers and the arch below the pommel.

4. **Have a helper lift the horse's left foreleg and pull it forward while your fingers are in between the top of the horse's shoulder blade and the pommel.** As the horse's shoulder moves, make sure the saddle doesn't impede shoulder movement. Perform the same test on the horse's right side.

5. **Stand behind the horse and look through the saddle (between the underside of the saddle and the horse's back).** If the saddle fits, you should see a tunnel of light shining through. If you don't see any light, the saddle is too snug. You likewise need to make sure that the saddle isn't too long for the horse. The seat panel shouldn't reach past the main part of the horse's back onto the loins.

WESTERN SADDLES

To make sure that a western saddle fits correctly, follow these steps:

1. **Place the saddle on the horse's back with a one-inch thick (or so) saddle pad underneath it.** Tighten the cinch so that it's snug but comfortable.

TIP

When you try to tighten the cinch, you may find that it's too short for the horse's barrel. Don't reject the saddle simply because the cinch is too short. If you really like the saddle and it fits, you can always buy a longer, replacement cinch. Meanwhile, borrow a cinch that fits so you can continue to try out the saddle.

2. **Have a rider sit in the saddle with his or her feet in the stirrups.** Be sure that you can fit at least three fingers between the arch of the pommel and the horse's withers.

3. **Examine the width of the saddletree, or frame, as it sits on the horse and compare it with the shape of the horse's back.** On a horse with a wide back and lower withers, the tree needs to be wide. On a narrower back with higher withers, the tree shouldn't be too wide. Place your fingers sideways (on a flat hand) between the saddle and the top of the horse's shoulder to help determine the width of the tree. If the fit is so tight that you can't squeeze your fingers between the saddle and the top of the horse's shoulder, the tree is too wide for your horse. If you can put your entire hand between the saddle and the top of the horse's shoulder, the tree is too narrow.

Fitting the rider

The saddle has to fit the horse, sure, but it also needs to fit you. Otherwise, you'll be miserable when you ride. The good news is that finding a saddle that suits you is much easier than finding one that suits your horse.

TIP

The seats of English and western saddles are measured in inches. If you're taking lessons, or using a friend's saddle and you like the feel of it, find out the measurement of the seat. Armed with this information, you can rule out saddles that don't have the same seat measurement. You can also try sitting in different saddles in a tack shop and take note of which size suits you best.

ENGLISH SADDLES

To determine whether an English saddle fits you, try it out in the store or on the horse, whichever is easier. We think you need try several saddles in the store first so that you don't find one that fits your horse perfectly but doesn't work for you.

Sit in the seat with your stirrups at the length you prefer (see Chapter 15 for information about determining the right stirrup length) and gauge how comfortable the saddle feels. You need to have about four inches of saddle in front of your body and four inches behind it.

If you like the way the saddle feels and you take it home to try on your horse, check the fit on the horse's back first. If it fits your horse, then put a pad under the saddle and take it for a spin to see how it feels. Ask a trainer or other person experienced in English riding to watch you and point out any problems with the saddle that he or she may see.

WESTERN SADDLES

Western saddles usually are easy to try out in the store, because they're often displayed on wooden sawhorses. If for some reason you can't try the saddle on a sawhorse, take it home and try it on your real horse. Make sure that it fits your horse's back first.

Adjust your stirrups to the proper length (see Chapter 15 to find out how). Sit in the saddle with your feet in the stirrups, and judge the comfort of the saddle. You need to have about four inches in between the front of your body and the pommel. Your derriere needs to rest against the base of the cantle but not be squashed against the rise of the cantle.

If the saddle appears to fit you and your horse upon initial inspection, get on, and ride in it. After half an hour of riding, it still should feel comfortable.

Tack It Up: Other Riding Requirements

Saddles are a major purchase, but the shopping doesn't stop there. Plenty of other accessories are needed before you can get up on your horse and start riding.

Getting a heads-up on bridles

Bridle is the word that applies to the headgear used on the horse during riding. A bridle consists of a *headstall*, the part that goes over the ears and connects to the bit; *reins*, the leather straps that attach to the bit and are held by the rider; and a *bit*, the piece, usually made of metal, that goes inside the horse's mouth — or a substitute for a bit. We cover bits (which you buy separately from a bridle) in more detail in the following section.

Each riding discipline has its own style of bridle, but bridles within each discipline's style also vary. The needs of your horse are the determining factors in the kind of bridle you ultimately buy.

REMEMBER

Bridles have buckles on them and are adjustable, so you don't need to worry much about matching your horse's head to a particular bridle — most bridles fit most horses. The exceptions to this rule are horses or ponies with a very small heads or draft horses like Belgians or Clydesdales with a very large heads. In either situation, you need to buy bridles that are specially suited to the horse's head sizes. Similarly, you occasionally may run across a bridle that is meant for an average-sized horse but turns out to be too small.

TIP

Before you go bridle shopping, have an experienced horseperson help you determine the type of bridle your horse needs. Figure 6-6 shows a variety of English and western bridles. The remainder of this section explains the different bridles.

The English disciplines of hunt seat, dressage, and saddle seat use several different types of bridle styles. The basic bridle for each is virtually the same, but you'll find these following variations:

>> **Hunt-seat bridle:** Hunt-seat riders typically use a standard snaffle bridle with a snaffle bit. This bridle consists of a headstall strap, a browband that goes across the forehead, a throatlatch that attaches under the horse's jowl, and a noseband that goes across the nose and under the jaw. Variations of this bridle exist, including ones with a drop noseband and a flash noseband to keep the horse from evading the action of the bit by opening his mouth.

>> **Dressage bridle:** The aesthetics of the dressage bridle are somewhat different, but riders also use the snaffle bridle in dressage.

TIP

Although many of the same bits and headstalls used in hunt seat also are used in dressage, some levels of dressage competition don't allow certain bits and nosebands. If you intend to show in dressage, contact the ruling dressage federation in your country to find out the latest rules.

>> **Saddle-seat bridle:** Horses ridden saddle seat typically wear a double bridle, which is similar to a snaffle bridle but has an additional cheek piece to hold an additional bit.

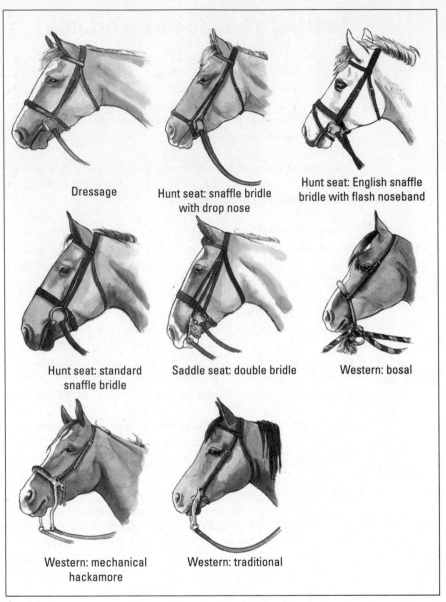

Dressage

Hunt seat: snaffle bridle with drop nose

Hunt seat: English snaffle bridle with flash noseband

Hunt seat: standard snaffle bridle

Saddle seat: double bridle

Western: bosal

Western: mechanical hackamore

Western: traditional

FIGURE 6-6: English and western bridles have several variations.

© John Wiley & Sons, Inc.

Bridles for western riding come in a few styles. Each has a headstall and reins. Some western bridles are *split-ear* style, which means a piece of leather at the top of the headstall is attached for the horse's ear to fit through. Other western bridles have browbands instead. And still others have neither browband nor split-ear design, and simply rest behind the horse's ears.

Within western styles, bridles differ mostly based on whether you use a bit. The material of western bridles likewise varies of late, and western riders can find not only traditional leather bridles but also brightly colored and elaborately patterned nylon bridles. The following list explains some of the types of western bridles:

>> **Traditional western bridle:** The traditional western bridle consists of a split-ear, browband, or plain headstall design with a bit attached. If the bit you use has a *curb shank* (a long, curved piece between the bit and the part where the reins attach), a curb chain or strap under the chin is included. A pair of reins finishes off the bridle.

>> **Western hackamore bridle:** Not all western bridles have bits; some are fitted with a device called a *hackamore,* which is a nosepiece that enables the rider to control the horse without using a bit. Hackamore bridles are split into these two main types:

- A bosal hackamore bridle is a rolled leather training device that's used to school young horses. It fits over the horse's head like a noseband.

- A mechanical hackamore bridle is a device that not only is for training, but also for general riding. The mechanical hackamore consists of a metal device that has a rolled leather noseband with metal parts beneath it. The reins attach to the metal piece, which helps you control the horse by putting pressure on the nose, chin, and poll. The entire hackamore piece is attached to a western headstall.

Breaking down bits

If you ever feel like being overwhelmed, go into any large tack store and take a look at the bits. There are easily as many bit styles as there are breeds of horses. Why such a huge number? Horse people throughout the centuries have endeavored to invent a bit for every equine riding problem, and they've nearly succeeded.

The purpose of a bit (which is usually made of metal) is to apply pressure to the horse's mouth and thus convey messages to stop, slow down, turn, and so on. The shape of the mouthpiece determines how that pressure is applied. Some bits are mild, meaning they apply minimal pressure. Others are harsh, demanding the horse's undivided attention by stricter means.

TIP

Beginning riders need to ride with a relatively mild bit until they develop their skills, because a harsh bit in inexperienced hands can result in pain for the horse. Ask a trainer for help on properly bitting your horse.

Western and English riding use different bits. The curb bit is the most common bit in western riding, while English riders typically use a bit called the loose ring snaffle. See Figure 6-7 for examples of some types of western and English bits. You can use any type of western or English bit with any type of bridle, as long as both the bridle and bit match the same discipline — western bits with western bridles and English bits with English bridles.

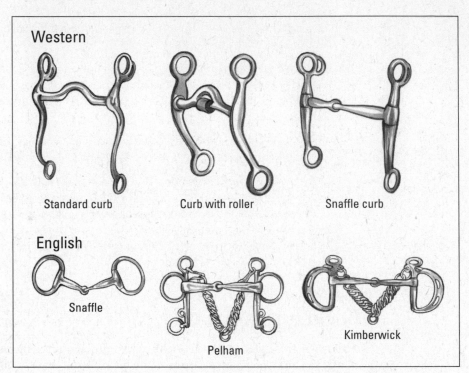

FIGURE 6-7: Western and English bits come in several different styles.

© John Wiley & Sons, Inc.

When buying a bit for your horse, you need the measurement of your horse's mouth, in inches. Figure this out by trying different bitted bridles on your horse. The average bit size for a horse is 5 inches.

TIP

Ask a friend with several horses or a trainer to loan you bits in a range of different sizes. Try the bridles on your horse and see which bit fits the best. The best fitting bit protrudes only a fourth of an inch on each side of the horse's mouth. Just to be sure of the size, measure the actual mouthpiece of the best fitting bit with a measuring tape. The measurement in inches is the bit size you need for your horse.

Checking out assorted riding aids

The number of contraptions that have been invented through the years to aid in riding is almost mind-boggling. The following sections list some of the most common gear. Some of these things are necessities, but others are luxuries.

Girths/cinches

In English riding dialect, the piece of equipment that holds the saddle onto the horse's body is the *girth*. In western lingo, it is known as the *cinch*. You obviously need one of these if you plan to ride your horse.

When you buy an English saddle, you have to buy a girth, too, because the two rarely come packaged together. You can purchase a leather girth or one made from a man-made material — either is fine (see nearby sidebar, "A great debate: Synthetic versus leather tack," for more information). Before you buy, be sure to measure your horse's girth area (underneath the horse) from one side of the saddle to the other. The resulting number in inches is the size girth you need.

When you purchase a western saddle, a cinch normally comes with it. If not, you can buy one in leather, nylon, or another synthetic material, such as Neoprene. Measure the area of your horse's girth from the right side of the saddle to about one-third of the way up the left side past the horse's elbow. Buy a cinch that is closest to that length.

TIP

For your horse's comfort, consider buying a girth cover for your English girth or western cinch strap made of fleece (or synthetic fleece). This fuzzy covering keeps the strap from rubbing on your horse's skin.

Stirrup irons and leathers

Only English riders need to worry about buying stirrup irons and leathers, because western saddles come with the stirrups and leathers attached. In case you're wondering, *stirrup irons* are those metal doohickeys you keep your feet in while you ride. Stirrup leathers are what hold the irons onto the saddle.

Stirrup irons (usually made of stainless steel, despite the name, which is a throwback to ancient times) are relatively standard items. Make sure that you buy a pair that fit your feet while you're wearing riding boots or shoes, of course, and invest in some rubber pads to go on the stirrups. The pads help your foot stay securely in the stirrup. Be sure to get the right size pads for your stirrup irons. If you aren't sure of the size, take an iron with you to a tack store and ask a store employee to help you.

TIP

Find stirrup leathers that match the leather of your saddle so the entire saddle looks like one unit. If your saddle is brown, don't get black stirrup leathers!

Artificial aids

When riding, the legs, hands, and voice are *natural aids* that you use to communicate with the horse. Any external device that you use to send a message (other than the bridle) is called an *artificial aid*, including the following:

>> **Spurs:** English and western riders wear spurs on occasion. English spurs are blunt tipped and come in either short or long lengths. Western spurs come in a variety of styles, nearly all with something called a *rowel*, or star-like wheel. Spurs attach to the heel of your boot with a leather or nylon strap.

   You use spurs to prompt a horse forward. Horses that aren't responsive to leg aids usually respond to the prodding of spurs. If used properly, spurs are not inhumane but merely send the horse a stronger message than a leg squeeze.

   WARNING

   In the wrong hands, spurs can be cruel and dangerous devices. Before you strap on a pair of spurs, make sure that you understand the proper way to use them. Learn this skill from a trainer or riding instructor. Only riders who have considerable training in the saddle should attempt to use spurs.

>> **Whips:** Each discipline of riding has its own design of whip.

   - Hunt-seat riders use a crop, a short stick with a leather bat on the end.

   - Dressage riders use a dressage whip, which is longer than a crop with a tiny tassel on the end. Saddle-seat riders sometimes carry a dressage whip.

   - Western riders traditionally use something called a switch, which is, in essence, a big tassel (plenty of western riders also use crops because they're more readily available).

   For longeing a horse, a long longe whip is used to keep the horse moving in a forward direction. (For more information on longeing, see Chapter 13.)

   Although whips typically are thought of as instruments of brutality, riders shouldn't use them that way. Whips usually serve as visual aids for riders who want to send any number of messages to a horse. In some cases, the whip actually makes contact with the horse, but merely as a tap, and never to deliver a beating.

   WARNING

   Beating a horse is inhumane and even illegal in many places. Never use your whip to punish your horse, and don't stand by and allow other people to do it either. A whip should never be used in anger.

Exercising your options on training gear

A few of the items used in training — or at least in the management of the horse — are worthy of your attention:

>> **Longe line:** To exercise your horse from the ground by longeing him (see Chapter 13 for more about longeing), you need a longe whip, mentioned in the previous section, and a longe line.

A *longe line* is a cotton or nylon rope ranging anywhere from 15 to 30 feet in length. One end of the line attaches to the horse's halter (we cover halters later in this chapter), cavesson (a headpiece made just for the purpose of longeing), or bridle, the other end is held in your hand.

TIP

We prefer cotton longe lines because they're less likely to give you the rope burn that synthetic lines can if the horse pull it through your hands.

>> **Longe cavesson:** You can longe your horse in a snaffle bridle or halter, but a longe cavesson actually is preferable. This item fits on the horse's head like a halter, but unlike a halter, it features a series of rings on the top part of the noseband. The longe line attaches to the center ring and gives the handler good control over the horse during longeing.

>> **Stud chain:** A stud chain is a steel-link chain usually about a foot long, with a ring at one end and a clip at the other. The chain fits around the horse's muzzle in conjunction with a halter, and is used to apply pressure to help control the horse.

Stud chains derive their names from being used on stallions during breeding. Ordinary horse people tend to use them on horses that have poor ground manners and problems leading. If you ever have to lead a horse that prefers to drag you rather than walk beside you, a stud chain is a literal lifesaver.

Considering a bareback pad

A bareback pad is not a necessity, but just a fun item to have around. If you ever have a day that you don't feel like throwing on the saddle, but would rather just have a relaxing stroll around the barn or countryside, a bareback pad helps make your ride more comfortable for you and your horse.

Bareback pads are usually brightly colored and made from synthetic fleece. Most have a nylon hand strap sown on near the horse's withers specifically for the rider to grab when security is needed. The pad attaches to the horse via a nylon girth that buckles on either side of the horse. If you have a pony, you'll need to buy a bareback pad made in pony size. Bareback pads for regular-sized horses are generally one-size-fits-all.

Most bareback pads don't have stirrups, although some do. We don't recommend you ride your horse extensively in a bareback pad with stirrups because this practice can result in a sore back for your horse.

WARNING

Although bareback pads are great whenever you don't feel like dealing with your saddle, they can be dangerous if not properly secured to the horse. One of the most common causes of horseback riding accidents is a bareback pad that has slipped off the horse. Make certain your pad is firmly secured to the horse with the girth that comes attached to the pad. If the girth is too loose and you can't make it any tighter, add more holes to it using a hole punch, or put a saddle blanket underneath it.

Ground Work: Horse-Care Items

Riding is only one part of horsemanship. True horse people are just as dedicated to caring for their horses from the ground. A trip to your local tack store or a flip through an equine mail-order catalog or website shows you no shortage of horse-care items. Making heads or tails out of all that stuff can be a challenge — unless you have this book to show you the way!

Understanding the importance of halters

REMEMBER

The halter is probably the piece of equine equipment that you use most often. Just about everything you do with your horse involves a halter. In fact, halters are so important that wearing one is the first thing a horse learns to do.

Halters differ from bridles in that halters have neither a bit nor reins. Instead, halters exist solely to provide control of the horse from the ground. When you take your horse out of his stall or pasture, groom your horse, bathe him, clip him, or tie him, you use a halter.

Halters are available in expensive leather designs and inexpensive, yet colorful nylon versions. When you buy a halter, get one big enough to fit your horse's head. The halter should be comfortably loose, but not so loose that it falls way down on the horse's nose. See Figure 6-8 for a correct fit of a halter.

WARNING

If you need to leave a halter on a horse that's loose in the stall or pasture, choose a breakaway model that snaps under pressure to avoid snagging the halter on something and trapping the horse.

TIP

We recommend that you keep more than one halter on hand. You never know when you may need a second one in an emergency.

FIGURE 6-8:
A correctly fitted halter with a lead rope attached.

© *John Wiley & Sons, Inc.*

Looking at lead ropes

You can't own a horse and not own a lead rope. Without one, you can't maneuver your horse while you're on the ground. Trying to lead the horse by only his halter can leave you vulnerable and unable to maneuver if a problem arises.

The lead rope attaches to the ring at the bottom of the halter's noseband, underneath the horse's jaw (as shown in Figure 6-8). You tie your horse with the lead rope and hold it as the horse walks beside you.

TIP

Lead ropes are available in cotton, leather, or synthetic material. Leather lead ropes are on the expensive side, and are usually only used at horse shows. And although synthetic lead ropes come in bright colors and in sets with matching synthetic halters, we recommend you purchase a cotton rope (which is also available in colors but not as bright and fancy). Cotton is less likely to burn your hands when your horse pulls back while you're holding the rope.

Cleaning up with grooming supplies

How do you keep a 1,000-pound horse clean? With specially made equine grooming tools, of course. Scores of different kinds of brushes, combs, and other doodads exist for the express purpose of horse grooming. If you like to spend money, go ahead and buy some of them. But the list that follows is all you really need to get started. See Figure 6-9 for illustrations of the different basic grooming tools and Chapter 9 for specifics on grooming procedures.

FIGURE 6-9: You can choose from a variety of grooming tools for your horse.

Stiff brush

Soft brush

Mane & tail brush

Sponge

Sweat scraper

Hoof pick

Rubber curry comb

Sweat scraper/Shedding blade

© John Wiley & Sons, Inc.

Brushes and grooming tools

You need to have these types of brushes and grooming tools in your tack organizer to properly groom your horse. Each brush serves a different purpose:

>> **Currycomb:** A rubber currycomb can be used to loosen the dirt in your horse's coat before you go over him with the stiff brush.

>> **Stiff brush:** Also known as a dandy brush, this handy tool helps you get the dirt out of your horse's coat — which is no easy task.

>> **Soft brush:** A gentler version of the stiff brush, the soft brush gets that top layer of dust off your horse's coat and makes it shine. This brush also is perfect for grooming your horse's face.

>> **Mane & tail brush:** Some people use a comb to groom their horse's mane and tail, but we think that a vented brush with plastic bristles is best for untangling hair without breaking it.

>> **Shedding blade:** This metal blade with teeth does wonders to get rid of loose hair when your horse is shedding out his winter coat.

WARNING

Before using brushes that have been used on other horses, disinfect them first by soaking them in a solution of one part bleach to four parts water. You're less likely to spread potential fungal infections between horses.

Clippers

If you want to keep your horse's errant hairs trimmed, you need to purchase a pair of horse clippers. Horse clippers look much like barber's clippers, but they're specially made for horses in that they tend to be quieter and smaller so as not to intimidate the horse.

Several manufacturers make horse clippers in a variety of styles. For regular maintenance, you need only a small pair. If you intend to do serious body clips on a regular basis, you may want to consider investing in a larger pair to use just for that purpose.

TIP

When you buy your clippers, pick up a couple of extra blades, too. Nothing is worse than having to clip a horse with a dull clipper blade because it's the only one you have. When your blades become dull, have them sharpened by a clipper service, referred to you by your local tack and feed store.

Other tools

In addition to brushes and clippers, you need a couple of other nifty items:

>> **Buckets:** You can never own too many buckets when you own a horse. Buckets have many uses, including giving baths, serving commercial feed, and providing water in an emergency or when on the road (to name just a few uses). Be sure to buy your buckets from a horsy source so you're sure that you're getting specially designed horse buckets. Regular buckets like the kind sold in grocery and hardware stores are not heavy-duty enough for use with horses. Avoid rubber buckets because they collect bacteria and are hard to clean effectively.

- » **Hoof pick:** The standard hoof pick has a colored, rubber handle and a metal, V-shaped head for cleaning out the underside of the horse's hooves. You can also find hoof picks made of solid plastic with scrapers attached and picks with nylon brushes for cleaning feet.

- » **Sponges:** Sponges are good for giving baths and for wiping off sweat and other things that stick to your horse. Horse-friendly sponges are available in different sizes, shapes, and colors. The ones you buy are a matter of personal preference.

- » **Sweat scraper:** Sweat scrapers come in two styles: long, straight plastic wands; and metal bows with one straight ridge and one toothed ridge and each end of the bow attached to a plastic handle (see Figure 6-9 to get an idea of what each of these scrapers looks like). The toothed side of the metal sweat scraper functions as a shedding blade for removing loose hair during the horse's springtime shed.

TIP

Despite the name of this tool, we recommend that it be used only for scraping water off a freshly bathed horse. Merely scraping off sweat isn't healthy for your horse's skin — water should be applied to remove the salts.

- » **Tack organizer:** Rather than throwing all your grooming tools into a shopping bag, keep your equipment in a tack organizer. A tack organizer is a plastic box with different compartments and a handle. You probably already have one for your gardening tools. Buy a tack organizer at a tack store, or get the same product at your local gardening center. Be sure to buy yourself an organizer in a really cool color!

Playing Dress-Up: Horse Clothes

People wear clothes, so why not horses, too? Actually, horse clothes exist for some very practical reasons. The following sections look at some common items of horse clothing and their functions.

Putting on coverups

Horses somehow managed to survive for a long time before humans began dressing them in coverups. Now, it seems, they can't do without them!

When you go to most busy stables in either summer or winter, you see several different kinds of coverups in use. Although they may all look pretty much the same to your as-yet-untrained eye, each one has a unique purpose.

Blankets and sheets

The term *blanket* applies to coverups that are used specifically to keep the horse warm in cold weather. Blankets come in different styles and materials, but most fit over the horse's shoulders and reach to the horse's tail. The body is covered to midway down the legs. Straps sown into the blanket fit around the horse's girth and back legs to keep the blanket in place.

Blankets can be quilted and lined with wool. Or, they can be thin, breathable, and water-resistant. Whatever blanket need your horse has, a blanket exists to fill it (see Figure 6-10 for a couple of examples of horse blankets). Here are a couple of types of blankets on the market in the United States and Canada:

>> **Stable blanket:** Horses in stalls and small paddocks wear stable blankets, which either are thick and very warm or very lightweight. A huge variety of different stable blanket designs are out there, suited to different weather needs and horse-owner tastes.

>> **Turn-out blanket:** Turn-out blankets are for horses that spend most of their time outdoors at pasture. These blankets are usually warm, water resistant, and durable. They are fitted with special straps that prevent the blanket from getting twisted when the horse rolls.

TIP

Not every horse needs to wear a blanket in the winter. If your horse is very old or very young, sick or recovering from illness, has a thin winter coat, or is body clipped, he may need a blanket. If your horse doesn't fit one of these descriptions, chances are that a blanket isn't necessary. The coat that Mother Nature gave the horse gets the animal through the cold of winter.

Some coverups are to keep horses warm — others have a different purpose. Refer to Figure 6-10 for examples of these coverups:

>> **Coolers:** You use coolers specifically to help a horse cool down after a workout without catching a chill. Coolers fit over the ears and stretch to the back of the horse, covering everything but the head and lower legs. Coolers are worn only when the horse is being handled, never when the horse is unattended in his stall or pasture.

>> **Antisweat sheets:** The purpose of an antisweat sheet is to help a horse cool down after a workout by absorbing the sweat and letting it evaporate off the body. Woven in a pattern that encourages circulation, the sheet fits over the horse like a blanket and keeps the horse warm while enabling sweat to dry quickly.

>> **Flysheets:** Flysheets are for use mostly in the summer to protect the horse's body from biting flies. The sheets are made of lightweight, breathable material woven tightly enough so flies cannot fit their mouth parts through the weave.

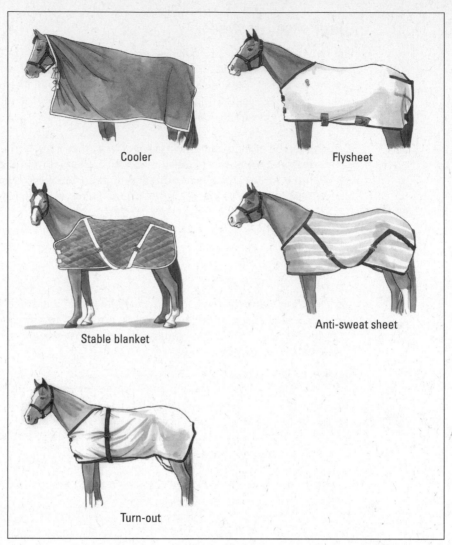

Cooler

Flysheet

Stable blanket

Anti-sweat sheet

Turn-out

© John Wiley & Sons, Inc.

FIGURE 6-10: Examples of several different types of coverups.

Leg protectors

Considering how important a horse's legs are, it's no wonder so many leg protection devices exist. Our favorites include the following:

>> **Bell boots:** Bell boots protect a horse from nicking his front pasterns (ankles) and stepping on his front shoes with his back hooves during exercise, known as overreaching. Rubber bell boots fit over the horse's front hooves.

>> **Splint boots:** Controversy rages over whether splint boots really do any good, but their purpose is to support the horse's tendons during workouts. Some people put them only on the front legs, while other riders dress all four legs with splint boots. Splint boots are usually made from synthetic material and are attached to the leg with hook-and-loop-fastener enclosures.

>> **Polo wraps:** Originally used on polo ponies to help protect their legs, cotton polo wraps now are traditionally used by dressage riders as protection for the tendons during hard workouts. Riders in other disciplines use them, too. No scientific proof exists that polo wraps, which are applied like wrapped bandages, do indeed help hard-working horses, but many riders swear by them.

WARNING

Before you attempt to put splint boots or polo wraps on your horse's legs the first time, you need a trainer or experienced person to show you exactly how to do it. Improperly applied leg protection can actually harm your horse's legs.

Paying attention to assorted apparel

So many items are available for horses to wear; describing them all in this book is impossible. Here are three of our favorites:

>> **Fly mask:** Whoever invented the fly mask did a great service for the domestic horse. Fly masks are mesh hoods that fit over the center part of the head. They shield the horse's eyes from face flies that feed on the eyes' moisture. Some fly masks also have ear covers that protect the horse's ears from biting gnats while also protecting the horse's eyes. (Although many inexperience people think a horse wearing a fly mask has been "blindfolded," in reality, the horse can see out of the mask, just as you can see out of a screened window.)

>> **Fly wraps:** These plastic mesh wraps keep flies from biting the horse's legs, the insects' favorite part of the horse. The wraps go on all four legs and fasten with hook-and-loop fasteners.

>> **Tail bag:** They may look goofy, but tail bags are the answer to growing a long, luxurious tail. As the name implies, the tail bag is just that: a bag that holds a loosely braided tail. It serves as protection for fragile tail hairs, keeping them clean and unbroken. Usually made from nylon, tail bags often have a tassel or fringes at the end that helps the horse chase away flies when it swings the encased swisher.

Looking Good: Your Own Riding Wear

The horse world has much tradition, and nowhere is this more obvious than in riding apparel. Unlike the ready-to-wear market where fashions change, equestrians have been wearing the same basic outfits for decades.

Just like with other sports, horseback riding has its own distinctive look. You wouldn't play tennis in jeans and a flannel shirt unless you wanted to give the impression that you didn't know what you were doing, right? Well, the same thing holds true with riding. If you want to look like one of the gang, you'd better dress like the gang, especially if you plan to show your horse.

The apparel in each discipline has its own distinct look, of course, just like the tack. In this section, we describe the appropriate apparel for each riding style, both for the show ring and for *schooling* (regular riding). Although you may see riders donning variations of what we describe here, if you follow our advice, you won't find yourself in the horse-world equivalent of plaid golfing pants.

TIP

Riding apparel for children is virtually the same as it is for adults, just in miniature. When you buy riding clothes for kids, get a comfortable size that really fits. No one is more miserable than a kid trying to ride in boots or breeches that are too big or too small.

Donning formal hunt-seat garb

Hunt-seat riding is based on British tradition and has a very formal appearance. The only thing that seems to change periodically is the color of jackets and breeches. We've seen green, rust, and beige come and go in popularity during the past 20 years or so:

>> **Show:** Hunt-seat riders in the show ring wear a white or pinstriped cotton riding shirt, long-sleeved preferred. The women's shirt has a band collar that usually bears a monogram. Men wear shirts with a standard straight collar and a regular necktie. Both genders wear breeches and dress (riding) or field boots. (Although breech colors go in and out of style — avoiding white if you ride hunt seat is always a safe bet.) A dark-colored or gray pinstriped, tapered wool riding jacket tops off the ensemble for men and women, along with a black velvet hunt cap or riding helmet. See Figure 6-11 for a drawing of this apparel.

>> **Schooling:** Male and female hunt-seat riders wear breeches for schooling, along with dress boots, field boots, or paddock boots and chaps. Tops are casual — anything from a T-shirt to a turtleneck. A schooling or velvet-covered show helmet also is worn.

© John Wiley & Sons, Inc.

FIGURE 6-11:
Male and female hunt-seat apparel is formal.

Dressing in elegant dressage attire

Everything about dressage is elegant, including the clothing. Very traditional in style, dressage apparel never seems to change much:

>> **Show:** Most dressage riders wear white cotton shirts with long or short sleeves. Both sexes sport a stock tie, fastened with a gold horsy pin over a band collar. In the lower levels and at smaller shows, riders often wear light-colored breeches, black dress (riding) or field boots, a black or dark dressage or hunting jacket, and a hunt cap or regular black helmet.

In the upper levels and at bigger shows, male and female riders wear white breeches, black dress boots, a black derby, and a black dressage jacket or shadbelly coat. See Figure 6-12 to get a look at dressage show apparel.

>> **Schooling:** Dressage riders dress more casually when schooling than they do in the show ring. Many wear any color breeches, dress boots, field boots, or paddock boots with chaps or half-chaps, and T-shirts or mock turtlenecks. They also wear schooling or show helmets.

© John Wiley & Sons, Inc.

FIGURE 6-12:
Male and female dressage riders look elegant in show apparel.

Slipping into saddle-seat apparel

Although hunt-seat and dressage apparel have a distinct European look to them, saddle-seat apparel has an old-fashioned, all-American appeal:

>> **Show:** In the show ring, both male and female saddle-seat riders wear a white shirt, dark jodhpurs, and a riding derby. They both wear saddle-seat coats, day coats, or saddle-seat suit jackets, and jodhpur boots under the jodhpurs. Women sometimes wear tuxedo shirts with feminine bow ties or rosettes, and both genders wear wingtip or straight collars with men's bow ties or neckties, respectively. A vest sometimes is worn under the coat. See Figure 6-13 for saddle-seat show attire.

>> **Schooling:** Saddle-seat riders of both sexes usually wear jodhpurs for schooling, along with jodhpur boots. They sometimes wear regular breeches and paddock boots. Their tops are often casual T-shirts or mock turtlenecks. They also usually wear a schooling helmet or hunt-seat show helmet.

FIGURE 6-13: Saddle-seat attire for men and women is distinctly American.

Wearing western gear

Formal western attire is only required in the show ring, and then only in "rail" classes like western pleasure, horsemanship, and trail. Otherwise, the western look is casual and comfortable, and a favorite of male riders:

>> **Show:** In classes calling for formal western attire, female riders wear tuxedo shirts alone or with long-sleeved western jackets, or western riding vests, and feminine bow ties or rosettes. They also wear jeans and fringed chaps, western paddock boots or riding boots, and broad-brimmed western felt hats. Male riders wear straight-collared western shirts with a western tie, along with jeans and fringed chaps. Both also wear paddock boots or western riding boots, and a broad-brimmed western felt hat tops off the outfit. Both wear leather belts with large silver, western belt buckles. See Figure 6-14 for formal western show ring apparel.

Riders showing in performance classes such as reining, barrel racing, and cutting need only to wear a western hat, jeans, fringed chaps, western boots or paddock boots, and a western shirt. A western tie is a nice touch.

REMEMBER

When buying western boots for riding, pick out a style designed specifically for riding. Most western boots for sale in regular shoe stores are for street wear and don't have the right style heel for safe riding. Boots designed for riding have soles that prevent the rider's foot from slipping through the stirrup and help keep the rider's foot in place. Shopping for your boots at a tack store is the best way to find appropriate riding boots.

>> **Schooling:** Western riders usually wear loose-fitting jeans or special riding jeans that combine elastic with denim for a comfortable fit. They often ride in paddock boots or western boots, and wear just about any kind of shirt including T-shirts, western shirts, or mock turtlenecks. Cautious western riders school their horses in helmets. Western style riding helmets are a newer addition to the riding helmet world, and help riders maintain their western look.

FIGURE 6-14: Formal western show attire for men and women is comfortable.

Kicking around in comfortable clothes

For days when you aren't riding but are instead doing equine–related chores like grooming, longeing or simply mucking stalls, wear the following apparel for comfort and safety (see Chapter 17 for details):

>> **Pants:** Jeans or stretch tights are the most comfortable pants to work in around the stable.

>> **Shirt:** Wear a T-shirt, sweatshirt, mock turtleneck, or flannel shirt. Make sure that the shirt is loose-fitting and comfortable. Make sure that it's something you don't care too much about, too, because your shirt is sure to get pretty dirty.

>> **Shoes:** Paddock boots, barn shoes, or hiking boots are best around the stable when the weather is dry. Rubber barn boots are good if the ground is muddy or you plan to muck stalls. Never wear tennis shoes to work around horses because they don't provide your foot with much protection if a 1,000-pound

klutz steps on your toe. Of course no functional footwear provides 100-percent protection if you get stepped on, but the heavier the shoe, the better off your toes are, should it happen.

Using your head by wearing a helmet

Riding can be a dangerous sport. Not because horses are vicious creatures, but because the laws of the universe dictate that falling off a horse is way too easy.

Falling off a horse usually results in nothing more than muscle soreness, but if you fall and hit your head, serious injury or even permanent brain damage or death can result. To prevent these dire consequences, most riders wear helmets. Some riders, however, don't wear helmets because they're hot during the summer. Helmets are also the cause of the female tragedy known as helmet hair. Riders who don't wear helmets are risking the health and well-being of an often-ignored organ known as the *brain* every time they mount up on a horse.

REMEMBER

Although fashion and peer pressure may dictate that you should not wear a helmet (western riders are notorious for not wearing them), we recommend that all riders wear a helmet whenever possible. If you are jumping horseback, you really have no choice. When jumping, you absolutely *must* wear a helmet.

TIP

When you shop for a helmet, make sure you buy one for equestrians (bike helmets will not do) that provides significant protection to your skull. In the United States, the American Society for Testing and Materials (ASTM) sets standards for helmet construction. If a helmet meets these standards, it receives a seal of approval from the Safety Equipment Institute (SEI). Only buy an SEI-approved helmet.

REMEMBER

Helmets are especially important for children, whose growing skulls are more fragile than the skulls of adults. Make sure your child always wears a riding helmet when he or she gets up on a horse.

Transporting Your Horse

If you want to show your horse, trail ride away from home, or do anything other just ride around in your local arena, you'll want to consider buying a horse trailer. Having a horse trailer gives you the freedom to take your horse to group trail rides, horse shows, and even to a veterinary hospital if necessary.

Buying a horse trailer

A horse trailer can be a major investment or just another accessory for your horse, depending on how much money you want to spend and what you want to do with your trailer. If you want to haul one or two horses to nearby shows, trail heads, or other equine events, you'll probably be happy with a simple, two-horse trailer. If you have ideas about going horse camping (what fun!) or want to be able to haul all your friends' horses to trail rides, you may want to consider a horse trailer with living quarters (essentially a small camper inside the front of the trailer) or one big enough to haul three of more equines.

Your budget will likely dictate what kind of trailer you'll be getting. Also, keep in mind that horse trailers can last a long time with good care, and you can probably find a good used trailer for a lot less than you would pay for it brand new. Just make sure to have a qualified trailer mechanic exam the trailer before you make the purchase.

When shopping for a trailer, read reviews of the different brands and types. Go to a trailer lot — a lot like a car lot — and take a gander at the different sizes and types. Do plenty of comparison shopping, and ask other horse owners what trailers they like. When you find the trailer that best suits your fancy, you'll know it.

Horse trailer designs

Before you run out and buy the first trailer you see on the lot, it's a good idea to understand the basics of horse trailers.

Aside from the number of horses a trailer holds, the size of a trailer depends on its design. Three different design types are out there, based on the type of horses you want to haul or just what you prefer in terms of roominess for your horse:

>> **Quarter Horse size:** The majority of two-horse, straight-load trailers are considered Quarter Horse trailers. That's not because they are only meant for Quarter Horses! They are actually designed for small to average-sized horses, and since Quarter Horses are the most popular breed out there, the name stuck. Stalls in these types of trailers are normally 6 feet in height. Horses that are on taller or longer than the average Quarter Horse may be too big to be comfortable in a trailer of this size.

>> **Thoroughbred size:** Designed for horses that are somewhat taller than the average Quarter Horse yet have considerably longer bodies, Thoroughbred trailer stalls usually measure 7 feet in height. Length varies from model to model.

>> **Warmblood:** A relative newcomer to the North American market, warmblood trailers usually feature stalls that are 7½ feet tall. The length of the stall is longer than even a Thoroughbred trailer to accommodate the overall size of most warmbloods. Smaller horses can also travel in this size trailer very comfortably.

Hauling types

Horse trailers also come in two different hauling types:

>> **Bumper-pull:** Also called tag-a-longs, these trailers attach to the bumper of a towing vehicle with the use of a hitch. Bumper-pulls can be used with any towing vehicle, regardless of design. Tight turns are more easily negotiated with a bumper-pull trailer. The downside is that with bumper-pulls, there is more potential for sway.

>> **Gooseneck:** The front of a gooseneck trailer fits over the bed of a pickup truck and attaches inside the truck bed. Gooseneck trailers are more stable than bumper-pulls, and they offer better control for the driver. On the other hand, sharp turns are harder to make with a gooseneck trailer. Greater tongue weight can tip the towing vehicle, making headlights shine higher. Goosenecks are more expensive than bumper-pulls, and they weigh more.

Interior styles

Horse trailers also come in different interior styles:

>> **Straight-load:** Also known as side-by-side trailers, the straight-load design places the horses facing straight ahead with a partition between them. This is the most common design seen in two-horse trailers. Some horse people believe that straight-load designs are harder on the horse because of the weight shifts from front legs to back during braking and acceleration. Horses that are difficult to load and are poor haulers can be especially troublesome with a straight-load.

>> **Slant-load:** Trailers with a slant-load design place the horse at an angle during travel, facing to the left. Many horse people believe that slant-loads make travel easier on a horse because the design enables the horse to shift its weight from side to side during braking and acceleration. Trailers with slant-load designs can also hold more horses in a shorter trailer length. Some people believe that the horse is not built to bear its weight from side to side, which is inevitable in a slant-load trailer. Slant-load trailers tend to be wider than straight-loads, and so allow for decreased driver visibility.

>> **Stock:** Stock trailers are open trailers with no partitions. The upper portion of most stock trailers are slatted, providing a lot of ventilation. Stock trailer design allows horses to move about at will, choosing the position that provides them the most comfort during travel. In hot weather, stock trailers stay cool because of the slatted upper portion. On the flip side, some horse people believe that stock trailers are not safe for use with horses, since they are designed primarily for cattle and smaller livestock. Wind and cold weather can provide discomfort for horses because stock trailers don't offer much in the way of protection from the elements.

Equine entryways

Horse trailers also have different types of equine entryways:

>> **Step-up:** Trailers with a step-up design require the horse to go straight from the ground directly into the trailer, and out again, without a ramp. Some horse people prefer step-ups because they believe horses load more safely with this design. On the other hand, some horses that are not experienced haulers will resist going into a step-up trailer, and they may have difficulty backing out.

>> **Ramp:** Trailers with ramps feature a door/ramp combination that lowers to the ground for loading and unloading. People who like these kinds of trailer designs believe that ramps are safer for loading and unloading. Conversely, a ramp can be inconvenient for the hauler since it needs to be raised and lowered for loading and unloading.

Construction

So what are horse trailers made of? They can be constructed from steel, aluminum or both:

>> **Steel:** Steel has been the standard material for horse trailers for decades. Most trailers in this category are made exclusively of steel. Steel trailers are durable and long-lasting, and tend to be priced lower than aluminum models. However, rust can be a big problem with galvanized steel.

>> **Aluminum:** Aluminum trailers are made mostly from aluminum with steel axles and chassis. Aluminum trailers are lightweight, immune to rust, have a higher resale value and are easier to maintain. They are more expensive than steel trailers, though, and are more prone to wear and tear.

>> **Steel/aluminum combinations:** Some trailers combine aluminum wall construction with steel frames. Steel frames provide strength while aluminum provides protection from rust. The downside is that rubber must be placed between steel and aluminum connections to prevent corrosion.

>> **Other stuff:** While the majority of horse trailers are made from either steel or aluminum, other materials such as fiberglass/wisaform/steel combinations are also available.

Custom features

If buying your horse trailer new, you get the fun of adding custom features to your rig. Here are some options:

>> **Electronic brake system:** Electronic brakes are the most popular brakes offered on horse trailers, especially on trailers made for two to four horses. They help stop the trailer when the brakes are applied to the towing vehicle.

>> **Floor mats:** A necessity with any trailer, floor mats provide traction for your horse. They need periodic removal for cleaning because urine can become trapped underneath. Depending on whether the horse paws or wears heavy shoes, floor mats may wear out and have to be replaced over time.

>> **Wall pads:** Wall pads provide protection for the horse while in transit. Should a horse be thrown to the side of the trailer, or kick the walls, wall pads can protect the horse from serious injury. While styles vary from manufacturer to manufacturer, all are designed to be soft yet durable.

>> **Ventilation windows:** The more ventilation in a trailer, the better for the horse. Ventilation windows provide airflow, which is especially important when trailering in hot weather. Ventilation windows also allow moisture to escape from the trailer. Opt for as many ventilations windows and air vents as you can afford.

>> **Interior lights:** Interior lighting is actually very important in a trailer. Horses tend to load easier into a lit trailer than a dark one, and good lighting will allow you to see what you are doing inside the trailer, especially at night. There should be one inside light for each horse you intend to haul.

>> **Tack compartment:** Tack compartments are usually horizontal holding areas situated under the manger of the horse trailer. Figure out how much space you'll need before deciding on this feature. You'll want enough room to keep more than one saddle, bridles, helmets, buckets — all the items you want to take along when you trailer. Make sure there's an interior light here, too.

» **Dressing room:** An upright dressing room to change in and out of your show clothes and keep your tack and accessories comes with many trailer models. You may have options on the size of the dressing room. The bigger you can afford, the better. Just make sure it doesn't cut too much into the room your horse has inside the trailer.

» **Escape doors:** Escape doors are a very important feature on any horse trailer, and they are usually a standard feature. They are located on the sides of the trailer and provide another way to access the horse besides the rear entrance. In an emergency situation, escape doors can mean the difference between getting to your horse or feeling helpless outside, knowing your horse is in distress. Escape doors also keep you from become trapped inside the trailer should a problem arise during loading.

» **Outside tie rings:** Outside tie rings give you a place to tie your horse to the trailer while you are tacking up or even camping with your horse. Make sure that the rings aren't so low that the lead rope will dangle but yet aren't so high that you can't easily reach them. There should be at least one tie ring for each horse you intend to haul.

» **Removable partitions/butt bars:** Trailers with removable partitions and butt-bars are more versatile because they let you give more room to a horse that is a difficult traveler. Removable partitions can even allow you to convert your trailer to haul other non-horsy items.

Hauling with the right vehicle

You can get a horse trailer without breaking the bank, but having the right vehicle to haul it with is another story. If you don't already have a heavy duty truck or SUV that can tow significant weight, you will need to buy or lease one if you want to pull a horse trailer.

WARNING

Although your crossover SUV may claim 4,800 pounds of towing capacity and your horse trailer weighs 4,000 pounds with two horses loaded up, you *don't* have enough power to safely pull that load, no matter what the car salesman tells you. **You need at least 7,000 to 9,000 pounds of towing capacity to safely pull a loaded two-horse trailer.**

Here are factors you need to consider when deciding on a tow vehicle:

» **Towing capacity:** This is the maximum weight that a vehicle is rated to tow. You need to figure out how much your empty trailer weighs, and then add the weight of your horses and tack, feed, water and whatever else you are carrying. This cumulative weight cannot exceed the gross trailer weight rating (GTWR) indicated by the vehicle manufacturer.

» **Curb weight:** The curb weight is the weight of your vehicle without passengers or cargo. The curb weight of the vehicle should be *heavier* than the loaded trailer, which ensure that the vehicle controls the weight of trailer, and not vice versa.

» **Wheelbase:** When it comes to towing, the longer the vehicle's wheelbase — that is the distance from the front axle to the rear axle — the better. A too short wheelbase will cause a teeter-totter effect with the trailer.

» **Chassis design:** For most tow vehicles, it's important to have a body-on-frame design. Most cars and regular-sized SUVs have unibody chassis, which makes them unsafe for towing. Some high-end SUVs are the exception.

» **Tow package:** A vehicle with a tow package will have a factory-installed ball hitch, stronger suspension and brakes, a larger radiator, and a transmission capable sending more power to the drive wheels. All this results in more power and easier towing. Some tow packages also feature extended mirrors that make it easier to see around the trailer.

Chapter **7**

Housing Your Horse Comfortably

Horses are pretty big creatures. Unlike a dog or cat, your horse can't just move in with you and start sleeping at the foot of the bed. No, you have to do plenty of thinking and planning on the subject of where and how to house your horse.

People who own horses in today's world basically have two choices when it comes to equine housing: Keep the horse on their own property or board the animal elsewhere. These options are vastly different logistically, and your choice has a significant impact on your lifestyle.

If you bought this book because you own property that's zoned for horses, and if you dream of a having a horse in your backyard, you may not need to ponder the question of where to keep your equine buddy. But, maybe you live in an urban or suburban area, have only a small backyard barely suitable for your Labrador retriever, and think that you have little choice other than to board your horse at your Uncle Jasper's house 70 miles outside the city limits.

Ultimately, you need to attain the most convenient and economically feasible housing arrangement for your horse. You want your horse to be happy and healthy, and you want horse ownership to be both fun and manageable for you. Keep these points in mind when making your decisions about housing.

Before you decide where your horse can call home, we urge you to read this chapter to get an idea of both backyard horsekeeping and boarding, along with details on how to correctly do both. After you discover the pros and cons of backyard horsekeeping and boarding, you'll be able to make a much more intelligent — and ultimately correct — decision.

Away from Home: Boarding Stables

A boarding stable is a commercial establishment that provides housing and limited care for horses. Boarding stables earn their income by charging horse owners a monthly fee for boarding their horse. Some boarding stables also offer horse owners additional horse care, such as exercising or blanketing their horses.

Most people who utilize the services of boarding stables live in urban or suburban areas. They can't keep their horses on their own land, so they board them at a nearby stable. Accommodations for horses vary greatly from stable to stable and region to region, with the more luxurious offerings costing more than the ordinary ones. Generally speaking, keeping your horse in a *box stall* (an indoor, barn-like enclosure — see "Housing your horse indoors" later in this chapter for details) will cost you more than pasture boarding.

TIP

Even if you have your own horse property, you still need to consider boarding. Boarding offers many benefits, particularly to first-time horse owners. Even if your dream is to have your horse in your backyard, explore the possibility of boarding for at least the first year that you own your horse.

In the following sections, we cover the advantages and disadvantages of boarding your horse, your boarding responsibilities, and ways to find and choose a suitable boarding stable (either commercial or private).

The pros and cons of boarding

Plenty of really good reasons exist for boarding your horse, especially if you're a first-time horse owner:

>> **Convenience:** When you board your horse, you're hiring someone else to do much of the daily upkeep needed to maintain a horse in good, healthy condition. And that means the boarding stable staff is responsible for feeding your horse every day, providing water, and cleaning his stall. If you choose to board your horse, not only do you avoid these chores, but you also avoid worrying about things like buying and storing hay and bedding material, and disposing of equine waste.

>> **Help with your horse:** Boarding stables are places where horse owners of varying experience congregate. Most boarding stables also have trainers available for hire to boarders. First-time horse owners who board their animals often find they're surrounded by people who can help them with just about any equine problem that comes up. That's a big contrast to being alone at home with your horse.

>> **A place to learn:** You can find out a great deal about horse care and handling just by being around other boarders. You may see others make mistakes to avoid, and you can figure out the right way to do many things by observing your fellow boarders.

>> **Riding facilities:** Most boarding stables have arenas for exercise, wash racks for bathing, mechanical hot walkers for exercising your horse, and access to riding trails. These facilities are available to horse owners as part of their boarding fee. You may not have access to these amenities at home.

>> **Social atmosphere:** Boarding stables are wonderful places to meet and make new friends who share your interest in horses. Many stables even foster the inherent social aspect of the environment by holding events like barbecues, parties, and play days. Boarding stables also are good for your horse's social life, too. Your horse will find himself with plenty of built-in equine friends.

Of course nothing is perfect, and boarding has its downside:

>> **Expense:** If you figure out the day-to-day expense of keeping a horse, you discover that you spend more boarding your horse than you do keeping him at home. Of course, you're paying not only for the horse's feed when you board, but also for the services that the stable provides. The amount of money you pay for monthly board depends on where you live and the type of facility you choose. Board can range from $100 a month for a pasture in rural areas to $700 a month or more for a full-service facility in an urban area.

>> **Inaccessibility:** Boarding can be very convenient because you don't need to worry about feeding and cleaning up after your horse daily. However, you *do* have the chore of driving to and from the stable every time you want to see your horse (as opposed to merely stepping outside your back door).

>> **Politics:** Just as in any situation that involves humans, boarding stables have their politics. Boarders get into squabbles, talk behind each other's backs, and sometimes even try to make trouble for one another with stable management. Of course, you can avoid much of this by keeping to yourself, but then you miss out on many opportunities for camaraderie.

>> **Instability:** You may keep your horse at a wonderful boarding stable for years, only to wake up one morning to find out the place has been sold. The new owner may be someone who couldn't care less about the business, or even worse, a developer who wants to knock down your horse's stall and build condos instead. Both of these situations — and particularly the latter — occur in the boarding stable world more than you may think. If it happens to you, you have to start shopping for a new place to keep your horse.

Knowing a boarder's responsibilities

If you think that boarding sounds like a good idea, keep in mind that you also have certain responsibilities as a boarder. You must:

>> **Be considerate of other horse owners.** In this book, we provide you with all the information you need to be a responsible and considerate horse owner. If you board your horse, you have a significant obligation to follow the rules of safety and protocol. Handling your horse carelessly can jeopardize the safety of your fellow boarders and their horses.

>> **Be courteous.** If you find a really nice boarding stable that you're happy with, count your blessings and be considerate to the staff. It's amazing how many boarders behave rudely to staffers whenever they want something done or have a problem. You get further with staffers by being nice rather than demanding.

>> **Consider the community:** Boarding stables and horse property in general are becoming more and more scarce these days. Land developers are gobbling up rural areas for housing and commercial buildings, minimizing the amount of places where horses can live. Homeowners in many once-rural-now-suburban neighborhoods also are looking to push horses out of their communities.

If you're boarding your horse in an urban or suburban area, your stable's very presence in that area is tenuous. Be considerate to the people who live in the surrounding community so they maintain a positive opinion of the stable.

>> **Pay your board:** Most boarding stable owners who run clean, well-kept operations aren't making profits hand over fist; they put a significant amount money back into the stable's upkeep. So paying your board *in full, on time, every month* is important. Don't expect the stable to carry you for a few months because you want to buy yourself a new TV. If enough boarders pay late in any given month, the stable can experience cash flow problems.

Selecting a commercial boarding stable

Boarding stables are just like any another type of business: Some are really good, and others are really bad. The good ones provide safe, comfortable accommodations for horses; have caring, conscientious, and knowledgeable staffs; and offer excellent facilities for riders. The lousy ones are just the opposite: They sport unsafe conditions for horses, have staffers who couldn't care less, and have little to offer boarders in the way of conveniences or facilities.

REMEMBER

Before you commit to keeping your horse at any commercial facility, we strongly recommend that you thoroughly check the place out. If you haven't already discovered boarding stables in your area, you can find local facilities to tour by looking online or asking at a local tack and feed store. Take a look at as many stables as you can, and spend some time walking around and talking to other boarders at these facilities. The things you're looking for include

>> **Safe, sturdy accommodations:** Inspect the box stalls, paddocks (small corrals, usually with some kind of shelter), and pastures. Make sure that each of these enclosures is well constructed and well maintained. Check to see whether gate latches are secure and horse-proof (that is, they can't be opened with a flip of the nose).

WARNING

Do not board your horse at a stable that uses barbed wire as an enclosure. A close encounter with barbed wire can seriously injure your horse. If you find a stable you really like that uses barbed wire, politely ask them to switch to a safer fencing. If they decline, consider boarding your horse elsewhere.

If you choose to board your horse in a pasture or paddock, look for accessibility to shelter from rain, snow, wind, and hot sun. If you plan to keep your horse in a box stall, check to make sure that the horses are given at least 8 inches of bedding in their stalls.

>> **Clean, safe surroundings:** The stable property should appear well maintained. Be wary of a place that has junk lying around and an unkempt look. If they don't take care of their own property, they probably won't take very good care of your horse either.

>> **Security:** Find out whether a guard or caretaker is on duty at the stable 24 hours a day. Not all boarding stables provide this kind of protection, but we recommend that you hold out for it if you can. If you can't find one in your area, look for a stable that provides some kind of security to ensure your horse won't be stolen.

>> **Water:** Find out how water is provided to each enclosure, and scout around to make sure that each horse at the stable has a generous supply of water at all times. If you live in a cold climate, find out how the management keeps the water from freezing in the winter.

>> **Quality feed:** If quality pasture isn't available to your horse, then hay needs to make up the majority of his diet. Make sure that the stable you're considering offers hay as an option for feeding, and provides at least two feedings a day. Ask to take a look at the stored hay on the stable property, and inspect it for quality. (See Chapter 8 for information on determining hay quality.)

WARNING

If the stable stores grain, be certain that it's kept securely locked up so that the horses can't get to it. Any escaped horse that gets into the grain is in danger of colicking or laminitis. (See Chapter 11 for more about preventing and reacting to these and other maladies.)

WARNING

Use caution with stables that feed only commercial pelleted feed with no other options, because a diet consisting solely of pellets is unhealthy for your horse. If a stable that you like feeds only pelleted feed as part of your regular boarding agreement, make sure that they agree to feed your horse hay if you provide it.

>> **Good care:** Have a talk with the stable manager and find out about the daily care the horses receive. Make sure that your horse's stall is cleaned at least once a day, every day, and that your horse is fed at least twice daily. Also, ask the manager about the stable's pest control program. Find out what steps are taken control flies, rodents, and internal parasites, and what method the stable uses to dispose of its waste. (See Chapter 8 for more info on general horse care.)

If you want extra care options for your horse, such as daily exercise, blanketing, and supplemental feeding, find out whether these options are available at the stable and, if so, at what cost.

>> **Health requirements:** Determine which, if any, inoculations the stable requires for horses to board. The more inoculations the stable requires, the less likely your horse will become ill. The stable you choose should require regular inoculations for influenza/rhinopneumonitis and equine encephalomyelitis, at the very minimum. Boarders also need to show proof of regular dewormings or negative results of a fecal test. (See Chapter 10 for more details on preventative healthcare for horses.)

>> **Riding facilities:** Look for good-sized, well-maintained riding arenas, turn-out pens, washracks, and hot walkers. Look for good footing in all riding arenas, which means the dirt is soft — without being too deep — not hard. If you live in an area that gets a lot of rain or snow, consider holding out for a stable with a covered or indoor arena so you can ride all year long regardless of the weather.

WARNING

If you plan to trail ride, ask the manager for a map of the local trails (or at least detailed directions) and find out how you can access them. Beware of trails that require you to spend too much time riding on busy roads before gaining access to them.

>> **Tack storage:** You need a secure place to store your saddle, bridles, halter, grooming equipment, and everything else you need to care for your horse (see Chapter 6 for horse gear details). Find out whether the boarding stable rents on-site tack lockers or storage sheds to boarders. If not, you have to provide your own or keep your equipment at home and bring it with you every time you visit your horse.

>> **A professional demeanor:** The boarding stable management should expect you to sign injury liability waivers and a boarding agreement, and fill out other official papers stating the name of your veterinarian and a person to contact in case of an emergency. Reputable stables also require proof your horse is up-to-date on his vaccines. Stable management also needs to provide you with written rules of the stable. Be wary of any boarding stable that has an overly casual attitude about your boarding agreement. They may also have an overly casual attitude about caring for your horse.

Choosing private boarding

Boarding your horse at a commercial facility isn't your only option. Plenty of people who own horse property rent out stalls, paddocks, and pasture to individual horse owners to help offset the costs of keeping their own horses. You can find these individuals by looking at ads in your local equine publication, your daily newspaper and often from flyers tacked up at feed stores.

Some people who offer private boarding don't have a riding arena on their property. If you're a beginning rider, you need access to a riding arena where you can safely develop your skills. Before you visit a property where you may decide to board, ask the owner whether you have access to an on-site riding arena or a nearby community riding arena.

Staying Close: Having a Home Stable

If you're one of the many who dreams of seeing a horse every morning when you look out your kitchen window, a home stable may be the right housing option for you — provided you live on property that has been zoned for horses. If you live in a suburban or even rural neighborhood that forbids the keeping of livestock, you have no other option than to board.

Double-check your zoning laws by contacting officials in the city or county where you live before you run out and buy a horse to put on your land. If it turns out that you can keep a horse or two on your property, then you can discover the joys of at–home horsekeeping. Knowing that your backyard horse is waiting for you whenever you get the urge to ride or simply share in some relaxing equine company is a wonderful feeling. Plus, something about the feel and smell of horses on the property makes even the most modest home feel very special indeed.

The pros and cons of a home stable

Here are some really good reasons to keep a horse in your own home stable:

» **Easy access:** No driving to the stable when you want to ride! Your horse is right there in your yard, just outside the back door. And if your horse needs special care like a blanket put on every night, feeding of extra or special feed, or medicating, his close proximity is convenient.

» **Security:** If you like to keep a close eye on your horse, a home stable provides a chance to watch your equine buddy nearly 24 hours a day.

» **Cost:** Keeping a horse on your own property is less expensive on a monthly basis than boarding him. At a boarding stable, you pay for daily feeding, cleanup, and the use of the facilities. With an at-home horse, you do the work yourself — your only cost in this regard is time.

If you determine that you want to keep your horse at home, you may find that the disadvantages can easily outweigh the benefits:

» **Hard work:** With an at-home horse, you're responsible for the daily chores of feeding and cleaning. If you work full-time, you may find that mucking your horse's stall is the last thing you want to do either before or after work.

» **Being tied down:** Because horses need to eat at regular times each day, you need to be home during these times to put out the feed. If you can't be home, you need to make arrangements with a responsible neighbor or a professional horse sitter.

» **Maintenance responsibilities:** Keeping a horse in your yard means storing hay on your property and possibly maintaining a quality pasture. Add to that list storing and disposing of the waste your horse creates and building and maintaining proper facilities for your animal.

» **No support system:** New horse owners who keep their animals at boarding facilities have the benefit of asking other horse owners and professional trainers for help. If you keep your horse at home and you run into a problem, chances are you have no one to turn to for immediate hands-on advice.

>> **Limited riding facilities:** Most owners of single-family horse properties don't have the space, time, or money to build and maintain their own riding facilities. If you're one of these people, you may not have access to an arena in which you can ride — a real problem if you're a beginning rider. And if your property isn't near riding trails, you won't have that option for riding, either.

>> **Liability:** All kinds of potential liabilities fall on the shoulders of horse owners. You need to have a talk with your insurance agent to determine exactly what kind of property insurance you need to have with a horse at home.

Knowing your responsibilities at home

If you decide to keep your horse at home, you must uphold a number of responsibilities:

>> **Cleanliness:** You have an obligation to your horse and to your neighbors to keep your property clean and well maintained. If you don't, you may even get in trouble with the law.

>> **A good image:** In urban and suburban areas everywhere, horse owners are facing a growing challenge to their hobby. Whereas horse property was commonplace at one time, it's becoming harder and harder for horse owners to find communities that are accepting of horses. You can do your part by being friendly and considerate toward your neighbors, and make every effort to resolve any horse-related problems that arise.

>> **Continuing education:** Because you and your horse are pretty much on your own, you need to learn as much about horses and horsekeeping as possible. If you don't continue to learn, your knowledge of all things equine won't advance, and you'll end up shortchanging yourself and your horse. Read plenty of books and magazines on horses, check out responsible discussion groups and well researched articles on the Internet, and most important, join an equestrian group in your community.

Committing yourself financially

Purchasing property that's zoned for horses is more costly than purchasing property that isn't zoned for horses. If you're lucky enough to get horse property that is already outfitted with safe and comfortable equine accommodations, consider yourself fortunate. If you buy a place that is zoned for horses but not set up to house them, you have expenses ahead of you. Adequate shelters, enclosures, waterers, feeders, and other items all have to be installed before your property is ready for a horse (see the next section for more details).

Upkeep on horse property is costly, too. You need to keep your property in good working order, with the fences painted and the grass trimmed (unless you have your horse do the lawn mowing for you). You need to factor these upkeep fees into your annual budget.

Don't forget about the cost of owning a horse, which you have to consider whether you keep your companion at home or board him. Include veterinarian and shoer bills, feed, tack, and other equipment in your budget.

Setting Up Backyard Accommodations

Okay, suppose you decide to keep your horse at home, on your own property. Where do you keep him and what exactly are your housing options? Well, you have a few options, and we give you a close-up look at each in the following sections.

Keeping your horse outdoors

In nature, horses live outdoors, where they constantly roam and graze. Outdoor enclosures confine horses in open air and are popular places to keep horses because they are more natural. Most horses prefer to be outdoors and seem to do best there as long as you meet their needs for food, water, and shelter.

When it comes to outdoor accommodations for your horse, you have two choices: pastures and paddocks.

REMEMBER

You need to keep the enclosure you choose for your horse free from debris. For your horse's safety, don't use the enclosure to store old pipes, car parts, or anything else.

Grazing your horse in a pasture

A *pasture* is defined as a substantial portion of fenced land where high-quality grass grows for equine consumption.

If you have the land, motivation, and ability to create and manage a high-quality pasture for your horse, a pasture is the best way to go. Horses that live on pastureland suffer the least from colic, leg problems, breathing disorders, stable vices (see Chapter 2), and other maladies that tend to afflict horses confined in stalls. Pastures usually can accommodate more than one horse at a time, too, providing an opportunity for its occupants to live together in groups, as nature intended. Pastures can range in size from a half acre to hundreds of acres, depending on how much land you have available.

TIP

Starting and maintaining a pasture is hard work and takes some know-how. We don't have room in this book to give you a crash course on how to grow a pasture, but we have enough space to tell you to go to your local agriculture office (look at your local government listings online for the County Extension office) for help. Find a good book with information on growing a pasture, and follow it. One such book is *Horsekeeping on a Small Acreage* by Cherry Hill, published by Storey Publishing.

REMEMBER

Even if your horse is on pasture, you still may need to supplement the animal's diet with hay during times when the grass is not growing or is lacking in quality. Don't assume that the grass alone will provide enough sustenance to the horse. Overgrazing, drought, and other problems can render a quality pasture into a field of starvation for a horse. (See Chapter 8 for more about feeding horses.)

Don't forget to provide your horse with shelter from hot sun and inclement weather. Add a shed to your horse's pasture so the animal can get out of the weather if he wants to.

Putting your horse in a paddock

A *paddock*, by our definition, is a small outdoor enclosure that is void of viable pasture grass, and contains dirt as footing. In certain parts of the Eastern United States, a paddock typically is thought of as a large pen with board fencing. In the more populated areas of the Western United States, most horses live in small 12-by-12-foot or 12-by-24-foot paddocks made of a pipe enclosure, known as a *pipe corral.*

A paddock is the next best thing to pasture because it gives the horse room to move around. Because paddocks are outdoors, they also provide good ventilation and more opportunities for mental stimulation for your horse than a box stall does. For information on setting up a paddock, contact companies in your area that install paddocks (search for "horse fencing" online).

If you decide to keep your horse in a paddock, make sure that you provide him with a place where he can seek shelter from the rain, snow, wind, and hot sun. A three-sided, run-in shed is a good option.

Focusing on the right fencing

A number of options exist regarding pasture and paddock fencing, including wood, pipe fencing, and polyvinylchloride (PVC), to name just a few. Whatever type of fence you choose, we strongly suggest that you only use fencing material that is designed with equine safety in mind.

The best material to use, in our opinion, is PVC, arranged in a post-and-rail design. PVC is attractive, durable, and easy to maintain. It can be expensive to install, but will last a very long time. Wood, although traditional and charming, is expensive and destructible (horses love to chew it). You also need to paint wood fencing on a regular basis, whereas PVC never needs painting.

Pipe fencing, on the other hand, is also safe and more affordable than PVC, but it isn't as attractive. Pipe fencing is most commonly seen in Western states, often with a corrugated metal roof. The advantages of pipe fencing, along with cost (it's the least expensive of the fencing mentioned here), are easy maintenance and adaptability. Paddocks made of pipe fencing and panels can be more easily rearranged than wood or PVC fencing into paddocks that are bigger or smaller.

Although wood is high maintenance and can be expensive, some people prefer to use it because of its innate beauty. If you want wood fencing, consider putting a hotwire above the top rail to keep your horse from chewing it. A hotwire gives your horse a mild zap of electricity if he tries to chew the fence and thus protects your wood from being gnawed. Even if you protect your wooden fence from your horse's teeth, you'll still need to paint it every so often to keep it from looking faded and worn. Use a quality, nontoxic paint for maintenance.

Don't enclose your pasture with barbed wire. Barbed wire is dangerous to use around horses. Horses easily become tangled in barbed wire and can be sliced to ribbons by the wire in short time as they struggle to get free.

Your pasture fence needs to be high enough to discourage your horse from jumping out, so the posts need to stand at least 5 feet high, after they've been inserted into the ground. And don't forget to include a gate! Make the gate at least 4 feet wide to accommodate you and your horse.

Sheltering your horse with a run-in shed

An old standby in the way of equine shelter is something called a run-in-shed. The run-in shed is a three-sided rectangular shelter with one open side that offers the horse a place to get out of the rain, snow, wind, and hot sun.

You can buy a prefabricated run-in shed from a barn manufacturer (ask at your local feed store for references of companies in your area or look online), or build your own from scratch using wood or corrugated metal. Make sure that the shed is big enough to safely accommodate however many horses you keep together in your pasture or paddock. Occasionally, members of the herd want to crowd into the shed at the same time.

The best location for your run-in shed is the highest ground on your pasture or paddock, with the opening of the shed facing away from the direction that winter winds typically blow. Keep fresh bedding in your shed to make it comfortable for your horse to lie down (see the next section for bedding options), and clean it every day.

Housing your horse indoors

The majority of horse owners keep their horses in outdoor enclosures, but some owners keep them inside, at least part of the time. Indoor accommodations for horses nearly always consist of a *box stall,* which is just what it sounds like: a stall in the shape of a box.

Keeping a horse in a box stall has a couple of advantages:

>> **Stall-kept horses stay cleaner and neater.** They don't end up muddy when it rains, or dusty when it's dry.

>> **Stall-kept horses avoid bites and other scars.** Horses kept outdoors in pastures or paddocks (which we cover earlier in this chapter) usually suffer more from such maladies.

WARNING

The downside of keeping a horse in a box stall is that it is less healthy for the horse than living outdoors. A horse that stands in nearly the same place for hours on end is more prone to colic, leg problems, and boredom, which can result in stable vices (see Chapter 2). Because ventilation isn't as good in a stall as it is outdoors, stall-kept horses also are more prone to respiratory disease.

If you choose to keep your horse in a box stall, make sure that the stall is at least 12-by-12 feet in size, or larger if you can manage it. Provide the horse with at least one window to see through to give him something to do and to improve ventilation. House another horse next door to him for companionship, if possible, and put a window between them so the horses can see each other and interact.

If you have room on your property, attach a small outdoor paddock to the stall so the horse can go outside whenever he wants. The stall's design also needs to allow for plenty of cross-ventilation without being drafty.

TIP

When it comes to designing and building a box stall, we recommend you purchase a prefabricated box stall made from wood or aluminum from a barn manufacturing company, or hire a well-recommended professional to design and build the stall. Either of these methods ensures that your horse is housed in a stall that is appropriate in size, design, and material.

REMEMBER

Don't forget to keep the stall floor covered with a rubber stall mat and at least 8 inches of bedding to protect the horse's legs and resting body from the hard concrete floor. Horses need bedding in their stalls or shelters to be comfortable. A thick layer of bedding material protects their legs and joints from the hard ground and their hooves from damaging moisture in wet weather. It also absorbs urine and keeps ammonia fumes to a minimum if it's cleaned frequently. Plus, horses just love clean, fluffy bedding. Just watch them roll in it when you first put it down.

You may find that buying one type of bedding over another is easier, depending on where you live. Stick with bedding that your horse seems less likely to eat, because such a habit is neither healthy for the equine digestive system nor your wallet. And make sure that whatever you use is specifically made with horses in mind. Bedding is available at your local feed store. Some common bedding options include:

>> **Paper:** Recycled paper bedding, made from newsprint, is absorbent, soft, and nearly dust-free. The downside of this bedding is that it can become easily packed down by a horse that walks around a lot in his stall.

>> **Peat:** Peat bedding is made from partially decomposed sphagnum moss from wet bogs or peatlands. This type of bedding is known for being very absorbent, taking in 10 times its weight in moisture and for neutralizing ammonia in the stall. Peat also composts easily, and doesn't make horses' hooves dry the way some wood bedding can.

>> **Sawdust:** Sawdust bedding is made from woods including pine, cedar, and fir. It's highly absorbent, easy to find, and economical. The downside of sawdust is that it can cause respiratory problems in sensitive horses.

>> **Straw:** Straw, sold in bales, isn't as absorbent as wood shavings but is less dusty, very soft, and warm. It is the bedding of choice for mares with foals. The downside is that it's particularly attractive to flies.

>> **Wood pellets:** Pelleted wood is high in absorbency, readily available, and easy to use. Pellet bedding is typically made from soft, nontoxic woods like pine.

>> **Wood shavings:** Wood shavings, available loose or packaged, offer a thick, comfortable bed, and are easy to buy and store in bulk. The best wood shavings for horses are made from pine and/or other wood mixtures. Shavings marketed as low in dust are the best choice.

WARNING

Wood shavings made from black walnut are toxic to horses and must be avoided for your horse's health!

Making Room for Work and Play

Regardless of whether you board your equine buddy or keep him at home, you still need to make sure that environment you provide for your horse includes equipment that specifically makes caring for and riding your horse safer and more enjoyable. If you plan to keep your horse at home and need the following amenities installed, talk to a trainer or other equine expert for advice on how to create your facilities.

Storing your gear in a tack room

You need a place to keep your saddle, bridle, grooming tools, horse blanket, and other items you use on or for your horse (see Chapter 6 for more about equine gear). This storage place can be as luxurious as a shed equipped with a saddle rack and pegs for your bridle and halter or as modest as a large trunk that you store inside a barn or other weatherproof building.

If you plan to board your horse, find out whether you can rent a tack room or locker for a fee or supply your own. If you're keeping your horse at home, take advantage of the fact that you own the property and erect the nicest tack room that you can. A roomy, well-designed tack room can enhance your enjoyment of your horse.

REMEMBER

When designing your tack room, think bigger than merely housing the amount of tack that you have at this point — you'll probably want to grow into it. Leave plenty of wall space for bridle racks, and don't forget shelving for items like shampoo, clippers, supplements, and other accessories.

Staying safe in a spacious work area

Horses' bodies take up a lot of room, so you need to have a decent amount of space for grooming, bathing, and tacking up your horse regardless of whether you board or keep your horse at home. Besides adequate space, your work area needs:

>> Crossties or hitching posts to secure your horse while you work on him (see Chapter 13 for more about safe means of restraining a horse).

>> A washrack with a cement floor and nearby crosstie or hitching post, water spigot, and hose for bathing your horse.

   The cement floor prevents your horse from having to stand in the mud while you're bathing him.

>> Tack storage (or full-sized tack room) situated nearby so you have easy access to your equine tools and equipment.

A sheltered work area is preferable so you can attend to your horse even during inclement weather. A roof over your work area not only protects you and your horse from rain or snow, it also keeps you both out of the blistering sun.

A contractor can do the work of putting all this in for you.

Sharpening your skills in a riding arena

REMEMBER

Having a safe, enclosed place to ride is extremely important, especially if you're a beginning rider. In an arena, you can perfect your riding skills and gain the confidence you need to take your horse anywhere beyond the stable.

Good riding arenas have well-constructed fencing at least 4 to 4 ½ feet in height, along with adequate footing to help cushion the shock to your horse's legs as you ride. Covered arenas are best because they shelter you and your horse from the sun, rain, and snow as you ride.

If you plan to board, make sure that the facility you choose has at least one good-sized, well-maintained arena. If the stable has more than one arena, all the better! Multiple arenas mean you rarely have to ride in crowded conditions.

If you plan to keep your horse at home, consider building your own arena, if you have the money and the room. Build the largest arena you can fit onto your property, because the more room you have to ride, the happier you'll be. If space is limited, make your arena at least 60 by 100 feet in size, which gives you the minimum amount of room you need to effectively ride your horse.

The type of fencing you use for your arena depends on your budget. Pipe fencing is adequate, but wood and PVC fencing are much more attractive, albeit expensive. If you plan to turn your horse out in the arena, you want to make the fence higher — at least 5 feet — to discourage him from jumping out. For more fencing details see "Focusing on the right fencing" earlier in this chapter.

If you don't have room for an arena on your property, find out whether the neighborhood you live in has a community arena where you can ride. Ask fellow horse owners — they know where the local arenas are situated.

Utilizing a round pen

Another type of arena that many horse owners find valuable is a round pen (sometimes called a bullpen). Unlike a standard riding arena, which tends to be rectangular or oblong in shape, a round pen is exactly what it sounds like: a perfectly round pen. Much smaller than a typical riding arena, a round pen can measure anywhere from 30 to 100 feet in diameter. Most round pens are 50 feet. The sides are typically 6 feet high and made of wood, pipe corral, or PVC fencing. The sides are sometimes solid, allowing no view from the outside. Others are open, like a traditional riding arena.

Round pens are helpful because they provide a smaller, more contained area where you can ride or work your horse from the ground. They can be particularly valuable to inexperienced riders because they provide a more confined area, making it easier to control the horse. It's safer and less scary to learn to ride in a round pen.

Accessing trails for a fun time

Few things are as relaxing and soul-enhancing as a horseback ride on a wilderness trail. The soothing feel of your horse's rhythmic step and the singing of the birds can melt away your stress.

If trail riding is an activity you want to enjoy with your horse, be sure to house your horse at a stable that has access to plenty of equestrian trails. Or make sure that trails are nearby when you consider keeping your horse at home.

WARNING

Don't put yourself into a situation in which you must travel on busy streets via horseback for an extended amount of time before you reach a trailhead. Horses and traffic don't mix (ever see *The Horse Whisperer*?), so limiting the amount of riding you do on major thoroughfares is wise. (If possible, avoid a situation where you have to trailer your horse out to a trailhead, too, especially if you're not ready to buy a horse trailer.)

Buying a Ready-Made Stable

If you plan on keeping your horse at home but don't have that special property yet, you should keep some points in mind while dong your search. Getting the right property with the right setup can make a big difference in the quality of your equine life.

Shopping for horse property

If you're looking for a place where both you and your horse can live, then the horse property should be your primary focus. You'll need to let your realtor (or your real estate app) know that buying a property zoned for horses is your primary concern.

Aside from the usual concerns when buying a home — school district, safety from crime, aesthetic appearance, and price — you should also keep these points in mind when shopping for horse property:

>> **Community:** While you want to live in an area that is safe for your kids and pretty to look at, if you plan to keep a horse, make sure your neighbors are on the same page. Don't buy a property where you are surrounded by non-horse

owners—especially if horse property is rare in the area. While some non-horse people enjoy living near horses, many do not, and you may end up with hostile neighbors. You may even find yourself facing a change in your zoning if enough neighbors complain to your local government.

» **Proximity to trails:** Unless you plan to only ride in an arena or don't mind trailering your horse whenever you want to leave the property, try to buy a home that has riding trails nearby. Scope out the path to the nearest trail-head, and make sure you won't have to cross busy streets or ride on the shoulder with cars zooming by.

» **Facilities — or not:** Some people prefer to buy a horse property that already has horse facilities set up. Others want a bare slate where they can create their own setup. Decide which route you prefer, and set your sites accordingly. The benefits of buying a home with existing horse facilities mean all you have to do is move in with your horse. No additional time, work or expense needed. On the other hand, the setup might not be exactly what you had in mind.

Getting the right setup

If you think you might like to buy a property that already has horse facilities in place, look for the following before you buy:

» **Quality fencing:** Makers sure the horse enclosures are made of good quality fencing, and that it's in solid shape. If the fencing needs repair, this will mean added costs for you before you can put a horse inside the enclosure.

» **Adequate shelter:** Inspect the area where your horse will live. If it's a full scale barn, have an inspector examine it just like you would any other important structure you plan to purchase. You want to make sure it is free from structural damage, leaks, dangerous electrical issues and more. If your horse will be sheltered in a simple run-in shed or other kind of cover, check it out carefully to make sure it's in good, safe condition.

» **An arena:** If you are a new rider, having an onsite arena is particularly important. You'll need to be able to ride in an environment where you can develop your skills and get to know your horse. Even a 50-foot round pen is suitable if a full-sized arena isn't included.

» **Convenient amenities:** Keep in mind that you'll need a place to keep your tack, tie up your horse and give him a bath. Are all these amenities included in the facility, and are they to your liking? Are they in good condition, and do they function properly?

3
Taking Care of Your Horse

Chapter **8**

Establishing an Everyday Routine

Owning a horse means caring for him every single day. You may find that you actually look forward to the time you spend in the stable cleaning up after your horse and tending to his needs. Or, you may think of it as nothing more than a necessary chore. The truth of the matter is that regardless of whether you feel like it, you *have* to do it, even on those days when it's freezing cold out, or rain is falling like mad and the last thing you want to do is trudge through the wind, mud, or muck to get to the barn.

As a horse owner with a horse on your own property, you must deal with three major factors in your horse's care: feeding, exercising, and managing the horse's environment. If you handle all of these areas properly, you not only will be highly regarded by your neighbors and fellow horse owners, but your horse will love you for it, too.

REMEMBER

If you're boarding your horse rather than keeping him on your own property, don't think that you're completely off the hook. Making sure that your horse's boarding facility adheres to the standards we describe regarding feeding, watering, and stable management is your responsibility. Although the boarding stable does this part of the job, you still must provide the horse with daily exercise and hands-on care.

Handling Your Horse's Hunger and Thirst

Food is very important to a horse, probably even more important than it is to humans. Nature designed the horse to spend the majority of his time chewing, swallowing, and digesting. The equine digestive system is meant to be constantly on the go and to process vast quantities of fibrous foods.

The following sections cover foods that your horse needs and different methods you can use to feed your horse properly.

Looking at feed

Much confusion exists in the horse world about the best food to feed a horse. The reason for this confusion probably lies in the fact that individual horses have different requirements. Factors in determining the best diet for a horse include where and how the horse lives and what kind of work the horse does in addition to the horse's own physiological makeup.

REMEMBER

The best person to guide you when it comes to your horse's diet is your vet. Your vet is familiar with your individual horse and his nutritional needs and should also be up on the local availability of different kinds of hay. (See Chapter 10 for more details on finding a vet.)

The following sections proves some general information on horse feeds to get you started. (All of these feeds, with the exception of pasture grass, can be purchased at a local feed store.)

Hay

Hay is a feedstuff composed of plants that have been cut, dried, and baled. Square bales of hay are available from feed stores, which provide individual feedings called *flakes*. Round bales, which are much larger than square bales, are also an option for pastured horses.

Two different types of hays exist: legumes and grasses. Alfalfa is the legume horses most commonly eat, but clover is another option, depending on where you live. Timothy, orchard, and Bermuda are the most common grass hays. Coastal, brome, fescue, oat, and rye are other grasses to try.

REMEMBER

Hay — also known as forage — is the best feed for horses because it provides roughage in addition to proper nutrition. It should serve as the foundation of your horse's diet. Forage keeps the horse's digestive system working properly and satisfies the horse's natural urge to chew.

The quality of what you feed is just as important as the feed itself. If you buy cheap, poor-quality hay, your horse will suffer for it. Don't scrimp on this most important aspect of your horse's care.

Look for the following factors in any hay you buy to ensure its quality:

>> **Plenty of leaves or blades:** Make sure that 60 percent or more of the hay consists of leaves or blades as opposed to woody stems. Leaves and blades contain most of the hay's nutrients.

>> **Good scent:** Good quality hay has a pleasant smell. Moldy hay has a foul odor and needs to be avoided at all costs. (You can tell if hay is moldy based on the smell and also the presence of a white powder between the flakes.) Dusty hay should be avoided.

>> **Purity:** The bale needs to contain only hay. That means no sticks, dirt, weeds, rope, or other foreign objects.

Hay cubes

You can feed your horse concentrated blocks of grass or legume hay called hay cubes. Hay cubes tend to be cheaper than hay, count as forage, and are good for

>> Older horses with worn-down teeth because cubes break apart quickly when chewed.

>> Horses with respiratory problems because cubes are less dusty than regular hay.

>> Horses that have trouble keeping on weight.

However, most horses prefer baled hay to cubes because baled hay better satisfies their need to chew.

Pellets

Another form of concentrated forage is pellets made from alfalfa, Bermuda, or other types of hay. Pellets are even cheaper than hay cubes, but they're not at the top of our list of recommended feeds unless you have a horse that has respiratory problems or trouble keeping on weight. Horses can easily choke on pellets, and pellets provide little in the way of chewing satisfaction for the horse. Pellets can make a good supplement to a diet consisting primarily of hay, however.

WARNING

When feeding pellets, be sure to soak them in water first to soften them. This reduces the likelihood of choking.

Pasture

Horses do best when they can graze in a pasture because grazing is most natural for them; however, providing your horse with nutritious pasture requires work and knowledge. If you live on property where pasture has already been cultivated, your task is to carefully maintain it. If you want to start a pasture from scratch, you need help. Contact your local agricultural agency for assistance in starting and maintaining a quality horse pasture. You can find this government agency in your telephone directory. (Check out Chapter 7 for more tips on setting up and maintaining a pasture at home.)

You can grow a number of different kinds of pasture grasses for equine consumption. Timothy, bromegrass, fescue, bluegrass, and orchard grass are among the types that horses enjoy. Talk to your veterinarian about which of the grasses that grow in your area best suit your horse.

WARNING

Do not graze a pregnant mare on fescue because doing so can cause the mare to spontaneously abort the foal.

Horses need to be started gradually on pasture grass so it doesn't upset their digestive systems. Allow only an hour of grazing per day for several days, and then increase to two hours, and so on.

If your pasture doesn't yield a substantial amount of good-quality, nutritious grass year-round, supplement your horse's diet with a daily ration of hay. If you don't, the horse may suffer from malnutrition. To verify that your pasture is of good quality, call your local agricultural office and ask an expert to inspect your pasture and help analyze its nutritional content.

Pay attention to weed control. Any number of toxic plants can invade your pasture, causing liver disease, and neurological disorders. Contact your agricultural office for a list of plants in your region that are toxic to horses.

Grain

When it comes to horse food, people often think of grain as a staple of the equine diet. However, if your horse is receiving only moderate exercise, he probably doesn't need any grain. Grain is a high-energy carbohydrate that increases the get-up-and-go of racehorses and other serious equine athletes but usually does little for the average horse other than leave him with too much energy. One exception to this rule is a horse pastured in extremely cold weather that needs the extra source of energy to stay warm.

Commercial feeds

Horse owners have access to good-quality commercial horse feeds. Available in tack stores, these pelleted feeds range from simple mixes like alfalfa and molasses (great for mixing with vitamins, supplements, and medications) to complex *extruded* feeds, which get their name from the way they're made (many extruded feeds are designed for older horses, very active horses, horses with trouble keeping on weight, and young horses).

TIP

We're big advocates of complex extruded feeds in place of grain because they're designed specifically with horses in mind and balanced with vitamins, minerals, carbohydrates, and fats. Talk to your veterinarian to find out whether your horse may benefit from a commercial feed.

Treats

Few things rate as high on a horse's list of favorite things as treats. All kinds of commercial horse treats are available at your local tack store. Or you can stick with two old favorites: carrots and red apples cut up in small pieces to prevent choking (especially important with ponies). The proverbial lump of sugar is okay only once in a while as it provides absolutely no nutritional value and isn't very good for the horse. (You can give healthy treats to your horse as often as you like.)

Fat

Horses tend to get very little fat in their diets, even though this nutrient is required for basic equine function. If your horse is worked consistently and has trouble maintaining his weight, talk to your veterinarian about supplementing him with flaxseed oil or another type of vegetable oil containing Omega 6 and Omega 3 fatty acids. Your vet will know whether your horse needs this as a supplement in his diet.

Vitamins

Horses need plenty of vitamins and minerals for good health. Many small problems ranging from lameness to colic to infection can result from vitamin and mineral deficiencies. We recommend that you give your horse a dose of equine multivitamin supplement every day or every other day. Talk to your vet about what your horse's individual vitamin needs may be.

Minerals

Provide your horse with access to a mineral salt block in his feeder or paddock, or give him a mineral supplement designed for the type of diet he's on. For example, horses eating only grass hays need a different supplement than those getting both legumes and grass. Your veterinarian can provide guidance in this area.

Determining how much to feed

Your horse's weight, along with the amount of exercise he gets, his age, your climate and his breed will all determine how much you feed him.

In general, horses should be given a daily ration of food that weighs 1.5 to 3 percent of their body weight. To figure out your horse's weight, use a weight tape, available at tack stores or online from equine products websites. Weighing your hay is the most accurate way to know exactly how much you are feeding. You can use a regular bathroom scale by stepping on it while holding the feed. Or if you'd prefer not to find out how much *you* weigh every day, get a fishing or luggage scale that you can hang.

If you keep your horse stabled (instead of in a viable pasture with good, nutritious grass or constant access to a round bale), it's imperative that you provide him with the proper amount of hay for his weight. Keep in mind that legume hays like alfalfa will generally help your horse maintain his weight more than feeding him strictly grass. If your horse has trouble keeping weight on, consider including alfalfa in his diet. (Consult with your veterinarian about how much food and what type of forage your particular horse should be receiving.)

REMEMBER

For some horses, a diet strictly consisting of grass hays is best. Horses with metabolic disease (see Chapter 10) or those that are very easy keepers (meaning it doesn't take much feed to keep them at an optimum weight) do best just on grass hay. Your veterinarian can provide you with guidance on whether your horse should only be eating grass hay.

Doling out the chow

REMEMBER

Although feeding your horse only once a day would be easier for you, a horse's digestive system isn't meant to handle only one large meal. Small, frequent meals are the way to go when feeding horses. Provide a minimum of two feedings of hay per day. Most horse owners feed once in the morning and once at night. Feed three times a day if you can because this is the best arrangement for your horse. Be sure to do so consistently.

We discuss different feeding ideas to consider in the following sections.

Using a feeder for meals

Always feed your stabled horse out of a feeder. The feeder can be something as simple as a plastic barrel with a side cut out or a commercial hayrack purchased at a feed store.

The purpose of a feeder is to keep your horse from eating directly off the ground. A horse that eats off the ground can easily ingest sand with the feed, resulting in colic or poor absorption of food. Slow feeders are another great option because they not only keep the hay off the ground, but they also slow down the horse's consumption. You want your horse's hay to last as long as possible because the horse's digestive system is designed to run all day long. The longer your horse takes to eat his hay, the healthier it is for him.

Slow feeders come in different styles, including hay nets and barrel-type designed to slow down the intake of feed.

WARNING

If you decide to feed your horse a commercial feed, offer it in a shallow bucket or rubber pan. Many commercial feeders are designed so you simply dump the grain or feed directly into them.

Switching feed slowly

If your horse is eating a particular kind of feed and you'd like to change him over to something different because of a change in availability or as result of directions from your vet, be sure to do so very gradually. Sudden, abrupt changes in feed can result in a very sick horse.

By gradually we mean over a period of two weeks. Add a quarter of the new hay to the feed the first few days, and then switch over to half for a few more days. Go to three-quarters new hay at the beginning of the second week, and change over completely to the new hay toward the end of that second week.

Feeding treats by hand or by feeder

People are divided when it comes to how to feed their horses treats. Some swear that feeding treats from your hand causes a horse to become bratty and obnoxious. Other people find that their horses don't misbehave when treats are handfed; they believe that feeding by hand helps foster the bond between horse and human.

Here's our position: If your horse acts like a spoiled kid when you hand feed treats to him (starts pushing and crowding you, demanding that you hand over all the goods), then your horse is not a candidate for hand feeding. We also recommend against hand feeding whenever you plan to show your horse at halter or another event where the horse needs to behave perfectly when standing at your side. In these cases, give your horse his treats in a bucket or in his feeder.

On the other hand, if your horse is gentle soul who politely waits for you to hand over delectables and doesn't have a job that requires him to behave a certain way, you can go ahead and feed your horse by hand.

Watering your thirsty horse

We can't overemphasize the importance of providing plenty of water as part your horse's daily care. Your horse needs water — lots of it — to stay alive and to ensure a healthy digestive system. (The average horse drinks 8 to 14 gallons a day, and that's with minimal exercise.) Access to water is particularly crucial for horses that are eating hay because of the dry nature of grass and legumes. Without enough water to drink, horses can develop intestinal impactions from dry feed. That's why it's vitally important that your horse have constant access to clean, fresh H_2O at all times.

A few of the different ways that horse owners can provide water include:

>> Installing an automatic waterer that automatically refills by using a float system whenever the horse drinks from it (available from feed stores or through equine product catalogs and online).

>> Manually filling a large watering trough (available at feed stores) whenever necessary. If you opt for this method, you have to be diligent in keeping the trough full. The benefit of this approach is that you always know how much water your horse is drinking, which can be valuable information when your horse is feeling under the weather (your vet will need to know).

In either case, keep the waterer clean and free of algae and other debris. You'll know when your water needs a good scrubbing because it will turn green from algae or you'll see hay and other stuff floating on the top.

TIP

If you live in a climate where temperatures fall below freezing, you also need to keep your horse's water supply from turning to ice. You can do so with a heating element made especially for horse waterers (available at your local feed store, through equine product catalogs, or online), or by manually breaking the ice whenever it forms. We recommend the heating element because it requires less work on your part and keeps the water at a warmer temperature, which encourages your horse to drink it.

White horses are solid white with pink muzzles and light-colored hooves. Don't confuse white horses with gray horses. Gray horses have some colored hairs in their coats — whites do not. White horses are sometimes seen with blue eyes (these horses are also called cremellos) or brown eyes.

HORSES BY COLOR

Gray horses come in a variety of shades, ranging from nearly white to a darker, dappled coloration. White hairs mix with darker hairs of any other color to produce a gray coloration. Gray horses are often born solid colored and lighten as they get older. One variety, called *flea-bitten gray,* is usually seen on older horses.

Pinto

Pinto markings consist of patches of dark color against white. Only certain breeds have pinto coloration.

Grulla

Grulla horses have a dark, smoky body coloration with a black mane and tail. Grullas usually have a dark stripe down their backs and dark legs.

Buckskin

The true buckskin has a yellow or gold body coloration with a black mane and tail. The lower legs are usually black and can have white markings. Many horse lovers believe that a horse must have a dark stripe down the back to be considered a buckskin, but in reality, true buckskins have no dorsal stripe.

Palomino

Palominos have a golden yellow body coloration with white manes and tails.

Dun

Gemma Giannini

Dun horses have a gold body color and a black or brown mane and tail. The most distinctive indication of a dun coloration is a dark stripe running down the length of the horse's back. Sometimes, you may see a transverse stripe across the withers as well as horizontal stripes on the legs. The dun coloration is considered the closest thing to a natural "wild" color in the horse

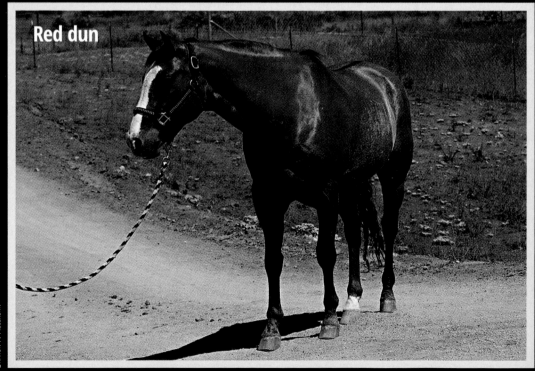

Red dun

Sharon P. Fibelkorn

Red duns are a type of dun with a reddish tint to their coats. They have a dark stripe running down the back and have a reddish or flaxen (blond) mane and tail. The horse in this photo is a classic red dun. He also has some roan characteristics.

Chestnut (light)

Chestnut-colored horses have a distinct reddish color on their bodies and usually have the same color in the mane and tail. Chestnut colorations come in a variety of shades, from dark to light. A light chestnut horse is shown here.

Chestnut (liver)

Chestnut horses can be a dark reddish color, as in this classic liver chestnut.

HORSES BY COLOR

Sorrel

The body color of a sorrel horse is light red. Sorrels are sometimes hard to distinguish from chestnuts. The main difference between the two is that sorrels usually have more of a yellow tint to their coats than chestnuts do. Sorrels tend to have a mane and tail color that matches the body color, although sorrel horses sometimes have flaxen manes and tails.

Bay

Bay horses have bodies that are anywhere from dark tan to reddish brown. Their manes and tails are always black, and they often have black on the lower parts of their legs.

Brown

Horses described as brown have a brown or light black body coloration with a lighter color around the muzzle, flank, and inside upper legs. The mane and tail are always black.

Red roan

The bodies of red roans are covered with a uniform mixture of white hairs mixed with red hairs. The head and lower legs are usually darker than the rest of the body because these areas have a proliferation of red hairs. The manes and tails of red roans can be black, red, or flaxen.

Blue roan

Blue roans have a uniform mixture of white hairs mixed with black hairs, which gives the body a bluish appearance — hence the name. The heads and lower legs of blue roans are usually darker than the bodies. The mane and tail are nearly always black.

Black

For a horse to be considered a true black, his body color must be a solid black with no light areas anywhere on his body. The mane and tail are black as well.

Appaloosa

The Appaloosa's most distinguishing characteristic is its spotted coat. Represented in several different patterns, including the popular *leopard* (shown) and *blanket with spots* (a dark body color with white over the rump, which is covered with dark spots), this characteristic sets the breed apart. Other physical traits include white sclera in the eye, striped hooves, and mottled skin. Some Appaloosas also have thin manes and tails. The height range for an Appaloosa is 14.3 to 16 hands.

Arabian

Arabians are known for their elegant and graceful beauty. The head of the Arabian is small and has a concave, or dished, face. The Arabian's ears are small and curve inward, and its neck is long and arched. Most Arabians have only five spinal vertebrae, as opposed to the six vertebrae typically found in most other breeds. This one less vertebra gives Arabians a shorter back than a lot of other breeds. Arabians are small horses that rarely measure much over 15 hands in height.

GEMMA GIANNINI

Miniature

Miniature horses are the dwarfs of the equine world and number one in the "adorable" category. The Miniature horse has all the physical and psychological characteristics of a regular horse in a very small package. The Miniature horse, which stands anywhere from 6 to 7 hands high, is kept primarily as a pet. Tiny tots can ride Miniature horses, but anyone over the age of four years old is probably too big to ride a Miniature horse.

SHARON P. FIBELKORN

Morgan

Morgans have small, elegant heads and strong, highly arched necks. They also have very deep chests, giving them considerable endurance. Just like their founding sire, Justin Morgan, Morgans tend to be smaller horses and rarely reach more than 15.2 hands in height. They are eager to please and willing to do whatever is asked of them.

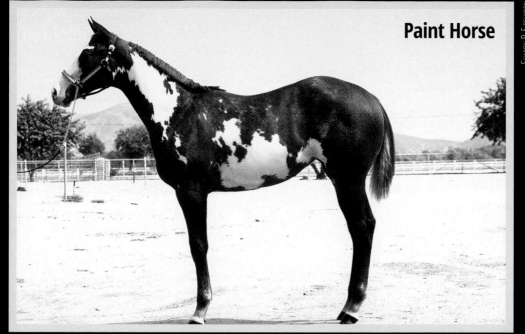

Paint Horse

SHARON P. FBELKORN

Paint Horse coats come in a variety of different patterns, most of which fall under the heading of *tobiano* (a white base with dark patches) or *overo* (a dark base with white patches, shown). The breed's conformation is identical to that of the Quarter Horse, with a height range of 15 to 16 hands. Its temperament is very much like the Quarter Horse's, too: mellow, easygoing, and eager to please. (The Paint Horse in this photo is a yearling.)

Quarter Horse

GEMMA GIANNINI

The Quarter Horse is a sturdy horse with a small head and a muscular neck. The breed's hindquarters are powerful, and the legs are straight and solid. Quarter Horses have a big height range, standing anywhere from 14.3 to 16 hands tall. One of the Quarter Horse's most outstanding features is its disposition. Its quiet temperament is a big reason behind the Quarter Horse's huge popularity.

GEMMA GIANNINI

Saddlebred

The Saddlebred is a *gaited* horse, capable of performing a rack and a stepping pace in addition to an animated walk, trot, and canter. Saddlebreds typically have long, arched necks and fine heads that they carry rather high. The Saddlebred's body is rather lithe and lean, almost like that of a human ballet dancer. Saddlebreds range in height from 15 to 17 hands.

Standardbred

CLIX PHOTOGRAPHY

Standardbreds have an inborn ability to move at great speeds without galloping. Some members of the breed are natural-born trotters and can trot at nearly 30 mph. Others are born *pacers* (where the legs on one side move in unison) and can attain these same speeds. Standardbreds can also gallop. The Standardbred is closely related to the Thoroughbred, although the Standardbred is considerably heavier in muscle. Standardbreds have rather large heads and powerful thighs. They usually measure anywhere from 15 to 16 hands.

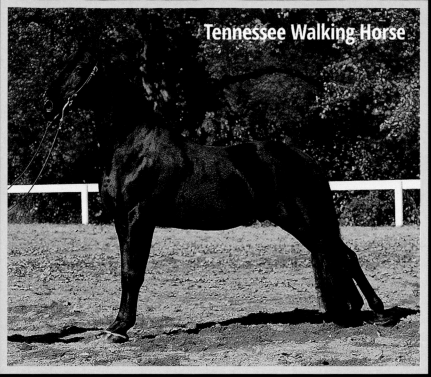

Tennessee Walking Horse

The Tennessee Walking Horse is a gaited horse and can perform, in addition to the walk, trot, and canter, a fourbeat running walk for which it is famous. A Tennessee Walking Horse has a straight head with larger-than-usual ears. The breed has a gracefully arched neck, prominent withers, and large hooves. Ranging in height from 15 to 16 hands, Tennessee Walking Horses have very docile temperaments.

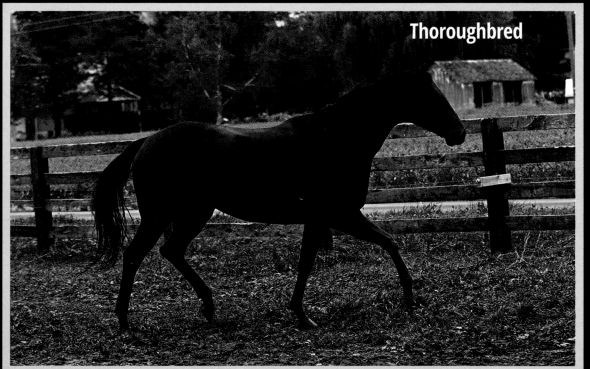

Thoroughbred

The typical Thoroughbred has a straight head, high withers, and long, fine legs. Standing anywhere from 15 to 17 hands high, Thoroughbreds have a lean, lanky appearance that sets them apart from other breeds. Thoroughbreds are willing horses but can sometimes be too spirited for beginning riders. This depends on the individual horse, however. Some Thoroughbreds do make good mounts for beginners.

CLIX PHOTOGRAPHY

Andalusian

The Andalusian horse, also known as the Pure Spanish Horse, is one of the most spectacular studies in horse flesh on the planet. You see this horse in museum pieces and paintings from the Middle Ages. Leonardo da Vinci sculpted this horse, and the winged Pegasus was based on this breed. Andalusians' necks are heavy and arched; their manes and tails are long and wavy. The breed is between 14.3 and 15 hands in height. With a regalness about them that is hard to equal, even a relatively untrained eye can easily spot this breed.

Belgian

CLIX PHOTOGRAPHY

The Belgian is an old European draft breed that's gaining popularity in the United States. American Belgians, such as the one in this photo, are slightly larger and heavier than their European counterparts. American Belgians are around 18 hands in height and are usually sorrel with a flaxen mane and tail. Most Belgians are used for pulling, although some are also ridden.

Dutch Warmblood

SHARON P. FIBELKORN

The result of Trakehner, Gelderland, and Thoroughbred crossings, the Dutch Warmblood was developed to be the consummate performance horse. Standing 16 to 17 hands high, Dutch Warmbloods are especially known for their skills in jumping, dressage, and carriage driving.

Peruvian Paso

AUDREY PAVIA

Developed in Peru in the 1800s to carry plantation owners across vast areas of land, the Peruvian Paso possesses three gaits: the *paso llano*, the *sobreandando*, and the *huachano*. Each of these gaits is designed to be comfortable while covering considerable ground. Peruvian Pasos that are in top condition can maintain these gaits for hours on end. Peruvian Pasos are small to medium in size, measuring 14.1 to 15.1 hands in height. They have well-muscled necks and long, thick manes and tails.

Racking Horse

Racking Horses have a graceful build, with a long, sloping neck. Their legs are smooth, and their hair is finely textured. The typical Racking Horse averages around 15.2 hands. What makes the Racking Horse so special is that it's a *gaited* breed, able to perform a four-beat racking gait in addition to a walk and a canter. Racking Horses are willing to work and eager to please their handlers.

Welsh Pony

Welsh Ponies come in four different types: the Welsh Mountain Pony, the Welsh Pony, the Welsh Pony of Cob Type, and the Welsh Cob. Each of these four names represents different heights and conformation types within the Welsh breed. It's easiest to think of each type in terms of its height: The Welsh Mountain is 12.2 hands or shorter; the Welsh Pony is 12.2 to 13.2 hands high; the Welsh Pony of Cob Type is 13.2 hands high or less; and the Welsh Cob is actually horse-sized at 14 to 15.1 hands tall.

Taking Care of Other Maintenance Tasks

Daily horsekeeping requires more than just feeding and watering. You also have to keep a close eye on your charge, exercise the critter, clean up after him, and work at keeping pests at bay. All these things are an integral part of maintaining a horse.

Giving your horse the once over

Horses may seem like rather independent creatures, but in reality, they're more like half-ton toddlers. They easily get themselves into trouble and sometimes develop problems through no fault of their own.

That's why your horse needs what we like to call *the daily once over*. Every day, you must take your horse out of his stall or pasture and examine him from head to toe. This task is easier to do when you are grooming, because grooming calls for close contact between your hands and eyes and the horse's body. Plus, grooming usually is enjoyable for the horse and helps the two of you bond. (Check out Chapter 9 for the complete scoop on grooming.)

As you go over your horse, check for the following signs of trouble:

>> Lumps or bumps

>> Scabs or hair loss

>> Swellings or hot spots, especially around backs of pasterns, lower legs, and tendon areas (see Chapter 2)

>> Rocks in hooves

>> Discharge from eyes or nose; swollen or squinty eyes

>> Foul smells, especially in the nose and mouth areas

>> Limping, or walking stiffly

>> Lack of appetite, depression, unresponsiveness, or sleepiness

For more information about what to do when you discover a problem during your daily once over, see Chapter 11.

Exercising your horse for optimum health

Stabled horses need daily exercise to keep their minds and bodies in good working order. Pastured horses don't need as much exercise as their stabled counterparts, but they still require time under saddle if they are to stay in good physical shape.

Give your horse a minimum of 30 minutes of exercise per day — more if you have the time (although don't overdo it if your horse isn't used to a lot of work). If you don't have time to tack up and ride, you need to at least take the horse out and walk him for half an hour. On the other hand, 30 minutes of just walking every day isn't enough exercise for the average horse, so you have to find time to give your equine buddy a good work out at least a few days a week. If you don't, your horse will start getting a bit crazy from all that pent-up energy, and you'll pay for it with misbehavior on the rare days when you do ride.

Although riding is the best way to exercise your horse, you can also vary the routine by occasionally longeing, or exercising him on a rope (see Chapter 13 for information on longeing). Don't overdo the longeing, however. Too much of it can put severe stress on your horse's legs and result in lameness.

Managing manure

One of the least fun things about owning a horse is cleaning up after him. Horses are virtual poop machines that never seem to stop evacuating their bowels. Of course if your horse is producing plenty of waste, that means his digestive system is in good working order. Try keeping that happy thought in mind every time you pick up your manure fork.

Manure is not the only waste product your horse produces. Horses also eliminate several gallons of urine per day, creating soiled bedding to clean up if your horse is stabled.

A WORD ABOUT TURNING OUT

Taking a stabled horse and giving it turn-out time, where it can exercise on its own in an arena, is a common practice in the horse world. Advocates of this practice see it as a way for a confined horse to expend some of his pent-up energy by bucking, rearing, running, rolling, and basically just being a horse.

Although turn-out time sounds good in theory, we've seen plenty of problems arise from this practice. Leg injuries, like bowed tendons and even irreparable fractures, often occur during turnouts. The reason is that horses that are cooped up all day tend to go berserk during turn-out time and end up hurting themselves.

If you need to turn a horse out for behavioral reasons, or want to turn him out so he can roll (rolling is good for horses because it helps them stretch out their spine and back muscles), warm him up first with a 5- to 10-minute walk, dress him with protective legwear, and turn him out alone (instead of with another horse).

We can give you a slew of really good reasons to pick up after your horse on a daily basis, regardless of whether he is pastured or stabled. Here are some of the biggies:

>> Your property begins to smell pretty bad if you let manure and urine-soaked bedding pile up.

>> Your horse's health suffers if he is forced to stand in his own waste.

>> The accumulated manure and urine provide a breeding ground for bacteria, flies, and internal parasites (covered in the next section).

>> You can get in trouble with your neighbors and the law if you don't clean up.

Scooping manure is really not a difficult job to perform, provided you're in decent physical shape and have a reasonably healthy back. All you need to do is scoop the poop into a wheelbarrow by using a manure fork, a wonderful invention that separates the manure balls from the dirt or bedding. It's available at feed stores.

Cleaning urine-soaked bedding is a little more difficult, although the shavings, straw, or whatever you chose for your horse's bed sticks together when it's wet and so isn't that hard to remove. You can use your manure fork for this part of the job or a shovel, being careful not to take too much clean bedding with you as you scoop. Remember to replace the removed bedding with clean, fresh stuff when you're done. (Chapter 7 has more details on bedding.)

You can dispose of the gathered waste by either dumping it in a trash receptacle for pick up or keeping it to compost. Whatever you do, be sure to follow the regulations in your municipality regarding equine waste disposal. If you aren't sure what those rules are, contact your county or city government for information.

If you want to compost your horse's manure and soiled bedding to use in your garden or to spread on the surface of a riding arena, make sure that you age the waste for at least eight weeks. We also suggest that you get a good book on composting so you can find out all about this method of waste disposal. Keep a close eye on your manure pile. Compost piles filled with manure have been known to catch fire as a result of internal combustion caused by the heat of decay.

Controlling pests

Where you find horses, you also find bugs. Flies, gnats, and intestinal worms tend to congregate at stables, dining on the horses and making their lives a living hell. These pests are a cold, harsh reality of the horse world, and all owners can do is try their darnedest to control them.

REMEMBER

If you follow the instructions regarding waste control in the previous section, you'll already be doing a great deal to control pests in your horse's environment. Many species of flies and intestinal parasites need access to horse manure to complete their life cycles. So, if you get rid of the manure quickly, the pests can't reproduce. This factor is especially true of internal parasites, many of which reinfect a horse when he accidentally ingests larvae in his environment.

In addition to diligent waste removal, you can control flies by

>> **Hanging fly strips or traps around the barn.** These products are good for snagging flies.

>> **Purchasing biological controls from companies that specialize in this aspect of pest control.** A tiny species of predatory wasp in the *Chalcididae* family that feeds on fly larvae is a popular choice among horse owners. (This wasp is barely noticeable in the environment and won't bother you or your horse.)

>> **Feeding a fly-control supplement.** A variety of dietary supplements are on the market designed to control flies. Some are all-natural products consisting of herbs and other ingredients that are reported to deter flies after the horse ingests it. Other products are chemical in nature and work by affecting the insect's ability to reproduce in the horse's manure once the horse passes it.

>> **Applying fly sprays or wipes to your horse daily.** Also, consider installing an automated insecticide system in your barn.

>> **Dressing your horse in a fly mask, fly sheet, and special fly-screen leg wraps to keep flies from biting him (see Chapter 6).**

The bad news is that you can never completely eliminate flies from a horse's environment. The good news is that, with hard work, you can keep their pesky numbers in check.

Chapter 9

Keeping Your Horse Clean and Pretty

Few things make a horse lover happier than being up on a horse that looks really good. Mane and tail flowing, coat glowing — you'll feel proud passing other riders on the trail as you sit astride such a glamorous beast.

Of course, your trusty steed isn't going to come out of the pasture looking so great — you have to make it happen. Although cleaning up a half-ton animal after he's been milling around in the dirt for days may not sound like a picnic, we consider grooming is one of the most enjoyable parts of horse ownership. And besides, most horses absolutely love the attention.

If you groom your horse every day, the effects are cumulative. His coat shines more every; his tail is silkier. He looks pretty darn good, even when he's just standing there eating in his stall, provided he hasn't just rolled in the mud, that is. In this chapter, we give you the essential information for making your horse look his best.

Getting Down to Business: Grooming Basics

Take a look in any tack store, equine supply catalog, or horse products website and you'll see oodles of grooming tools for sale. That's because grooming is an important activity in the horse world. You'll soon discover just how important it is after you spend more and more time around horses. But for now, several of the really good reasons for grooming your horse on are that it

>> Removes sweat and dirt from your horse's coat, helping keep his skin healthy.

>> Prevents chafing and skin irritation by removing dirt, burrs, and other material before you put on the tack.

>> Gives you a chance to inspect your horse for any unusual lumps, bumps, or blemishes. You're more likely to notice changes or problems as they arise if you're familiar with your horse's body.

>> Helps build that all-important bond between you and your horse.

>> Gives your horse the attention on which he thrives.

>> Earns the high regard of other horse people, who will respect and admire your dedication to your horse.

>> Helps you (and your horse) relax, and reduces the daily stress in both your lives.

>> Makes your horse look handsome and well cared for.

If you're still not convinced that you need to take time out as often as you can to groom your horse, then hear this: Regular grooming is important to your horse's health and welfare, and it's a requirement of every horse owner, pure and simple.

REMEMBER

Grooming your horse isn't hard. In fact, it's one of the easiest and most enjoyable aspects of horsemanship, and it needs to be done as often as possible. The optimum schedule is to groom your horse once a day. You'll get great results if you do. If you can't spruce him up every day, grooming your horse before and after you ride him is imperative. When you groom after you ride, make sure that the horse is completely cooled down (no longer hot and wet); trying to groom a sweaty coat is aggravating and nearly impossible.

With only slight variations for personal style and preference, horse people around the world use the grooming procedures described in the following sections. If you hope to fit in with the horsy set, you must practice proper grooming procedures and protocols. After becoming familiar with the basics, you can vary the steps to suit your own personality. For example, some people prefer to clean the hooves before grooming the body, and others tend to the horse's head only after taking care of every other part of his anatomy.

Starting with the right tools and setup

The first thing you need to do is assemble all of your grooming tools in a tack box or organizer. Make sure that everything is clean and in good working order. At a minimum, your tools need to include the following items:

>> Rubber currycomb

>> Stiff brush

>> Soft brush

>> Shedding blade

>> Cloth (any old soft, clean rag will do)

>> Mane and tail brush

>> Hoof pick

>> Hoof brush

You can find descriptions of these items and their uses in Chapter 6.

After you organize your tools, put a halter and lead rope on your horse, and lead him to a roomy area in the stable where you can tie him securely, either in cross-ties or at a post.

REMEMBER

Never try to groom a horse that is loose in a stall or pasture. You won't have control over his movements, and it teaches him to disregard you while he's being groomed. When the weather is inclement, you also want to find a spot to shelter you and your horse from wind and wetness. (Directions for leading and tying up your horse are in Chapter 13.)

Working the body

Start with the biggest part of the horse: his body. The body includes the head, neck, legs, rump, and everything in between.

Everyone knows that horses are covered in hair, but unless you've spent some time around horses, you may not realize that a horse's hair is a trap for every speck of dirt, mud, and dust that he comes into contact with. Your job as a groomer is to get as much of that grunge off the horse's coat as you can, exposing the clean-looking, shimmering coat beneath.

If your horse is stabled indoors all the time, the amount of dirt in his coat will be minimal. Horses that live in pastures or paddocks, however, usually require a bit of elbow grease to get them clean.

Use a rubber currycomb, stiff brush, soft brush, and cloth to clean the body of your horse. With these tools at your disposal, follow these steps:

1. **Use the currycomb to bring the dirt to the surface of the coat by rubbing in a circular motion. (If your horse has a very thin coat, proceed gently or skip this step altogether.)**

TIP

Start on your horse's left side with your currycomb in your right hand (although if you are left-handed, you'll probably be more comfortable holding the comb in your left hand). Begin rubbing at the end of your horse's neck (where it joins the head) and work down toward the horse's body. (See Figure 9-1 for the correct way to stand and groom.) The order in which to groom is: neck, chest, shoulders, back, belly, rump, and haunches.

WARNING

Be gentle when working around the horse's flanks and underbelly. Some horses are sensitive in these areas and may kick out if you tickle them.

If mud is caked on the horse's legs, use a gentle circular motion to shake it loose. Do so only with dry mud; wet mud is impossible to remove with a brush.

After finishing the left side, move over to the right side, switching the currycomb to your left hand and repeating the process. If your horse is the least bit dirty — and we're sure he is — the dust comes to the surface of his coat.

2. **Use the stiff brush to dissipate the dirt into the air by brushing in short strokes in the direction of the coat.** Again, start on the horse's left side with the stiff brush in your right hand (or left hand, if you are a lefty) and start at the top of the neck, moving down the horse's neck, to his chest, shoulder, back, barrel, belly, rump, and haunches. You can also use the stiff brush to loosen the dirt from your horse's legs, but you need to be gentle.

After finishing the left side of the horse, move over to the right side and repeat the process with the stiff brush in your left hand.

3. **Use the soft brush to remove the remaining dust from the coat, brushing along the lay of the coat by using short strokes.** Again, start on the horse's left with the brush in your right hand (or left, if you prefer) and move from the horse's neck, to his chest, shoulder, back, barrel, belly, rump, and haunches. Move to the right side of the horse with the brush in your left hand, and repeat the brushing process. You should begin to see a shine on your horse's coat.

As you brush your horse with the stiff and soft brushes, clean the brushes continually by rubbing them against the rubber currycomb. Doing so helps to get rid of the dust that has accumulated in the brushes and keeps the dirt from going back onto the horse.

4. **Complete the body-grooming process by wiping down the horse's body with the cloth.** This step gives the coat even more shine and removes any dirt and dust you may have missed.

5. **Use the cloth to clean out the insides of your horse's nostrils, where dirt and mucus tend to accumulate.**

6. **Use the soft brush to gently groom your horse's head with long, soft strokes.** Stand at the side and in front of your horse to do this step.

Although most horses enjoy having their heads groomed, some don't. Be sure to calmly approach your horse's head with the brush, showing it to him and letting him smell it before you use it on his head. Be careful when brushing his ears because some horses are funny about having their ears touched. If your horse objects to having his ears brushed, try grooming them with a soft towel.

When your horse is shedding (something that occurs in early spring), you can use your shedding blade to remove the loose hair from the coat. Use the blade before you groom, starting on the left side of the horse, moving down the body, and then starting again on the right.

FIGURE 9-1:
To groom a horse, start at the top of the neck and move along the body.

© John Wiley & Sons, Inc.

Shedding blades work best on horses with thick winter coats. If your horse has a thin winter coat and is shedding only minimally, you can use a shedding stone (made of pumice) or metal currycomb to remove the excess hair.

WARNING

Use care and caution whenever you use the shedding blade. The sharp teeth on this tool can injure your horse's skin. Apply only minimal pressure, and *never* use this tool on your horse's legs.

Managing the mane and tail

Your horse's mane and tail are made up of hair not unlike human hair. And as with human hair, regular cleaning and brushing helps keep it looking luxurious.

You need the soft brush and the mane and tail brush to tend to your horse's mane and tail whenever you're grooming him. You may also want to use a mane-and-tail detangling solution — the kind you apply when the mane and tail are dry, not wet.

Follow these steps for grooming your horse's mane and tail:

1. **Using your fingers, pick out any shavings, burrs, or other foreign material lodged in the mane, tail, or forelock.** The *forelock* is the area of the mane that hangs between the horse's ears and down onto his forehead.

2. **Separate tangles in the mane and tail with your fingers, if you can.** If the hair is badly tangled, use dry-detangling solution (available in tack stores). Put some of the detangler in the palm of your hand and work it into the mane and tail for later combing.

3. **Using your soft brush, groom the base of the horse's tail, where the hairs are short.** Try to reach the skin when you do this step, because brushing helps stimulate the circulation.

4. **Using the soft brush, groom the base of the mane, where it joins the crest of the neck.** Again, let the brush reach the skin to help with circulation.

5. **Using the mane and tail brush, brush out the hair of the mane and tail, gently removing any tangles with your fingers first, until you get a silky look.**

Attending to the hooves

The health of your horse's hooves is extremely important, and you should try to clean them daily, if possible. Hooves that are not cleaned regularly can develop thrush (a fungal disease), stone bruises (sore spots on the bottom of the hoof), and other problems. (See Chapter 11 for more information on maladies that can affect the hoof.)

MANAGING THE MANE WITH A PULL

Some horse owners like their horses to have long, flowing manes. Others prefer a shorter, thinner look. In fact, people who show their horses in western rail classes — such as western pleasure, equitation, trail, and horsemanship — must keep their horse's manes short and trim. The same goes for those who show in English events like dressage and hunt seat, where manes are often braided for competition and need to be kept short and manageable.

Keeping your horse's mane short and thinned out is not as simple as you may think. You can't just take a pair of scissors and cut it. If you do, it will look thick and chopped up. Instead, what you need to do is *pull the mane,* using a mane comb.

Here is how you pull a horse's mane:

1. **Shift the horse's clean, dry mane, to one side of the horse's neck. Stand next to the horse on the side where his mane hangs down.**

2. **Beginning at the center of the horse's neck, hold your mane comb in your right hand and take a 1-inch wide section of mane in your left hand, between your forefinger and your thumb.**

3. **Stretch down the mane hairs you're holding. Then, using the same fingers with which you're holding the hairs, push up some of the hairs that you are holding. This leaves you with several hairs still between your fingers.**

4. **Wrap these remaining hairs in the metal mane comb and yank down in a short, quick pull to remove some of the longer hairs, leaving shorter mane behind.**

5. **Perform this step repeatedly over the length of the entire mane until you have a nice, neat look.**

If you use short quick pulls, mane pulling shouldn't bother your horse. If it does, ask an experienced horse person to help you get the hang of it. If your horse is extremely sensitive when it comes to having his mane pulled, you may have to have a veterinarian come out and give the horse a sedative before you can proceed.

You need a hoof pick and hoof brush to properly clean your horse's hooves, and your horse needs to be securely tied to a hitching post or crossties.

Picking up the feet

Before you can clean your horse's hooves, you have to be able to pick up his feet. Standing on the left side of your horse, facing toward the horse's back end, bend down and run your left hand along your horse's left front leg, starting above the knee and moving down toward the *pastern* (ankle). Some horses pick up their feet for you automatically. If yours doesn't, lean your shoulder against your horse's shoulder to shift his weight to the opposite leg, and squeeze the back of the leg you're hoping to lift. The horse should then pick up his foot, enabling you to cradle the left hoof with your hand. Be sure to bend the leg back at its natural angle and not off to the side. Support this uplifted foot in your hand and begin cleaning.

Some horses are trained to pick up their feet if you gently squeeze the horny growth on the inside of their elbows and hocks called the *chestnut*. Give this a try if you're having trouble getting a new horse to lift his feet.

Cleaning the hooves

To clean out the inside of the uplifted hoof, take the pick in your right hand, with the handle in your fist and the point of the pick facing away from you. Stand at the horse's left side at his shoulder, looking toward the back of the horse. You'll know you're in the right position if your left shoulder is next to your horse's left shoulder. Ask your horse for his hoof (see the previous section), and then support this uplifted foot in your left hand and start scraping out the dirt with the tip of the hoof pick. (Figure 9-2 shows the correct way to hold the hoof and the hoof pick.) Be sure to clean out the areas around the *frog* (the triangular area on the underside of the hoof), but don't scrape the frog itself. Look for rocks, nails, or other items that may be lodged around the frog.

FIGURE 9-2:
Support your horse's hoof in one hand as you grip the hoof pick in your other hand.

© John Wiley & Sons, Inc.

Get to know the anatomy of a horse's foot so you can scrape in just the right areas. See Chapter 2 for details on what the underside of the hoof looks like under all that dirt.

After you dig out the dirt and debris from the hoof, use your hoof brush to wipe away any excess dirt in the foot. You get a good view of the foot after you do this, so you can spot any stones or other objects that may be lodged inside.

When you're satisfied that that first hoof is clean, move to the hind leg on the same (left) side. Facing the back of the horse, again run your hand down the horse's leg and lift the foot off the ground. If the horse doesn't lift his foot right away, push gently on his thigh so he shifts his weight to the other leg.

TIP

After you finish the hooves on the left side, move over to the right. Don't start with the front leg on the right side, though. Tradition dictates that you move from the left foreleg to the left hind leg to the right hind leg, then to the right foreleg. Face the back of the horse with your shoulder to horse's right shoulder, and lift the horse's right leg with your right hand. The hoof pick should be in your left.

After you clean out each hoof, use your hoof brush to clean off any dirt clinging to the outside of the hoof. If the outside of your horse's hooves are caked with dirt, you can also use the brush to clean them off.

Taking action when your horse refuses to lift its feet

Some horses simply won't lift their feet when you try to clean out their hooves. Among the different reasons for this problem are

>> A lack of training — horses have to be taught to have their feet handled at a young age.

>> A lack of balance — horses have to learn to stand on three feet.

>> A prior bad experience — a horse may have fallen when having his feet worked on or may experience pain or discomfort in one of his legs.

If your horse refuses to lift his feet for cleaning or for the *farrier* (a specialist in trimming and shoeing horse hooves), have him examined by a veterinarian to make sure he isn't experiencing pain in one or more legs. Doing so is especially important whenever you have an older horse that is stiff when he moves or is somehow lame.

If your horse is sound and still won't lift his feet, he needs to be trained how to have his feet handled. Calling in a patient, gentle, experienced trainer or horse person is best for solving a foot-lifting problem, as opposed to trying to deal with it yourself.

Sticking to safety rules

Although grooming is a relaxing activity for you and your horse, you don't want to get too comfortable while doing it. Remember these safety tips when you're working on and around your horse:

>> **Never duck under your horse's neck or belly.** If you want to get from one side of the horse to the other, walk around.

>> **Never stand directly behind your horse when grooming him.** Stand off to the side in case he decides to kick.

>> **Never kneel down or sit while you're working on your horse's legs.** Stay in a bending or squatting position so you can move out of the way quickly if necessary.

>> **Never stand directly in front of your horse's legs when grooming.** Stay to the side of the legs to avoid being struck if the horse moves forward or strikes out.

>> **Never groom a horse that is loose in a stall or pasture.** Always make sure that the horse is correctly secured before you begin grooming.

>> **Never assume that a strange horse is open to grooming.** When grooming a new horse, use caution, especially when brushing the flanks and underbelly.

Scrub-a-Dub: Bathing Your Horse

Bathing a horse isn't that much different from washing a car, except that with a horse, you don't need to wax. Both objects are large, however, and require plenty of soap, water, and elbow grease.

You can choose any number of ways to bathe your horse, but we show you one of the fastest and easiest methods in this section.

Knowing why and when horses need baths

Why wash a horse? In nature, horses don't get baths. In fact, the only time wild horses ever get wet is during a rainstorm.

Captivity is essentially the main reason for washing horses. Humans like to be around clean horses, and most horse owners see their horses as extensions of themselves and want their equine companions to look just as good as they do.

Likewise, the fact that humans take pleasure in riding horses, more or less demands that we keep them clean. A dirty horse is prone for trouble after tack is placed on his body. Sweat and dirt underneath a saddle and girth can cause chafing, itching, and sheer misery. Tack can also be a breeding ground for fungus that can infect your horse's skin.

No firm rule exists for determining when and how often to bathe your horse. Some horse owners bathe their horses once a month like clockwork; others do it just before a show. Some people wait until the horse is really, really dirty. Still others, by necessity, wait until the weather warms up or simply until they have time to do it.

How often *you* bathe your horse depends on several factors, including:

>> How dirty your horse is

>> The purpose for which you're using your horse

Because they're graded on their looks, show horses get more baths than noncompetitive equines. On the other hand, bathing a horse too often isn't good because the shampoo can strip natural oils from the horse's skin and coat.

TIP

If your horse works hard and gets dirty and sweaty often, you can simply opt to rinse him all over with clear water, without the shampoo. Clear water doesn't hurt him and keeps his skin and coat free of irritating debris.

REMEMBER

Because horses live outside, check out the weather forecast before you give your horse a bath. If you live in a cold climate, for example, and it's the dead of winter, bathe your horse only if you can provide him with warm water and a place to wash and dry him that is warm and free of drafts. Otherwise, only sunny warm days are good days for a bath.

Making preparations to bathe your horse

Don't start washing that horse unless you're prepared. Consider the following:

>> Be sure that your horse is amenable to being washed. If you can, find out the horse's history with bathing. Short of that, you can try bringing him into the washrack with the help of another person and watch his reaction carefully as you administer the bath. Most horses are fine when tied in a washrack (a place made especially for bathing horses, complete with asphalt or concrete flooring and hitches for tying the horse) and when hosed or sponged down with water. However, until you know for sure that your horse won't panic in the confines of a washrack or freak out at the sight of a garden hose, hold off on the bath.

>> Make sure that you have enough time to do the job right before you get started. Washing a horse is a big chore. It takes at least 20 minutes, maybe more, to thoroughly wash and rinse a horse and another 30 to 45 minutes to get him dry, depending on the weather.

>> Have a good place to bathe your horse. Use a specially designed washrack, or a roomy, hard-floored area where you can securely tie the horse to a hitching post or crossties (see Chapter 13 for information about tying your horse).

>> Use a nylon halter and lead rope if you can. Nylon halters and lead ropes can best withstand the rigors of being soaked with water.

>> Make sure you have access to running water. Garden hoses are the most convenient way of bringing water from the faucet directly to your horse's body.

>> If the water from your faucet comes out very cold, have at least 72 gallons of lukewarm water on hand.

>> If you don't have access to running water, warm the water in buckets using an electrical device called a bucket warmer, available in tack and feed stores.

>> Wear clothes and shoes that you don't mind getting wet: Bathing a horse is messy business (see Chapter 6 for more about proper footwear).

Having the right tools on hand

Assemble your bathing tools before you bring your horse to the washing area. You need to have the following on hand:

>> **Shampoo:** Plenty of equine shampoos are available at tack and feed stores or from equine catalogs and online horse supply retailers. You can also use human shampoo on your horse if you prefer. (Some humans prefer to use horse shampoo on their own hair instead of human shampoo, in an attempt to have full and glossy manes.)

>> **Conditioner:** Some equine (and human) shampoos have a conditioner built in. Or, you can add one later as a second step. Some horse owners use conditioner only on the horse's mane and tail. This decision is strictly a matter of personal preference.

>> **Body sponge:** For sale in tack and feed stores, body sponges are large sponges that are good for working the shampoo into your horse's coat.

>> **Face sponge:** You use this sponge, usually a natural sea sponge, to clean delicate areas of your horse's face.

>> **Sweat scraper:** The sweat scraper is great for removing excess water from your horse's coat after the bath.

>> **Towels:** Use towels to dry the horse's face (and probably your own) and to clean up any other wet areas. You also want to use a towel to dry the back of your horse's pasterns to prevent the growth of any fungus in this area of the leg.

>> **Cooler or sweat sheet:** If you're bathing your horse on a hot summer day, you won't need this piece of horse clothing. However, if your horse will be exposed to drafts while you are walking him to dry him off, a cooler or sweat sheet (see Chapter 6) is necessary.

Washing your horse properly

With your horse securely tied in a wash area and your tools assembled, you're ready to start scrubbing. Now, follow these steps to give your horse a bath:

1. **Starting on the left side of your horse (you wash and rinse only one side of the horse at a time), run lukewarm water from the garden hose on the horse's legs if your washrack has a hot water faucet or the water comes out lukewarm.** If not, you have to use warm water from a bucket for this step. Wetting down the legs first enables your horse to get used to the water and to the idea that he's about to be bathed.

2. **After the horse adjusts to the water, slowly move the hose up to where the neck joins the head and wet the body all the way to the rear end of the horse.**

3. **Apply shampoo to your sponge and begin lathering your horse's coat, starting where the neck joins the head and working your way down across the body.** Be sure to scrub underneath your horse, where the girth lies, and along the back where the saddle sits, because sweat and dirt tend to accumulate in these areas. Wash your horse's legs and the outsides of his hooves.

4. **After you're confident that you've loosened the dirt and sweat from your horse's coat, take the hose or a bucket of water and begin rinsing the shampoo from your horse's coat.** Warm water is best if you have access to it, but if not, cool water from the hose will do.

   Rinse thoroughly; you don't want to leave behind any soap residue that can irritate your horse's skin.

REMEMBER

5. **Shampoo, condition, and rinse the horse's mane.** If the mane is on the right side of the horse, move over to that side.

6. **Repeat Steps 1–4 for the right side of the horse.**

7. **Wash the horse's tail.** Wet the tail with water and apply shampoo. Be sure to work the lather into the tail so that you lather up all of the hair. Rinse, condition, and rinse again. Be sure to rinse out all of the soap residue from the base of the tail. Soap residue can irritate the horse's skin, and he'll probably rub his tail on whatever he can find, dirtying those luxurious locks. (See the nearby sidebar "Making your equine's locks more luxurious" for additional tips about maintaining your horse's tail and mane.)

8. **Wash the horse's head.** This step can be tricky, depending on the horse. Most horses are cooperative when having their faces cleaned. Others have had bad experiences or are wary of the process and give you trouble. In either case, be gentle and considerate when washing your horse's face.

   Wet the horse's face with a sponge and warm water. Don't forget to wet and wash the forelock when you do the head.

WARNING

   We recommend that you just rinse the face with a clean sponge and water and avoid using shampoo on your horse's face. Shampoo is difficult to rinse off thoroughly, and it can get in the horse's eyes — ouch! Avoid the temptation to wash your horse's face by squirting it with the garden hose. Some horses tolerate it, but all clearly hate it.

There is a right way to bathe a horse and a wrong way. Your horse wants you to do it the right way by adhering to the following list of do's and don'ts:

>> **Do have patience with your horse when bathing him.** Bathing makes no sense to horses; they put up with it only because we ask them to.

>> **Do have consideration for your horse during the bath.** Use a comfortable water temperature and appropriate water pressure.

>> **Do talk to your horse when bathing him**. Constantly reassure him and tell him what a good horse he is.

>> **Don't spray your horse in the face with water.** How would you like it if someone did that to you?

>> **Don't get water in your horse's eyes, ears, or nostrils.** Doing so not only causes the horse fear and discomfort, but it also can result in medical problems.

>> **Don't put your horse back in his pasture or stall while he's dripping wet.** Let him air dry first while tied and under supervision.

MAKING YOUR EQUINE'S LOCKS MORE LUXURIOUS

Soft, silky manes and tails are both made and born. Although Mother Nature certainly has much to do with the quality and texture of your horse's lovely locks, you can do plenty to enhance what's already there, such as:

- **Keeping it clean.** Washing your horse's mane and tail once a month or so with a good shampoo keeps them looking really good and prevents them from getting dirty, sticky, and stringy. Use a gentle shampoo, one made especially for horses.

- **Condition, condition, condition.** If you put a really good made-for-equines conditioner on your horse's mane and tail every time you wash them, your horse will sport some glorious tresses. Buy a premium conditioner, one that moisturizes. Be sure to rinse it all out after you apply it.

- **Brush it out.** Before every ride and after every washing, brush that mane and tail with your horse's body brush to keep snarls from getting out of control. Avoid using a comb or any other implement that can break and pull out the hairs.

- **Wrap it up.** Protect that magnificent hair when your horse is at pasture or in the stable with braids and bags. Large, loose braids in the mane keep the hair from getting dirty and tangled, and keeping a braided tail in a tail bag protects its' hair from knots and mud. Just be sure to undo the braids every three to four days to keep the hair from falling out.

If you want your horse's tail to grow, keep it loosely braided and in a tail bag.

Caring for your horse after his bath

After giving your horse a bath, it's time to dry him off. How fast your horse dries depends on the thickness of his coat, the air temperature, and the humidity. Here's some advice to help you get that 1,000-pound, dripping-wet animal dry in the shortest time and safest manner possible:

>> Whisk away as much excess water on the body as you can by using your sweat scraper. Start at your horse's neck on the left side and scrape in long strokes in the direction the hair grows, working your way across his body. Do the same for the right side of his body. Finish by scraping the front of his chest and his belly.

>> Dry your horse's face with a towel, being careful not to scare him with it. Move slowly and talk to him gently and give him a chance to sniff the towel before you put it on his face.

>> Walk your horse around in the sun, if the weather is hot and sunny, preferably on a hard surface or on grass so dust doesn't stick to his newly washed legs and hooves. If your horse is amenable to going on a hotwalker (a mechanical merry-go-round of sorts), you can put him on one of these contraptions as long as you stay there to supervise.

>> Cover your horse with a cooler or sweat sheet before walking him if the air temperature feels cool to you.

WARNING

Never put your horse back in his stall, paddock, or pasture while he still is soaking wet. Not only is this unhealthy for the horse (he can get a chill if the weather is cold), but all your hard work goes down the drain when he gets down and rolls in the dirt!

PRIVATE PARTS

Like it or not, the private areas of the horse need to be washed on a regular basis. In the wild, the normal course of equine reproduction keeps these areas clean, healthy, and in working order.

When cleaning your mare or gelding's private areas, use a mild soap or a gel product made specifically for that purpose. It's available in tack stores. You also want to have a supply of latex gloves on hand for these kinds of procedures.

If your horse is a mare, your job is relatively easy. All you need to do for her is to clean out the waxy substance that builds up between the teats, located underneath her body between her back legs. Wet the area with warm water and apply shampoo between the teats. Manually remove the wax that builds up there — the latex gloves come in handy for this task. Rinse thoroughly to remove all that soap. Be aware that your mare may not like all this attention and may try to kick out at you. Be cautious until you know how she reacts to this process.

If your horse is a gelding, you need to clean his sheath at least once a year. A lovely little item affectionately known as *the bean* can form from a build-up of secretions in the pocket at the end of the penis and result in irritation and swelling. The bean needs to be removed annually, sometimes more often.

If you've never cleaned your gelding's sheath, we recommend that you have a veterinarian do it the first time. Some geldings react violently to interference in this very delicate area — who can blame them? — and it's best to have a trained professional deal with this situation.

If your vet tells you that your gelding is amenable to having his sheath cleaned, you can try doing it yourself. Start out by putting on a latex glove and covering your hand with a very small amount of soap. Wet the area with warm water and loosen and remove the built-up material inside the sheath. If your horse is very cooperative, he will drop his penis, which enables you to wash that, too.

After you finish cleaning your horse's private parts, rinse the entire area thoroughly with lukewarm water, making sure to remove all the soap. Any residue left on the horse's private parts will irritate him.

Although you can try clean your own gelding's sheath, the truth of the matter is that most geldings are uncooperative when sheath-cleaning time comes and require a sedative before they allow their genitals to be handled. Don't feel that you're cheating if you opt to skip performing this aspect of horse care. It's perfectly reasonable to have your vet do the cleaning each and every time.

Carefully Clipping Your Hairy Equine

You've seen those before-and-after makeover photos, right? Well, the equine equivalent to those images are before-and-after clipping photos. *Clipping* is the practice of shaving a horse's hair, or sections of his hair, so the hair is close to the skin. If you clip a horse that hasn't been clipped in a few months, chances are you won't recognize the beast afterward. And just like in the makeover pictures, the *after* photo looks a whole lot better than the *before* shot.

Clipping is a simple and easy way to make your horse look good. Even a less-than-beautiful horse can be made to look much more handsome with a simple head and leg trim.

Several ways of clipping exist. Basic maintenance clipping involves trimming the head and legs. More extensive clipping is necessary in body clips, where large amounts of hair are removed from the horse's coat to help him cool down quickly after a workout.

The type of clippers you use depends on what you plan to clip. Maintenance clips require nothing more than a good pair of small horse clippers. Body clips, on the other hand, call for heavy-duty equipment: body clippers. (See Chapter 6 for more information on clippers.)

Clipping your horse is a relatively simple chore, provided your horse cooperates. A simple maintenance clip shouldn't take more than 15 or 20 minutes at most. Body clips can take anywhere from half an hour to all day, depending on the extent of the clip.

The scoop on maintenance clipping

To keep your horse looking nice and neat, perform a maintenance clip on him at least twice a month, which means trimming the long hair under the jawline, clipping the excess hair from his ears, and removing the overgrown hair on his fetlocks (ankles). Unless you show your horse in a discipline that forbids it, you may also want to trim your horse's bridle path (the area of the mane just behind the horse's ears, measuring about four inches in length) as part of this routine.

Before you clip your horse, make sure that the clipper blades you're using are sharp and well oiled. Read the instruction manual to learn about setting the clipping depth, and make sure your horse is clean and dry before you clip. Several hours after a bath when the horse's coat is completely dry is a good time to remove hair.

Follow these steps to perform a maintenance clip on your horse. Remember to move the clippers along the hair in the opposite direction that it grows:

1. **Tie your horse securely at a hitching post or at crossties (see Chapter 13).** If you're not sure whether your horse is amenable to clippers, ask someone to hold the lead rope while you do your clipping instead of tying your horse. If your horse is cooperative, you can tie him up next time.

2. **Stand to one side and start clipping your horse's head at the jaw line, lightly trimming hair that extends beyond the horse's jaw line.** Clip up to the level of the jaw, removing that shaggy look. Many horses are frightened of having their heads trimmed. If your horse gets panicky when you try to clip his head, recondition him to tolerate the clippers.

   TIP

   If you have a clipper-phobic horse, try trimming his fetlocks, bridle path, and possibly whiskers with scissors. Most horses afraid of clippers don't mind being trimmed this way.

3. **Trim the whiskers from your horse's muzzle gently, one whisker at a time.** Although a muzzle full of whiskers isn't pretty, some equine experts believe that horses use their whiskers as feelers in the dark. If you prefer that your horse keep his whiskers, simply skip this part of the process. Nevertheless, you need to be sure to leave the long whisker-type hairs around the horse's eyes intact. Experts believe these hairs help keep horses from injuring their eyes on objects in the dark.

4. **Move up to the horse's ears and trim the hair protruding around the edges.** Don't trim the inside of the horse's ears because the horse needs that interior hair to protect the inner ear from insects, dirt, and other intrusions.

5. **Shave a bridle path for your horse, just behind the ears.** The length of the bridle path depends on the discipline in which you ride your horse and/or your horse's breed (see Chapter 14 for discipline details). If you plan to show your

horse, this detail may be important. Talk to other equestrians who ride in your discipline to find out the proper length of bridle path for your horse.

If you aren't showing but just want to create a comfortable landing strip for the top of your horse's headstall so his mane doesn't get tangled in the bridle (the actual purpose of a bridle path) clip back about three inches of mane from behind the ears.

6. **Check the back of your horse's fetlocks to see whether your horse has *ergots*, soft, horny growths at the point of the fetlock joints.** If so, take scissors and cut down the ergots so they're only about half an inch long. (If your horse has particularly tough ergots, you may have to cut them just after a bath when they are damp.)

7. **Trim your horse's fetlocks.** Before you start clipping, use your hand to feel the shape of the bone at your horse's ankle. The object here is to clip short the hair around the anklebone.

8. **Trim the long hair that hangs over the coronet onto the top of the hoof (see Chapter 2 for a diagram indicating the exact location of the coronet).** Clip the hair gently until the line between the top of the hoof and the coronet is straight and void of shaggy hairs.

WARNING

When clipping your horse, don't ever put your head in front of or behind your horse's legs or under his belly. Doing so puts you at risk for getting kicked in the head.

Caring for your clippers

If you take good care of your clippers, they'll take good care of your horse. Follow these rules of clipper care:

>> **Keep your clippers well lubricated.** Buy quality clipper lubricator and lubricate the clippers before, while, and after you use them. You can buy clipper oil at the same place where you got your clippers. Most tack stores carry clipper oil, or you can buy it online.

>> **Use only sharp blades on your clippers.** Ensure that you use blades specifically made for your model, and make sure they're sharp. Take them to a blade sharpening service for maintenance. Places that sharpen scissors and knives often sharpen clipper blades, too. Some tack stores also offer this service.

>> **Don't let your clippers overheat when you are using them.** Check them often while you're clipping. If they get hot, turn them off and let them cool so you don't burn your horse.

>> **Keep your horse from stepping on the clipper cord.** If the cord breaks, the horse can be shocked or electrocuted.

>> **Check the cord and plug regularly.** Make sure that they aren't frayed or broken.

>> **Dismantle and clean your clippers periodically.** Clean all the various parts with a soft rag.

>> **Store your clippers in a dry place.**

The basics of body clipping

One of the banes of the busy horse owner's existence is the equine winter coat. If you live in a cold climate where you don't ride much in the winter, and if your horse is out in a pasture, this wad of fuzzy hair is a blessing to your horse — he needs it to keep warm. However, if you live in a temperate or, worse yet, a mild climate, and if you ride in the wintertime, then that long shaggy coat can be a real pain in the you-know-what.

Here's the dilemma with winter coats: Nature designed this shaggy hair to keep the horse warm in the coldest of winter months. In the wild, this warm fur coat works great. Wild horses do little in the winter besides forage for food and huddle together for warmth. But the domestic horse has a whole other lifestyle. He is usually ridden in the winter and often is kept indoors in a stall, where a thick winter coat is unnecessary.

When a horse in full winter coat is ridden, he sweats profusely, and it's no wonder. Imagine moving furniture all day dressed in a down coat! After the horse's workout, the thick hair is filled with sweat, and it can take hours to dry out. In the meantime, the horse is subject to draft, chill, and ultimately illness, while you, the poor horse's owner, spend half the day desperately trying to get the horse to dry.

Humans have found a way out of this predicament: body clipping. By removing some or all of the horse's body hair in the wintertime, you can avoid having to deal with the time and trouble it takes to properly cool down a hot and hairy horse. And another perk: Clipped horses are easier to keep clean.

WARNING

Of course, body clipping has its downside. In cases where horses receive substantial body clips, you must keep the horse constantly blanketed, which is only logical because body clipping removes the horse's natural means of staying warm in winter. If you choose to clip your horse, you need to make sure your horse wears a blanket in cold weather and that the blanket comes off when the weather heats up. And if you have a particularly hairy horse, you may have to do a body clip more than once during the cold weather season.

Surveying types of body clips

If you plan to ride your horse often in the wintertime, you may want to consider body clipping. Depending on your horse's living conditions, work schedule, and your personal preference, you can choose from several different types of clips, shown in Figure 9-3.

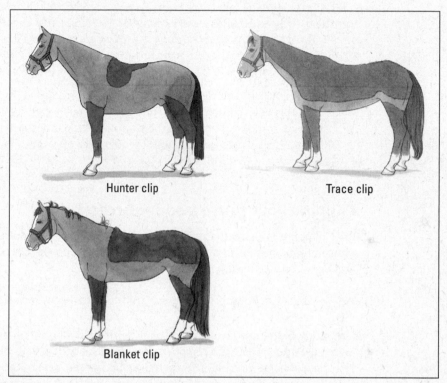

FIGURE 9-3: You can choose from several different types of body clips.

The following list explains the uses of the different clip styles:

>> **Trace clip:** The trace clip is a good choice for horses that live outdoors and do moderate work in the winter. With the trace clip, only the bottom third of the horse's coat is removed. The underside of the neck, belly, and chest are trimmed. With this clip, the horse sweats less during workouts, but still retains enough coat to stay warm outdoors in temperate weather. In cold weather climates, a horse with a trace clip must be blanketed on cold days and every night.

- **Blanket clip:** This clip requires removal of the hair on the horse's head, neck, chest, shoulders, and the lower portion of the abdomen and hindquarters. The blanket clip is good for horses that work hard in the winter but still need some protection from the cold on their legs, back, and hips. Horses with blanket clips must be blanketed on cold days and every night during the winter.

- **Hunter clip:** The hunter clip is helpful to horses that work hard out on the field, such as foxhunters, cross-country event horses, and endurance horses. This clip leaves a patch of hair on the back where the saddle lays and a patch of hair on the legs. The rest of the horse is completely clipped. Horses with hunter clips must be blanketed on cold days and every night in the winter.

- **Full clip:** With the full clip, the entire winter coat is removed from the horse's body. This clip is chosen by many riders who compete with their horses in events year-round or who work them hard. This clip is best used on horses that are stabled indoors. A blanket is required for cold days and every night in the winter.

Clipping your horse's body successfully

Body clipping is an art that takes a bit of practice. You may want to find an experienced horse person to help you show you how to do the clipping the first time around — or to at least get you started, anyway.

Before you start clipping, assemble everything you need to do the job:

- **Body clippers:** If you plan to do a full clip, blanket clip, or hunter clip, you need a good pair of body clippers. (You can usually do a trace clip using regular horse clippers.) If you don't want to invest in a pair of body clippers, you can usually rent them from a local tack and feed store. Make sure the blades are sharp before you begin your task.

- **Clipper lubricant:** To keep your clippers from getting jammed or overheated, keep lubricating them as you clip. You can purchase clipper lubricant at a tack and feed store or online.

- **White chalk:** For any clip other than a full clip, use a piece of white chalk to draw the outline of the clip before you start trimming. You're better off with grooming chalk purchased at a tack and feed store rather than blackboard chalk simply, because grooming chalk draws better on horsehair. (If you have a horse with white body hair, you'll have to go with a different color chalk so that you can see it.)

>> **Towels:** Wipe the oil and hair from your clipper periodically with a towel. You can also use a towel to wipe the hair from yourself. Clipping is messy business, especially on windy days.

>> **Work goggles:** You need goggles to protect your eyes from flying horsehair, if you're clipping on a windy day.

When you're ready to do the actual clipping, keep these pointers in mind:

>> **Wear work clothes.** You'll be covered with horsehair by the time you finish. Consider wearing a windbreaker suit that you can just strip off before you get in your car or go back into your house.

>> **Feed your horse.** Give your horse a hay net filled with hay to occupy him as you clip.

>> **Make sure that your horse is clean and dry before you start clipping.** A dirty coat is nearly impossible to clip.

>> **Lubricate your running clipper blades frequently.** Lubricate before you start trimming and frequently as you go along to keep the clippers cutting smoothly; remove hair fragments with a brush.

>> **Start at the front of your horse and work backward.** Start on one side of the horse first and then work your way to the other side.

>> **Clip against the lay of the hair.**

>> **Hold the clipper so the blades lay flat against the horse.** This keeps you from cutting too deep.

>> **Give your horse frequent breaks.** Clipping not only is tiring for you, but also for the horse. He has to stand still for long periods of time. Consider doing your clipping in segments over two or three days.

>> **Check the temperature of the blades frequently.** If they start to feel hot, let them cool down before you continue.

>> **Sweep up the clipped hair after you finish.** If you're boarding your horse, sweep up as a courtesy to others who use the facilities. If you keep your horse at home, clean the hair up before the wind scatters it around.

If you clip your horse in the early spring, consider leaving some of the hair on the ground. Birds love to use it as nesting material.

GROOMING YOUR HORSE FOR SHOW

If you're planning to show your horse, you may have your work cut out for you in the grooming department, depending on which riding discipline you've chosen (see Chapter 18 for details on competitions). Although some events like reining and cross-country jumping don't call for special grooming, some of the more popular types of showing require that your horse look a certain way.

We're not going to try to explain every aspect of how to groom a show horse for every possible discipline. You can find out this information from your trainer or from your fellow equestrians after you become immersed in the show world. But we can give you some general advice on how to make your horse look good in the ring:

- **A good trim.** All show disciplines have one thing in common, and that's the requirement for a neatly clipped horse. Ears, muzzle, and fetlocks must be properly trimmed. In some breeds, the bridle path (the area of the mane just behind the ears) also needs to be clipped. To find out how to clip these areas, see "The scoop on maintenance clipping" earlier in this chapter.

- **Winning sheen.** No matter what type of showing you plan to do, your horse stands a better chance of winning if his coat is clean and shiny. Bathe your horse a day or so before the show to give his coat time to regain some of its natural oils. On the day of the event, you can apply any number of commercial coat polishing products meant to add sheen to a horse's coat. (Don't apply them to the area where your saddle will go; they make the hair too slippery.)

- **Beautiful braids.** A number of disciplines — including dressage and hunt seat — call for the horse's mane (and sometimes the tail) to be braided. Although we could describe these procedures for you here, we don't think a written description will help you that much. The best way to find out the proper braids for your discipline is to have a trainer or fellow competitor show you how. Don't be shy about asking for help. Everyone has to learn sometime, and most knowledgeable horse people are happy to teach newcomers the braiding ropes.

- **Proper manes and tails.** Some disciplines, such as western pleasure and saddle seat, require trimmed mane and tail styles. Learn the particulars of your discipline and acquire the skills needed to make your horse look like it should for the show ring.

Chapter **10**

Preventing Equine Health Problems

Despite their size and physical strength, horses are actually rather delicate creatures when it comes to their health. When a horse gets sick, life can get difficult for his owner: Bills can add up quickly; a sick horse means time lost in the saddle; and horses are notoriously difficult to medicate. Plus illness causes suffering for the horse. For these reasons and more, horse owners need to work hard at preventing equine illness. Horses require regular preventive care to keep them healthy and able to perform the tasks asked of them.

The Doctor Is In: How a Vet Helps Your Horse

The best way to take care of your horse's health is to find a good veterinarian and work with him or her to establish a preventive care plan for your horse. Although the cost of preventive care may tweak your wallet a bit, anteing up is well worth the money. In return, you'll have a happy, healthy horse who can do whatever you ask, and lower vet bills in the long run.

In the following sections, we cover how to find the right vet for your horse and the procedures that a vet usually handles for keeping a horse healthy.

Understanding horse vets

Like medical doctors, most veterinarians focus their practices on a particular type of medicine. Small animal vets treat dogs and cats; exotics vets treat rabbits and reptiles; bovine vets spend their time treating cattle. Vets who are the most knowledgeable about treating horses are equine veterinarians.

The best choice for your horse's healthcare provider (preventive, regular, and emergency care) is an equine veterinarian, meaning a vet who *specializes* in horses. Equine veterinarians are specially trained to diagnose and treat equine illnesses, and they have more knowledge of horse issues than their small-animal counterparts. In most cases, equine veterinarians treat only horses, which means their knowledge of the species is quite vast.

Some rural areas do not have vets who treat only horses. These so-called "farm vets" treat a variety of livestock and pets. If you can't find a vet in your area who deals exclusively with horses, make sure that the vet you choose has at least moderate experience in equine medicine.

Searching for a vet

One of the most important things you can do for your horse's health is to find a good equine veterinarian. Just like human doctors, veterinarians vary in skill, knowledge, dedication, and bedside manner. Finding a horse doctor who can provide you with these elements ensures that both you and your horse feel well taken care of.

WARNING

Choose a veterinarian *before* you find yourself in an emergency situation. A vet already familiar with your horse can be a huge plus during an emergency. If you're a regular client, your request for an emergency barn call receives priority treatment over a similar request from a non-regular client.

Start your search for a vet the moment you realize you're adding a horse to your family. The timing may be after you have purchased your horse but before you bring him home.

Locating a good equine veterinarian usually takes a bit of research. Don't settle for the first name you see in the phonebook or use the vet your next-door neighbor is using without doing some investigation first.

Follow these steps to finding a vet who really knows equine stuff:

1. **Get referrals.** Unlike cat and dog owners, horse owners religiously share veterinary information with each other — and that includes opinions on local vets. You can easily identify the veterinarians in your area who have the best reputations among horse owners just by listening to conversations around the stable or in your riding group concerning vets. You can even go so far as to ask your fellow horse owners which vets they prefer. Make note of the names you hear time and again in a positive light, and put them on the top of your list.

   If horse owners are few and far between where you live — or if equine veterinarians are scarce — search online for horse vets in your area, and check out their reviews.

2. **Ask questions.** After you're armed with a couple of names of equine veterinarians, call or email each one to get more information. Because most equine vets have limited or nonexistent office staff, you may be posing your questions directly to the actual veterinarian. Find out whether more than one doctor works in the practice and whether the vet or vets are available 24 hours a day for emergencies. (The answer should be "yes.") Also, ask about the qualifications of the doctors in the practice. Look for a specialization in equine medicine and several years of experience. Make certain the vet provides routine care for horses, and doesn't just specialize in one area of equine health.

3. **Meet the vet.** Based on what you hear from other horse owners and over the phone or by email from the veterinarian or practice staff, decide which vet or practice is your first choice. Then schedule an appointment for your horse's next inoculation or deworming. When the vet comes out to see your horse, talk to him or her and try to get a feeling for the vet's bedside manner. Pay close attention to the way the vet behaves with your horse. The vet should answer all your questions in a clear and understandable fashion. You're looking for someone who feels comfortable around horses and who knows how to handle them.

   At this point in the process, you can pretty much go on gut instinct. If you like and feel comfortable with the vet, make him or her your permanent vet. If not, call the vet who came in second on your list and perform the same evaluation.

TIP

If you already went through an evaluation process when choosing a veterinarian who performed the pre-purchase exam on your horse and were happy with the service you received, consider this individual as your horse's regular vet. See Chapter 5 for more about pre-purchase exams.

Taking a shot at vaccinations

A number of dangerous infectious diseases plague the horse world, but the good news is that vaccines exist for many of them. To keep your horse in his optimal state of health, you need to commit to a regular vaccination program, developed with your veterinarian, to protect your horse from serious illness.

Although a host of other vaccines exist, the four that follow represent the absolute minimum your horse needs.

>> **Influenza/rhinopneumonitis:** These two respiratory illnesses strike with the same kind of regularity as human flu viruses and with similar symptoms. Your veterinarian may recommend that your horse be inoculated with flu/rhino vaccine as frequently as every three months, or only twice per year if the horse is at minimal risk of exposure, meaning he isn't exposed to many other horses.

>> **Equine encephalomyelitis:** Three strains of the same encephalomyelitis illnesses — Western equine encephalomyelitis (WEE), Eastern equine encephalomyelitis (EEE), and Venezuelan equine encephalomyelitis (VEE) — can infect horses through mosquito bites. Encephalomyelitis attacks the central nervous system and can cause severe neurological symptoms and even death. Your veterinarian can recommend inoculation against one or more of these diseases at least once per year.

>> **Rabies:** Although it's not common, horses can contract rabies if they are bitten by an animal that has the infection. The virus shows itself in horses most often as lameness in one leg that spreads to other legs. The horse can also appear dull and stagger when he walks. No cure exists, and death may follow. An infected horse can also spread the disease to humans through a bite. Your veterinarian can administer an effective equine-specific vaccine for rabies as part of your horse's annual vaccines.

>> **Tetanus:** Tetanus isn't contagious but can be contracted through open wounds. This bacterial disease can result in serious neurological symptoms, such as extreme sensitivity to touch and spasm of the neck and jaw muscles, and ultimately death in many cases. Because horses are particularly susceptible to tetanus, veterinarians recommend an inoculation of tetanus toxoid for your horse at least once per year.

>> **West Nile virus:** The insidious West Nile virus has now spread across the United States and Canada, threatening the lives of thousands of horses. Humans, birds, and equines are the only creatures seriously affected by the disease, which is spread by mosquitoes and attacks the nervous system. Horses that contract West Nile virus can become permanently damaged, and death often results. Vaccinating your horse once or twice per year (depending on which vaccine your vet uses) is vital to protect him from this terrible disease.

Reputable boarding stables require that all horses on the property be kept up-to-date on inoculations against contagious diseases. If your horse is boarded, maintaining a consistent schedule of inoculations is imperative.

Getting the bugs out with deworming

Horses, like most other animals, are quite susceptible to a number of internal parasites. These parasites, more commonly known as worms, can cause serious damage to your horse's internal organs. When left uncontrolled, they can result in chronic colic (stomach pain) and even death.

Approximately 150 different species of internal parasites can infect the horse. Don't worry. We won't bore you with all 150, but the more common ones include strongyles, roundworms, pinworms, and bots.

Although keeping worms from infecting your horse is nearly impossible, you can control their numbers. Regular deworming with a chemical agent that is safe for horses kills parasites in their various stages of growth and is a necessary part of your horse's preventive care. Another option is having your horse's manure tested regularly for worms before deworming. Discuss your horse's deworming needs with your vet so the two of you can come up with an effective program.

Several over-the-counter dewormers are available to horse owners at feed stores and can be used on a regular basis under your vet's supervision. You can also ask your veterinarian to deworm your horse for you and or recommend a dewormer rotating schedule to ensure the parasites in your horse's gut don't develop a resistance to any one product.

Keeping track of teeth

Your own dentist probably preaches the importance of brushing, flossing, and maintaining your choppers. Horses depend on their teeth just as much, if not more than humans. Because the food they eat is so difficult to chew and digest (try downing a sprig of hay sometime and you'll see what we mean), maintaining your horse's healthy teeth is vitally important.

To combat the normal wear that occurs from chewing such tough, fibrous foods, nature has equipped the horse with teeth that slowly erupt from the gum as the top layer wears off. However, the horse's upper jaw is wider than his lower jaw, so the upper outside teeth and lower inside teeth have nothing to wear against as they erupt, and ridges and sharp points result. These ridges and points restrict the horse's normal side-to-side rotary chewing motion, resulting in poor and painful chewing and the dropping of food. Horses with this condition tend to chew up and down instead of side to side, making horses with neglected teeth prone to problems like choking and colic. These sharp points also hurt the horse when the noseband is tightened and when the bit hits the horse's teeth.

REMEMBER

To keep sharp points from interfering with your horse's ability to chew and subsequently digest his food, have your veterinarian file down those pointy teeth as often as once or twice a year, depending on how fast they grow. Called *floating,* this procedure is an absolute must in preventive care.

Have your veterinarian examine your horse's teeth at least twice a year to determine when his teeth need floating. During these exams, the vet can also spot other dental problems that may be developing, such as infected teeth or abnormal wear.

If the Shoe Fits: The Work of a Farrier

Nearly as important as finding a veterinarian for your horse is finding a skilled and qualified *farrier,* a specialist in trimming and shoeing your horse's hooves. Choose your farrier wisely: The health of your horse's hooves and legs depends on it.

REMEMBER

Whether to shoe your horse or allow him to go barefoot is a choice you can make along with your veterinarian. Some horses have tough feet that don't require the protection of shoes. If you choose not to put shoes on your horse, you still need a farrier to trim your horse's hooves every four to eight weeks, depending how fast they grow.

In the following sections, we discuss the selection of a farrier and the health-care tasks usually assigned to a farrier.

Finding a farrier

The best way to locate a good farrier is through a referral, and the first person to ask for a referral is your vet. Most equine vets are well acquainted with the farriers in their area and can recommend one or two good ones.

You can ask other horse owners for referrals as well. If you go this route, be sure to take a consensus and see which farriers get the most thumbs up. Don't base your decision on the comments of only one owner — you want to get a feeling for which farriers are able to successfully handle horses with different hoof care needs.

Before you settle on a farrier, find out where the person was educated and how long she has been in business. You want to select a farrier who has a strong background in the trade, through both education and hands-on experience. Pick someone you're comfortable with who seems willing to discuss your horse's needs in a friendly and articulate manner. Find out whether this person is available if your horse needs corrective shoeing to fix a leg problem, or if your horse loses a shoe. If you opt to keep your horse barefoot, make sure your farrier is comfortable with that concept.

After you have chosen a farrier, monitor his work closely. Does the farrier come when he is supposed to, or do your horse's feet go weeks overdue because the farrier doesn't show up on a regular basis? Does your farrier trim or shoe your horse too frequently, just to pad his pockets? Most horses need shoes and/or trimming every four to eight weeks. If your farrier wants to work on your horse more often than this, ask him for a detailed explanation as to why.

Consider how your horse feels after being shod. Is he "ouchy," walking gingerly after a trim, or stumbling a lot after he gets his new shoes? Does he become lame often (start limping), with a diagnosis related to poor trimming or shoeing? If so, your farrier isn't doing a good job.

If your horse is having trouble with his hooves or legs, consider the job your farrier is doing, and talk to your vet about the possible causes. A farrier can make or break a horse's soundness (ability to move without pain).

Caring for a horse's hooves

If you want your horse to do more than just look good, you have to take care of his feet. A horse with poorly treated feet can be plagued with chronic lameness and may eventually end up unrideable. Regular trimming and/or shoeing by a qualified farrier are keys to good hoof care.

Trimming

Horses' hooves are always growing, just like human fingernails. For your horse to stay sound, his feet must be kept neatly trimmed at an angle parallel to the slope of his *pastern* (ankle). No one is better qualified to perform this trimming accurately than a professional farrier.

Each horse's feet grow at a different pace, so the frequency between trimmings varies from horse to horse. The time range for most trims can be anywhere from four to eight weeks. No horse should ever go longer than eight weeks without a trim.

Shoeing

The vast majority of horses ridden for pleasure and show wear metal shoes for protection. Shoes guard a horse's hoof from cracking and splitting, two problems that can result with normal riding, especially in horses that don't have particularly hard hooves.

If your vet believes your horse needs shoes, consider this option. Depending on the strength of your horse's hooves and what you're using him for, you can opt to have your horse shod on all four feet or on just the front hooves where the majority of pressure exists during exercise. (Your vet can advise you on this issue.)

REMEMBER

If you ride your horse lightly or he has very tough hooves, he probably doesn't even need shoes. In addition, horses that spend all their time at pasture rarely need shoes. Because each individual horse is different, discuss your particular shoeing needs with your veterinarian and your farrier.

WARNING

Every now and then, one of your horse's shoes may fall off. In other words, the horse throws a shoe. Never ride your horse with a shoe missing from his hoof. Doing so can result in damage to the bare hoof and possibly to the other legs. If you're riding when the shoe comes off, dismount, retrieve the shoe, walk your horse back to the stable, and call your farrier to have it nailed back on. You can also keep an item known as a *hoof boot* with you when you ride, and use this as a substitute for a shoe until you make it back to the barn. If you find your horse in his stall with a shoe missing, skip riding until the farrier replaces the shoe.

In Control: Understanding Your Role in Preventive Care

In addition to having a good veterinarian and farrier, two other factors play a large part in determining the general well-being of your horse: food and exercise. You can have the best veterinarian and farrier in the world, but if you don't feed and exercise your horse properly, you won't have a healthy horse.

Feeding time

The quality of the feed you provide, the frequency with which you feed it, and the feed's consistency are big factors in your horse's health:

>> **Quality:** Good feed is vitally important when it comes to your horse's general well-being. Poor hay or pasture lacks nutrients and may cause vitamin and mineral deficiencies. Moldy or diseased hay can make your horse sick. Don't scrimp on your horse's feed. Buying poor quality hay, or grazing your horse on poor pasture just to save a few bucks will come back to haunt you in the form of poor health for your horse. (See Chapter 8 for details on determining the quality of hay.)

>> **Frequency:** Horses evolved as grazing animals, and so they need to eat often. Their digestive systems can't tolerate long periods of time without eating. If you force your horse to go too long between meals, you're asking for trouble in the form of gastric ulcers, colic and other problems. Feed your horse at least twice a day at regular times, with three times a day the ideal. Or, supplement your horse's regular feedings with low-calorie grass hay to keep him occupied. Even better: Keep your horse in a pasture that provides access to quality grass at all times.

>> **Consistency:** Any sudden change in feed can cause considerable disruption and even serious illness to your horse and his digestive system. If you want to change your horse's feed from one type to another, do so gradually over a period of at least two weeks. The same goes for changing the amount of feed you're giving your horse. If you want to increase the amount, do so gradually during a week or two.

Getting exercise

Nature designed horses to be on the go all the time. Wild horses walk constantly as they graze, and stand still only for a few hours a day to sleep. Contrast this reality with the life of a typical stabled horse, who spends most of his time standing around and moving only a few hours a day! The result of this sedentary life can be a host of leg and digestive problems for your horse.

In the same way your own doctor has espoused the importance of getting your rump off the couch and exercising, the same goes for your horse. If you keep your horse in a stable, you need to make special efforts to keep his body in good working order. Provide a minimum of 30 minutes of exercise a day to increase circulation, loosen muscles, and provide mental stimulation. Be sure to warm up and cool down with at least 10 minutes of walking before and after a workout to help your horse's body stay healthy. (See Chapter 8 for more about daily exercise.)

Exercise is not only necessary for your horse's physical well-being but also for his mental health. If you spent most of your time standing around inside a box with nothing to do, you'd get pretty bored. Horses are no different, and need time and exercise outside their stalls to keep from developing neurotic habits (known as stable vices; see Chapter 2) and other assorted misbehaviors.

If your horse lives in a pasture and can graze at will, the need for structured exercise is less important than for a stabled horse.

Coping with weather

Horses can withstand all kinds of weather under the right conditions. As a horse owner, it's important that you provide your horse what he needs to handle the climate in your part of the world.

>> **Hot and humid:** If you live in an area where summers are hot and humid, be sure to provide your horse with plenty of a shade and fresh water, and limit his exercise to the cooler part of the day. Horses can become overheated in hot and humid weather when they exert themselves. Horses sweat to cool themselves, and humidity makes it difficult for the sweat to evaporate from the horse's skin, which can cause his body temperatures to rise to dangerous levels.

If you have a barn on your property, you can help your horse cope with the heat by setting up large fans indoors and bringing him in during the heat of the day. He can go back outside in the evening when the weather has cooled down. Be sure to keep his drinking water cool by changing it frequently and keeping it in the shade. Horses don't like hot water, and if your horse doesn't drink enough, he can become dehydrated or develop colic.

>> **Hot and dry:** Horses seem to tolerate hot and dry climates better than humid conditions. As long as your horse has shade and cool, fresh water, he should be able to handle desert-type summers. On super hot days, wait until evening to exercise your horse. Both you and your horse will function better once the temperature drops. If you do a lot of riding in the heat, talk to your vet about the possibility of adding electrolytes to your horse's regimen.

>> **Rain:** Your horse should have a place where he can shelter to get out of the rain. That said, many horses will stand in the rain instead of going indoors. Your horse should have a choice, however, especially if downpours are common where you live. Most horses don't like to be pelted with pouring rain. If your horse is out in a pasture, you may want to consider providing him with a waterproof blanket to help him stay dry.

>> **Hail:** Some areas are prone to hail storms, which can actually be dangerous to horses if the hailstones are big enough. Make sure your horse has a shelter where he can go if hail starts to come down.

» **Snow:** Horses can do fine in snowy weather with the right care. If your horse is out in a pasture, make sure he has a three-sided shelter. It will not only keep out the snow but will also provide your horse with a shield against the wind. Keep an eye on his hooves, too. Ice and snow can become impacted in your horse's feet and cause discomfort. Ask your farrier about fitting your horse with snow pads to prevent snow and ice from balling up in the hoof.

» **Cold:** Most horses can tolerate temperatures around freezing without much help thanks to the winter coats they start growing in early fall. Very frigid temperatures below 0 degrees Fahrenheit (–18 degrees Celsius) are another story. Hypothermia and frostbite are real possibilities if a horse doesn't have proper care in frigid weather. If you live in a place where winters bring very cold temperatures, you'll need to provide your horse with some help to get through the season. Indoor housing in a barn is a must in this kind of weather, along with an insulated horse blanket or two. Provide your horse with extra food in cold weather; he will be burning a lot of calories trying to keep warm. You'll also need to keep his drinking water from freezing. Water heaters made for buckets and troughs are mandatory when the temperature dips below freezing.

Chapter **11**

Examining and Treating Equine Health Troubles

People who spend significant amounts of time around horses often wonder about the sanity of the guy who coined the phrase, "Healthy as a horse." Horses are notorious for getting sick. Whether a self-inflicted injury, a bout with colic that requires surgery, or simply the arthritis that comes with old age, some horses seem to require more veterinary attention than do cats or dogs. In fact, a vet has to treat the average horse about twice a year — not including preventative care.

Okay, now we've scared you. But really, you don't need to panic. The majority of vet calls are for fairly common problems that the vet resolves with short-term treatment — as long as you address the problem right away.

In this chapter, we show you some of the more common ailments and conditions that can afflict your equine friend during his lifetime. Armed with this knowledge, you'll be able to recognize early symptoms of these ailments and get help for your horse in a timely manner.

Tracking Symptoms (and Recognizing an Emergency)

Not every equine ailment requires a frantic phone call to the nearest veterinarian. You can deal with some problems at home, or at least monitor them *before* making that call.

Taking temperature

If your horse ever appears sick, you need to take his temperature before you call the veterinarian. Taking your horse's temperature isn't the most fun part of owning a horse, but you still need to know how to do it. The horse's temperature helps the vet decide whether the situation is an emergency or can wait until later, or the next day.

TIP

Before you can take your horse's temperature, you need to purchase a veterinary thermometer from a pet supply, tack or online store, or you can simply buy a human rectal thermometer. (Most thermometers are digital these days.) Veterinary thermometers are better because they have a loop at the end; you can tie some string or yarn onto the device, making it easier to hold onto while taking the horse's temperature. You need lubricant, too. K-Y Jelly or another human-grade lubricant is sufficient. Stay away from petroleum jelly because it can irritate the sensitive lining of the rectum. In a pinch, you can use your own saliva as a lubricant.

Here's how you actually do the deed:

1. **Prepare the thermometer.** If your thermometer is the old-fashioned mercury type, shake it down so it reads 96 degrees F (35.5 degrees C) or below. If the thermometer is digital, simply turn it on.

2. **Lubricate the thermometer.** Apply a good amount of lubricant to the thermometer's tip so it slides in easily.

3. **Prepare your horse.** Some horses are very calm when you take their temperature; others freak out. If you have the kind of horse that doesn't appreciate the procedure, ask someone to hold the horse's head before you insert the thermometer and position the horse against a wall so he can't move away from you. Be patient and try to reassure the horse that nothing terrible is about to happen to him.

4. **Insert the thermometer.** Stand to the side of and not directly behind the horse to avoid being kicked. Hold the thermometer at an angle parallel to the horse's back, lift the tail, and slowly insert the thermometer about 3 inches into

the horse's rectum. The thermometer should slide in gently. If the thermometer stops part way in and won't move forward, do not force it. Instead, pull it out and reinsert again, angling it slightly up or down until it gently slides in.

5. **Wait three minutes.** Keep the thermometer inside the horse's rectum for three minutes, holding onto the end or the string the entire time.

6. **Read the thermometer.** After three minutes (or when the thermometer beeps), you can remove the thermometer and read it. Normal adult equine body temperature ranges from 99–101 degrees F (37–38 degrees C). Foals are 100–102 degrees F (37.5–39 degrees C). If your horse's temperature is above or below normal, call a veterinarian immediately.

Looking for signs of trouble

Here are physical signs to look for when your horse seems under the weather. If your horse has one or more of these symptoms, the condition is an emergency that warrants a call to and a possible visit from the vet:

>> **Bleeding:** If your horse is bleeding heavily from any place on his body, try applying pressure with a towel or cloth to stop the flow. Even if you can stop the bleeding, call the vet. (See "Taking Care of Horse Wounds" later in this chapter for details on how to control bleeding.)

>> **Blood in urine:** If you see your horse urinating blood, a severe infection or bladder injury is a possibility.

>> **Choking:** A horse is choking if he coughs and salivates with his head down while watery food exits his nose and mouth, backs away from his food, acts anxious, and/or swallows repeatedly. (The horse can still breathe when this is happening, so don't panic.)

>> **Colic:** If your horse is sweating profusely, lying down and getting up, pawing the ground, standing with his legs outstretched, rolling, and/or biting or kicking at his abdomen, he's suffering from colic. Remove his food and lead him around at a walk until the vet arrives. We cover colic in detail later in this chapter.

Not all colic symptoms are severe. If you see your horse behaving in any way that indicates he may be having even slight stomach pain, you still need to call a veterinarian.

TIP

If you see signs of colic but aren't sure whether your horse is actually sick, a good way to tell is to offer him a carrot. No healthy horse *ever* turns down a carrot. If your horse refuses it, he's suffering from abdominal distress or some other health problem and needs to see a vet right away.

>> **Diarrhea:** Severe, very liquid, foul-smelling diarrhea can be life-threatening.

>> **Inability to stand:** A horse that cannot or will not stand up is a very sick horse. A horse that staggers or has trouble staying on his feet also is in an emergency situation.

>> **Injury:** Wounds that are deep or that expose the bone are emergencies, and so are puncture wounds, which can easily become infected. You also need to contact your vet if a less serious injury that doesn't require sutures begins to appear infected.

>> **Labored breathing:** Rapid breathing, raspy breath, or heavy coughing can be life threatening for a horse.

>> **Painful eye:** Call the vet if one or both of your horse's eyes suddenly becomes teary, the horse holds the lids partially or completely closed, the white part of the eye is red, the eye is sensitive to light, or the surface of the eye is cloudy. We cover eye problems in more detail later in this chapter.

>> **Refusal to eat:** When a horse won't eat, you're often seeing a sign of serious illness or possibly mild colic.

>> **Severe pain:** A veterinarian needs to immediately examine any horse that appears to have severe pain in any part of his body, including any of his legs.

>> **Straining:** If your horse is straining to defecate or urinate and nothing or very little passes out, an intestinal or urethral blockage is likely.

>> **Swelling:** Whenever any part of the horse's body is swollen and hot to the touch, call the vet.

Understanding Common Health Problems

Although horses are susceptible to a wide variety of ailments, the same handful of problems routinely crop up. Some of these illnesses have the potential to be serious, while others are simply annoyances to the horse and the human. In each situation, prompt treatment by a veterinarian is important to keep the problem from getting out of hand.

This section outlines the most common equine health problems, along with their symptoms, usual treatments, and general prognoses. Your veterinarian can give you even more information — specific to your individual horse — on any one of these conditions.

Cancer

Fortunately, horses don't often get cancer. But when they do, the prognosis can be poor, depending on where the cancer is located.

Horses can get any number of cancers, including the ones that affect the skin and lymphatic systems. Diagnosis calls for a biopsy in the case of lumps or tumors that appear, usually on the eye, skin, or genital area. Some cancers are harder to diagnose because symptoms are vague. Horses that aren't thriving and don't respond to traditional treatments may be suffering from cancer, which can include tumors on the internal organs.

Treatment for cancer includes surgery to remove the growth, radiation treatment, chemotherapy, cryosurgery (freezing off the tumor, in the case of skin cancer), immunotherapy (support for the immune system), and laser therapy.

The only type of cancer that can sometimes be prevented is skin cancer. Cancerous areas on light-skinned horses may be avoided by keeping these fair-complexioned equines out of the sun. (See the sections "Melanomas" and "Squamous Cell Carcinoma" later in this chapter for specific information on skin cancer.)

Colic

Colic is actually a symptom, not a disease. The term *colic* refers to abdominal pain, which can have any number of sources. Because horses are designed to be grazers, they're meant to ingest plant material at a slow and constant rate. The equine digestive system often is upset when humans confine horses and give them concentrated feeds.

REMEMBER

Colic is a rather common problem among horses. It can be serious or it can be mild, but it's *always* a cause for concern and *always* warrants a call to the vet.

Horses suffering from colic usually are in a great deal of pain. They express their discomfort by doing some or all of the following:

>> Biting at the flanks or abdomen

>> Kicking at the belly

>> Lying down

>> Pacing

>> Pawing

>> Rolling

>> Standing with legs stretched out

>> Straining

>> Sweating profusely

>> Swishing the tail violently

These bouts of pain often come in waves, so the horse may seem all right one minute but frantic the next. The pain also can start out mild and get progressively worse, or simply remain mild.

REMEMBER

If you suspect that your horse has colic, call a veterinarian immediately. Take away the horse's food and walk him while you wait for the vet to arrive. Get a read on your horse's temperature so you can provide that information to the vet before he or she arrives. (See "Taking temperature" earlier in this chapter.)

WARNING

If a well meaning trainer or other horse person offers to give your colicking horse an injection of painkiller, politely decline. Your veterinarian needs to be the one to determine the course of action for your horse's particular case. A layperson, however good his or her intentions, should not be treating your horse's pain without knowing exactly what is causing the colic.

Colic classifications

Colic has two classifications: medical or surgical. Here's a look at each and the problems that usually cause them.

>> **Medical colic:** Colics that can be fixed with simple medical treatment — usually without having to transport the horse to a hospital — are considered medical colics. Medical colics are the most common classification of colic and usually are caused by gas or *impactions* (blockages). Each of these causes has its own symptoms and treatments:

- *Gas colic:* This type of colic is the result of gas that has built up inside the large intestine. Consumption of spoiled food is one common cause of gas colic, and so is eating too much of a new food. The horse's digestive system becomes dominated with gas-producing organisms, resulting in excessive gas.

   Gas colic usually isn't life threatening, but it is extremely painful and requires immediate veterinary attention. Your vet may give your horse a pain reliever and monitor him to determine if further treatment is required.

- *Impaction colic:* This colic is caused by an impaction in the large intestine. Any number of things can cause an impaction in the intestine, but lack of sufficient water intake often is to blame, resulting in manure that is dry, hard, and difficult to pass. Horses with teeth problems often develop impaction colic caused by their inability to properly chew their food. The ingestion of sand — which can happen when horses eat hay directly off the ground, graze at pasture, or deliberately eat sand in a turn-out arena — and dehydration also can cause impaction colic. Veterinarians typically treat impaction colic with pain relievers and oral administration of oil that works as a laxative. The goal is to get the horse to pass the impacted manure.

>> **Surgical colic:** Surgical colic refers to a colic that requires surgery for repair. This type of colic can be caused by a number of issues, including impactions, enteroliths (stones that form in the intestines), and other conditions that can cause parts of the intestine to die off. In most cases of surgical colic, the horse will die without the surgery.

Colic prevention

The good news about colic is that in many cases, it is preventable. Follow these guidelines to keep your horse's digestive system working properly:

>> **Feed often:** Feeding your horse as frequently as possible is a good way to ward off colic. The equine digestive system seems to function best when it's constantly working to digest fibrous foods. Keep your horse at pasture whenever possible, or if he's stabled, try giving him three meals a day. Two is the absolute minimum. See Chapter 8 for more info about feeding your horse.

>> **Feed hay:** Veterinarians have discovered that fibrous particles inside the intestine tend to stimulate the horse's gut and therefore reduce the incidence of colic. Give your horse a diet that includes hay to ensure he gets plenty of fiber. However, avoid feeding the hay off the ground, so the horse doesn't ingest sand particles that can cause colic.

>> **Provide high-quality feed:** When you feed your horse, give him only the highest quality hay. Don't try to save a buck by purchasing cheaper (and therefore lower-quality) feed. Avoid hay that contains mold, weeds, and other contaminants, such as dirt.

>> **Provide plenty of water:** Another way to prevent colic is to ensure that your horse has access to plenty of fresh drinking water. Be sure to keep waterers and troughs clean. In the wintertime, be certain that the horse's water supply hasn't frozen over. A water heater is a good investment for horse owners who live in frigid climates.

TIP

Keeping your water in liquid form isn't the only service a water heater can provide; it can also keep the water at a comfortable temperature. Horses are less likely to drink water that is extremely cold, so keeping water lukewarm even in winter encourages your horse to drink.

If you live in a hot climate, be sure your horse's water stays cool in the summer. Horses are reluctant to drink hot water. Add cool water to troughs frequently, and bury water lines so they aren't exposed to direct sun. Check out Chapter 8 for details on watering your horse.

>> **Use electrolytes:** In any situation where your horse may not be drinking enough water (like on cold winter days) or may be losing a good deal of body fluids and salts (during the hot summer or when exercising heavily), supplement his feed with an electrolyte mixture. Electrolytes increase the salt level in the horse's body, thus stimulating his thirst. Several commercial electrolyte products for horses are available through tack and feed stores; you can mix them with the horse's grain or administer them directly into the mouth in paste form.

WARNING

Although some manufacturers' labeling on electrolyte products suggests adding the product to the horse's water, we don't recommend that you do because the taste can discourage the animal from drinking.

>> **Provide exercise:** Regular exercise is another way to help prevent colic, because it stimulates gut motility. Given this fact, your horse needs to receive some kind of exercise daily — especially if your horse is stabled. Even if you have time for only a half-hour walk around the property, the exercise helps keep your horse's digestive system in working order. Flip to Chapter 8 for more info about regular exercise.

>> **Warm up and cool down:** When you ride your horse, be sure to make time for gradual warm-ups and cool downs before and after exercise. Don't work your horse hard without at least a 10-minute walk/trot warm-up first, and be sure to finish up your ride with at least 10 minutes of walking.

Be certain that your horse is completely cooled down before you let him have anything to eat or drink. Eating or drinking immediately after strenuous exercise can bring on a bout of colic.

>> **Care for those teeth:** Horses that have problems chewing don't properly masticate their food before swallowing it, making them more susceptible to impaction colic. Have a vet check your horse's teeth at least twice a year to determine whether they are healthy. (See Chapter 10 for details on tooth care.)

Choke

The term "choke" is slang for *esophageal obstruction.* When a horse "chokes," it's not as bad as it sounds. Unlike a choking human, a horse can still breathe.

A horse chokes when food is trapped in the esophagus. The food doesn't block the airway, so the horse can still get air, but you should still call the vet right away. The trapped food can cause damage that will result in scarring and subsequent narrowing of the diameter of the esophagus. This narrowing causes the horse to be more prone to choking in the future.

You can tell your horse is choking if food particles mixed with saliva are coming out of his nose or mouth. The horse may also act depressed and show difficulty swallowing. He may stretch his neck out, cough, rock back, paw, and get very agitated.

Depending on what caused the obstruction and how bad it is, the horse may be able to cough it out. If the horse relaxes, the obstruction may soften, and the normal movement of the esophagus will send the food down to the stomach. This typically happens within the first 30 to 60 minutes. That said, don't wait to call the vet if you horse is choking. A blockage in the esophagus can cause a horse to become dehydrated. The horse may also aspirate food or other material into the lungs, which can cause pneumonia. In severe cases, the esophagus can rupture. This is why it's vital to call the vet as soon as you suspect your horse has a blockage.

Your vet has a few options for treating the problem. The first is to give your horse intravenous pain medications, anti-inflammatories, antibiotics, and heavy sedation. Next, your vet will insert a flexible plastic tube through your horse's nostril to help coax the blockage down into the stomach. Lubricant and water may be inserted through the tube to help move the blockage along the esophagus.

Once the blockage is cleared, the horse has to eat soft, moist food for a period of time to allow the esophagus to heal. Some horses that experience choke become susceptible to having it happen again if this special diet isn't followed.

TIP

You can prevent choke by making sure that hard food pellets or dried feeds, like beet pulp, are thoroughly soaked and softened before you feed them. If your horse has a tendency to gulp down his hay, use a hay net or a slow feeder to restrict him to smaller bites. Also, make sure he always has access to fresh water while eating.

Equine infectious anemia (EIA)

A nasty, contagious disease among horses is equine infectious anemia (EIA). Horses with an acute case of EIA have a high fever and are lethargic, depressed, and anemic. They often develop thrombocytopenia (lack of blood platelets), which causes hemorrhages to occur on the gums and elsewhere. They may also exhibit stocking-up (swelling) of the lower legs and along the bottom of the abdomen.

The signs of EIA develop 7 to 30 days after exposure to the virus. Horses can die from EIA or become chronic carriers of the disease. Infected horses will have an intermittent fever, weight loss, and hind limb incoordination.

Equine infectious anemia is caused by a virus that is spread between horses via biting horseflies. It can also be spread by using needles, dental floats, and other contaminated equipment between horses.

The best test for EIA is something called the Coggins test. Because EIA is so serious and must be reported by law to state health authorities, blood for the Coggins test must be drawn by a licensed and accredited veterinarian. The sample is then submitted to a state-approved lab.

If a horse tests positive for EIA, he must be euthanized or quarantined for life because there is no treatment this disease, and infection is permanent. The infected horse must be kept a minimum of 200 yards from any other equine. The virus only lives for 15 to 30 minutes in the horsefly, so keeping horses this far apart means the virus usually dies before the infected fly can travel to get another blood meal.

Once a horse is deemed positive for EIA, most states also require an obvious brand on the animal. Check with your veterinarian to find out your state's requirements for frequency of the Coggins test.

Before transporting your horse across state lines, check out the health requirements for transporting. All large horse show and competitive venues require a current Coggins test prior to competition.

TIP

To help protect your horse from EIA, be sure you only board your horse at a facility that is vigilant about requiring proof of negative EIA status for all horses. Never use any needle or syringe more than once, and be diligent that equine professionals clean all instruments before using them on your horse. Also, make certain you know the EIA status of any horse you purchase.

Equine influenza and rhinopneumonitis

People aren't the only ones who get the flu. Horses have their own versions of the virus, known as equine influenza and *rhinopneumonitis* (the latter caused by the equine herpes virus). Like the human version of the flu, these viruses spread across the country every fall and winter. They're just as contagious as the human version of the virus (not to humans, however!) and result in a respiratory infection that attacks the upper and lower respiratory tracts of the horses it affects.

Although equine influenza and rhinopneumonitis are two different viruses, they both cause the same symptoms, and veterinarians handle the two infections identically. If your horse has a mild case, he may just have a runny nose and seem a bit lethargic for a few days. If his case is moderate to serious, he runs a high fever, has runny eyes and nose, is coughing, and appears stiff. He may also lose his appetite. Your vet will provide supportive care in the form of fever reducers if your horse has an above-normal temperature and may prescribe an antibiotic if a secondary bacterial infection is present.

You can reduce your horse's chances of contracting equine influenza or rhino-pneumonitis in two ways:

>> **Vaccinate:** The same as with the human flu vaccine, the equine version is not foolproof. However, it can go a long way toward keeping your horse from contracting the diseases. The number of times per year you need to vaccinate your horse depends on how much exposure he receives to other horses. Follow your veterinarian's recommendations regarding the frequency of flu/rhino vaccine. Check out Chapter 10 for more about vaccinations.

>> **Practice equine hygiene:** During flu/rhino season, which usually is in the fall and winter, try to minimize your horse's contact with other horses that may be carrying the virus. Don't allow him to sniff muzzles or drink from the same trough as other horses, even those who appear healthy, because horses can shed the virus before showing any symptoms of the disease. If you board your horse, make sure that the stable management requires all boarders to be current on their flu/rhino (EHM)

Equine protozoal myeloencephalitis (EPM)

Equine protozoal myeloencephalitis — EPM for short — is a common neurological disease that occurs mostly in the central and eastern United States where opossum populations are high. Many horses are exposed to the illness by coming into contact with opossum feces. Some horses develop antibodies to the disease, which creates some protection. Other exposed horses develop varying neurological signs. The infections can be sudden and severe or subtle and lingering, making it hard to recognize.

A protozoa called *Sarcocystis nerona* causes EPM, and it affects the spinal cord and brain, resulting in a variety of possible symptoms. These include uncoordinated movement of some or all of the horse's limbs, spastic movements of one or more legs, tilted head, muscles that waste away in the face or one of the hind legs, and seizures.

Diagnosing EPM isn't easy. Sometimes a horse seems only slightly lame, or may just perform poorly. Most often, a horse with EPM suffers from an obvious lack of coordination, looking almost as if he is drunk when he walks. The only way to diagnose EPM is through laboratory tests, even though they're not 100 percent reliable. Diagnosis usually is confirmed only if the horse responds to treatment, which consists of oral anti-protozoal medications.

To prevent EPM, you must keep opossums far away from your horse, which is no easy feat, because opossums are common wildlife in most suburban and rural areas. You can do much to keep opossums from contaminating your horse's feed, though. Follow these simple horsekeeping rules to prevent opossums from soiling your horse's food:

>> **Close it:** Keep commercial feed and other supplements in tightly lidded containers.

>> **Lift it:** Feed your horse in a trough or bucket — never on the ground.

>> **Clean it:** Wash feeders with soap and water on a regular basis.

>> **Toss it:** Throw out feed that falls on the ground.

Exhertional rabdomylitis ("tying up")

Imagine the worst Charlie horse you've ever had, and then imagine it throughout your entire body. This is what *exhertional rabdomylitis* — or tying up as it's commonly called — does to a horse.

For a long time, veterinarians believed tying up was caused by a build up of lactic acid, which caused damage to the muscle. Recent research has proven this theory wrong, showing that the problem is related to calcium in the muscle cells.

The symptoms of tying up — anxiety, abnormally heavy perspiration, and unusually fast pulse — usually come on 15 minutes to 1 hour into exercise. The horse begins to experience intense stiffness and takes painful short steps. He may also refuse to walk. In severe cases, horses ultimately collapse.

If you suspect that your horse is tying up, don't force him to move. Instead, call a vet immediately. Diagnosis is made by observing the horse's symptoms and a blood analysis taken 24 hours after the incident. A horse that is tying up will show high levels of muscle enzymes in the blood that have been released as a result of muscle damage.

If your horse has symptoms of tying up, your vet will likely give him a sedative and may possibly treat him with other medications, depending on the situation.

To prevent your horse from ever having to experience the anguish of this condition, follow these guidelines:

>> **Provide regular exercise:** Provide your horse with exercise on a daily basis to keep his metabolism functioning properly. (Pastured horses tend to exercise

themselves and so are less prone to tying up.) See Chapter 8 for details about including exercise in your horse's daily routine.

>> **Warm up, cool down:** You must spend at least 10 minutes warming up your horse by walking and trotting. When your ride is over, walk the horse for at least 10 minutes to help him cool down. Horses that are properly warmed up and cooled down are less susceptible to tying up.

>> **Cut feed rations:** During times of long inactivity for your horse (bad weather, lameness, and so on), reduce his intake of higher calorie foods like alfalfa (a particularly high-protein hay) and high-calorie commercial feed you may be giving him. If the lay-up is short (only a day or two), stop the commercial feed only. Too much protein and carbohydrates while inactive can result in tying up when the horse returns to work. Supplement the diet with low-protein timothy hay or orchard grass and a fat source such as vegetable oil or rice bran so that your horse still has enough hay and energy in his diet. Chapter 8 has more info on feeding.

>> **Provide supplements:** If your horse has repeated attacks of tying up, talk to your vet about supplementing the horse's feed with vitamin E, selenium, and fat sources such as rice bran. These additives can help protect the horse from a recurrent attack.

Eye problems

Horses sometimes come down with ailments that affect the eye. The most common ones are corneal ulcers, equine recurrent uveitis, and cataracts.

>> *Corneal ulcers* by far are the most common eye problem and often the result of a foreign body entering the eye and causing damage to the cornea. Bacteria can infect the damaged area and begin to erode the cornea. (Some corneal ulcers seem to form for other reasons that vets aren't sure of.) Symptoms include squinting, tearing, and an obviously painful eye. Treatment for this problem often requires application of ointment to the eye several times a day until the ulcer heals. To help prevent corneal ulcers, don't let your horse hang his head out the window of a horse trailer, where a foreign body can blow into his eye. If your horse shows signs of eye discomfort, contact your vet immediately because corneal ulcers worsen quickly without treatment.

>> *Equine recurrent uveitis (ERU)* is the number one cause of blindness in horses. This painful inflammatory condition has unknown causes, although some researchers believe exposure to the leptospirosis bacteria, believed to be carried by some wildlife and in contaminated streams and ponds, may play a part in the development of ERU. (This bacteria can be difficult to avoid, especially for horses that live in pastures with natural water sources. A vaccine

for leptospirosis exists, but there's some controversy about whether it can actually prevent ERU.) Anecdotal evidence also suggests that Appaloosas, warmbloods, and draft horses are genetically prone to the disease. Symptoms include pain, tearing, and sensitivity to light. Treatment involves the application of steroidal ointment in the eye to reduce inflammation. In some cases, an implant in the eye can provide ongoing medication. ERU eventually results in a loss of sight for the horse, but good management of the condition can keep this from happening later rather than sooner.

>> *Cataracts* can develop in adult horses, but they're most common in foals. Cataracts are an opaqueness that forms in the lens of the eye and restricts vision. The causes of equine cataracts are not completely understood, although injury, diabetes, and ERU are three suspected culprits in adult horses. A horse's cataracts can be removed with surgery.

Gastric ulcers

Humans aren't the only species that get stomach ulcers. Horses also are prone to this malady. Equine gastric ulcers take place when the lining of the stomach is eroded because of an overexposure to stomach acid that occurs when the horse isn't allowed to eat often enough and when the horse is under stress. In fact, research has shown that hauling horses and stabling them away from home makes them more susceptible to developing ulcers.

Gastric ulcers can be hard to diagnose because symptoms are subtle. Poor appetite, an unattractive coat, and decreased activity all can be signs of gastric ulcers. Horses with severe cases repeatedly suffer bouts of colic (covered earlier in this chapter). They also have performance problems, such as irritability during work and resisting work.

Diagnosing equine gastric ulcers requires use of an endoscope so the examining vet can see what is going on inside the stomach. Horses suffering from gastric ulcers are prescribed more frequent feedings, more interaction with other horses, and a decrease in grain. Some horses may require medication for their ulcers.

The most common medication for the treatment of ulcers is omeprazole. This drug has also been shown to prevent ulcers at a lower dose. The drug can be given daily while traveling and while the horse is away from home to help prevent ulcers.

If your horse is suffering from gastric ulcers, your vet will likely recommend more frequent feedings, more interactions with other horses, pasture access, a decrease in grain, and an increase in calcium-based hays, like alfalfa.

Heaves

Heaves is the common term for *chronic obstructive pulmonary disease (COPD)*. The illness is similar to asthma in humans in that the horse has difficulty breathing in, and even more difficulty breathing out. Heaves causes inflammation and spasm within the lungs and usually is brought on by airborne allergies to mold, dust, and pollen, or by poor air quality. Horses suffering from heaves may experience shortness of breath during exercise, chronic coughing, and wheezing. Because heaves is chronic by definition, these symptoms persist over a period of time.

TIP

Horses with heaves often have something called a *heave line,* which is a line of developed muscle along the belly that forms as a result of the horse's struggle to push air out of his lungs. Presence of a heave line is a good way of telling whether a horse suffers from heaves.

Veterinarians usually treat the disease by recommending changes in the horse's environment. In severe cases and to get the condition under control, a vet may also prescribe corticosteroids, a bronchodilator, and possibly antibiotics.

Horses are born with a predisposition to heaves, but you still can do plenty to help keep your horse from developing the condition:

>> **Supply good air.** Horses need quality air to breathe, just like humans. Try to give your horse as much ventilation as possible. If you're stabling him in a box stall, choose one that has ample windows so fresh air can enter. Buy bedding and hay that is low in dust, and change the bedding often to avoid ammonia build up. Avoid using straw bedding because allergy-inducing mold spores flourish in it. (Check out Chapter 7 for details on bedding and housing.)

>> **Move the horse:** When cleaning your horse's stall, move your horse out of the immediate area so he doesn't breathe in an excessive amount of dust and other particles.

>> **Keep him outside:** If your horse has a tendency toward heaves, keep him outdoors in a pasture instead of in a stall.

>> **Feed low:** Provide your horse with a feeder that requires him to keep his head down when eating. Doing so encourages nasal drainage.

WARNING

Although you want to keep your horse's head down while he eats, don't feed your horse directly off the ground if he's in a pasture or paddock because he may ingest sand and develop colic (which we cover earlier in this chapter).

Metabolic diseases

affect their health. As a horse owner, it's important that you know how to recognize the symptoms of these diseases early on so that you can notify your veterinarian.

Anhydrosis

Some horses can develop a metabolic problem called *anhydrosis*, which is the inability to produce normal amounts of sweat.

The condition has a range of seriousness: from the extreme of a horse that has no functioning sweat glands to a horse that simply produces less sweat than he should at certain temperatures and levels of exercise. The problem can be seasonal, as some horses with this problem do fine in the cooler seasons but have trouble when the weather heats up and humidity elevates.

Your horse depends on sweating to regulate body temperature. Sweat is critical so that evaporation can cool him down and keep his body temperature from becoming dangerously high. When a horse stops sweating, he tries to cool himself by panting, which not very effective. The body temperature of a horse that can't sweat may elevate as high as 103 degrees. (The normal body temperature for a horse is 101.) Add exercise to the equation, and the horse's body temperature can go as high as 108 degrees. Brain damage is highly likely when body temperature exceeds 106 degrees.

Your horse should normally cool down within 30 minutes after exercise. If your horse doesn't seem to be cooling off, check his rectal temperature. If it is above normal and your horse is also breathing rapidly, has decreased energy, depression, and a lack of sweating, contact your veterinarian.

If your vet suspects anhydrosis, he or she can test your horse to see if the sweat glands are functioning. If they are, your horse has a form of anhydrosis that may respond to some treatments, including a combination of cobalt, vitamin C, L-tyrosine, and niacin. Some horses benefit from dopamine and electrolytes. Other horses respond to acupuncture and traditional Chinese veterinary medicine. It's important to remember that treatment is not 100-percent effective in all cases of this no-sweat conundrum.

Pituitary pars intermediary dysfunction (PPID)

Pituitary pars intermediary dysfunction (PPID) — often referred to as Cushings disease — is a condition that involves the horse's pituitary gland. When a horse has PPID, his body doesn't properly regulate the chemical secretions of his pituitary gland, which can lead to a host of different symptoms.

Common physical signs of PPID are a long, curly coat that doesn't shed out in the spring; chronic infections; excessive sweating; loss of muscle mass, leading to a pot-bellied appearance; and weight loss. Laminitis sometimes occurs as well.

Your vet can diagnose PPID with a blood test. Oftentimes, if your horse has a long, curly coat that never sheds out, the vet will make a diagnosis just on his appearance.

No cure exists for PPID, but it can be treated with a medication called pergolide, and can be managed for many years. Horses over 15 years old should be tested for PPID if they develop laminitis with no apparent cause since this syndrome is actually the most common cause of laminitis in older horses. Management of PPID does take diligence and dedication because frequent testing and readjustment of medication is needed.

Equine Metabolic Syndrome (EMS)

Horses with EMS gain weight easily and often suffer from insulin dysfunction. The consequence is a high risk for developing laminitis, which is a devastating hoof disease (see the subsection "Laminitis" in the "Dealing with hoof issues" section later in this chapter.)

A high starch diet and obesity can contribute to a horse developing EMS, which is why it is so important not to let your horse get fat, and especially from overfeeding high starch diets.

EMS is diagnosed by blood work to check insulin levels. It can't be cured, but is managed by controlling the horse's weight, reducing the levels of carbohydrates in the feed, and increasing exercise. Studies have shown that regular exercise that raises the horse's heart rate and causes him to sweat can do a lot to help lower insulin levels.

If your horse is diagnosed with EMS, your vet will help you plan a diet and exercise program to help manage the condition.

Skin problems

A number of different skin problems plague horses. Allergic reactions bring on some of them, while others are the result of parasitic infections and various other biological reactions. Some of the most common skin ailments are fly allergies, fungal infections, hives, melanomas, sarcoids, and squamous cell carcinoma. Each of these problems has unique symptoms, causes, and treatments.

Fly allergies

For horses, flies are probably the worst thing in the world to be allergic to, because where you have horses, you have flies. Sure, you can and should do plenty to keep flies under control, but getting rid of them completely is impossible. A fact of equine life is that flies are here to stay.

Flies are annoying enough to horses, but when a horse is allergic to these obnoxious insects, the situation becomes unbearable. If your horse has areas of skin that are scabby and itchy, and the flies are out in force, he probably has a fly allergy. Your vet will recommend that you bathe your horse a couple of times a week to remove the itchy scabs and apply a steroidal ointment on a daily basis. The ointment is safe because it's applied topically, and it may contain an antibiotic, if the sores are infected. Your vet may also give your horse a cortisone shot to relieve the inflammation or recommend regular allergy shots to reduce your horse's sensitivity to fly bites.

REMEMBER

The only way to prevent your horse from developing a fly allergy is to keep him from ever being bitten by a fly — a virtually impossible task. So, all you can do is implement a strict pest control program in an effort to keep the fly population under control (see Chapter 8 for tips) and minimize your horse's exposure to bites. You also need to use a fly mask, flysheet, and fly-screen leg wraps to minimize fly contact with your horse (see Chapter 6 for information on these items.)

Fungal infections

Several different kinds of fungal organisms can affect a horse's skin. Among these culprits are rain scalds and ringworm. Each of these infections has different symptoms and treatments.

>> **Rain scalds** (technically called *dermatophilosis*) is a genetic anomaly that's sort of a cross between a fungus and a bacteria. The organism comes to life in damp weather and often shows up on horses when weather conditions are wet, such as during rainy seasons or in tropical regions.

The organism that causes rain scalds can only enter the skin at a break. An insect bite or minor scratch that is invisible to your eye is all the organism needs to gain entry. After the condition takes hold, you see areas of matted hair on your horse's coat that look like paintbrush strokes. These patches are mostly around the back area where the saddle lies, on the hindquarters, and on the thighs. Crusty scabs accompany the matted coat.

Veterinarians usually recommend that rain scalds be treated with a 10 percent iodine scrub. Exposure to sunlight also helps gets rid of rain scalds.

TIP

Keeping your horse dry in wet weather helps keep rain scalds away. Give your horse adequate shelter to escape from rainy weather. If you can't keep him completely dry, provide him with a waterproof blanket to wear during rainstorms.

>> **Ringworm** is one or more round lesions on the horse's skin, often found near areas of the abdomen where the girth sits or on the back. The center of the lesion is hairless, and can be raw or covered with a scab. Ringworm is highly contagious to humans and other horses. The disease usually occurs in the winter when the conditions are dark and damp and horses are being kept indoors.

TIP

Ringworm actually goes away by itself in six to eight weeks, but to keep it from spreading to other areas of the horse — and to other people and animals — wash the lesion with Betadine scrub, which contains iodine and is available from your local tack store or online. Aside from being sensitive to iodine, ringworm also is vulnerable to sunlight and dry conditions. You can also treat the area with an over-the-counter ringworm medicine meant for humans.

To prevent ringworm, keep your horse clean and dry. Sweat is a good food source for the organism that causes ringworm, so wash or sponge your horse down after every workout. Turn your horse out in the sun frequently, because the organism doesn't like sunlight. Another way to prevent ringworm is to avoid using tack and grooming equipment that has been used on other horses. If you have to borrow equipment, at least disinfect brushes, saddle pads, and other washable items with a solution of mild bleach (one part bleach to four parts water). Leave the solution on the item for eight minutes and then be sure to rinse thoroughly, because bleach residue will irritate your horse's skin.

Hives

Plenty of humans get hives, and they know how unpleasant these little lumps can be. On horses, hives usually cover the entire body or a section of the body, are anywhere from half an inch to a few inches in diameter, and are uniform in shape. When you touch the hive, it gives to the pressure. Hives can be itchy or not itchy, and swelling of the face and eyelids sometimes occurs with them.

In horses, just as in people, hives are the result of an allergic reaction to a substance, either airborne or eaten. Horses prone to hives typically get them from inhaling certain pollens and eating some feeds.

REMEMBER

Because hives are the result of an allergy, you can't do much to prevent their onset. Pay close attention to your horse and notice any possible outbreaks right away. The sooner you address the problem, the less your horse suffers. In severe cases, your vet may prescribe an antihistamine or give your horse a corticosteroid injection. Your vet will also suggest removing the allergen from your horse's environment.

Melanomas

Melanomas are rather common tumors in horses. A predisposition to developing these tumors seems to exist in certain individual horses and in certain breeds (Arabians and Percherons in particular). Horses that are gray in coloring also tend to develop melanomas as they age. In fact, 80 percent of gray horses over the age of 15 develop melanomas.

Melanomas take on the form of black growths on or under the skin, usually about an inch in diameter. Sometimes the lesions are hairless and ulcerated. They can be single or clustered in groups and can grow rather large in size. These tumors typically appear on the horse's genitals (both male and female), under the tail, near the anus, and on the eyelids, throat, and mouth, but they can be found anywhere on the horse's body.

In gray horses, melanomas usually are nonthreatening, slow-growing tumors. You need only to remove them if they're interfering with the horse's function (tumors on the anus can interfere with defecation, for example). *Note:* Gray horses are the only mammals known to science that can host a cancer that is not usually life-threatening.

In horses that aren't gray, melanomas can be much more serious because they can *metastasize* (spread to other areas of the body) quickly through the bloodstream and affect the major organs. A melanoma in a horse that isn't gray usually is serious and should be surgically removed by a veterinarian. If you notice any growths on your horse's skin, contact your vet right away.

Experts have yet to discover a way to prevent melanomas.

Sarcoids

Sarcoids are common, benign skin tumors. You typically see them on the horse's head, stomach area, or legs. Sarcoids sometimes come in groups and are usually about an inch to a few inches in size. They occasionally appear in wounds that are healing.

Sarcoids are most commonly seen in two forms: flat sarcoids and proliferative sarcoids. Veterinary researchers believe that sarcoids are the result of a virus, although no conclusive evidence exists to prove this theory. Some sarcoids are very aggressive and grow rapidly.

Veterinary science has yet to discover the exact cause of sarcoid tumors, leaving horse owners with no way to prevent the problem. Treatment usually involves removal of the tumor, either through conventional surgery, through laser surgery, or by freezing it off using cryosurgery — although the tumors sometimes return. Some veterinarians treat sarcoids with a topical cream first before resorting to surgery, or they'll combine topical treatment with surgery to remove the tumor.

If you notice a lump anywhere on your horse, contact your veterinarian right away.

Squamous cell carcinoma

Horses are prone to a cancer that usually starts on the skin, called squamous cell carcinoma. It shows up as a red sore or bump that appears on the horse's eye, vulva, sheath, or other place on the body where skin and mucus membranes come into contact with each other. It is most common in horses that have pink skin in these areas.

Squamous cell carcinoma is treatable at the skin stage but can ultimately be fatal if it travels to areas within the horse's body, like the bone or lymph glands. This is why it's important to catch this cancer before it has a chance to spread.

Your vet can treat squamous cell carcinoma in a number of ways, depending on where the cancerous lesion is located. Cryotherapy, radiation, localized chemotherapy, laser therapy, and topical drugs are all options.

TIP

Since the sun's UV rays can be a cause of this cancer in light-skinned horses, keep a UV-protection fly mask on your horse on sunny days to protect his eyes. You may also want to keep him stabled out of the sun during the summertime, turning him out only after the sun has gone down.

Strangles

Strangles, a condition caused by bacteria known as *Streptococcus equi,* takes hold around a horse's neck and upper respiratory tract, forming abscesses within the lymph nodes. The illness results in fever, lack of appetite, runny eyes and nose, and a dry cough. The horse sometimes acts depressed and refuses to eat, and stands with his head down. In more severe cases, the lymph nodes enlarge (about two weeks after the disease hits) as abscesses develop. You can see these abscesses as big lumps under the horse's throatlatch (the area under the jowl). Often, these lumps break open and drain externally.

Strangles is a contagious disease that spreads from one horse to another through direct contact with secretions from the mouth and respiratory tract that are left behind on food and water troughs or other objects. Flies also spread it.

The only way to know for sure whether your horse has strangles is to have a veterinarian examine him. If your horse is diagnosed with this disease, the abscess that forms will be cut open and drained. Some vets also prescribe antibiotics.

Many veterinarians recommend yearly inoculations with a strangles vaccine to guard against the disease, especially if your horse is exposed to a number of other horses.

REMEMBER

To keep your horse from contracting strangles and other infectious diseases, don't allow him to drink from community watering troughs at horse shows and other places where strange horses gather. Instead, bring your own bucket and fill it with water when you horse needs a drink. Keep him from making nose-to-nose contact with the other horses because any horse he meets is a potential carrier of the disease.

West Nile virus

West Nile virus was discovered in Uganda in 1937 but wasn't diagnosed in the United States until 1999. Since then, the disease spread from the East to the West Coast through mosquitoes. After biting an infected bird, the mosquito then bites a horse, injecting the virus into the horse's bloodstream. One-third of the horses that are bitten by an infected mosquito get sick. One-third of these sick horses die from the disease.

The West Nile virus can cause mild-to-severe neurological symptoms in horses, including lack of muscle coordination, stumbling and weak limbs (ataxia), partial paralysis, muscle twitching (especially around the muzzle), hypersensitivity to sight or sound, head drooping, lethargy, and depression. Some horses fall asleep at inappropriate times, such as while eating. These symptoms show up seven to 10 days after an infected mosquito bites the horse. Some horses also run a fever early on in the disease. In cases where horses are seriously affected by the disease, they can be left with permanent neurological damage.

Treatment for West Nile virus includes supportive care to help the horse's body battle the effects of the organism. This care includes intravenous fluids to prevent dehydration and anti-inflammatory drugs. An antibody for the West Nile virus also has been introduced to help fight off the illness in horses.

The best way to protect your horse against West Nile virus is with an annual vaccine (see Chapter 10 for details). You also need to practice mosquito control on your property by eliminating standing water where mosquitoes breed (see Chapter 8 for details on pest control).

Rabies

Although rabies is not common in horses, a horse can contract the disease if bitten by an infected animal. (Raccoons and bats are notorious carriers of rabies.)

Rabies in horses typically shows up as a lameness in one leg that gradually spreads to the others. The horse may also appear depressed and stagger when he walks.

If your horse contracts rabies, any people who have handled him are considered exposed and have to be evaluated for the disease. If your horse bites someone, you may get a visit from authorities, who will want your horse quarantined for rabies.

No treatment for rabies exists, but an effective vaccine for horses is available and recommended by most vets as part of an annual vaccine protocol.

Getting a Grip on Leg Woes

Many of the ailments that plague horses are related to their legs, which probably has a great deal to do with the way people keep and ride horses. In the wild, horses walk almost constantly as they graze, keeping their muscles loose and flexible and their circulation up. Wild horses also trod on nicely cushioned, plant-covered soils. Compare these scenarios to the life of stabled horses, standing for hours on end as their muscles tighten and their joints become stiff. Look, too, at the riding horses that regularly walk on tightly packed trails and even asphalt and concrete. These same horses are asked to perform rather unnatural maneuvers like trotting or cantering in tight, collected circles and while jumping, and performing other discipline-specific maneuvers.

Another important part of the problem is that rather delicate bones, tendons, and ligaments make up the equine leg. A horse's legs are expected not only to support the animal's weight, but also the rider's — on less-than-ideal footing and during strenuous activity. Considering all these factors, you can easily see why leg problems are so common.

The following sections take a look at the five most common leg ailments affecting horses, and we tell you how you can help manage and prevent them.

Arthritis

People aren't the only ones who get arthritis. Horses do, too — and often. Simply put, *arthritis* is an inflammation of a joint. It's the most common form of lameness in horses. Horses with arthritis limp — some very mildly, others dramatically. (To find out how to determine whether your horse is lame, see the nearby sidebar "Detecting lameness in your horse.") Several different forms of arthritis exist.

Degenerative joint disease

The most common type of arthritis is what is collectively known *as degenerative joint disease (DJD).* This disease starts out mildly with an inflamed joint capsule and can progress into erosion of the cartilage and fusion of the joint.

DJD can affect young and old horses, and the causes vary. Fifty to sixty percent of the time, the hocks are the affected joints. The knees are the next most common sites. Other joints such as the fetlocks and stifles can be affected, too, although DJD in these joints tends to result in less lameness (see Chapter 2 for a diagram showing the parts of the horse). Poor conformation, hard work, trauma, and old age are other main causes of arthritis (see Chapter 4 for information on conformation).

Several treatments exist for DJD, and whether they're used depends on the severity of the problem. All are aimed at stopping the cycle of inflammation and restoring the health of the joint fluid and joint surface cartilage.

REMEMBER

You can't always prevent arthritis, especially when it strikes a young horse or when poor conformation is the cause. Sometimes, just the wear and tear of carrying people around takes its toll on a horse's joints. Honestly, nature didn't intend horses to carry humans around on their backs while doing dressage, jumping, reining, and other equine sports. But shoeing your horse properly, riding him on surfaces that provide good footing, and refraining from working him too hard can help keep arthritis at bay.

TIP

You can also opt to give your horse intravenous hylauronic acid, Adequan, yucca, chondrotin sulfates, and glucosamine as preventatives against DJD. The use of these supplements is aimed at keeping the joint healthy before arthritis sets in.

Ringbone

Ringbone is another type of arthritis that affects the pastern and coffin joints. Extra bone development occurs around the joint or in the joint itself. When the coffin joint is affected, the condition is termed *low ringbone*; when the pastern joint is affected, it's called *high ringbone*.

In the early stages of ringbone, bone development usually is mild and lameness tends to be present but not severe. As the disease progresses, more of the joint becomes affected and the lameness increases. In high ringbone, the joint may actually fuse completely, which can be quite painful — most horses with this problem are extremely lame.

Researchers don't fully understand why horses develop this condition, but they think that part of the problem is genetic and part has to do with uneven trimming of the hooves. When the hooves are not trimmed completely level, they land on the ground unevenly, causing trauma to the joint.

Treatment usually involves *therapeutic shoeing,* special trimming and shoeing techniques that ensure a balanced foot. Shortening the toe during trimming also helps to ease stress on the joint. All of the other arthritis treatments also apply to this disease.

Because uneven trimming of the hooves can bring on ringbone, make sure that you use a skilled and reputable farrier. See Chapter 10 for more about finding a farrier.

Bowed tendons

Bowed tendons, or *tendonitis,* are a lower-leg problem. Bowed tendons occur when tendons at the back of the leg become overstretched and strained or torn. The back of the leg becomes very swollen, hot and painful to the touch, and lameness usually results. Overexertion of the tendons either through jumping, galloping, or galloping in deep footing causes bowed tendons.

A veterinarian usually uses an ultrasound of the affected tendons to diagnose and determine the severity of the problem. Severely bowed tendons have tears in the tendons, while mildly bowed tendons have swelling and enlargement.

Treatment is aimed at reducing the swelling by using icing, anti-inflammatory drugs (such as phenylbutazone), and stall rest. All tendon injuries require long periods — six months to a year — of rest and controlled exercise to heal properly.

TIP

You can help prevent bowed tendons by providing proper shoeing and riding sensibly in good footing that isn't too deep, slippery, or muddy. Despite precautions, however, bowed tendons are sometimes unavoidable.

Fractures

It's a myth that a horse with a broken leg must be destroyed. While this can be true in cases of severe fractures of the larger bones in the leg, a fracture is *not* an automatic death sentence — at least not these days. Medical technology can go a long way in helping a horse's leg heal.

Catastrophic injuries such as a fall, a kick from another horse, or a trailer accident can result in the fracture of a large, long bone in the leg. You can tell if a horse has a severely broken leg because he won't put weight on it; it may swing abnormally; the horse may not be able to get up from the ground; and the horse will be in obvious pain.

Fortunately, the more common leg fractures seen in horses are of the smaller bones in the leg. These fractures can cause lameness but can often be helped to heal. Horses can sometimes develop fractures in the shoulder or back, too.

Fractures are diagnosed using a range of methods, including X-ray, ultrasound, bone scintigraphy, MRI, and CT scan. Treatments can range from simple reset to therapeutic shoes, stem cell injections, shockwave treatments, and surgery.

The prognosis for a fracture depends a lot on the injury, the treatment, and the individual horse. Some horses can return completely back to normal, while others may need to be retired out to pasture.

Dealing with Hoof Issues

Have you ever heard the expression "no hoof, no horse"? No truer words were ever spoken. Without healthy hooves, horses can't be themselves; they need their hooves to walk, run and stand. As a horse owner, keeping your horse's hooves healthy is one of your most important tasks.

Hoof abscesses

When an abscess forms in a horse's hoof, it can cause severe lameness. The abscess is an infection that starts at the bottom of the hoof or the sole and travels up the lamina (also called the white line), and often breaks open at the coronary band, where it drains. A puncture wound or infection in the bottom of the hoof usually causes the abscess. Horses with this problem appear fine one day and suddenly very lame on one leg the next.

Vets base their diagnoses of hoof abscesses on symptoms of severe and sudden lameness on one leg, increased pulse in the leg, and sensitivity to hoof testers. Your veterinarian will make a final diagnosis when the abscess is found.

Treatment involves opening the abscess, which allows it to drain, and soaking the hoof in Epsom salts. Soaking in a warm Epsom salts solution draws out the pus from the abscess and kills the bacteria within it. Your horse also may be prescribed anti-inflammatory/painkilling drugs such as phenylbutazone (bute) or Banamine or possibly antibiotics. Most horses recover fully from this problem in three to five days and return to full, regular work without any problems.

TIP

Help prevent hoof abscesses by cleaning your horse's feet daily and by getting regular hoof trimmings from a competent farrier. Keep your horse's bedding clean and dry to discourage bacterial growth.

Bruising

Have you ever stepped on a rock while walking barefoot? If so, you know what a hoof bruise feels like to a horse.

Hoof bruises occur when a horse does something that traumatizes the sole of his hoof, such as stepping on a rock, pawing at a gate, kicking at a wall, and hitting one hoof with the opposing hoof while moving, to name just a few possibilities.

A horse that has sustained a hoof bruise will be lame on the effected leg. The lameness will probably be subtle, but if you know your horse, you'll be able to tell that he's off.

Your veterinarian can diagnose a hoof bruise with a device called a hoof tester. The tester is like a giant pair of pliers, and it can show the vet if the sole of your horse's hoof is sensitive. Your vet will also ask you if your horse has done anything lately that may have caused a hoof bruise, such a galloping on a rocky trail.

Treatment for a hoof bruise most often involves giving the horse anti-inflammatory medication, along with rest and soft bedding and footing. Most hoof bruises resolve on their own in two to six weeks. Some bruises can be severe enough to develop into abscesses or cause lameness for long periods of time. In this case, your vet may recommend an MRI, X-ray, or scintigraphy to help get to the bottom of a stubborn bruise.

Hot nails

Horses have been wearing shoes for centuries, and while the craft of horseshoeing has evolved over the years, one thing remains: the use of nails.

When a horse is fitted with a shoe, nails are driven through the bottom of the metal shoe through special holes into the hoof wall. Proper nail placement is the mark of a skilled farrier and a source of great pride in those who shoe horses for a living. However, mistakes happen.

If a nail is accidentally placed in the wrong spot, an area in the horse's hoof called the lamina becomes traumatized, inflamed, and very painful. In fact, this "hot nail" can cause the horse so much pain that he may not be able to bear weight on the leg. In other cases, the lameness may be subtle.

If your horse is lame, your veterinarian can diagnose a hot nail using a hoof tester, or by performing nerve blocks in your horse's lower leg. If a nail problem is detected, the veterinarian will recommend removing the shoe, soaking the affected hoof, and giving anti-inflammatory medication, in addition to other actions. Most horses recover completely within five to seven days of removal of the offending nail.

Laminitis

Laminitis, which also is known as *founder,* is a devastating disease that affects an area within the hoof known as the *sensitive lamina,* the connective layer between the hoof and the coffin bone that holds the coffin bone in place. Laminitis occurs when the lamina becomes inflamed and the coffin bone begins to separate from the hoof. With severe laminitis, the coffin bone may actually come out of the bottom of the hoof.

In the milder forms of laminitis, the horse appears to be *walking on eggshells*, moving tenderly on his feet. As the disease progresses, the horse feels greater pain and adopts a *rocked back* stance, with his weight shifted toward his rear, in an attempt to take weight off the front hooves. The horse also resists walking. As more damage occurs and subsequent pain develops, the horse starts lying down often to take the weight off his feet.

Causes of this disease are plentiful and include trimming the feet too short, galloping on hard ground, absorbing toxins from the gut during bouts with colic (which we cover earlier in this chapter), eating too much grain or rich pasture grass, keeping the horse on black walnut shavings, and sometimes, receiving steroid medications.

If your horse demonstrates sensitive hooves (particularly at the toe) and an increased pulse in the leg, he may have laminitis. Consult your vet, who needs to X-ray the affected hoof. *Rotation,* the separation of the bone from the hoof, shows up on X rays.

Treatment of this disease varies depending on the severity of the problem. The basics include complete stall rest on very soft footing (preferably soft sand or very deep shavings), therapeutic shoeing, changes in the diet, administration of anti-inflammatory drugs such as phenylbutazone, Banamine, DMSO, and drugs that increase the blood flow to the foot (acepromazine and nitroglycerine are two).

WARNING

Laminitis can become so severe that the horse can die. If the horse survives, he is prone to relapses. Each relapse means more damage, with chances of recovery lessening with each episode. Many horses that survive also are lame for life. If you find yourself in this situation, discuss your horse's condition with your veterinarian to determine whether the horse's quality of life is such that euthanasia may be warranted (see the section on "Coping with Euthanasia" later in this chapter).

REMEMBER

Provide proper shoeing; feed balanced diets that are not too rich in carbohydrates; and ride and stable your horse on good footing.

Navicular disease

Navicular disease involves a small bone called the navicular bone, which acts as a fulcrum between something called the *deep flexor tendon* and the coffin bone. Researchers still are debating exactly what causes the disease, but the traditional belief is that it occurs when the bone undergoes degeneration and — as a result of decreased circulation to the bone itself — forms cysts and large channels inside its center. Horses with this problem typically are lame in both front legs, and their pain tends to be isolated at the heel area.

A vet usually diagnoses this disease through the use of nerve blocks and X rays of the navicular area. This disease has no cure, but the condition can be managed. Treatment usually involves therapeutic shoeing (usually in the form of a bar shoe, which is a type of horseshoe with a special bar at the bottom to support the foot), drugs to help increase the blood flow to the navicular bone, and anti-inflammatory and painkilling drugs. In the most severe of cases, where the horse stops improving with medication and shoeing, nerves to the heels are cut so that the horse no longer feels the pain from the disease.

Prevention of this disease is difficult because researchers don't fully know how it develops. Veterinarians suspect a genetic link, so not breeding horses with this problem may be a way of preventing of the disease. Be sure to provide proper shoeing, a balanced diet, and regular exercise to help avoid navicular.

Thrush

Black goo never seems good, and in the case of your horse's hoof, this is especially true. Called *thrush*, the black goo of horse hooves is actually an infection of the foot caused by a bacteria or fungus (vets aren't sure which). The infection takes hold when the pathogen starts thriving in wet conditions where oxygen is scarce, which creates the perfect conditions for an infection.

Thrush is one of the most common problems afflicting horses today. Horses that don't undergo regular feet cleaning are prone to this disease, as are horses kept in wet environments. The infection takes hold if the foot is routinely packed with mud, soiled bedding, and manure.

Horses with thrush have a foul-smelling black discharge on the bottom of the hoof surrounding the frog (the triangular-shaped area on the underside of the hoof — see Chapter 2 for a diagram). When you scrape the bottom of the hoof with a hoof pick, a clay-like material comes off, leaving deep grooves in the hoof.

Left untreated, thrush can result in a more severe foot infection that can also damage the horse's tendons. In serious cases, thrush can cause lameness (which we cover in this chapter).

If you suspect that your horse has a mild case of thrush (odor and some discharge, but no lameness), you can try treating the condition yourself with an over-the-counter thrush medication that's available at your local tack and feed store or online. If this treatment isn't effective or if thrush seems to be severe and causing your horse pain when he stands or walks, call your veterinarian who will make a diagnosis by conducting a visual inspection of the foot. Your vet can treat the condition with more powerful medication. In severe cases, it may be necessary to cut away the infected part of the frog.

DETECTING LAMENESS IN YOUR HORSE

Determining whether your horse is going lame, and on which leg can be a tricky business. Although some lamenesses are painfully obvious to even the most casual observer, you need a trained eye to detect the more subtle limps.

If you suspect your horse is limping, or if someone else tells you your horse appears to be lame — a common occurrence in the horse world because lamenesses are most obvious while the horse is being ridden — take these steps to help figure out whether your horse indeed has a problem. (If he does, a call to your veterinarian is in order.)

- **Examine the legs:** Do a visual inspection of your horse's legs, shoulders, and hips, searching for swelling.

- **Check the feet:** Lift each of your horse's feet up one at a time and examine the frog and the sole of the foot for bruises or foreign objects (see Chapter 2 for a diagram showing parts of the hoof). If the frog is filled with dirt, get a hoof pick and clean it out so you can clearly see around the frog. Check the outside of the hoof for cracks.

- **Feel around:** Run your hand down each of your horse's legs, feeling for heat, swelling, cuts, or unusual bumps.

- **Step back:** Tie your horse up or ask someone to hold him. As your horse is standing, check to see whether he's putting his weight evenly on all four feet. If one leg is raised or cocked, it may be causing him pain.

- **View from the front:** Most lamenesses are visible when the horse is moving. If you've been unable to locate any swelling or injury, try watching your horse move. Ask someone to walk and trot your horse on a loose lead rope. As the horse comes toward you, notice whether his head bobs up as he lands on one of his forelegs. The leg his head bobs up on is the lame leg. You can also judge which leg is hurting by watching the horse's stride. The lame leg will move faster with a shorter stride.

- **View from the back:** Have someone walk and trot the horse on a loose line as you view him from behind. If the horse's hop rises higher on one side as he moves, his hind leg is lame on that side. The horse's stride on that leg is also faster and shorter.

TIP

Providing your horse with good foot care goes a long way toward keeping thrush at bay. Follow these guidelines for healthy hooves:

>> **Clean 'em:** Using a hoof pick, clean out your horse's hooves every day (see Chapter 9 for instructions).

>> **Keep 'em dry:** The bacteria that causes thrush loves moisture. Keep your horse's feet dry by providing clean, dry bedding. Don't let your horse stand around in urine-soaked bedding or accumulated manure. Avoid keeping your horse in a muddy paddock or pasture.

Taking Care of Horse Wounds

If you spend much time around horses, you soon discover that first-aid knowledge is a godsend. Horses are big animals, and they sometimes get hurt. Knowing just what to do when an accident occurs not only helps your horse, but also makes you a hero around the barn. You may just save your horse's life — or another's — as you wait for the vet to arrive.

WARNING

If your horse is injured, let him quiet down before attempting to release him from any situation in which he may be trapped. Injured horses often thrash about, sometimes causing injury to themselves and others. Horses that are hurt often have trouble recognizing their owners and tend not to respond to humans the way they normally do.

Here are some important things to keep in mind when your horse is injured:

>> **Stay calm and call for help.** Hysterics only frighten the horse further and aggravate the situation.

>> **Make human safety first and foremost.** If a human gets hurt trying to help an injured horse, the human becomes the priority.

>> **Avoid contaminating a wound with bacteria.** Before you handle any wound on your horse, wash your hands first and wear latex gloves.

The first thing you need to do when your horse gets hurts is determine what kind of wound your horse has suffered, and then act accordingly. The list that follows tells you about the four most common horse wounds and what to do about them.

>> **Abrasions:** Abrasions are the most superficial of wounds. They tend to result when a horse scrapes himself against something rough surface. Abrasions can also happen when saddles or blankets fit poorly and rub the skin away. As long as a fall doesn't cause the abrasion, they're not usually critical, but they are among the most painful of wounds.

When treating an abrasion, stop the bleeding by applying pressure, rinse the area with Betadine, and apply an antibiotic ointment. Do not bandage the area. If the cause of the abrasion is a fall, call your veterinarian.

» **Animal bites:** Horses frequently bite each other, and on occasion, these bites can be severe. Sometimes, horses also suffer bites from other animals like dogs, cats, and wildlife.

If your horse receives a deep bite from either another horse or another animal, call your veterinarian right away. Bites tend to become easily infected, and an injection of an antibiotic can ward off this possibility.

If your horse is bitten by another horse but the wound is superficial and isn't bleeding, you can leave it to heal on its own. Horse bites, however, are susceptible to tetanus, so get your horse a tetanus shot if he hasn't been vaccinated within six months prior to the bite.

» **Lacerations:** A laceration is a cut anywhere on the horse's body that can be large or small or superficial or serious, depending on the size and amount of bleeding.

If the wound seems minor, flush it out with water from a garden hose to get rid of any foreign objects that may be inside. If dirt and other materials continue to adhere to the skin, use water and Betadine on a sponge to gently clean it. Apply antibiotic ointment to the wound and let it heal on its own.

If the laceration is large and deep, do not apply any ointments or sprays and call your veterinarian immediately. Control the bleeding by applying pressure to the wound with a gauze or clean cloth.

Note: When lacerations heal (both the major and minor kind), they can develop something called *proud flesh*. Proud flesh is the normal first layer of healing tissue that occurs in a wound. In horses, this first layer of tissue tends to overproduce. This granulation tissue can become so large that it interferes with the wound's healing and can be unsightly. When this condition occurs with your horse, you need to have the vet come out and remove the proud flesh. The vet then treats the area with a special ointment so the proud flesh won't grow back.

» **Puncture wounds:** Puncture wounds are potentially the most serious of wounds, because they tend to penetrate far into the horse's flesh, deeply implanting bacteria into the horse's body.

Nails and other sharp objects that plunge straight into the skin usually cause puncture wounds. Puncture wounds in hooves result from stepping on protruding objects such as nails. If the wound is in the back third of the hoof, bacteria may get into an area called the *navicular bursa,* where an infection can travel up the entire leg and the horse can lose his life.

Don't attempt to stop the bleeding, unless it's profuse, but call a veterinarian right away — especially if the wound is in the hoof. The vet probably will opt to give the horse a series of antibiotic injections.

Heavy bleeding usually comes with serious equine wounds. Take these precautions if your horse is bleeding freely:

>> **Know the bleeding.** Understanding the type of bleeding helps you gauge the seriousness of it. If blood is spurting from your horse, chances are that an artery is involved, and you need to take immediate action to stop the flow. In the blood is dark and oozing, it's coming from a vein and isn't immediately life-threatening.

>> **Keep the horse still.** Calm your horse by talking softly to him and making him stand in one place. Keep other people (especially children) and dogs quiet. Hysterical people make for hysterical horses. The more the horse moves around because he's upset, the more the wound will bleed.

>> **Apply pressure.** Regardless of whether the bleeding comes from an artery or a vein, always bandage the wound securely. The pressure of the bandage reduces the blood flow. If the bleeding is coming from an area that is too large to bandage, hold a piece of gauze or other clean, absorbent material firmly against the wound. If the blood is coming from an artery and you don't have a bandage or a cloth, use your bare hands to create the pressure. (Wear a latex glove, if you can, to avoid infecting the wound.)

>> **Make a tourniquet.** When an artery is spurting blood and regular pressure won't stop the flow, make a tourniquet. Tourniquets are most practical for leg wounds. Wrap a clean towel or piece of cloth around the leg above the wound (between the heart and the point of bleeding). Tighten the tourniquet with your hands and tie it firmly until the blood flow stops. Note the time you applied the tourniquet. Call a vet immediately, explain the situation, and get advice as to whether the tourniquet will cause any harm. Your phone call also helps the veterinarian determine the seriousness of the situation and how fast he or she needs to get there. While waiting for the vet to arrive, loosen the tourniquet every 15 minutes for a few minutes at a time to allow blood to temporarily flow back into the leg.

Putting Together a First-Rate First-Aid Kit

Every good horseperson has a first-aid kit on hand to deal with any possible emergencies that come up. What's great about having an equine first-aid kit is that many of the items in the kit also come in handy for humans.

TIP

Store your first-aid kit in an easily accessible place near your horse's tack. Make sure that you can get to it quickly in case of an emergency. The last thing you need when you're frantic is a first-aid kit you can't find.

You can go out and buy yourself a preassembled equine first-aid kit at a tack and feed store or online. Or you can put one together on your own. Most items for your kit are available at your local drugstore. If you opt to create your own kit, you need:

>> **Antibiotic ointment:** Triple antibiotic ointments or Betadine provide the best protection against infection for minor wounds.

>> **Antiseptic cleanser:** Betadine is your best choice and a staple for every equine first-aid kit.

>> **Container:** Use one of those medium-sized plastic bins that sell for a few dollars at the discount store to hold all your first-aid supplies. You can easily take this type of container with you whenever you travel to a horse show or other event.

>> **Bandages:** Elastic bandages made specifically for use on horses are best. You have to purchase these at a tack store or through a mail-order or online equine supply catalog.

>> **Disposable diapers:** You can use disposable diapers, which are very absorbent and thick, to apply pressure to lacerations.

>> **Gauze pads:** Sterile gauze pads are useful when dealing with wounds, abscesses, and other breaks in the skin. You can get a few different sizes for use with varying types of wounds.

>> **Serrated knife:** Because horses sometimes get tangled in ropes and other equipment, a jagged knife is a good item to have in your kit. You can use it to cut away an entrapping strap or rope.

>> **Lubricant:** A product such as K-Y Jelly is useful for lubricating your thermometer. Don't use petroleum jelly, which can irritate the sensitive lining of the rectum.

>> **Rubbing alcohol:** You can use rubbing alcohol to disinfect your thermometer between uses.

>> **Scissors:** A pair of scissors is useful for cutting bandages and clothes in an emergency.

>> **Tweezers:** In the event your horse gets a splinter or other object lodged in his skin, a pair of tweezers can come in handy.

>> **Veterinary or human rectal thermometer:** A thermometer is good to have around. If your horse seems ill, taking his temperature before calling the vet helps give the doctor a better idea of what's wrong.

Coping with Euthanasia

Sometimes, a horse's illness is incurable. The horse may simply be too old to fight off whatever it is that's plaguing him. Or, the horse may be gravely ill and veterinary science may be unable to provide any hope for the animal. In many situations, care and treatment for a horse can be so costly that the owner simply can't afford to pursue it. In a number of these cases, a poor prognosis makes trying at all unfeasible.

Euthanasia is the humane process of taking an animal's life. Veterinarians use a barbiturate, which they inject in large quantities into a horse's bloodstream. The drug stops brain function almost instantly, and the horse loses consciousness. The horse then stops breathing, and his heartbeat ceases.

Euthanasia is a fact of horse ownership that no horse owner likes to think about. At some point in your horse experience, you may have to cope with this unfortunate reality. The following sections give you some helpful information.

Making a difficult decision

The decision to put your horse down is incredibly hard. You probably will feel all kinds of emotions, the strongest of which is doubt. Humans are not often put in the position of playing God, and when they suddenly find themselves forced to make a life and death decision over an animal they love, the experience can be confusing and extremely upsetting.

REMEMBER

Should you find yourself struggling with this terrible dilemma, remember that the act of euthanasia can be a gift to a horse that is suffering. Without you to make that decision and allow him a painless, dignified end, your horse will undoubtedly suffer. Think about your horse's quality of life and put yourself in his place. Would you prefer to stay alive in his condition, or would a peaceful death be a welcome relief? Thinking of the subject in these terms and seeking your veterinarian's advice can help you decide what's best for your horse.

Handling the grief

Losing a beloved horse can be an incredibly painful experience. As your horse's caretaker, you feel profound loss, sadness, and even guilt. Your thinking process at this time won't be very rational, and even though you may think you did something terrible by having your horse euthanized, in time, you'll probably realize that you made the right choice.

Sometimes, horse lovers can have difficulty finding a sympathetic ear when they're grieving. People who don't care much for animals will tell you to just "get over it," or ask you what the big deal is. During your time of grieving, try to surround yourself with other animal lovers who understand what you're going through.

TIP

During the past several years, a number of organizations have set up grief counseling hotlines for horse people and other pet owners who have lost a beloved animal. Make use of these services. They can help you work through the grieving process and recover from your loss.

Knowing what happens to your horse's remains

You may be wondering what happens to your horse's remains after euthanasia. The sad reality is the disposal of equine remains is not as easy as it is with smaller animal companions, such as dogs or cats.

If you're fortunate enough to own a large amount of property and your zoning laws allow it, consider burying your horse on your land. If you don't have land, another option is burial in a commercially run pet cemetery, if you can afford it. It can cost upward of $3,000 to bury your horse in a pet cemetery, depending on where you live.

Because most horse owners have neither the land nor the money to bury their horses, they're faced with the unpleasant reality of sending their horse's body to a rendering plant — the least expensive and most convenient method of disposal. This method usually costs less than a few hundred dollars for removal and disposal of the body.

Another option is cremation. If you are fortunate enough to have a crematorium near you that will accommodate a horse, and you can afford a couple thousand dollars, you may choose this route as an alternative to rendering or burial. Some or all of your horse's ashes may be returned to you for burial on your property or placement in an urn. Urns for pet owners are available on the Internet and can be a nice final resting place for your horse.

Chapter **12**

Giving Up Your Horse

U nfortunately, nothing lasts forever, including human/horse relationships. Your horse may get so old that you can no longer ride him. Perhaps lifestyle changes prevent your having time for your horse. Maybe your first horse has taught you so much that you've outgrown him. You may find yourself wanting a horse that can provide a new challenge.

When these situations arise, do the right thing by your horse. He deserves it. A horse isn't an object to be discarded when he has outlived his usefulness. Horses are feeling creatures capable of suffering, and so are deserving of consideration. In this chapter, we first warn you about the dangers of public auctions and slaughterhouses, and then tell you about telltale signs that you've outgrown your horse and provide several options on how to give up your horse.

Beware of Killer Buyers

Every year, more than 80,000 American horses are slaughtered and the meat sold for human consumption in parts of Europe and Asia. This fate befalls not only old, lame animals, but young, rideable horses in their prime. In fact, according to the Humane Society of the United States, 92.3 percent of American horses sent to slaughter are healthy. How can this be? A perfectly rideable horse can land at a slaughterhouse merely because the horse was sold at an auction and purchased by a *killer buyer*. The killer buyer gets the horse at a price that's less than what the horse will be worth as meat, making the animal worth more dead than alive.

A movement is at work in the United States to make purchasing a horse for slaughter illegal, but until a law preventing this act goes into effect, every horse is at risk of being slaughtered if it ends up in the wrong hands. Horses purchased for slaughter spend days journeying in packed trailers to slaughterhouses in Canada and Mexico, with no food or water for the duration of the trip. All the horses suffer under these conditions, but the infirm, the very old, and the very young suffer the most.

Debate rages in the horse world over the issue of slaughter. Some people believe that slaughter is a practical solution for the disposal of thousands of unwanted horses and argue that as soon as the horse arrives at the slaughterhouse, his death is quick and painless. Others offer proof that the end doesn't always come swiftly and feel that slaughter is no way for an animal to end up after serving his life as a companion to humankind.

Humane groups in the United States are currently working on national legislation to ban the practice of buying horses for the purpose of slaughtering them. Until a nationwide ban goes into effect, horses in the U.S. will continue to be sold for slaughter for human consumption elsewhere in the world.

REMEMBER

We aren't telling you this news to bum you out but rather to make you aware. We want you to be aware of what happens to horses that are casually sold or given away after they've outlived their usefulness or are simply unwanted. If you don't give much thought to what happens to your horse after you sell him, he may well end up at a public auction, where he may be bought by a killer buyer and shipped to slaughter.

We assume that you love your horse too much to see him end up this way. With this fact in mind, we tell you how you can protect your horse so that he doesn't find himself in this situation, while at the same time meeting your own needs to get a different horse or get out of horse ownership altogether.

Figuring Out if You Need to Move On

You may have trouble imagining a time when you don't want to or can't ride your companion anymore. Yet it happens to horse owners all the time. If you lose interest in riding or if your horse can't be ridden, your decision not to ride your horse anymore is pretty cut-and-dried. But if you simply outgrow your horse, the decision to stop riding him isn't so easy. This is a gray area, where the question of whether your skills have surpassed your horse's skills is a bit subjective. Emotions can muddle the situation even more, making the decision an agonizing one.

Seeing signs of outgrowing your horse

One day, you may look at your horse and realize that you've learned more from him than you ever could have imagined. He served as your guide to an exciting but uncertain world. But now you feel both comfortable and confident in that world, and life with your horse is beginning to get a bit stagnant. If you suspect you're outgrowing your horse, certain signs can help you determine the truth. Examine yourself for these feelings and situations:

>> You used to love riding your horse, but you're getting bored. You've varied your riding routine and pursued different riding activities, but nothing makes riding your horse fun. You're certain the problem isn't riding itself because whenever you ride someone else's horse, you find the experience exhilarating.

>> You enjoyed learning to ride on your horse, but now that you're more competent, you want to get involved in a competitive activity (see Chapter 18 for details). Your horse is a great beginner's horse but he's not a show horse. You have no hope of moving into competition if you keep him as your mount.

>> You feel you've mastered the basics of horsemanship and now want to move up to the next level within your discipline so you can become a better rider. Or maybe you want to change to a different discipline (see Chapter 14 for discipline details). Your horse is holding you back because he doesn't have the athletic ability to help you get to the next level or to work in another discipline.

If any of these scenarios apply to you and your horse, talk with your trainer or another equine expert who is familiar with both your riding ability and your horse to see whether that person agrees that you're outgrowing your horse.

Deciding your next step

When you're certain that you've outgrown your horse, you must decide what you're going to do. If moving on in your riding is important to you, you need to get a new horse. You can keep your first horse and care for him in addition to your new horse, or you can find a new life for your first horse and replace him with another horse.

If your urges to learn more aren't more important than your relationship with your horse, consider keeping him and continuing to ride him while taking lessons on other horses, or put your desires to grow aside. Although many horse people believe that you may be doing a disservice to yourself by following this latter option, there's something to be said for loyalty, dedication, and commitment to your equine friend.

Looking at Options for Your Old Friend

After you make the decision to stop riding your first horse in favor of getting another one (or even leaving the hobby completely), think long and hard about what you're going to do with Old Faithful. You can protect your horse from the slaughterhouse, and we tell you how in the following sections.

Selling

Selling your horse outright is the riskiest option for your horse in terms of his long-term future, especially if he's in the upper age range (20 years or older). Yet selling is the most common way of divesting oneself of an unwanted horse. If you're determined to sell your horse and recover your investment but are concerned about where the horse ends up, follow these guidelines:

>> **Find out the meat market price for horses in your area (usually around 50 cents to $1.25 per pound, depending on location), and price your horse considerably higher than what he would sell for at slaughter.** This way, killer buyers won't be interested in him because they won't be able to make money by reselling him for slaughter.

>> **Don't consign your horse to a public auction.** The majority of horses purchased for slaughter come from public auctions.

>> **Don't sell your horse to a horse dealer who ships horses to slaughter (ask him if you aren't sure).** Your horse may end up on a truck to the slaughterhouse instead of being purchased by someone who wants to ride him.

>> **Sell your horse only to a good home.** Screen potential buyers by asking them questions such as whether they've owned a horse before (and if so, what happened to him), their intended uses for the horse, the type of housing the horse will receive, and what they plan to do with your horse when they no longer want him. Ask to see where the horse will be kept, and check out the facilities to make sure they're well maintained. Watch the prospective buyer ride the horse, and think about whether the horse is a good match for the buyer. If it doesn't appear that the horse and the buyer get along (the horse seems unhappy when being ridden by this person), decline to sell the horse. Selling your horse to someone who isn't a good fit may result in your horse being resold at some point down the line. (Realize that this may happen anyway. Once you sell your horse, his fate is out of your control.)

>> **Be cautious about potential buyers.** Unscrupulous people in the horse world sometimes pretend to be buying a horse to ride when in reality they intend the animal for slaughter. Combat this problem by asking potential buyers plenty of questions about themselves and their intent for the horse,

and don't hesitate to say no if you get a bad feeling. Keeping your horse's price tag well above meat value helps keep these buyers away.

>> **Offer a buy-back option on the horse.** Tell the buyer you want to buy the horse back at the purchase price at any time in the horse's life if the owner decides he no longer wants the horse.

Leasing

If your horse is still healthy and sound, the best alternative to selling him is to lease him. (Chapter 4 has full details on leasing.) When you lease your horse, you still maintain control over his ultimate destiny while divesting yourself of the time and financial responsibilities of ownership. In a lease situation, the lessee pays you a sum for use of the horse, in addition to whatever other costs you want to charge (board, shoes, and preventive veterinary care are the norm in full leases). The lessee cares for and rides the horse while you collect the fee.

The three typical types of leases are

>> A *full lease,* where someone rides and cares for your horse off your premises.

>> A *full lease with stipulations,* where the lessee rides and cares for your horse on your property or at an approved facility.

>> A *partial lease,* where the lessee shares use of the horse with you or another partial lessee.

WARNING

Some headaches come with leasing. If the horse develops a major health or training problem, you need to get involved. If your lessee stops making payments to you or backs out of the lease, you have to deal with the problem. But if you truly care about your horse's future, leasing is surely the best way to go.

Donation to a program

If your horse is healthy and sound, donation to a special riding program is an excellent alternative to selling him because most centers for therapeutic riding accept donations of horses. Centers typically look for horses that are sound, quiet, gentle, and forgiving to inexperienced riders. In turn, the horse receives excellent care. Plus, you may even be able to go visit him from time to time.

If you contact a therapeutic riding center and offer your horse for donation, center personnel will want to evaluate the horse to make sure that he has the right disposition for the job. If the horse passes muster, you can grant the center legal possession and receive a charitable tax write-off for your trouble.

Although this option can be great for an older horse, we want to caution you about two things regarding donating your horse:

>> **Make sure that you donate your horse to a legitimate organization.** Con artists often present themselves as representing a therapeutic riding program when they're really procuring free horses to sell for slaughter. Ask for proof of the group's nonprofit status, and pay their stables a visit. If in doubt, contact your state government to determine whether the group is registered as a nonprofit therapeutic riding program.

>> **Find out the therapeutic riding program's policy on disposing of horses who are no longer needed.** Most therapeutic riding organizations euthanize horses that are too old or ill to perform their duties. However, some organizations sell the horses at an auction or to a horse dealer, where the horses are at risk of going to slaughter. Get the group's policy in writing. If the group sells horses at auction or to a dealer, decline to donate your horse or stipulate in writing that you're donating your horse only if you're allowed to take the horse back or buy him back at meat price when he's no longer needed in the program. The horse may be returned to you when he is very old and sick, but at least with this arrangement, you can have the horse humanely euthanized instead of sending him off to slaughter.

Gift to a family member

If your horse is rideable but you've outgrown him, consider passing him along to someone in your immediate family. Perhaps your oldest child is getting more interested in riding and wants her own horse. Maybe your spouse hasn't been riding much but wants to and could benefit from the teachings of your old veteran. Of course, this option only works if your family can afford to keep two horses. If not, consider passing your horse along to a relative who seriously wants to get into riding. You can sell the horse to your relative for a nominal fee or even give the horse away, but only under one condition: that the relative won't eventually resell the horse, but will instead sell or give the horse back to you. Get this agreement in writing so the relative feels obligated to stick to it.

Retirement

Probably the kindest option for an older horse is to retire him. Retirement is also practical because older horses tend to be harder to sell. After years of service, older horses often need and deserve a break from regular work. A pasture is the best place for a retired horse, but you can't put him out there and forget about him. He still needs daily care, grooming, veterinary care, and TLC.

WARNING

Retiring a horse to pasture is a good idea, but retiring a horse to a stall or a small, grassless paddock is *not* the best route to take unless your horse will receive daily turnout. If your horse has nothing to graze on and is confined in a small space, he will deteriorate due to the lack of exercise and mental stimulation. If you don't have your own pasture, you can keep your horse at an equine retirement facility. Try to find a retirement facility that isn't too far from where you live so you can check on your horse on regular basis.

You can find retirement facilities in your area by asking your veterinarian or searching online. Before committing to keep your horse at a retirement facility, visit the stable first. Check to make sure that the facility is well maintained and that the resident horses look happy and healthy.

Euthanasia

If you're no longer riding your horse because he's old and lame, and you can't afford to retire him, consider euthanasia. Although losing a companion after all he's done for you is painful, euthanizing him is a much kinder end for him than ending up in the slaughterhouse. You can think of the minimal cost of the euthanasia and disposal of the body (either by burial on your own property, cremation by a pet cemetery, or livestock removal service to a rendering plant) as your final gift to your old friend. See Chapter 11 for more information on euthanasia.

4

Handling Your Horse with Ease

IN THIS PART . . .

Handling your horse from the ground and in the saddle

Learning all the different ways you can ride a horse

Competing with your horse and riding just for fun

IN THIS CHAPTER

» Knowing how horses should act

» Approaching horses confidently

» Putting a halter on your horse

» Leading and tying horses correctly

» Longeing a horse with ease

» Dealing with naughty horses

Chapter **13**

Working with Your Horse from the Ground

Most people associate horses with riding, and understandably so. Nearly every equine image they're exposed to depicts a human sitting on a horse. But what most people don't think about is that before you can get up on the horse, you have to handle him from the ground.

Because horses are such large creatures — weighing nearly 10 times as much as most humans — you need skill and tact (not to mention tack!) to handle them from the ground. The fact that most horses are gentle and enjoy human company makes the job easier, but accidents still occur whenever humans are careless. Even though most people worry about falling off when they ride, humans actually are more vulnerable to horse-related injury while on the ground.

In this chapter, we give you a crash course in horse handling from the ground up. You'll find out the safest and most effective ways to deal with your horse before you get up on his back. As you discover how to handle your horse, you'll also explore the deep bond that develops between a human and a horse just from hanging out together.

Establishing the Right Manners

Horses are herd animals, which means that they are genetically programmed to be social. A big part of being social for a horse is fitting into the herd hierarchy. In horse-herd politics, a self-appointed leader tells the other horses what to do. When you handle your horse on the ground, you become the leader. If you get your horse's buy-in, he listens to you and you have the basis for a good relationship on the ground — one that translates into good rapport in the saddle.

Understanding your responsibilities

Before you begin handling your horse from the ground, know that you have certain responsibilities. As the leader of your small herd, you must hold up your end of the bargain by being firm, consistent, and confident. If you aren't, your horse will dismiss you as leader and take over the job himself. Or, if you're too rough, your horse may come to think of you as a predator rather than a benevolent leader.

To help you establish the right tone with your horse, do the following:

» **Be firm.** When you handle your horse from the ground, remember that you're the one in charge, not the horse. Don't allow your horse to push you around — literally or figuratively. Don't ever let the horse think that he is the one making the decisions. If he ever tries to boss you around, a firm jerk on the lead rope and a loud "Quit!" should get the message across.

» **Be fair.** Require the horse to do your bidding, but do so in a way that shows compassion and understanding. For example, if you're leading your horse and he's walking obediently beside you until a bale of hay falls from a nearby rafter, scares the heck out of him, and makes him pull away and nearly knock you off your feet, don't punish the horse. He's merely reacting in a normal way to something outside of his control. Instead, understand the circumstances of your horse's behavior.

» **Be patient.** Think of your horse as a 1,000-pound toddler. Sometimes he knows what he needs to do but doesn't feel like doing it. Sometimes he's at a total loss and can't figure out what you want. Have some compassion for your horse; he'd much rather be out in a pasture eating with other horses rather than doing things that make no sense to him. Think before you react, make sure that your horse understands what you want before you assume that he doesn't, and above all, be patient.

>> **Be anger-free.** Unfortunately, taking anger out on those we love is an all-too-human trait. Despite the horse's large size, he's a rather gentle creature, quite vulnerable to the abuses of humankind. (If you ever saw or read *Black Beauty,* you know what we mean.) Never lose your temper with your horse and never take out your daily frustrations on him.

>> **Be calm.** Because horses are prey animals, they tend to be nervous sorts. Whenever you're around your horse, move slowly and speak quietly. Loud voices and quick movements make horses nervous. And whatever you do, avoid waving your arms over your head when you're around a horse. For some reason, waving arms scare the daylights out of some horses.

>> **Be consistent.** Don't be wishy-washy when you deal with your horse. Expect the same behavior from him day in and day out. The more consistent you are when you handle him, the more consistent he'll be in his responses to you.

Recognizing your horse's responsibilities

Humans aren't the only ones expected to act a certain way during on-the-ground interactions. Horses need to have "good ground manners," which means they need to behave themselves when a human is handling them on the ground. Horses that do *not* have good ground manners are a hazard and a liability, and need to be trained.

Good ground manners that you must expect from your horse include:

>> **Standing still:** When your horse is being haltered or tacked up, he needs to stand quietly until you signal him that it's time for him to move.

>> **Being nice:** While you're working around your horse, he needs to have a pleasant attitude, meaning no attempts to bite or kick you and no threatening facial expressions.

>> **Walking alongside:** As you lead your horse, he should walk quietly beside you, taking your cue as to speed and which direction to turn.

>> **Respecting your space:** Your horse should always respect your physical space, never intruding on it. He should respond immediately to your requests for more space (see "Your horse crowds you" later in this chapter for more about asking your horse for space).

Approaching Your Horse in the Stall or Pasture

Before you can do anything with your horse, you have to catch him. This means approaching him in his stall or pasture, placing a halter over his head, securing it, and leading him out. If your horse is well behaved in this regard, this part is pretty easy. If he isn't well behaved, you may have a real tough job on your hands. Either way, handle the situation with safety first and foremost in your mind.

Retrieving your horse from a stall

Horses are much easier to catch when they're in a stall or small paddock. The horse realizes he has nowhere to go and rarely puts up a fight. The exception to this rule is a horse that fears his handlers or simply hates to be handled, both of which are often the result of mistreatment.

Assuming that your horse likes you and doesn't mind being caught, attach the lead rope to your horse's halter by snapping the lead rope clip onto the ring of the halter (see Figure 13-1) and follow these steps when you go to retrieve him from his stall:

1. **Speak to your horse to let him know you've arrived before you enter the stall or paddock.**

2. **Enter the stall or paddock.**

3. **Approach the horse at his left shoulder rather than directly at his face.** Horses can't see directly under their noses or directly behind them. If the horse's hindquarters are facing you as you enter the stall or paddock, make sure that the horse knows you're there before you get too close. Talk to him and try to wait until he faces you before you proceed to the next step. If he doesn't turn to face you, approach his front end from his left side.

4. **As you get closer to the horse, extend your hand, palm down, and let the horse sniff you.** This greeting assures the horse that you're friend, not foe.

5. **Loop the other end of the lead rope around the horse's neck and slip the halter over his head.** See "All Strapped In: Haltering Your Horse" later in this chapter for details on how to put a halter on your horse.

FIGURE 13-1: Stand at your horse's left shoulder when you put on a halter.

Heading toward your horse in a pasture

Catching a horse in a pasture can be tricky if the horse doesn't want to be caught. Fortunately, most horses don't mind it and will cooperate, provided the human handler approaches the horse in the right way.

Catching a horse in a pasture is different from catching him in a stall, because in a pasture, the horse has much more room to move away from you. Follow these steps for the best way to approach a horse that is loose in a pasture with other horses:

1. **Walk quietly toward the horse with your hands at your side and your halter and lead rope in hand, making sure that he sees you.**

2. **Approach the horse at his left shoulder, never directly from the front or back.** As you make contact with the horse, gently pat or scratch his neck, speaking softly.

3. **Place the lead rope around the horse's neck in a loop as you continue speaking to him.** Holding the noosed lead rope, proceed to put on the halter as we describe in the next section.

REMEMBER

Whatever you do, don't let your horse get away without being caught. After you make an attempt to catch the horse, keep trying until you succeed. If you don't, the horse quickly learns that capture can be easily eluded.

WARNING

Some people take treats out in a pasture to help catch a horse, but we don't recommend doing so when other horses are in the pasture. The group may get nasty and competitive with one another over the treats, leaving you vulnerable to a misplaced bite or kick.

Turning your horse loose in the pasture after you're finished with him requires some finesse, too, so that he doesn't develop the habit of bolting away right after you remove his halter. Take these precautions for a safe release:

>> Noose the lead rope around the horse's neck before you take the halter off.

>> Secure the horse with the lead rope with your hand, and then slip the halter off the horse's head.

>> Release the noose and allow the horse to walk away.

>> If your horse tries trot off before you have released the noose, tell him "whoa" and make him stand still. Don't release him until he is standing still.

All Strapped In: Haltering Your Horse

The fundamental tool for controlling a horse on the ground is the halter. Most horses are amenable to having a halter placed on their heads because they've been wearing one since they were foals.

TIP

Before placing the halter on your horse, check to make sure that the crown strap of the halter is unbuckled and that the lead rope is attached. The hardest thing about learning to halter a horse is visualizing where all those straps are supposed to go. Study horses wearing halters before you attempt to put one on your horse. Become familiar with the way the straps sit on a horse, and then hold a halter in your hand, imagining the horse's head inside it. See Chapter 6 for more details about halters.

REMEMBER

Your horse needs to stand quietly as you halter him. If he doesn't, you have a behavior problem on your hands — one that a professional trainer or experienced horseperson needs to deal with.

To halter your horse, follow these steps:

1. **Facing the same direction as your horse while standing at his left shoulder, place the lead rope in a loose loop around the middle of the horse's neck.** Don't tie the rope, but hold it together with your right hand. Doing so secures the horse and keeps him from walking away from you. When the lead rope is over the horse's neck and the horse is standing still, you can release it momentarily so that your hands are free to put on the halter.

2. **With the buckle side of the strap in your left hand and the crown strap in your right hand, slip the horse's nose through the noseband of the halter by reaching your right hand underneath the horse's neck, as shown in Figure 13-1.**

3. **When the horse's nose is through the halter, bring the crown piece up behind the horse's ears and buckle it so the halter fits comfortably — not too tight and not too loose.**

4. **Take the lead rope from around the horse's neck and fold the excess in your left hand while holding the attached rope just below the halter with your right hand.** You're now ready to lead your horse out of his stall or pasture.

On the Ropes: Leading Your Horse

Your role as your horse's leader is never more literal than when you're actually, physically leading him. Provided your horse is well trained and well behaved and you're confident and adept, leading a horse can be fun and easy.

Leading the right way

For safety reasons, you need to lead a horse the right way, and that means standing on your horse's left side and holding the end of the rope closest to your horse's head in your right hand as described in the previous section. Some other tips that can help you lead your horse the right way:

>> **Hold onto the lead rope with your right hand about 6 inches from the halter.** If your lead rope has a chain at the end, hold the rope just below the chain so you don't injure your hand if the horse pulls back.

   If you find you need more control when leading your horse, gain it by moving your hand closer to the halter.

>> **Never coil the remaining lead rope around your left hand.** If you do and the horse pulls back, the coil can tighten, trapping your hand.

>> **Always lead your horse from his left side.** See Figure 13-2 for the correct position for leading a horse.

>> **Give the lead rope a gentle pull with your right hand as you begin to walk forward.** The horse should begin walking, keeping pace with you so you remain at his shoulder.

>> **Turn the wrist on your right hand either left or right to turn your horse in either direction**. Turning the horse away from you is always best because it keeps your toes away from his big clumsy hooves and reinforces to the horse that he should stay out of your space Your horse should follow your lead.

>> **Stop your horse by saying, "Whoa!" and by stopping yourself and giving a backward tug on the rope with your right hand**.

FIGURE 13-2: You should stay at your horse's left shoulder when you lead.

© John Wiley & Sons, Inc.

When leading your horse, keep in mind that he doesn't know which way you intend to go at any given moment. Remember that your horse is much heavier and longer than you, and can't turn as fast or stop as quickly as you can without warning. You know that you're about to turn or stop, but your horse doesn't.

Refraining from bad habits

Try not to forget just how big your horse really is when you're leading him. It's important, because if something should something happen — like your horse spooks or starts to misbehave (see "Handling Problems from the Ground" later in this chapter) — you can be in serious physical danger if you aren't leading the proper way.

Make sure you don't fall into these bad habits when leading your horse:

>> **Don't lead a horse by anything other than a halter and lead rope, or the reins of a bridle.** If leading by the reins, don't loop them over the horse's neck while leading but rather hold them free instead. Don't loop them around your hand, either.

>> **Don't coil or wrap the lead rope around your hand.** If the horse pulls back or runs off, the rope may tighten around your hand, and you can be dragged.

>> **Don't wrap your hand around the chain part of a lead rope (if your lead rope has a chain, that is — not all do).** If the horse pulls back, your hand can be injured.

>> **Don't put your hand in the halter to lead your horse in place of using a lead rope.** If the horse bolts and your hand gets caught in the halter, you may be dragged.

>> **Don't walk in front of your horse with him trailing behind you.** If your horse suddenly bolts forward, you can be trampled.

>> **Don't trot your horse when you're leading him, unless someone is evaluating the animal for lameness.** Leading a trotting horse is difficult for novice horse handlers.

In Knots: Tying Your Horse

To tie up a horse so that he can't walk off while you're saddling him, grooming him, or doing anything else that requires him to stand still, you just take a rope and tie him to a post. Right? Wrong. Although it may seem that simple, tying a horse is anything but. Horses must be secured in just the right way or they can get themselves into all kinds of trouble.

Pulling back when frightened is one of the most common and dangerous problems that occurs when a horse is tied (see "Your horse pulls back when tied" later in this chapter for solutions to this problem). Another problem involves the horse getting tangled up in the lead rope.

When tying a horse, follow these rules to ensure safety:

>> **Whenever possible, tie a horse in *crossties*, which are two ropes on either side of the horse that attach to the sides of the horse's halter.** Crossties need to be about the same height as the top of the horse's shoulders.

(See Figure 13-3 to see what crossties look like.) Tying a horse in crossties is much safer than tying a horse to a hitching post or other object.

Make sure that your horse is familiar with the feeling of being crosstied before you tie him this way. Gradually get him used to the idea by attaching one crosstie to his halter first and your lead rope to the other. That way, he gets used to the pull that comes from the crosstie without being completely confined in it.

And make sure that the crossties have a breakaway feature so the horse won't get hung up in the ties if he panics and thrashes around. Quick-release snaps are a good feature to have on crossties, so a frightened horse can be turned loose if he's in danger of hurting himself or someone else. Consider buying a cotton lead rope that's affixed to a panic or quick-release snap that you can release whenever the horse pulls back or gets tangled up. This rope is the safest kind for tying.

FIGURE 13-3:
When you secure a horse with crossties, you attach ropes on either side of the halter.

© John Wiley & Sons, Inc.

>> **Tie a horse only by a halter and lead rope, or halter and crossties.** *Never* tie a horse by the reins of a bridle. If the horse pulls back, the reins can break and the bit may damage the horse's jaw.

>> **Tie a horse only to an immovable object.** Horses need to be tied to solid fence posts, hitching posts made for this purpose, horse trailers hooked to a truck, crossties, or, if on the trail, to strong, secure tree trunks. The rope needs to be tied so that its height is stable and won't slip down toward the ground. Horses are strong, and if they spook and pull back when tied to something that isn't secure, they can drag the object or pull it right out of the ground.

>> **When tying a horse with a lead rope, use a safety, or quick-release, knot.** The knot can be released in an emergency by pulling on the loose end. Practice tying a safety knot and make sure you know precisely how to tie it before you use it to secure a horse. See Figure 13-4 for instructions on tying a safety knot.

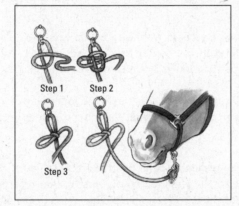

FIGURE 13-4:
You need to practice tying a safety, or quick-release, knot.

© John Wiley & Sons, Inc.

>> **Always tie a horse with the knot at about the level of the horse's withers, with no more than 3 feet of rope from the post to the halter.** Doing so keeps the horse from getting the rope over his head or from getting a leg caught in it. See Figure 13-5 for a drawing of a horse safely tied.

>> **Never tie a horse with a chain shank run through his halter.** If the horse pulls back, the chain can injure him.

>> **Never leave a horse alone and unsupervised when tied up.** You'd be amazed at how quickly a tied horse can get into trouble.

FIGURE 13-5:
A horse is safely tied when there is no more than 3 feet of rope between the halter and a hitching post.

© John Wiley & Sons, Inc.

Circle Around: Longeing Your Horse

Riding is only one way of exercising your horse. You can also do something called *longeing*, where you stand in the center of an imaginary 60-foot circle as your horse, attached to a rope that you're holding, moves around you.

REMEMBER

Why longe your horse? Can't you just ride the horse for exercise? You can, but then you'd be passing up on all the benefits that longeing provides you and your horse. For example:

>> **Longeing is a way of providing controlled exercise to your horse on days that you can't ride.** It's safer than turning a horse out to run around on his own because with longeing, you can control the horse's behavior and keep him from doing something to hurt himself.

>> **Longeing before riding helps a horse get rid of excess energy that can create problems when you're in the saddle.**

>> **Longeing teaches your horse to respect your authority and respond to voice commands.**

The following sections tell you what you need to know to prepare your horse for longeing and longe your horse the right way.

Readying your horse for longeing

Before you can longe your horse, you must have the proper tools. These include:

>> A 25- to 30-foot long cotton longe line to attach to the horse and hold in your hand

>> A halter, longeing cavesson, or English snaffle bridle to go over the horse's head and attach to the longe line. Figure 13-6 shows how to rig up a horse for longeing (see Chapter 6 for more about these pieces of gear):

- If you're longeing your horse with a halter, attach the longe line to the halter by running the clip end of the longe line through the ring on the left side of the halter, pulling the longe line up over the horse's ears, and then clipping it to the ring on the right side of the halter. Make sure that the halter is snug so that it doesn't slide sideways on the horse's head when you begin longeing. (Run the clip end of the longe line through the ring on the left side when you are preparing to longe your horse in a counter-clockwise direction. Switch the clip end to the ring on the right side of the halter before you longe your horse in the other direction.)

- If you're using a *longeing cavesson,* outfit the horse with the cavesson and attach the longe line to the cavesson, by clipping the longe line to the ring on the cavesson in the center of the top of the noseband, which should be about 4 inches above the horse's nostrils. Make sure that the cavesson is snug on the horse's head so that it doesn't slide around.

- If you use a *snaffle bridle,* outfit the horse in the bridle, secure the reins, and attach the longe line to the bridle. Secure the reins by putting them over the horse's head as if you were going to ride, twisting them a few times, unbuckling the throatlatch, and then rebuckling the throatlatch with the reins underneath so they don't swing when the horse moves. Attach the longe line to the bridle by running the clip end of the longe line through the left bit ring and up over the horse's head behind the ears. Clip the longe line to the bit ring on the other side of the bridle. (Run the clip end of the longe line through the ring on the left side when you are preparing to longe your horse in a counter-clockwise direction. Switch the clip end to the ring on the right-side bit ring before you longe your horse in the other direction.)

>> A longe whip to encourage the horse to move forward (see Chapter 6 for details on this tool)

>> A secure, fenced area with good footing (not wet and slippery, and not hard) big enough to longe your horse

>> Leather gloves to help you keep a good grip on the longe line and to protect your hands

Before you start longeing the horse, you need to properly prepare and fit the pre-viously listed equipment. Have an experienced horse person who knows how to longe help you the first few times you try.

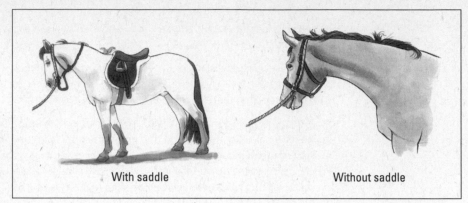

FIGURE 13-6:
The correct way to rig up a horse for longeing with a saddle and snaffle bridle, and using a halter.

If you plan to ride your horse after longeing him, you want to tack up the horse in his saddle, tightening the girth or cinch securely. Likewise, if you ride in an English saddle, be sure that the stirrup irons are run up to the top of the leathers so the irons don't bounce against the horse when he's moving. Wrap the leathers tightly around the irons to secure them. See Chapter 15 for more about tacking up your horse.

WARNING

Before you attempt to longe your horse, make sure that the horse has been trained to longe. If you're not sure whether he's been longed, ask an experienced horse person to try longeing the horse to see whether the animal knows what's expected of him.

Longeing your horse properly and safely

If your horse is trained to longe and is obedient, longeing can be an easy task, after you know what you're doing. Realize, though, that longeing takes practice.

REMEMBER

We strongly recommend having an experienced horse person help you the first few times you longe your horse to make sure that you and the horse are doing it right.

Take these steps when longeing your horse (Figure 13-7 shows the proper lunging position):

1. **Prepare your horse as described in the previous section, and take your horse to a secure area with plenty of room to work.**

2. **Imagine a large circle, and position your horse so that he's prepared to move in a counter-clockwise direction on that circle.** Hold the part of the

longe line attached to the horse's head in your right hand. Fold up the excess longe line in your left hand. Hold the longe whip in your left hand, too.

3. **Tell your horse "Whoa!" and step away from the animal.** As you back up, feed out some of the excess longe line loosely so you don't pull on the horse's head. If your horse tries to follow you, tell him "Whoa!" until he stops.

4. **Back up until you're about 4 feet from the horse. Point the longe whip toward the horse's hindquarters.** If your horse knows voice commands, tell him to "walk out." If not, cluck to the horse to get him to walk forward. As the horse starts to move, slowly back up until you're about 10 feet away from him.

5. **Adjust your position relative to the horse.** You should be standing at the top of an imaginary triangle in which the horse's body serves as the base, with the longe line and longe whip as the other two sides. Your body should at an angle that puts you behind the horse's eye. Staying in this position keeps the horse moving forward.

    Keep the horse walking in a clockwise direction for five minutes.

6. **Change directions.** Point the whip upright and tell the horse "Whoa!" When the horse stops, slowly approach his head, taking up the slack in the longe line as you go. Be sure to keep the whip pointing up so you don't confuse the horse.

7. **Place your hand on the longe line about 4 inches from where it attaches to the horse's head.** Turn the horse around so he faces the opposite direction. Switch the clip end of the longe line to the other side of the halter or bridle, as described in "Readying your horse for longing." Reverse the position of the longe line and whip. You now should be holding the part of the longe line attached to the horse in your left hand and the excess longe line and whip in your right.

FIGURE 13-7:
In the correct position for longeing, keep your longe line in one hand and your whip in the other.

© John Wiley & Sons, Inc.

8. **Ask the horse to "walk out" again, adjusting your position as in Step 5.** Work your horse at different speeds, changing direction every five minutes. To get the horse to go faster, tell the horse "Trot on" and then "Canter." If the horse doesn't know voice commands, cluck to him for the trot or kiss to him for the canter to him until the horse speeds up to the gait you're looking for. Cluck or kiss to the horse again if he breaks into a slower gait.

9. **To stop, step slightly out of your position so that you are even with the horse's head, and say "Whoa!"** The horse should halt on command.

10. **If your horse has worked up a sweat on the longe line, cool him down by walking him for at least 10 to 15 minutes, either on the longe line or by leading him, using the longe line as a lead rope, holding the excess rope in your left hand.**

Safety issues abound on the subject of longeing. Keep all of these points in mind when exercising your horse this way:

>> **Longe your horse only in an enclosed area in case he somehow gets away from you.**

>> **Get help while you're new to longeing.** Make sure that your horse is quiet and well behaved while longeing before you start doing it on your own.

>> **Don't longe for long periods (20 minutes is more than enough), or too often (twice a week maximum).** Exercising in a tight circle is hard on the horse's legs. Give your horse plenty of walking breaks, especially if he's out of shape. If your horse isn't used to being longed, build up slowly to longer work periods, starting out with a 10-minute session and gradually moving up in 5-minute increments per week.

>> **Never loop, coil, or wrap the excess longe line around your hand.** You can be seriously injured if the horse pulls away from you.

>> **Some horses get spunky when they're longeing, so stay far enough away that you won't be kicked if the horse start frolicking on the longe line.**

>> **Be cautious with the longe whip.** Don't use it to strike your horse, and be careful not to wave it around, especially in the horse's direction. Think of the whip as an extension of your hand, which is guiding the horse forward.

>> **Try not to talk while you're longeing except to give voice commands to your horse. That way you won't confuse your horse.**

>> **When giving voice commands, carefully enunciate and differentiate each command so the horse can distinguish between them.**

Handling Problems from the Ground

Sometimes, no matter how hard you try to do things right, your horse may make handling from the ground difficult for you. Horses are much like small children — they easily develop bad habits and often test you to see what they can get away with. At times, their misbehavior comes from fear; other times, it stems from sheer boredom or lack of training.

REMEMBER

The way you handle problem behaviors on the ground is important. If your horse discovers that he can get away with naughty behavior, he will keep doing it, and eventually, you'll have a serious problem on your hands. Conversely, if you let your horse know that you're wise to these shenanigans and you're consistent in correcting the bad behaviors, he soon gives up that behavior.

The following sections cover some typical stunts that horses pull when you're handling them on the ground and ways you can combat these behaviors.

Your horse resists being caught

Refusing to be caught is a much bigger problem with horses that live out in a pasture with other horses. Horses who have been worked hard or don't enjoy being around humans all that much, usually because they've been mistreated in the past, may come to associate being caught with something unpleasant. Horses that that experience pain or discomfort when being ridden often resist capture.

TIP

If your horse is hard to catch, consider having him checked out by a veterinarian to make sure the he isn't experiencing pain somewhere in his body that is being exacerbated with riding. If your horse refuses to be caught — or at least gives you a good run for your money before allowing you to get close (even though you've tried catching him by using the method we describe earlier "Heading toward your horse in a pasture") — the horse needs to be reconditioned to associate being caught with something pleasant. If he has a health problem, it needs to be resolved before you can begin retraining him.

Practice catching him alone in a small enclosure by using this method:

1. **Arm yourself with a favorite treat like a carrot or slice of apple.**

2. **Attempt to approach the horse by using the method described in the earlier "Heading toward your horse in a pasture" section.** Don't bring a halter with you because you're only practicing right now. Be nonchalant about your approach, and don't look the horse right in the eye.

3. **As you get closer to the horse, extend your hand so the horse sees the treat.** The horse probably will let you approach or may even walk toward you to get the treat.

4. **When you make contact with the horse, give him the treat, scratch him on the withers or in his favorite spot, and then walk away before he has a chance to leave.** Practice this a number of times over a period of a few days until the horse seems comfortable with your approach.

5. **Begin placing the halter on the horse after you give him the treat.** Don't take him out of the enclosure, though. Simply halter him, give him his treat, scratch him where he likes it, then remove the halter and leave.

   When you get the feeling that the horse is comfortable with this routine, move the horse to a larger enclosure and practice the same method for a couple of weeks, alternating times that you take him out of his enclosure to ride him, and times that you just halter him and remove the halter and leave him alone.

REMEMBER

   Make sure that you don't overwork the horse after you take him out of the enclosure. Many horses don't like to be caught because they're unhappy about what happens to them after they leave their pasture.

6. **After several weeks of practice, you can move your horse back to the original pasture and try this method in this larger area.** If other horses share the pasture, you have to skip the treats, because things can get dangerous if the other horses start fighting over the food. Instead of treats, give lots of scratches and kind words.

   If, after a month or so of working on this problem, you're not getting anywhere with your difficult-to-catch horse, you need to call in a professional trainer for help.

Your horse pulls forward when you lead

Few things are as aggravating as having a horse pulling you forward when you lead him. Plenty of horses demonstrate this bad habit, and it requires work to correct. Try the following techniques to cope with a horse that likes to pull forward:

>> **Lead the horse in a bridle instead of a halter and lead rope.** The bridle gives you more control and makes the horse less likely to rush forward.

>> **Keep the horse's head bent slightly to the left to keep the horse from pushing into you.**

>> **Repeatedly ask your horse to stop, then walk, on your command.** This repetition reinforces that he must stay with you and not pull you.

>> **Ask an experienced horse person to help you affix a *stud chain* (an 8-inch chain made for use on horses) to the horse's halter that goes over the bridge of the nose.** This chain makes pulling you along as you lead him uncomfortable for the horse.

JAILBREAK! CATCHING A RUNAWAY HORSE

Nothing can disrupt the quiet atmosphere of a stable like a horse that has gotten loose from his handler. The cry "loose horse!" makes human heads go up in a flash.

Something strange happens when a horse gets loose at a well populated stable. After they realize what's going on, other horses get excited and start bucking, whinnying, and dancing around. Here are some pointers on how to cope when an errant horse makes a bid for freedom.

- **Don't panic.** Stay calm and shout "loose horse!" at the top of your lungs to warn other people that an escapee is on the premises.

- **If the escapee isn't your charge, but you're leading, riding, or standing next to your own horse when the culprit gets loose, be aware that your horse is probably going to react with excitement when he discovers what's happening.** Stop in your tracks and dismount or untie your horse quickly. Hold on to your horse tightly and be prepared for some dancing around.

- **If a horse you're handling gets away from you, don't chase him.** Chasing the horse only makes him run away from you with increasing speed. Take it from us: You won't be able to outrun him.

- **Walk slowly in the direction your horse ran to see where he's gone.** Most horses that escape from a handler in a familiar setting don't go far — usually to the nearest food storage area. If you find that he stopped somewhere to eat, speak softly and walk up to him slowly, placing a lead rope around his neck to secure him. Remember not to give off any vibes that you're angry — if you do, the horse won't let you get close.

- **If your loose horse is not eating but just milling around, get a handful of hay or a carrot and slowly walk in his direction.** After the horse sees you, stand still and offer him the food in an outstretched hand as you speak softly to him. Most horses are more than happy to exchange their newfound freedom for a bite of something tasty. While the sellout is happily munching away, slowly place a lead rope around his neck.

- **If your loose horse has stopped to eat, but takes off again when he sees you approaching, you need the help of one or two other people.** Arm yourselves with halters, and walk in different directions with the idea of surrounding him by blocking all his exits. Most horses will realize their defeat and allow themselves to be caught.

WARNING

If you're a newcomer to horses and find yourself handling a horse that repeatedly pulls you whenever you try to walk alongside him, you have a serious problem. Have someone experienced handle this horse and work on solving the problem before you try to lead the horse. The experienced handler can teach the horse not to pull forward and can teach you what to do to avoid being dragged along. Horses that are prone to pulling forward tend to exhibit this behavior even more with inexperienced horse people.

Your horse pulls back when tied

Horses that are in the habit of pulling back when tied create terrible problems for owners. Some horses are so bad about pulling back that they can't be tied at all and must be held by hand whenever they need to be secured.

Occasionally, a horse pulls back when something frightens him at the tie rack. You can't miss it when this happens: The horse gets a terrified look in his eye and throws all of his weight on his haunches, practically sitting down as he pulls with all his might against his halter. If the horse breaks loose once or twice during such an incident, it can be the beginning of a bad habit — the horse has discovered that pulling back means freedom. Follow these guidelines to ensure that your horse doesn't develop the terrible habit of pulling back:

>> **Always tie your horse to something secure, using a lead rope or cross-ties.** See the earlier section "In Knots: Tying Your Horse."

>> **Tie your horse securely with a safety knot, using an unbreakable halter and lead rope.**

>> **Don't tie your horse with too little rope.** If the horse feels he can't move his head much, he may become claustrophobic and pull back.

>> **Be careful about how you approach your horse when he's tied.** Don't come at the horse suddenly with a strange object, spray the horse in the face or upper body with water or fly spray, or do anything else that may spook him and make him pull to get away.

>> **Anticipate what's likely to scare your horse.** If you have to do something to the horse's head that frightens or upsets him — applying eye medicine, for example — untie the rope first and hold the horse yourself so he doesn't have an opportunity to pull back when tied.

If a horse pulls back when tied to a hitching post or other object, try the following to get the horse to stop pulling:

>> **Pull on the loose end of the safety knot to release the horse from being tied.** Be sure to take hold of the rope so the horse can't run away. Don't allow the horse to break the halter. Most horses will stop pulling when they feel a release in resistance.

>> **Step behind the horse (well out of kicking range) and shout at him.** The horse will move forward to get away from you.

Be aware that when one horse pulls back, the other horses tied with him at the same post often pull back, too.

If you have a horse that is a chronic puller, enlist the help of a professional horse trainer to break this difficult-to-change habit.

Your horse bites you

Most horses are pleasant creatures, but you may run across one that is the equine equivalent of a crabby 2-year-old. These grumpy-grouches may be wonderful when you're riding them, but they try to bite you when you handle them from the ground.

Horses usually bite humans for one of two reasons: to play or to send an aggressive message. Either way, the results are the same — an extremely painful bite that usually leaves black and blue marks on tender human skin.

Some horses bite because they're in constant pain or because they're experiencing pain when being ridden and they now associate being handled and ridden with discomfort. If your horse is a biter, have him checked out by a vet to make sure he doesn't have a medical issue behind his bad attitude.

Most horses are taught at a young age not to bite humans in play or out of aggressiveness. Horses that haven't learned this lesson, however, must be trained in adulthood. If you have a horse that tries to bite you when you're grooming or leading him, follow these guidelines to break the habit:

>> **If your horse bites you or attempts to bite you, respond immediately by yelling "Quit!" and jerking once on the lead rope.**

>> **Get to know your horse and anticipate when he may try to bite.** If he bites when you're grooming him, let him bang the side of his head into your raised elbow as he turns around to bite. If he tries to bite you when you're leading him, hold your fist up near his mouth so he bangs into your knuckles when he swings his head around to bite.

TIP

We like the idea of feeding treats to horses, because we think it helps develop the bond between horse and human. However, if your horse is the nippy type, we recommend that you don't give him treats by hand, and instead, leave goodies for him in his feeder. Check out Chapter 6 for more info about feeding your horse.

Your horse kicks you

Kicking is a maneuver that nature gave horses to help protect them against predators. Unfortunately, it's also a maneuver that gets used on humans now and then (usually only with one hind leg rather than both at the same time). Although most horses don't go around kicking people, enough do to make this behavior worth mentioning.

WARNING

Most horses kick only when startled from behind; others kick deliberately to keep humans from doing something the horse finds unpleasant. Whatever the cause, a well-placed kick from a horse can do serious damage to the human body.

Here are some pointers to avoid getting kicked by a horse:

>> **Never approach a horse directly from behind because this area is one of a horse's blind spots.** Instead approach from the side, all the while speaking to the horse so he clearly knows you're coming.

>> **If you must walk past a horse from behind, give the horse plenty of room.** Walk far enough away so the horse's back leg can't reach you. If you don't have that much room, the next best alternative is to walk so close to the horse's hindquarters that you're nearly touching them. If the horse moves to kick, you'll only be bumped by his hock and not kicked by his hoof.

>> **If a horse suddenly turns his rump toward you, pinning his ears at the same time, the horse is threatening to kick you.** Yell "Quit!" as loud as you can and quickly get out of range.

>> **If you're grooming or saddling a horse and the horse pins his ears and kicks out at you, yell "Quit!" and slap the horse with an open hand on the shoulder or side.** Don't run away and leave the horse alone, which only reinforces the bad behavior. If your horse always reacts with a kick or kick threat when you groom a particular spot or tighten the cinch, consider whatever you're doing as potentially causing the horse pain. Have a veterinarian check out the horse.

>> **If you find yourself dealing with a chronic kicker, get help from a professional trainer to fix this dangerous habit.**

Your horse crowds you

Well-trained horses learn at a young age to respect humans. They know that when a human is standing nearby, they shouldn't crowd or invade that person's space.

WARNING

Horses who haven't been taught this lesson can be downright bratty when it comes to crowding. Although most horses don't have any intention of hurting you when they crowd, their sheer bulk can cause injury regardless of their intent.

If you find yourself dealing with a horse who repeatedly pushes into you when you're leading him, grooming him, or going into his stall or pasture, you have a crowder on your hands — a horse that needs professional help.

If your horse is generally well behaved in this area, you can reinforce his good habits by following these rules:

>> **Make sure that your horse always gives way to you when you ask him to move.** When you push on your horse's shoulder or hindquarters from the side, he should willingly move away from you. Practice this movement with your horse every so often to remind the horse that he needs to respect your space.

>> **Never allow your horse to push you up against a wall or other object.** If he does, yell "Quit!" at the horse and slap him with a flat palm on the shoulder or side.

>> **Don't let your horse get away with crowding you when you're leading him.** If the horse starts coming into your space, use your right elbow to jab him in the shoulder.

Chapter **14**

Selecting a Riding Discipline

One of the coolest things about horseback riding is that you can ride in so many different ways. Humans have been riding horses for thousands of years, so they've had plenty of time to create a whole bunch of different styles (*disciplines* in horse lingo), several of which still are in use today.

Before you buy a horse or even take riding lessons, you have to figure out which discipline is for you. Don't, however, confuse discipline with sport. One discipline can cover several sports. For example, cutting is just one of many sports within the western riding discipline. For a rundown of different equine sports, see Chapter 18.

In this chapter, we describe the most common forms of riding to help you get a handle on the style you want to pursue.

The Most Popular Ways to Ride

Nearly everyone who rides has a favorite riding discipline. As a budding equestrian, you need to find one, too, so you know in advance exactly how you'll be riding your horse. You don't have to be married to a discipline forever, but you need to at least start with a commitment to riding in it. You can always switch to another discipline later on.

REMEMBER

Your choice of a riding style is a very personal one. You need to choose a discipline that you find attractive and with which you feel comfortable. The style you choose may be one that you've always admired from afar or one that your friends participate in. Realize, however, that each discipline calls for different skills. You may have more talent for one than another.

TIP

Before you choose your riding discipline, do some research. Read up on the history of the discipline and the equine sports that ride in the discipline. Be sure to take some lessons in the discipline *before* you make the serious commitment of buying a horse trained in that style — and the tack (equipment) to go with it (see Chapter 6 for more about tack). What looks good to you from the ground may not feel comfortable when you're in the saddle.

The most popular riding styles in the United States and Canada today are hunt seat, dressage, saddle seat, and western. The following sections tell you a bit about the history of each style, the sports that utilize them, and some basics about riding in the different styles.

Showing off with hunt seat

Few feelings are more exhilarating than the sensation of cantering along on a horse in a hunt-seat saddle. When checking out this discipline, you'll discover that wonderful sensation. The English discipline of *hunt seat* gets its name from the British sport of fox hunting. Unlike fox hunting, most hunt-seat riding takes place in an arena, although plenty of hunt-seat riders also *hack* (ride on the trail). Hunt seat is probably the most popular discipline in the world.

The uses

Hunt seat is the style of choice for many people who participate in horse shows. In hunt-seat competitions, judges rate riders *over fences* (evaluating the horse and/or rider for their skill over a course of jumps) and *on the flat* (judging horse and/or rider in the arena at the walk, trot, and canter). Competitive hunt-seat class competition is conducted within different divisions determined by age and expertise of either the horse or rider.

Some riders who master hunt seat eventually move on to a sport called show jumping. *Show jumping* is similar to hunt-seat competition, but it isn't for the faint of heart, because the jumps are higher, and time and speed are of the essence. (See Chapter 18 for more about show jumping.)

People ride many different breeds in hunt seat, but Thoroughbreds are the horses you see most often in this discipline (see Chapter 3 for details on different breeds).

The tack

Logically enough, hunt-seat riding uses hunt-seat saddles. Varying only slightly in style from one to another (you more commonly see all-purpose saddles and show jumping saddles), these saddles enable the rider to maintain close contact with the horse's body. The seat is rather shallow, and the stirrups are kept relatively short.

Hunt-seat headgear for the horse usually consists of a single-rein bridle (one rein attaches to either side of the bit) with a bit that offers direct contact with the horse's mouth. One exception is the *pelham bit,* which uses two reins (see Chapter 6 for more about the tack that riders use in hunt seat).

The ride

Hunt seat is an excellent discipline to practice if you want to develop good balance on horseback. Hunt-seat saddles are small, and you have to learn to ride well to ride hunt seat.

When riding hunt seat for show, judges expect you to sit in the saddle — maintaining correct body position — as the horse walks. Figure 14-1 shows a hunt-seat rider in correct position. An imaginary line can be drawn up through the back of the heel and through the hip, shoulder, and ear. At the trot, you have to *sit the trot,* which means to sit firmly in the saddle. You must also *post the trot,* which is the action of lifting your rear end up out of the saddle and bringing it back down again, all to the rhythm of the horse's gait. At the canter, you lean slightly forward and move with the horse's body, with your seat firmly in the saddle. (See Chapter 2 for more details on how horses move.)

If you plan to jump on horseback (and most hunt-seat riders do), you have to master, or maintain, the *two-point position* (also known as the half-seat) while the horse actually negotiates the jump. Two-point requires you to position your torso forward over the horse's neck while lifting your bottom off the saddle.

Staying natural with dressage

Dressage, an English discipline, is one of the oldest riding styles in the world. Its roots lie in ancient European military maneuvers. Consequently, this type of riding has long been popular in Europe. Over the past several decades, dressage has become rather popular in North America, too.

FIGURE 14-1:
A rider in correct
hunt-seat
position sits tall
in the saddle.

© John Wiley & Sons, Inc.

The uses

Dressage is primarily a competitive discipline, although not in the same sense as other equine sports such as reining and show jumping. Dressage competitors strive to achieve different skill levels that are measured by tests. The dressage levels of mastery are called Introductory Level, Training Level, First Level, Second Level, Third Level, Fourth Level, and Olympic Level. At dressage events, the riders with the highest scores receive ribbons, but most dressage riders care more about the quality of their own test scores rather than those of the other competitors.

The discipline of dressage focuses on and emphasizes the horse's natural movements. For horse and for rider, this discipline is one of the most difficult to master. Riders trained in dressage work very hard, which ultimately ranks them among the best riders in the world.

Warmbloods are the most popular breed for upper-level dressage, and yet plenty of riders compete in regional and local events on Quarter Horses, Thoroughbreds, Appaloosas, Morgans, Saddlebreds, and many other breeds (see Chapter 3).

The tack

The discipline of dressage calls for a dressage saddle, which looks much like a hunt-seat saddle to the untrained eye. Closer scrutiny reveals that the seat of a dressage saddle is deeper than that of a hunt-seat saddle. The flaps of a dressage saddle also are wider and at a greater angle to the seat. Finally, you wear the stirrups lower in dressage than in hunt seat.

As far as bridles go, dressage bridles don't vary too much from the bridles you see in hunt seat. See Chapter 6 for the complete scoop on dressage saddles and bridles.

The ride

To master dressage, you and your horse must be pretty athletic. Many people compare dressage to ballet because it calls for the same kind of grace and discipline from the horse. You likewise have to become a very good rider to exact that sort of bearing from your horse.

If you pursue dressage, you practice riding at the walk, trot, and canter. At the trot, you're taught to *post* (move up and down in the saddle to the rhythm of the horse's movement) and to sit firmly in the saddle at the canter. Figure 14-2 shows a dressage rider in correct position in the saddle at the canter. The rider sits deep in the saddle, and an imaginary line comes behind the heel and goes up through the hip, shoulder, and ear.

FIGURE 14-2: A dressage rider in correct position at the canter.

© John Wiley & Sons, Inc.

Riding high with saddle seat

Saddle seat is considered an English discipline, although it is uniquely American. You don't see as much saddle seat as the other English disciplines in most parts of the country, but this riding style nonetheless has its very dedicated followers. The roots of saddle-seat riding lie in the American South, where the discipline is still popular today.

The uses

Competition is the main purpose of the saddle-seat discipline, although many saddle-seat riders also enjoy trail riding. Shows for American gaited breeds always contain saddle-seat classes, and so do many shows for Morgans and Arabians. Saddle-seat classes are judged either on the horse's action or the rider's position in the saddle (equitation). For a horse to be successful in saddle-seat competition, he must be a flashy animal.

You primarily see saddle seat on horses with high leg action, most often gaited horses like American Saddlebreds, Tennessee Walking Horses, and Racking Horses (see Chapter 3 for more information on gaited horses).

The tack

Saddle-seat riding uses a *show saddle*, which is a type of English saddle, although it's quite different from hunt-seat and dressage saddles. Show saddles are flatter than other English saddles, have a shallower seat, and feature a design that enables the horse's shoulders to move freely as the animal demonstrates high, front-end action. This design causes the rider to sit far behind the horse's withers, taking the rider's weight off the front part of the horse. The stirrups are worn rather long, similar to the length of the dressage rider's stirrups.

The bridle that saddle seat typically uses varies considerably from other English bridles. Called a *double bridle*, this piece of equipment features two bits and two sets of reins (as opposed to one bit and one set of reins used in conventional bridles). One set of reins controls the curb bit, which you use to establish and maintain the set of the horse's head (the position in which the horse holds his head relative to his neck). The other set of reins controls a snaffle bit, which helps keep the horse's head and neck up high. Riders need considerable dexterity and skill because they must use each set of reins separately rather than together, which is the usual tendency. See Chapter 6 for more details on show saddles and double bridles.

The ride

If you choose to ride saddle seat on a gaited horse, you'll notice the four-beat gaits of breeds such as the American Saddlebred, the Tennessee Walking Horse, and the Racking Horse provide a completely different experience than riding a so-called "trotting horse." The fact that you're sitting in a saddle that puts your legs out in front of you instead of beneath you like most other disciplines (see Figure 14-3) makes the ride even more unrivaled in feeling.

The most exciting aspect of the saddle-seat discipline is the way that it better enables you to show off the horse you're riding. Sitting astride an animal who commands the attention of spectators with his flashy style and assertive presence is an exhilarating benefit of the saddle seat discipline.

FIGURE 14-3:
A saddle-seat rider in the correct position keeps her legs out in front.

Taking it easy with western

Thanks to Hollywood, almost everyone is familiar with the discipline of western riding. Every cowboy movie showcases western riding, but it isn't the best execution of the style that we've seen.

Western riding and the saddle used with it are creations that arose in the American West and have become the most popular style of riding in the United States. This relatively large saddle was the perfect invention for ranch hands who worked cattle on the range from dawn to dusk and traveled long distances on horseback.

The uses

Cowhands who work cattle in the West still use western riding, but its biggest function is as a form of pleasure and show riding. Western shows and rodeos take place around the country by the thousands every year, sporting classes such as western pleasure, trail, gymkhana, reining, roping, and cutting. In each of these sports, the western saddle and the style of riding associated with it is the only discipline permitted.

The discipline of western riding is also a favorite of equestrians who ride for the sheer joy of it. Trail riders throughout North America ride in western saddles, primarily because of the saddle's comfort and the discipline's relaxed style.

The Quarter Horse has nearly cornered the western riding market, although breeds like the Appaloosa and Paint are popular western horses, too. Because of the western saddle's design, you don't often see rangy Thoroughbreds and other high-withered breeds that aren't suited to wearing the saddle in this discipline.

The tack

The tack you use in western riding is one of the neatest things about the discipline. The western saddle, with its high pommel and cantle (see Chapter 6) and its very distinct horn, differs considerably from the English saddle. This difference isn't surprising because the primary influences for the Western saddle came from Spain and Mexico, not Britain.

The western saddle's stirrups are also different in that they consist of large fenders and are sewn directly onto the saddle's body. Unlike English saddles, the stirrups themselves are not made of iron, but instead are wooden with a leather covering.

Even the girth of a western saddle — more correctly called a *cinch* — is different. Unlike the English version, a part of the saddle called a *latigo* strap holds the western saddle on the horse. You must loop the strap through the girth and knot it high on the cinch ring.

Western bridles also differ considerably from their English counterparts. Typically, western bridles consist of a leather headstall and not much else. Some bridles bear brow bands and throatlatches, but many don't. The bit is almost always a curb bit — although snaffles are becoming more popular and usually are used without curb shanks for training. A curb chain is present on every western bridle that bears curb shanks. See Chapter 6 for a complete explanation of the different parts of a western saddle and bridle.

The ride

If you like the idea of relaxing when you ride, western riding may be the discipline for you. You wear western stirrups long, and as you ride, you find that leaning back slightly and keeping a loose rein enable you and your horse to travel comfortably for hours. Figure 14-4 shows a western rider in correct position. Western riders sit back more than hunt-seat riders but still maintain an upright position with an imaginary line that runs behind the heel up through the hip, shoulder, and ear.

© John Wiley & Sons, Inc.

FIGURE 14-4:
A western rider in correct position has a relaxed but upright position.

In the western discipline, the horse's gaits are known as the walk, jog, and lope, as opposed to walk, trot, and canter in the English disciplines. These gaits are considerably slower than what you experience when riding English. Generally speaking, if you ride a western horse, you experience an animal that has been trained to have quiet, leisurely gaits. The exception is a competitive rodeo horse trained to sprint around barrels and chase down cows.

Other Cool Riding Styles

Hunt seat, dressage, western, and saddle seat are the four most popular riding styles in the United States and Canada. However, they're certainly not the *only* styles of riding. Equestrians around the country use other riding forms, each with its own unique history and particular usage. Some of these styles are actual disciplines, but others don't require formal training.

REMEMBER

If you want to pursue one of the actual disciplines we discuss here, you need to do some work finding a riding instructor who can teach them. Finding an instructor for a less-popular discipline isn't as easy as finding someone who gives western riding lessons, but the trouble with ferreting out an instructor may just be worth it to you when you come to appreciate the uniqueness of each type of riding. Contact a riding instructor association for a referral to a discipline specialist in your area.

Endurance

Several decades ago, North Americans discovered the wonders of the Australian stock saddle, a piece of tack that looks like a cross between a dressage saddle and a western saddle. Created by Australian riders who needed a light saddle with an easy seat for long rides through the outback, the Australian stock saddle became the saddle of choice for many trail and endurance riders.

The Australian stock saddle has since morphed into what is commonly known as an endurance saddle. Endurance saddles come in a few different styles, but each has two things in common: a comfortable seat for the rider and a comfortable fit for the horse. Those who ride many hours on the trail in endurance and competitive trail riding competitions describe endurance saddles as ideal for their sport.

In North America, riders — depending on their preference — use English or western bridles with endurance saddles. The use of a bridle isn't terribly important in this instance because riding in an endurance saddle doesn't call for the mastery of a new discipline. Riders who are experienced in hunt seat and dressage disciplines are most comfortable in an endurance saddle, although western riders may have little trouble adapting to it. (See Chapter 6 for more about this saddle.)

Peruvian

Despite the fact that several American gaited breeds exist, Americans haven't cornered the market on gaited horses. The Peruvian Horse is a gaited breed that is becoming more popular in the United States of late (see Chapter 3 for more information about gaited horses).

Although you can also ride them in the more common disciplines, Peruvians have a discipline that's unique to the breed. Tradition dictates that you show these horses in their native discipline. Some purists insist on riding Peruvians in the breed's native tack at all times, even when merely going for a jaunt on the trail.

In Peru, people ride the Peruvian Horse in an incredibly comfortable saddle that has wide, flat skirts, a high pommel and cantle, and a leather-hooded stirrup. The traditional Peruvian bridle is quite elaborate, featuring a bosal type halter, a piece called a *gamarilla* that holds the bit, and a wide brow band known as a *tapa ojo*.

Riding a Peruvian Horse in his traditional tack is very fun, although you must specifically learn the Peruvian discipline. Many of the skills you learn in English and western riding aren't applicable in this discipline. Saddle-seat riding probably bears the closest resemblance to the Peruvian discipline.

Sidesaddle

It's hard to imagine in this day and age that people used to consider it improper for a woman to sit astride a horse. Until the 20th century, however, this belief was essentially the social custom when it came to riding.

For women, the answer to this expectation was something called the *sidesaddle,* a piece of equipment that provided female riders a secure seat while keeping both legs on one side of the horse. In the sidesaddle, the left leg fits in the stirrup as it would in a conventional saddle, while the right leg rests over a fixed pommel situated on the left side of the saddle.

At first, society women simply rode sidesaddle when they needed to get from one place to another on horseback. Eventually, women were able to ride along on fox hunts, thanks to the invention of something called the *leapers horn,* which made them secure enough to sit on a jumping horse.

Today, a relatively small group of female equestrians are keeping the tradition of sidesaddle alive, praising its elegance and historical significance. Using modern sidesaddles in either English or western design with corresponding bridles, they ride in arenas and on the trail in this discipline. They also show in antique saddles, most from the 1800s, while wearing period costumes appropriate to the saddle's age. Some sidesaddle riders even compete in barrel racing and other daring events.

Sidesaddle calls for a skilled rider and an obedient horse. Unlike astride disciplines, the aside discipline of sidesaddle doesn't permit the rider to give leg cues from the right. Sidesaddle riders must use a sidesaddle crop to direct the horse on the right side, while using standard leg pressure on the left. To learn this discipline, you need an instructor who is well versed in this form of riding.

Bareback

Before the invention of saddles, human beings rode bareback. This riding method worked well for transportation purposes. Humans didn't decide they needed saddles until they figured out they could wage war on horseback.

Today, many equestrians ride bareback. Bareback riding is not a discipline per se, but actually just another way of enjoying your horse. Riders who indulge in bareback riding don't usually ride *only* bareback, but do so for an occasional change of pace. Some even show in bareback riding classes, usually seen only at western shows.

Bareback riding makes you feel closer to your horse. When cantering along without a saddle, you almost feel as though you are one with the animal. Our ancient ancestors must have savored this exciting feeling.

Bareback riding is good for beginners because it helps create a secure and confident riding seat. You can't rely on the confines of a saddle to keep you on the horse when you are riding bareback. Instead, you must learn to keep your balance to stay on. Another bonus of bareback riding is that it saves you time: You don't need to spend an extra 5 to 10 minutes saddling up your horse on the days you plan to ride bareback.

WARNING

Although bareback riding can help you develop a good seat, the downside is that falling off a horse is much easier when you're riding bareback. Gripping the mane can help, but if your horse is bucking, spinning, or pulling some other athletic stunt, chances are you're going to eat some dirt.

Driving

Humans have been putting the cart after the horse for millennia, and still do so today. For many elderly and physically challenged equestrians who are physically unable to ride — and for those who simply don't like to ride — driving is the equine sport of choice.

Many people hitch up their horses to carts and drive for the sheer joy of it, although others are serious competitors in the driving show ring. Several breed shows have driving classes that feature one or two horses pulling different types of vehicles, as well as events with six- to eight-horse draft teams hauling wagons the way they did before the advent of the automotive engine.

Horses must be specially trained to drive; some learn the style in their early pre-riding training. Horses who are trained to drive are taught to pull weight (instead of carry it), and they can be steered in a completely different way than when they're ridden. Drivers also must train for this discipline. This training includes learning to handle the reins used in driving, which are quite different from riding reins.

Chapter **15**

Getting Ready Before You Mount

Unless you're wealthy — or starring in a movie — you probably don't have the luxury of having someone bring your saddled and bridled horse out to you every time you want to ride. The task of *tacking up*, as horse people call it, falls squarely upon your shoulders. Of course, to truly become an accomplished horseperson, you need to be able to tack up a horse.

Although the basics of tacking up for English and western riding are essentially the same, the differences are enough to make the process a bit confusing. We unravel all those straps and buckles for you in this chapter so you have a fundamental understanding of how to prepare a horse for riding. (And for more about the basics of horse equipment, be sure to check out Chapter 6.)

Putting On a Saddle and Accessories

The saddle and accessories always go on before the bridle (the head piece consisting of the bit, headstall, and reins) when tacking up a horse; you need the horse's halter (a head harness of sorts) to secure him to crossties or a hitching post while you saddle up. After you finish bridling, the halter comes off.

REMEMBER

Before you attempt to tack up a horse, have an experienced horseperson demonstrate the steps. After you watch the process a few times, you're ready to try it on your own — with supervision. Don't attempt to tack up a horse alone until whoever is supervising you assures you that you have the process down pat.

Before you start saddling up, do the following:

1. **Tie your horse securely by his halter to a hitching post (using a quick release knot) or crossties.** (See Chapter 13 for more about tying.)

2. **Groom your horse thoroughly, being careful to brush down the hairs on the back and the girth area (check out Chapter 1 for a diagram showing the parts of the horse).** Make sure that no pieces of dirt, bedding, or other foreign objects are stuck to your horse's back or girth area. (Chapter 9 has the full scoop on grooming.)

3. **Check your saddle blanket and girth or cinch to make sure that no burrs, sticks, or other items are clinging to the underside.**

REMEMBER

Correctly positioning and fastening the saddle on your horse's back is extremely important. A poor saddling job can result in discomfort or injury to both you and your horse. The diagrams in Figure 15-1 show the correct placement of English and western saddles.

FIGURE 15-1:
The correct placement of English and western saddles on a horse's back is essential.

Western

English

© John Wiley & Sons, Inc.

TIP

Whether you're saddling your horse with an English or a western saddle, always begin on the left side. All tasks concerning the horse's body begin with a left-side approach. The tradition of working first on the left side of the horse goes back hundreds of years, and is part of horse handling protocol. Most horses are accustomed to being approached from the left as a result and are likely to be more cooperative if you maintain this tradition.

The English saddle

First, familiarize yourself with the parts of the English saddle (refer to Chapter 6). Know where all your equipment is. You need

>> A saddle pad

>> A girth

>> The saddle

Then follow these steps to saddle a horse with an English saddle, beginning on the horse's left side:

1. **Lay the pad over the horse's back.** Stand on the horse's left side and position the front of the pad a few inches above the horse's withers, at the base of the neck.

2. **Slide the pad backward a couple of inches so the front edge of the pad is still covering the withers.**

WARNING

   Don't slide the pad forward if you need to reposition it because doing so ruffles the hairs underneath, resulting in irritation to the horse while you ride. Instead, lift the pad off the horse's back and reposition it. Check both sides of the horse to make sure that the amount of pad is even on the left and the right.

3. **Pick up the saddle.** Grasp the front of the saddle in your left hand and the back of the saddle in your right. Make sure that the stirrup irons have been pushed up to the top of the stirrup leathers so they don't flop around while you handle the saddle.

4. **Place the saddle gently on the horse's back in the hollow just below the withers.** About 3 inches of the pad should be showing in front of the saddle, and at least 3 inches showing behind (if not, the pad is too small). To determine whether the saddle is correctly positioned on the horse's back, look to see whether the girth, when attached to the saddle, fits just behind the horse's elbows (refer to Figure 15-1 for the correct position of a English saddle).

5. **Slide the girth straps on the left side of the saddle through the tab on your saddle pad.** Go to the horse's right side and do the same.

6. **Fasten the girth to the right side of the saddle.** You usually don't store English girths attached to the saddle, so your girth will probably be detached. Three girth straps hang there, but you only need two. The third one is just in case one of the other straps breaks.

   Bring the girth over to the right side of the horse and fasten the girth's buckles to the two outside girth straps that are hanging from the saddle. Be sure you're fastening the part of the girth that has solid leather and not stretch material.

The stretch material attaches on the left side. (Some girths have stretch material on both sides — in that case, it doesn't matter which side you attach to the left or right.) Fasten the buckles about halfway up each girth strap.

7. **Fasten the girth to the left side of the saddle.** Move to the left side of the horse and reach underneath to grasp the girth. Follow the same buckling procedure that you did in Step 6. Be sure that the girth is resting just behind the horse's elbows, and that it isn't twisted. Buckle tight enough to make the girth snug.

8. **Gradually tighten the girth on the left side over a period of several minutes (so as not to shock the horse with one sharp pull) until it's snug enough that the saddle doesn't move.** If you run out of holes on your left-side girth straps, begin tightening the buckles on the right. Figure 15-2 shows how you tighten an English girth.

FIGURE 15-2: Gradually tighten the girth on an English saddle so you don't shock your horse.

© John Wiley & Sons, Inc.

9. **Check your stirrup length.** Before you mount, determine whether your stirrups are the correct length for your legs. You can check pretty reliably by holding the reins in your left hand while sliding your right hand, palm down, under the flap of the saddle where the stirrup leather attaches to the saddle. Using your left hand, grasp the stirrup iron and pull it toward the crook of your arm, allowing the stirrup leather to lay flush against the bottom of your outstretched arm. If the stirrup iron fits snugly in the crook of your arm, the stirrups are most likely the correct length for your leg. If the stirrups are too long or too short, the problem will be obvious relative to your arm length.

If your stirrups need lengthening or shortening, adjust them by using the buckle on the stirrup leather.

After you mount, you can determine whether the stirrups are truly the correct length. You should be able to stand up in the stirrups and have your body clear the saddle. Another way to check is to take your feet out of the stirrups while you are sitting in the saddle and notice where the stirrups rests against your foot. The irons should rest at the ankle when you legs are stretched down.

10. **Stretch the horse's legs to prevent pinching.** Standing at the front of the horse, pull the left leg toward you to stretch out the skin under the girth so it doesn't pinch the horse. Do the same with the horse's right foreleg.

REMEMBER

You may need to repeat Step 8 after leading your horse around, before you mount. Many horses have a tendency to puff up their bellies by holding their breath while you tighten the girth. Before you get on, make sure that the girth is snug enough that it feels tight if you put your fingers between it and the horse's body. If you can't get your fingers in there, the girth is too tight and needs to be let out a notch.

The western saddle

Before you start, familiarize yourself with the parts of the western saddle (refer to Chapter 6). Have your pad and saddle ready to go. Then follow these steps to saddle a horse with a western saddle:

1. **Lay the pad over the horse's back.** Stand on the horse's left side and position the front of the pad a few inches above the horse's withers, at the base of the neck.

2. **Slide the pad backward a couple of inches so the front edge of the pad is still covering the withers.**

WARNING

Don't slide the pad forward if you need to reposition it because doing so ruffles the hairs underneath, resulting in irritation to the horse while you ride. Check both sides of the horse to make sure that the amount of pad is even on the left and the right.

3. **Prepare the saddle.** On a western saddle, the cinch is permanently attached to the right side. Before you approach the horse, flip the cinch up and over so it drapes across the seat. Take the right stirrup and loop it over the saddle horn.

4. **Bring the saddle to the horse.** Grasp the front of the saddle in your left hand and the back of the saddle in your right. Approach the horse's left side.

5. **Place the saddle on the horse's back.** From the left side of the horse, swing the saddle up and over, and place it gently on the horse's back. The saddle needs to sit in the hollow just below the withers with about 3 inches of the pad showing in front and in the back. To determine whether the saddle is correctly positioned on the horse's back, look to see whether the cinch, when attached to the saddle, fits just behind the horse's elbows (refer to Figure 15-1 for the correct position of a western saddle).

6. **Walk around to the right side of the horse and undrape the cinch so it hangs down.** Unloop the stirrup from the saddle horn and let it hang.

7. **Secure the saddle with the cinch.** From the left side of the horse, reach underneath and take up the cinch. Run the latigo strap through the ring of the cinch, and then feed the strap through the same D-ring on the saddle where the latigo is attached. Continue to loop the latigo strap through the two rings until you have about 12 inches of free strap coming from the D-ring. See Figure 15-3 to find out how to tie the knot.

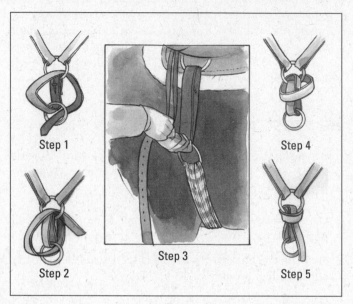

FIGURE 15-3: You tie a western cinch knot in five easy steps.

Step 1

Step 2

Step 3

Step 4

Step 5

© John Wiley & Sons, Inc.

8. **Check your stirrup length.** Before you mount, determine whether your stirrups are the correct length for your legs. You can check by holding the reins in your left hand while sliding your right hand, palm down, under the flap of the saddle where the stirrup leather attaches to the saddle. Using your left hand, grasp the stirrup and pull it toward the crook of your arm, allowing the stirrup leather to lay flush against the bottom of your outstretched arm. If the stirrup fits snugly in the crook of your arm, the stirrups are most likely the correct length for your leg. If the stirrups are too long or too short, the problem will be obvious relative to your arm length.

After you mount, you can determine whether the stirrups are the correct length. You should be able to stand up in the stirrups and maintain your balance for a few seconds in that position.

If your stirrups need lengthening or shortening, adjust them by using the buckle flap underneath the stirrup leather. (You need to dismount to do this, if you discovered a problem when you were already on the horse.)

9. **Make sure that the cinch is snug enough that the saddle doesn't move, but not so snug that you can't fit the fingers of a flat hand between the cinch and the horse's body.** To tighten the cinch, loosen the knot, and pull up on the outside layer of strap between the D-ring and cinch rings.

REMEMBER

Check the cinch again after walking your horse a little and before mounting. You may need to retighten the cinch if your horse has a tendency to hold his breath when you cinch him up.

Bridling Your Horse with Ease

The bridle goes on last, because after you bridle your horse, you can't tie him up again until you finish with your ride. If you've never bridled a horse, ask an experienced horse person to show you first before you attempt it.

Before you start to bridle your horse, do the following:

1. **Tie the horse securely by his halter to a hitching post (using a quick release knot) or crossties.** See Chapter 13 for more about tying.

2. **Groom and saddle the horse.** Chapter 9 has grooming info.

3. **Check the bridle to make sure that the *noseband* (the part that goes around the nose) and *throatlatch* (the strap that fastens around the horse's jowls) on an English bridle are unbuckled.** If you have a throatlatch on a western bridle, make sure it's unbuckled, too.

4. **Have an experienced horse person help you determine whether the bit size is correct, and how short the straps need to be on the headstall (the part of the bridle that goes over the horse's ears and is attached to the bit), if your horse has never worn this particular bridle.**

The steps for putting on an English and western bridle are nearly the same. Familiarize yourself with the parts of both bridles before you begin (refer to Chapter 6). Then, follow these steps to put on the bridle:

1. **Secure the horse with the halter.** Standing at the horse's left side, unbuckle the halter (which you had put on the horse before saddling), slide the noseband off, and then rebuckle the halter around the horse's neck. (Figure 15-4 shows how the halter fits around the horse's neck.)

2. **Put the reins over the horse's head so they lay on the horse's neck.**

3. **Hold the bit and headstall and stand at the left side of your horse's head, facing the same direction that your horse is facing.** Grasp the top of the headstall in your right hand and the bit in your left hand. Let the bit lay against your outstretched fingers. Stand next to the horse's head, facing forward in the same direction as the horse.

4. **Place your right hand (still holding the headstall) just on top of the horse's head, behind the ears.** If you can't reach above the horse's head, you can instead reach your arm under the horse's jaw and around to the right side of the horse's head so your right hand and headstall are just above the horse's forehead, or above the bridge of his nose.

5. **Open the horse's mouth and insert the bit.** With your left thumb, gently press down on the inside corner of the horse's lip to open his mouth and gently guide the bit into his mouth, being careful not to bang it against his front teeth. Raise the headstall in your right hand until the bit slides all the way into the horse's mouth.

6. **Gently slide the headstall over the horse's ears.** Adjust the horse's forelock (the hair on the forehead between the ears) and the area of the mane just behind the ears so the hair is smooth under the headstall. The bridle is now in place.

7. **Buckle the throatlatch and noseband, if any.**

    English bridle: The throatlatch and noseband need to be snug, but not so tight that you can't get three fingers between each of these straps and the horse's face.

    Western bridle: You probably won't have a noseband to tighten. If the bridle has a throatlatch, make sure that two fingers fit between the horse's cheek and the strap.

    Curb chain or strap: If one of these is attached to the bit, make sure that it's loose when you let the reins relax (one or two fingers should fit) but makes contact with the horse's chin when you pull the bit shanks back at a 45-degree angle.

8. **Unbuckle the halter from your horse's neck.** If you plan to mount where you are, leave the reins over your horse's neck. If you want to lead your horse to another area for mounting, remove the reins from around your horse's neck and lead the horse by the reins.

Figure 15-4 shows more detail on how to put on English and western bridles.

FIGURE 15-4:
The correct way
to put on English
and western
bridles.

English   Western

© John Wiley & Sons, Inc.

IN THIS CHAPTER

» **Getting into a good mind-set for riding**

» **Taking riding lessons**

» **Mounting your horse easily**

» **Understanding riding (and post-ride) basics**

» **Coping with equine misbehavior**

Chapter **16**

Taking Control in the Saddle

S omething amazing happens when a human climbs aboard the back of a horse. If the rider knows how to communicate with the horse, and if the horse is receptive, the resulting experience can be magical. Achieving this oneness of horse and rider requires hard work. Popular culture images make riding a horse look like a piece of cake, but it takes months of practice before you have a sense of what you're doing.

It's never too late to develop riding skills. With plenty of hard (albeit fun) work, you can become an efficient rider. But you have to start somewhere — like this chapter.

Preparing Yourself Mentally

Riding is more than just a physical activity — it's a mental one, too. You need to use your brain for riding, probably even more than your body, and that means understanding your role as a rider on an intellectual as well as an emotional level. Read on to see what we mean.

Beating your fear

We talk a lot about the horse's fear in this and other chapters of *Horses For Dummies,* 3rd Edition, but what about the fear you have?

If you are asking, "What fear?" right about now, then good for you. You're probably one of those brave souls who has no qualms about getting up on a half-ton animal and trusting him with your life. But more than likely, you're one of the great majority of beginning riders who finds the notion of riding a horse a bit scary.

REMEMBER

Being afraid to ride is okay, as long as fear doesn't keep you from trying. We feel confident that if you follow the advice in this book, you'll soon discover that your fears are unfounded and that riding a good horse is one of the most relaxing and enjoyable things anyone can do.

If you have a nagging reluctance, know that the more your riding skills increase, the more confident you'll feel on a horse's back. Remember, human beings have been riding horses for the past 4,000 years, and our species still survives!

Acknowledging your role as the leader

Before getting up on a horse for the first time (or if you've already been on a horse, make it before the first time you do it after reading this chapter), you need to have a basic understand of what riding is all about.

REMEMBER

The key to understanding why horses let humans ride them is *leadership.* Horses are herd animals that seek a leader in any social situation. Generally speaking, human beings have managed to convince the equine species that humans are worthy of that leadership position. So when a human gets up on a horse's back and tells that horse what to do, the horse obeys because he views the rider as his leader. (See Chapter 2 for more about the horse's psyche.)

This scenario works only when the rider has the leadership qualities that the horse expects. If a rider gets up on a horse without a clue as to what to do and how to do it, the horse quickly senses those lacking skills and takes over the leadership role.

Taking Riding Lessons First

Have you ever ridden a horse that ran away with you, tried to roll on you, rubbed you against a tree, or refused to move as soon as you got on? If not, you probably know someone who has. Unfortunately, many first-time riders have this kind of experience, and it sours them on horses forever. However, if they had taken riding lessons *before* they tried to go out on their own, their experiences may have been much better.

REMEMBER

We can't overemphasize the necessity for taking formal riding lessons before you go out and get yourself a horse or start riding regularly on your own. You probably wouldn't dream of going scuba diving without first taking lessons or doing something as benign as golfing without finding out the rules of the game. With horses, rider training is doubly important, because you need to understand the rules and develop the skills before you go it alone.

Deciding where to get lessons

Where can you get lessons? You have a number of options:

» **Commercial stables:** Many commercial riding establishments offer riding lessons, usually in several disciplines. These facilities aren't hard to find — all you need to do is search online for "riding lessons." Before you sign up, visit the stable and observe the lessons. Talk to the instructors and ask them about their experiences. Look for certified riding instructors with experience showing horses and tutoring clients who are successful in the show ring. Certified instructors have successfully completed a riding instructor certification program. If you like the stable and instructors, sign up for one lesson. If the experience is good, plan to take at least several months worth of lessons.

» **Horseback vacations:** The term *dude ranch* conjures up images of city slickers slumped in western saddles, timidly hanging onto the saddle horn as their horses pick their way over steep mountain trails. But these days, dude ranches and other horseback-oriented vacation spots do more than give trail rides to those with only a casual interest in riding. You can take formal riding lessons at many of these places, provided you pick a facility that caters to beginners. A horseback vacation spot actually is a great place to get started, because it not only combines a fun atmosphere with training but also provides you with one or two weeks of intensive riding. You can follow up this instruction with more lessons when you get home (see Chapter 19 for more details on riding vacations).

» **Riding clubs:** Horse lovers tend to congregate, which is good news for neophytes who take an interest in horses. Although clubs that exist specifically to teach newcomers usually are aimed at children, they actually offer opportunities for adults, too. One example is the Pony Club, an excellent U.S. and British organization that teaches children (most of whom do *not* own their own horses) horsemanship and riding skills. If you and your child want to ride horses, sign your child up with your local Pony Club chapter and volunteer as an adult helper. If you have a child of college age, consider getting involved with an intercollegiate or college riding program.

>> **An equine expert:** If you live in a small town or a remote area, you may have trouble finding a commercial riding stable or riding club nearby. In that case, try to find someone locally who can help you with your riding. Ask other horse owners in your town to help you locate an experienced horse person, such as a breeder, an equine veterinarian, or someone who shows extensively. Ask this expert whether you can hire him or her to teach you to ride. Most horse people are more than happy to help newcomers to the hobby provided those newcomers have a sincere and genuine interest. (Flip to Chapter 4 for tips on finding an equine expert.)

Avoiding mistakes

When seeking out lessons, you definitely want to avoid the following situations:

>> **Don't go to a stable that rents out horses by the hour without first receiving riding instruction.** Remember those friends of yours who've been on the back of a runaway horse and rubbed off on trees? Most likely, it happened in this type of place. Owners at most rent-by-hour stables allow the horses to develop bad attitudes and dangerous habits. Such horses are bad news for beginning riders.

>> **Don't let an inexperienced friend give you lessons on his or her horse.** If your friend is an experienced rider who owns a suitable horse for beginning riders, then by all means, ask your friend for help. But if your friend has only been riding a short time and has a horse he or she can barely control, politely decline the offer and opt for one of the alternatives we mention earlier.

Taking your time

The amount of time necessary for you to get the hang of riding depends on you. Some people pick it up faster than others. When you are to the point where you feel like you can competently control your horse, inside and outside of the arena, you know enough to begin doing some riding on your own. But remember: You can never know too much when it comes to riding. Heck, even the riders on the Olympic equestrian teams still take lessons!

The way you keep the relationship between you and your horse healthy is to provide continuing education for the both of you by:

>> Entering into training with a professional (where you and your horse will be schooled)

>> Taking lessons as often as you can

>> Practicing your riding skills and schooling your horse

Spend some riding time reinforcing the commands your horse already knows while you practice giving them. Work in an arena once a week or so and execute turning, backing up, stopping, and other skills that you pick up in formal lessons.

Getting into Riding Shape

You only need to be on a horse once to discover that riding utilizes muscles that you never knew you had. You don't need to be a super athlete to be a competent rider, but the stronger and more flexible you are, the easier riding is on your body.

TIP

If you don't already have a regular exercise routine, now may be a good time to start one. (Be sure to talk to your doctor first.) Here are a few things to work on that will enhance your riding abilities:

>> **Lose weight:** If you're overweight, it can be more difficult to mount, dismount, cue the horse, and stay comfortable when riding the horse's various gaits. Besides, your excess weight can be a hardship for the horse. Try to stick to a healthy diet of mostly protein and vegetables, with only a small amount of carbohydrates per day to keep your weight down and your energy level up Refined sugar should be avoided because it makes you gain weight and causes your blood-sugar levels to spike and crash. Avoiding preservatives, sugars, and processed foods whenever you can and eating mostly whole grains and fresh foods can keep your body strong and healthy for riding.

>> **Build muscle strength:** If you plan to ride English, a good amount of arm strength is needed to maintain contact with the horse's mouth via the reins. Women, especially, need to take note of this necessity, because unlike most men, they do not get sufficient arm strength genetically. (This can also be an issue for women who ride western and need to lift a heavy saddle onto a tall horse's back.) You also need strong legs to cue the horse, *post* the trot (move up and down in the saddle with the rhythm of the horse's gait), and do a number of other tasks when you are riding. Pilates exercises are a good way to build muscle strength in the areas you'll need it most for riding.

>> **Get flexible:** Most people notice soreness in their legs when they first train to ride. That's because sitting stretched out across a horse's back creates a big pull on the upper, inner muscles of the thighs. Do stretching exercises for your legs and the rest of your body several times to a week to stay flexible for riding. Yoga is another great way to stretch the muscles you'll need for riding.

>> **Build endurance:** If you plan to spend much time in the saddle, like on a long trail ride, you'll want to build up your endurance. You can do this with aerobics, jogging, or even walking, if you do it often and for long periods of time. Riding for longer amounts of time over a gradual period also helps your body become accustomed to long hours in the saddle.

After you've gotten into solid riding shape, you probably will ask: How long should I ride? The answer depends on a couple of things:

>> **Your horse:** Healthy horses are capable of going all day, provided they're properly conditioned. If you prefer to ride for an hour a day, once a day, you can slowly build your horse up to this level of conditioning. If you want to trail ride for hours on end several days a week, work your way up to that level over a period of months. If you ride only once a week (we recommend that you ride more often), don't expect your horse to go for hours on that day because he's pretty much out of shape and at risk of developing leg problems or a muscle condition called *azoturia* (see Chapter 11). We also recommend that you limit arena riding to no more than one hour per day. Arena riding is hard on your horse's legs and can be a real bore for your horse.

Keep in mind that although a horse can walk for an extended time without tiring, faster gaits, such as trotting and cantering, take much more energy. Be careful about spending too much time at these faster gaits if your horse isn't properly conditioned. And don't ride your horse in tight circles or on hard ground for extended periods; Both can do serious damage to his legs.

>> **Your time:** Most horse lovers would be happy spending most of their waking hours in the saddle. However, unless you're a working ranch hand, reality dictates that you'll ride much less that that. We recommend that you ride as often as you can, and take really long rides only on the trail and only if your horse has been conditioned for such activity. The time you spend riding is not only good for your horse, it's also good for your physical and mental well-being.

Swinging Up and Onto Your Horse

Before you can ride, you have to get on, and for most beginners, mounting is one of the greatest challenges of riding. Adults find it especially difficult, because they have much more bulk to get up into a saddle than does a child.

TIP

Mounting your horse with great ease and decorum takes practice. In the beginning, we recommend that you have an experienced horse person spot you and make sure that you're doing it right. While this person observes, have him or her hold onto your horse's bridle for the sake of safety.

Before you get up on a horse and go, check the footing of the area where you plan to ride. If you plan to ride in an arena, be sure the dirt is loose — that is, not hard packed. Conversely, make sure the dirt isn't *so* loose that your horse has to struggle through it. And be certain that the footing is dry. Wet arenas are among the most dangerous places to ride, longe, or turn out a horse. A horse can easily slip and fall on wet footing, seriously injuring himself or you in the process.

Many English riders use a mounting block to get on their horses, in large part because their stirrups are set shorter than those of western riders. The mounting block enables you to climb up nearly to the level of the horse's back, where you simply swing your leg over the saddle. A mounting block keeps the saddle from slipping as you mount the horse and reduces the amount of wear and tear on your horse's back. You can buy one of these at a tack store or a feed store, or through an equine Internet or mail-order catalog.

REMEMBER

Using a mounting block every time you get up on your horse is perfectly acceptable, no matter what discipline you ride. But even if you choose to use one, you also need to know how to get on from the ground. If you get off or fall off your horse out on the trail, or in a place where you don't have a mounting block, you can strand yourself if you can't get back get on.

TIP

Mounting in a western saddle is easier than mounting in an English saddle because western stirrups are longer and reach lower than English stirrups. Western saddles also are less likely than English saddles to slip as you're mounting, and you have more to hold onto with a western saddle.

To mount your horse from the ground, follow these steps (and see Figure 16-1):

1. **Lead your horse to the area where you want to mount.** Choose the inside of the arena where you plan to ride, or another safe area.

2. **Position yourself and stay in control of the horse.** To do so, you need to

   - Place the reins over your horse's head. If you're mounting English, rest them on his neck.

   - Stand at the horse's left shoulder, facing the back of the horse with the reins snug in your left hand. Never release the reins while you're mounting. You need to keep control of your horse at all times.

   - If you're riding English, grab a handful of mane at the base of the horse's neck with the same (left) hand. If you're riding western, grab hold of the pommel (the front of the saddle) with the same (left) hand.

3. **Using your right hand, grasp the stirrup and turn it toward you. Place your left foot in the stirrup.**

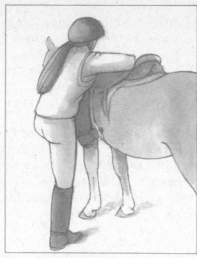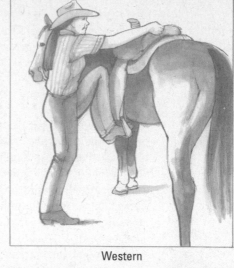

© John Wiley & Sons, Inc.

FIGURE 16-1:
Mounting a horse in both English and western styles takes practice.

English

Western

4. **Swing into the saddle.** Turn your body toward the horse as you grasp the cantle (the rise at the back of the saddle) with your right hand. Bounce on your right leg two or three times and then launch yourself up into the air, swinging your right leg over the horse's hindquarters, being careful not to touch them, and land gently in the saddle.

5. **Place your right foot in the stirrup.** Divide up your reins into both hands if you're riding English. If you're riding western, just gather up your reins in your left hand.

Focusing on Riding Fundamentals

Among the many things you practice when you take riding lessons are what we call *riding basics,* or the fundamental elements you must know to successfully ride a horse. In the following sections, we cover how to hold the reins, position yourself in the saddle, cue your horse, and ride along with your horse's gaits.

Holding the reins

Just as you figured out how to hold a knife and fork as a child, you must now figure out the right way to hold the reins when you ride. Holding the reins properly is very important, because the reins are one of the primary means of communication between you and your horse.

We describe how to hold the reins for both English and western styles in the sections that follow. In addition to reading our descriptions, we also recommend that you have a trainer or experienced horse person *show you how* to do it.

English

English bridles call for two hands on the reins. When you ride English, you hold the left rein in your left hand and the right rein in your right hand.

Even though the term *reins* is plural, be aware that English snaffle bridles technically have only one continuous rein that connects from one side of the bit to the other. However, the part of the rein that connects to the left side of the bit is the *left rein.* The part on the right side is the *right rein.*

To correctly pick up the reins, start with the reins resting on the horse's neck. Reach down and grasp the reins with your palms facing down and your thumbs next to each other. After you have the reins in your hands, rotate your wrists so that your thumbs are at the top (knuckles up) and the knuckles of your fingers are facing each other. Move your pinkies under each rein, so the rein rests between your pinkie and your ring finger. Hold your hands in a relaxed fist as shown in Figure 16-2.

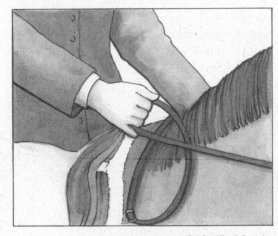

FIGURE 16-2:
When you hold your reins English style, make sure each rein rests between your pinkie and ring fingers.

© John Wiley & Sons, Inc.

A common mistake many beginning English riders make is that they tend to balance themselves in the saddle by leaning against the reins. If you do this, you're in essence using the horse's mouth to help keep you in the saddle, which is considered poor riding and unfair to the horse. Imagine having 100 pounds or more pulling on your mouth in an effort to keep from falling. Ouch! Nobody wants to do that to any horse, so we suggest that you work hard at developing balance and security in the saddle so you won't feel the need to weigh heavy on the horse's mouth.

Western

Western reins usually are *split reins,* which means you have two separate reins, one attached to the right side of the bit, the other attached to the left.

While you're still learning to ride, we recommend that you tie a knot in your western reins, right above the area where your hand normally is when you're holding them. Knotted reins are safer for beginning riders, because they won't fall out of reach if you happen to drop them while riding.

Western riding calls for the reins to be held in the left hand only. Doing so theoretically frees up the right hand for roping, an important task for the cowboys who originated this style of riding.

You can hold western reins in one of two styles: traditional and California. These two styles exist purely as regional distinctions, with California style being most popular in California, of course. Either way is correct, although your riding instructor may prefer one over the other.

To ride traditional style, grasp the reins in your left fist, with the part of the reins that leads to the bit resting between your thumb and forefinger. As you hold the reins, the nail on your thumb should face skyward while the thumb itself points toward the horse's head (see Figure 16-3).

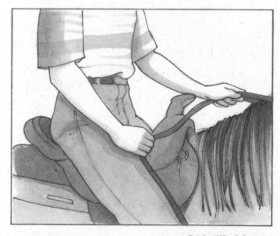

FIGURE 16-3:
Your thumb points toward the horse's head when you hold reins in the traditional western style.

© *John Wiley & Sons, Inc.*

To hold the reins California style, grasp the reins in your left fist, with your thumbnail pointed upward. The excess rein should be held in your right hand, which rests on your right thigh (see Figure 16-4).

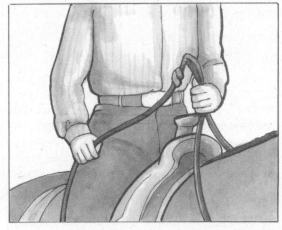

FIGURE 16-4: Your left fist holds the reins and your right hand is on your right thigh in the California western style.

Positioning yourself in the saddle

Many people don't realize how important your seat position is when riding. Although experienced riders may seem to just casually sit up there, attaining the proper position takes a certain amount of practice and concentration. The way you sit in the saddle affects your and your horse's comfort levels. It also determines how secure you are in the saddle. Riders with correct positioning are less likely to fall off if the horse suddenly moves in an unexpected direction.

Your exact position in the saddle depends on your riding discipline. (See Chapter 14 for discipline details.) The following basics apply to nearly everyone:

>> **Your back:** Keep your back straight when you sit in the saddle. Don't hunch forward, slump your shoulders, or arch your back. Just sit up straight like you were told to do in grade school.

>> **Your legs:** Generally speaking, your legs belong directly under you while you're in the saddle. They shouldn't thrust forward ahead of your body or lag behind. (An exception is when you're riding saddle seat, where your legs come out farther ahead of the body than in other disciplines.) Furthermore, the balls of your feet (and nothing more) need to rest in the stirrup, your toes should point up and straight ahead, and your heels should point down.

>> **Your derriere:** Before you get on a horse, and in the privacy of your own home, become familiar with your seat bones. The two bony points between your thighs and your buttocks (one on each side) make contact with anything firm that you sit on, provided you're sitting up straight. When you're in the saddle, you should feel these two points against the seat of your saddle, which indicates that your posture is correct.

TIP

If you don't feel your seat bones when you're riding, you're probably doing something wrong with your position. Ask a trainer, instructor, or experienced horse person for help aligning your seat in the saddle.

>> **Your arms:** If you're riding English, your arms need to be bent at the elbow, creating (theoretically) a straight line from your elbow to the bit. You need to hold your hands about 6 inches above the horse's withers (the area on the back at the base of the horse's neck). If you're riding western, your left hand goes a few inches above the saddle horn. Your left arm should be bent at an approximate 45-degree angle, while your right arm should be relaxed with your right hand resting on your right thigh.

Cueing your horse

After you're properly seated on the horse and are holding the reins, you're ready to start signaling the horse. Most horses understand the following basic commands:

>> **Forward:** Squeeze the horse's sides with both your legs (using your calf muscles) at the same time. Make sure that your reins are relatively loose as you do. If the horse does not respond, you may need to gently tap the horse with your heels and make a clucking sound.

>> **Stop:** Pull back on the reins with one steady motion as you say "Ho" (or "Whoa"). Maintain the pull on the reins until the horse stops.

>> **Turn left:** You use both your legs and the reins to communicate this message.

If you're riding English, pull back very slightly on only the left rein as you move your right leg back a little and apply some pressure. Your left leg applies pressure while staying stationary on the girth as a support for the horse to turn around. After the horse completes the turn, relax your hands and legs.

If you're riding western, move your left hand to the left so the right rein makes contact with the horse's neck (this is called *neck reining*). At the same time, move your right leg back a little behind the girth and apply some pressure to the horse's side. Your left leg applies pressure while staying in place on the girth as a support for the horse to turn around. After the horse completes the turn, relax your hands and legs.

>> **Turn right:** Turning right calls for the same commands as turning left, although in reverse. In English riding, pull back very slightly on only the right rein as you move your left leg back a little behind the girth and apply some pressure to the horse's side. In western riding, move your left hand to the right so the left rein makes contact with the horse's neck. At the same time, move your left leg back a little behind the girth and apply some pressure to the horse's body.

>> **Back up:** Pull back on the reins in one steady motion at the same time you apply leg pressure to both sides of the horse. For some horses, you may need to add a clucking sound. Continue this command for the entire time that you want the horse to back up. Be sure to keep your body straight in the saddle, as leaning forward will confuse your horse.

TIP

Coordinating the movements required to signal a horse takes practice. We recommend that you have an instructor, trainer, or experienced horse person help you with these basic human-to-horse commands.

Moving with your horse's gaits

As you begin to ride, you start out slow and work your way up to the faster gaits. Your first lesson is completely at the walk. As your seat and hands improve, your instructor moves you into a trot or job, and ultimately to a canter or lope. (See Chapter 2 for more about the different gaits.)

BLAZING TRAILS ON YOUR HORSE

Basic riding skills are just as necessary on the trail as they are in a riding arena. Out in the wilderness, you may find yourself in situations where you must turn your horse, back him up, and of course ask him to stop and go forward.

In addition to using your basic skills, you also need to use your head out on the trail. Stick to these trail basics to ensure the safety of your horse, other riders, and yourself:

- **Walk up and down hills.** Though your horse may want to, don't gallop downhill. Avoid the urge to trot uphill, too, if you can. The faster you go up or down a hill, the more dangerous it is. Riding faster up or down also is bad for your horse's legs, and it's a difficult habit to break after the horse is used to doing it.

  Lean forward in the saddle when going uphill and lean back when going downhill. This helps your horse by shifting your weight off the end of the horse that is bearing most of the animal's (and your) weight.

(continued)

- **Negotiate obstacles.** Sooner or later, you and your horse are going to come across an obstacle on the trail that your horse won't want to deal with. It may be a fallen tree trunk, a mud puddle, or a big rock. Chances are, the obstacle will be running water because many horses are afraid to cross creeks and streams. You can't allow your horse to successfully avoid the obstacle, or your horse soon figures out that he can dodge things he doesn't like rather than listening to you.

  If your horse refuses to cross an obstacle, first make sure it's safe enough to do so. Then get off and lead the horse through or over the obstacle. If that doesn't work, ask your trail buddy to take her horse first over the obstacle. Chances are, your horse will follow. If not, don't risk your safety by engaging in a huge battle with your horse. Continue your ride in another direction, and when you get home to the stable, find an experienced horse person or trainer who can take your horse back on the trail to get him over his fear of that particular object.

- **Don't allow jigging.** *Jigging,* a cross between a walk and a trot, is something horses do when they're anxious to get home and don't want to walk. If your horse starts jigging and gets away with it, you soon have a chronic jigger on your hands. If your horse starts jigging, insist that the horse walk. If he won't walk, turn him around in a continuous figure eight every time he starts to jig.

- **No eating!** Imagine you're a horse on a trail ride. Everywhere you look, you see all kinds of grasses, flowers, and shrubbery, just waiting to be eaten. Walking on the trail must the equine equivalent of strolling through a bakery.

  Horses being horses, they're inclined to temptation and will reach out and try to snag a nibble at the first opportunity. However, as mean as it sounds, don't let your horse have anything to eat on the trail, for three reasons: First, many poisonous plants exist out there. Even one mouthful of the wrong thing can make your horse very sick. Second, if you let your horse eat on the trail whenever the mood strikes, pretty soon your entire ride will be spent sitting on top of a grazing horse. And third, if your horse has a bit in his mouth, some of the roughage may get caught in his windpipe, causing breathing issues. (If you want to let your horse snack on a long trail ride, dismount and take the bit out of his mouth. Be certain the plant he wants to eat is not poisonous.)

- **Warn other riders.** If you have a horse that is particularly nasty to other horses — especially the ones that approach from behind — tie a red ribbon at the base of his tail as a warning to other riders that your horse might kick.

- **Walk him at the end of the ride.** Don't trot or canter during the last third of your journey home. Otherwise, your horse will think that rushing home is okay, and you'll soon have trouble controlling the horse when you turn toward the stable.

- **Be safe at night.** When riding at dusk or at night, wear reflective clothing (a vest is best), reflectors on your saddle, and/or reflective wraps on your horse's legs so that drivers can see you.

If you're like most beginning riders, you're anxious to try riding a horse while it gallops. We don't blame you: After all, riding a galloping horse is an exhilarating feeling. But you need to be patient and work your way up to that moment when you're secure enough in your basic riding skills where you can handle that kind of speed. If you work hard at riding, you'll soon experience the glorious sensation of pounding hooves and the wind in your hair.

Delving into Post-Ride Details

After you have your fill of riding for the day, you aren't finished with your horse. A few tasks remain: dismounting, untacking, cooling down, and grooming.

Getting off your horse

Before you can do anything else in your life, you have to get off the horse or *dismount*. Dismounting is much easier than mounting because you don't have to battle gravity. However, you still need to dismount correctly for your own safety and for the comfort of your horse. Dismounting is virtually the same for both English and western riders:

1. **Bring your horse to a complete halt.**

2. **Take your right foot out of the stirrup and position your left hand.** If you are riding in an English saddle, put the reins in your left hand, and grasp the horse's mane at the base of the neck with the same hand. Put your right hand on the pommel (the front of the saddle).

   With a western saddle, grasp the saddle horn or the pommel in your left hand as you continue to hold the reins.

3. **Swing your right leg over the horse's hindquarters — be careful not to touch the horse as you do — *and* at the same time, move your right hand to the cantle.**

4. **Turn so your stomach is flat against the horse and your legs are next to one another; remove your left foot from the stirrup.**

5. **Slowly slide down until your feet are touching the ground.**

Never let go of the reins while you're dismounting. You need to keep control of your horse at all times.

Untacking your horse

After dismounting, take the reins over your horse's head and lead him back to the hitching post or crossties where you left the halter. You're now going to remove the horse's tack. Untacking is basically the reverse of the procedure you followed when tacking up in Chapter 15.

TIP

If you ride English, be sure to *run up* the stirrup irons before you walk your horse back to his halter. The purpose is to keep the irons from banging against the horse's side as he walks. You can run up the irons by sliding them up the back strap of the stirrup leather so the irons lay flat against the saddle. Tuck the loop of stirrup leather through the stirrup iron to secure it. Follow these steps to untack your horse:

1. **Restrain the horse with the halter.** Stand at the horse's left side. As you hold the reins in your left hand, buckle the halter strap around the horse's neck to restrain him (see Chapter 15 for an illustration). The halter should still be attached to the hitching post with a lead rope or to a crosstie. Unbuckle the bridle noseband and throatlatch, if any.

2. **Remove the bridle.** With your right hand, gently slide the headstall over the horse's ears so that the bridle comes off the horse's head.

TIP

   Be careful not to pull the bit out of the horse's mouth when you're removing the bridle. Let the horse open his mouth to drop the bit before you pull the bridle completely off the horse's head.

3. **Return the halter to its normal position.** Loop the headstall and reins over your shoulder or a nearby post. Unbuckle the part of the halter that is around the horse's neck and lower the noseband just enough to slip the halter over the horse's head. Then buckle it again. Be careful not to remove the halter strap completely from the horse's neck as you do; otherwise, you have no restraint on the horse!

4. **Remove (English) or untie (western) the saddle's girth (or cinch).** With an English saddle, remove the girth by unbuckling first the left side of the girth, then the right. Remove the girth completely.

   If you are using a western saddle, untie the cinch knot first. Then, loop the latigo strap several times and tuck it into the D-ring. From the right side of the horse, lay the cinch over the seat of the saddle, and loop the right stirrup over the saddle horn.

5. **Remove the saddle.** Stand on the horse's left side, facing the saddle. Grasp the front of the saddle pad with your left hand and the back of the pad with your right. Lift the pad and saddle up together, up and off the horse's back.

6. **Put the saddle on a saddle rack.** The saddle pad should be on top of the saddle, with the wet underside of the pad facing up to dry. With an English saddle, you may want to lay the girth over the saddle pad, wet side up, to dry.

Cooling down and cleaning up

If your horse had a hard workout and you didn't already walk him for at least ten minutes at the end of your ride, you have to do so now. Remove your horse's saddle and bridle as described in the preceding section, and take the horse for a walk around the stable by his halter and lead rope. (See Chapter 13 for more on leading your horse properly.) Keep walking until the horse is cool. You can tell whether the horse is cool by putting your hand on his chest. If the horse's chest is hot and sweaty, keep walking. The sweat should be dried from the most of the horse's body by the time you finish with your walk, and his breathing should be slow and back to normal. (If the weather is warm, you can also sponge him or hose him off with water to help him cool down and to remove the sweat.)

WARNING

For the benefit of your horse's health, never allow your horse to eat or drink until he's completely cooled down! A horse that eats or drinks when hot is at risk for colic. (See Chapter 11 for details on this malady.)

REMEMBER

Your horse needs to be groomed after you ride as well as before. Clean out your horse's feet and brush the horse down using the methods we describe in Chapter 9. If your horse sweats a lot during the ride, wash the horse off with a hose or sponge.

Catching Tricks That Naughty Horses Play

Horses are much like children: They have a tendency to constantly test authority, just to make sure that it's still there. In your horse's mind, the best time to test your authority is when you're riding.

Many horses pull the stunts in the following sections just to see what they can get away with. In other cases, these behaviors stem from genuine fear, poor training, and insecurity on the horse's part. Either way, you need to call on your superior human intellect and leadership skills to convince the horse to change his behavior. To constantly reinforce your horse's compliance, make sure that every move you make when riding is *your* idea, not the horse's.

Bucking

You've seen bucking broncos on TV. Although they may look ferocious, they actually are made to buck with the use of a device called a bucking strap, tied around their flanks. Rodeo riders make these horses perform by taking advantage of the horse's natural tendency to buck when something unpleasant or frightening is on his back.

When an average saddle horse bucks, it isn't usually with the same force as a rodeo bronc. Nonetheless, even a moderate buck can still remove you from the saddle if you don't have good balance.

Average horses usually buck for one of two reasons: They have excess energy that they need to release, or they're in pain. If you find yourself on a bucking horse, sit squarely in the saddle and try to pull the horse's head up with the reins. A horse needs to put his head down to be able to buck.

TIP

If your horse bucks frequently when you ride, try giving him more exercise on a regular basis to release any pent-up energy. You may have to try longing him before you ride. If that doesn't help, have a veterinarian examine the horse to determine whether he is suffering from leg or back pain. If neither one of these works, contact a trainer. Your horse may be bucking to get out of having to work — something everyone does on occasion.

REMEMBER

If your horse bucks you off, be sure to get right back on (or have someone else get on) and continue riding, at least for a few minutes. You may not want to get back on board, but you need to do so to keep the horse from thinking he can get out of work simply by unloading his rider.

Rearing

When a horse *rears*, he stands up on his hind legs, lifting his forefeet off the ground. Most horses rear when they are very afraid of something that is approaching them from the front, when a severe bit or hackamore is hurting their mouths or nose, or when they're resisting the rider.

WARNING

Rearing while being ridden is an extremely dangerous habit that you should not tolerate. If your horse rears with you when you ask him to do something he doesn't want to do, you need to hang on and wait for the rear to end. (Don't pull back on the reins because doing so may throw the horse over.) Don't ride the horse again until a trainer has worked with the animal to cure him of this vice, or find out if pain is causing it.

Backing up without being asked

When a horse starts backing up even though you didn't ask him to, the horse is trying to resist you, probably because you asked him to do something that he doesn't want to do.

Make sure that you're not inadvertently telling the horse to back up. Be sure that your reins are loose whenever you squeeze the horse to move forward. If your reins are loose but the horse continues to back up, then the horse is trying to pull a fast one. To combat this maneuver, loosen your reins and prompt the horse forward by nudging him in the ribs with your heels. Keep nudging until the horse gives up and moves forward.

REMEMBER

If unwanted backing up is a repeated problem with your horse, call in the services of a professional trainer for some help.

Spooking

Horses are prey animals by nature, and so they're always on the alert. If something spooks a horse, his first reaction is to shy away from the offending creature or object. Because spooking usually comes along with quick and sudden movements in unexpected directions, riders sometimes become unseated.

Horses typically spook at the following objects: white plastic bags blowing in the wind, flags, balloons, umbrellas, deer and anything they haven't seen before that they can't identify. They also get nervous when they see an object in a place where they haven't seen it before.

If your horse spooks for some reason, he is most likely frightened of something he sees. Allow him to turn and face the source of the spook to get a good look at it. After the horse has a moment to carefully focus on whatever frightened him, he most likely will calm down. If the horse still refuses to move forward or wants to turn and run away, you may need to get off him and lead him past whatever it is or wait for the scary thing to leave. For some reason, horses are much braver when they are being led than when they are being ridden. If your horse is afraid of a stationary object, you can even try going over to it and touching it yourself so that your horse sees that it's harmless.

TIP

Many things on a trail can cause your horse to spook. Hikers with big orange backpacks, mountain bikers, and people walking their dogs are potentially scary things to a horse. If you come across someone on the trail that your horse is nervous about, ask the person to stand aside and refrain from moving so the horse can pass. Encourage that person to say something; many horses relax after they realize the strange object in front of them is the person they just heard speak. If the horse still is too frightened to approach the person, you may have to get off and lead the horse.

REMEMBER

If the horse seems deathly afraid of something and refuses to calm down, take the horse away from the object so he doesn't become panicky and dangerous. Ask a trainer or experienced horse person to help you work with the horse to get him over this particular fear.

Running away

Most well-trained horses wouldn't dream of running away with a rider, but on occasion, something can frighten a horse so badly that he takes off in a blind panic.

If you ever lose control of a horse that is running away with you, do your best to stay on without squeezing your legs against the horse (which only makes the horse go faster). Pull back on the reins in a continuous motion, and say "Ho" again and again in as calm a voice as you can muster. You also can try to turn the horse in a circle, because doing so often is a good way to slow the animal down. Turn the animal by pulling the horse's head around using one rein as you apply pressure with the leg on the same side as the rein you're pulling. Take this action slowly and gradually, however, because a sudden and dramatic jerk to the side while the horse is running can throw him off balance.

REMEMBER

If you have a horse that chronically runs away with you, you have a serious problem that needs to be handled by a professional trainer.

Refusing to move

When being ridden, horses sometimes refuse to budge. Because horses that are inclined to plant their feet usually are the kind that are good at sensing a lack of confidence in a rider, beginning riders often encounter this problem.

If you find your horse won't move when you first get up on his back, even though you apply leg pressure, you have a horse who isn't very responsive and is testing your authority. (Just to be on the safe side, have an experienced horse person observe you to make sure that you aren't doing something wrong.) You can deal with this problem by tapping the horse with your heels and clucking to the horse to encourage the animal to move.

REMEMBER

If this doesn't work, get a trainer or experienced horse person to help you deal with the problem. Spurs and a crop may do the job, but you need help to properly use these devices.

Another situation where a horse may refuse to move is if the animal is afraid of something up ahead. You can tell the difference between the two kinds of refusals by looking at the horse's body language. A frightened horse holds his head up high, rotates his ears forward, tenses his body, and shows the whites of his eyes. If that's what you see, follow our advice under the earlier section "Spooking." If the horse seems relaxed but simply refuses to move, you have a resister on your hands.

Being "barn-sour"

A horse that refuses to leave the stable for a trail ride or fights you out on the trail in an attempt to get back home is considered *barn-sour*. Barn-sour horses are potentially dangerous and a real problem to retrain.

If you have a horse that is barn-sour, your first step is to make sure that the horse doesn't have a physical reason for his attitude. Have a vet examine the horse's mouth, poll, girth, and back to make sure that the animal isn't in pain.

If the horse is okay, then the attitude results from a lack of respect for rider authority or lack of confidence in the rider. You need to gain the horse's agreement before you can expect the animal to allow you take him away from the barn, a place that he associates with food and security. Start by schooling the horse at home, in an arena. Practice moving forward, backing up, turning, and stopping. The horse needs to follow your commands completely before you attempt to take him out on the trail. (Be sure to reward him with a pat and kind words when he does what you want.)

When you go out for the first time after a couple of months of schooling, go with another rider for your own safety, just in case the horse misbehaves. Remind the horse throughout the ride that you're in charge by asking him to stop and back up. When it's time to turn around and head for home, keep the horse's gait at a walk for the entire ride back to the stable. Avoid feeding the horse immediately after you return to the barn.

Barn-sour horses are notoriously hard to retrain. If none of the above work, you have to bring in a professional trainer.

Rolling

Rolling on the ground is a natural horse behavior. Horses do it to relieve itches and just because it feels good.

Rolling in a pasture or turnout is fine and dandy, but rolling when there's a rider aboard is not okay. Some horses do it because their training is lacking, and they aren't completely tuned into their riders. They come across a spot that looks good for rolling (sand is a favorite), and they decide to go down. Many horses like to roll in water, and will stop in the middle of a water crossing to get down in the water.

One of the least favorite experiences you can have on a horse is having one roll when you're in the saddle. You will fall off as the horse is making his way to the ground, making it unlikely he will actually roll on you. Still, it's no fun!

Learn to recognize the signs of a horse who is about to roll. If you are crossing water or a sandy section of the trail and your horse stops on his own, watch out. If he starts pawing at the water or the ground, rolling is imminent. Pull his head up and start kicking him in the sides. The only way to stop him from sinking to his knees is to keep him moving forward.

If your horse frequently rolls with you, he may have learned that rolling is a way to get rid of his rider. Bring in a professional trainer or other equine expert to help you deal with this issue.

Ignoring cues

Some horses just won't listen to you when you're riding them. They may not go forward, stop, or turn when you request. While not usually dangerous, this behavior can be very frustrating, especially for a novice rider.

Horses who behave this way are most likely in need of a training tune up. If you are learning to ride on a horse that is starting to ignore you, he may need some time with a trainer or more experienced rider who can let him know that he needs to respond to his rider's cues.

TIP

You may need to have an experienced rider get on him at least once a week while you are honing your riding skills. This will help him stay tuned into his training.

Chapter **17**

Staying Safe on (and around) Your Horse

Horses are a real joy to be around, but the fact is, they're much bigger than we are. The average horse weighs almost ten times as much as the average human female. Consequently, humans have to be careful around horses to make sure that equine bulk doesn't end up somehow becoming a liability to the human body.

In this chapter, we give you the details you need to be safe around horses, regardless of whether you're on the ground, in the saddle, alone, or with other riders. This chapter also gives you tips about how to keep your horse safe from himself, too!

Dressing the Right Way

Believe it or not, the clothing you wear around horses and your safety go hand in hand. Wearing — or not wearing — something when handling these cumbersome beasts can mean the difference between an ambulance ride to the emergency room and going to bed that night unscathed. We cover helmets, pants, footwear, and jewelry in the following sections. Be sure to check out Chapter 6 for additional info on what to wear when you're around horses.

Wearing a safety helmet

Probably the most important part of your equestrian wardrobe is the safety helmet, because it protects your skull and brain. A safety helmet can protect you in the following ways:

>> **On the ground:** If you're planning to be around a horse that is known for being difficult to handle in certain situations (freaks out while loading in a trailer, has a deadly fear of clippers, needs to be given some bad-tasting medicine), wearing a helmet is a wise precaution.

>> **In the saddle:** The fall from a horse's back is not a short one, and it can take place at a high speed. In far too many instances, helmetless riders have fallen off their horses, hit their heads on a hard surface, and sustained permanent brain damage. Wearing a safety helmet designed specifically for equestrians can protect the most important part of your body — your brain.

REMEMBER

Wearing a safety helmet is especially important for children. Their heads tend to be more breakable than those of adults.

Putting on the proper pants

The same people who ride around in tennis shoes usually ride in shorts, too, and that's something we don't recommend. In fact, we're not really sure how people can stand riding in shorts. Bare skin has to rub against a leather saddle only for a few minutes to make you realize that shorts and riding don't go together. An occasional bareback rider can get away with riding in shorts, although that rider's skin doesn't stand a chance should he or she take a spill.

TIP

Your discipline determines the type of pants you should wear when you're riding. English riders wear riding tights or breeches. If you're riding western, wear jeans. No matter what, closely fitted pants are best to prevent chaffing when you ride. For the greatest comfort, buy pants made specifically for riding.

Stepping into safe footwear

You should always wear protective footwear whenever you're around horses. Always wear heavy leather boots whether you're planning to ride your horse or just going for a simple grooming session. Follow these rules to keep your tootsies safe:

>> **Wear heavy boots when working with a horse on the ground.** Heavy boots are the footwear of choice for horse handlers, for good reason. Sooner or later, if you spend enough time around horses, one of these hulks is going

to step on your foot. When he does, you'll have a few hundred pounds of pressure on your foot, conveniently punctuated with a weighty metal shoe if the horse is shod. If you're wearing tennis shoes or sandals when that happens, you'll be walking around with a cane for quite a while. We recommend wearing equestrian boots, which are heavier than your average shoe, for maximum protection.

>> **Wear riding boots when you're in the saddle.** You may've seen people wearing tennis shoes while riding — a major no-no in our opinion. Riding boots are made especially for equestrians. They're the safest form of footwear to don when riding. One reason: Riding boots have a heel that keeps your foot from sliding through the stirrup and trapping your leg — an important factor if you happen to fall from your horse.

Protecting Yourself on the Ground

You may not believe it, but the majority of your time around horses is spent on the ground and not on the horse's back. You'll groom, feed, and clean up your steed on a regular basis. All this time spent in close proximity to your horse means greater odds that an accident will occur when on the ground. That is one reason why ground safety is so important with horses.

Another reason is that when you're on the ground, you're vulnerable to being stepped on, kicked, or knocked down. Sure, if something goes wrong while you're riding, the ground is at least a five-foot plunge away. But when you're handling a horse from terra firma, more stuff can happen besides falling.

In the following sections, we cover how to stay safe when you're cleaning a horse's hooves, moving around a horse in close quarters, leading a horse, and tying a horse. We also give you a few warning signs that a horse is about to make a sudden move. Check out Chapter 13 for more info about handling a horse from the ground.

Caring for a horse's hooves

Horse people always are fussing with their horses' feet. Horses constantly are getting their feet cleaned, their fetlock (or ankle) hair clipped, or their hooves brushed with hoof polish.

The human urge when performing these hoof-related tasks (covered in Chapter 9) is to kneel down on the ground next to the hoof. After all, from this vantage point, you can get your work done much more efficiently. The problem, though, is that kneeling close to a horse's feet puts you in a dangerous position from which you can't easily retreat. If the horse suddenly moves to the side, he'll likely step on you. If something scares him, you can even be trampled.

TIP

When you're fiddling with a horse's hoof, bend or crouch instead of kneeling. By bending or crouching, you keep your feet beneath you, enabling you to move quickly if the horse's body comes your way.

REMEMBER

Don't hold the hoof by the tip; doing so won't give you enough control if the horse tries to pull the leg away from you. If you hold the hoof only by the tip, you can easily lose your grip on the hoof and drop it on your own foot! Instead, keep your hand under the hoof or under the pastern (the area between the hoof and the ankle). Check out Chapter 2 for information about horse and hoof anatomy.

WARNING

Keep your head out of the field of motion of the horse's leg; don't put your head in an area where the horse can inadvertently conk you if he quickly jerks up his leg to remove a fly or reacts to the tickle of clippers. As a child, one of your authors (okay, it was me, Audrey) stuck her head behind a horse's foreleg while clipping a fetlock and received a lump on her forehead roughly the size of Nevada.

Being in close quarters with a horse

When you find yourself in close quarters with a horse, the reality of the horse's mass becomes much more apparent. Your comparatively minute human form can easily be squashed if a horse pins you up against a wall.

Horses that are well trained know not to encroach on a human's space. With these horses, you can merely push on the too-close body and cluck your tongue to get the horse to move over and give you some breathing room. Unfortunately, not all horses have learned this lesson, which is why you don't need to take chances with your well-being by being in a position that enables a horse to pen you in.

Follow these simple rules to keep yourself out of harm's way in close quarters:

>> **Never wedge yourself between a horse and an unmovable object.** Find a way to move the horse if you don't have enough room to gain access to that side of the horse.

>> **Never enter a box stall with a strange horse without finding out whether the animal is okay with your presence.** Nothing is more terrifying than finding yourself inside a small space with a horse who hates you. If the horse pins his ears back, rushes at you, or turns his rear end toward you, stay away!

>> **Never stand directly behind a horse (especially one you don't know).** Although occurrences are rare, horses occasionally kick out at people walking or standing behind them, causing serious injury to the kick's victim.

If you need to pass close behind a strange horse, make sure that the horse knows you're there, and pass *very* close to the horse's body, nearly touching it. That way, if the horse tries to kick, you'll make contact only with the point of the hock (or elbow of the back leg) and not the full-force of the hoof.

>> **Make sure that the horse sees you:** When you approach a horse that is loose in a stall, speak to the animal first so that it turns around and looks at you before you enter the stall. Gauge the horse's body language to make sure that it is calm and receptive to your approach. (Read on, or see Chapter 2, to find out more about how to read equine body language.)

Recognizing some dangerous horse moves

Horses typically make maneuvers that put the humans in jeopardy — although to be fair to the horses, the poor creatures rarely mean to do so. Regardless of whether the move is accidental, you still need to know what to watch out for. Being forewarned about the following moves, you stand a better chance of getting out of the way in time:

>> **Head jerks:** If a horse wants you to get away from his head, he jerks it upward and sometimes to the side at the same time.

>> **Swinging body:** Remember these key points about equine physics: When a horse's front end moves to the left (he pivots on his front hooves), the back end concurrently moves to the right, and vice versa.

>> **Sideways moves:** If a horse is afraid of something on his right-hand side, he will leap to the left, and vice versa.

>> **Forward we go:** If something spooks a horse from behind, the horse moves forward — rapidly.

>> **Backward ho:** If you approach a horse from the front, holding something he wants to avoid (medication, dewormer, or a frightening object, for example), he will throw up his head, place all of his weight on his haunches, and back up at significant speed. If this happens, don't pull back on the lead rope because doing so only excites the horse more and causes further backing up. Just relax, hold the scary object behind your back, talk softly to the horse, and give the big guy a chance to settle down.

Leading a horse

Leading sounds simple enough — just walk with the lead rope and the horse follows, right? Well, yeah, but what happens if something scares the horse from behind? If you're directly in front of the horse, you're going to get trampled.

REMEMBER

Horse people have discovered that leading a horse from his left side, just at the shoulder, considerably reduces your chances of being stepped on or run over. If you lead a horse in this way, the worst thing your horse can do is step on your foot, and that's much better than being trampled, don't you think? (See Chapter 13 for an illustration showing the correct way to lead your horse.)

Here are some other points to remember when leading a horse:

>> **Never wrap the lead line around your hand or hold a coiled lead rope.** If the horse pulls back or takes off, the rope will tighten around your hand and you'll get dragged along on a rough ride. Instead, hold the part of the rope near the horse's head in your right hand and make loops of the loose end to be held in your left hand.

>> **Hold the lead rope close to the halter.** Doing so gives you better control over the horse's head and prevents you and the horse from tripping over slack in the line.

>> **Never lead a horse with your hand in his halter.** If the horse pulls back or runs away, your hand can get caught and you can be dragged.

Moving around a tied horse

Many horses feel vulnerable when they're tied to a hitching post or crossties. Something about having their heads restrained can really set them off. Chapter 13 has even more details about tying up horses and dealing with scary behavior, but to avoid accidents, follow these basic rules of safety around tied horses:

>> **Use a short tie.** Whoever came up with the phrase "enough rope to hang himself" must have known a horse. If you tie a horse up at a hitching post with too much slack in the lead rope, the horse inevitably gets a foot hung up in the rope or ends up with the rope over his neck. Always tie a horse with a short rope (12 inches of slack is a good length) so he can't get himself into trouble.

>> **Use safety restraints:** When tying a horse to a hitching post or horse trailer, always use a safety knot. A safety knot enables you to quickly release a

panicking horse's lead rope. If you're cross-tying your horse, use quick-release snaps on crossties and light ropes that break easily if the horse pulls back.

>> **Never duck underneath a horse's neck to get to the other side (even though you may be tempted to and even if you've seen other people doing it).** Instead, take the long way and walk around the horse's front or back. Many horses don't mind a human walking under their necks, but enough do that you can end up with a panicked horse and a seriously injured human.

>> **Use the frontal approach.** All horses have a propensity for freaking out and pulling back when they're tied. If you've ever seen a horse throw all his weight on his hindquarters and rip a hitching post out of the ground, then you know that pulling back is a terrifying and dangerous habit. Some horses do it routinely, but others need serious provocation before pulling this stunt.

To avoid instigating a horse to pull back, always be slow and quiet when approaching from the front. If you need to move toward the horse with an object in your hand, watch the horse's body language carefully to determine whether the horse is scared and a pullback is imminent (see Chapter 2 for details on equine body language).

Being Secure in the Saddle

You can have plenty of fun riding a horse, but you need to keep safety in mind at all times if you're going to *continue* to have fun. Getting hurt is a sure way to ruin the party.

When riding, several different safety angles come into play, such as checking your tack and knowing the etiquette for riding with other people. Remembering all the stuff in the following sections may take some concentration at first, but in time, it will become second nature. (Be sure to flip to Chapter 16 for general information about maintaining control while you're riding.)

Inspecting your tack first

Having quality tack (riding equipment) in good condition is pretty important if you want to have a safe horseback ride. Just like the timing belt in your car's engine, tack can break at the most inopportune times if you don't regularly inspect it.

Before every ride, do a cursory inspection of your tack to make sure that no accidents are waiting to happen. See Chapter 6 for details on the following items:

>> **The bridle:** Check it to make sure all the buckles are tightly fastened and all the pieces are securely attached. Check the stitching to make sure it's secure, too.

>> **The girth:** On English saddles, inspect the buckles on both sides to make sure they're securely fastened. On western saddles, be sure that the left latigo strap is snugly tied to the saddle's D-ring, and the right latigo is securely buckled to the cinch.

>> **The stirrups:** On English saddles, check to make sure that the stirrup leathers are securely buckled and positioned on the stirrup bar. For western saddles, inspect the stirrup buckle to make sure that it isn't loose.

TIP

If you ride English, run your stirrup irons up the leathers so the irons are flush with the saddle skirt after you dismount from your horse. Doing so keeps your irons from catching on anything and from banging around on your horse.

Riding by yourself

Riding alone can be a peaceful and relaxing experience. However, to ensure your safety when you're out on your own, follow these precautions:

>> If you'll be out on the trail, make sure that someone knows where you are going and when you plan to return.

>> Carry a cell phone with you. Keep the cell phone on your body, not attached to your saddle. That way, if you and your horse part ways, you still have a way to call for help.

>> Stay on marked trails and make certain that you have a map or know your way around.

Flip to Chapter 16 for additional safety info.

Riding with other horse folks

Riding is most fun when done in groups. Cruising the trail with your friends or riding around an arena with a buddy or two can be a blast. In situations where horses are kept at boarding stables and boarders share riding facilities, riding in groups is not usually a choice; it's mandatory simply because everyone is forced to use the same arenas and trails at the same time.

Riders must take certain safety precautions when they're around other riders and horses. Following the rules in the next two sections helps keep you and your fellow equestrians safe and makes you a popular person around the barn!

Adhering to arena etiquette

Riding is a dignified hobby, and riders are expected to behave a certain way when they're astride a horse. Nearly all of these expected behaviors are related to safety, and they keep you in good stead with the other riders and their horses.

Follow these guidelines when riding in an arena with other riders:

>> **Slow going:** When a cowboy wants to go for a ride in the movies, he simply leaps onto his horse and gallops off in a flurry. In the real world, equestrians don't behave that way unless they want to do harm to their horses and incur the wrath of everyone around them.

When you first mount your horse, walk slowly to the riding arena. Don't trot or canter through the aisles of the stable, and don't stress your horse by tearing off into a gallop from a standstill. This behavior labels you as a yahoo and puts you and your horse in all kinds of physical danger.

>> **Stay back:** When you're riding in a head-to-tail situation, such as around the perimeter of an arena, keep your horse several feet away from the horse in front of you. Most horses tolerate other horses behind them, but some won't. As a result, crowding can end up with your horse being kicked and even seriously hurt.

TIP

If you have a horse who kicks when other horses get too close, tie a red ribbon at the base of your horse's tail to warn other riders at horse shows, organized trail rides, or other events. Likewise, when you see a horse with a red ribbon on another horse's tail, stay back! The ribbon is a warning that your horse may be kicked if you get too close.

>> **Rear approach:** If you're approaching a horse from behind while in the arena, do *not* run your horse up behind that rider. If you do, the rider's horse almost certainly will spook or take off, and you can be the cause of a serious accident. Instead, if you're trotting or cantering and going to pass another rider from the rear while that rider is at the walk (her horse is walking), give the rider and horse a wide berth so you don't upset the horse.

>> **Passing:** When riding in an arena, you're bound to find yourself going in one direction while one or more riders are traveling the opposite way. When passing one another in a riding arena, riders use the *left-shoulder-to-left-shoulder* rule. When riders pass one another in opposite directions, their left shoulders pass each other. To accomplish this feat, you may need to stay close to the rail so the approaching rider passes you on your left. Or, you may need to stay to the inside

or middle of the arena, away from the rail, so that an approaching rider passes you to the left. (To understand left-shoulder-to-left-shoulder passing, see Figure 17-1.)

If you need to be on the inside or outside when you're approaching a horse and the left-shoulder rule won't work for some reason, you can call "inside" or "outside" to the other rider to indicate which direction you plan to go.

>> **Be quiet:** Again, the movies come to mind. Yelling, hollering, and yee-hawing while on horseback is fine for actors in westerns, but in real life, doing so frightens your horse, annoys others, and makes you look like a dope.

The only exception to this rule is when you're riding in gymkhana or some other competitive speed event where such vocalizations are considered acceptable because they encourage the horse to go faster (see Chapter 18 for more details about such events).

FIGURE 17-1:
Two riders pass left shoulder to left shoulder in an arena.

© John Wiley & Sons, Inc.

Staying safe on the trail

Trail riders also need to follow these rules of safety and etiquette while enjoying the wide-open spaces:

» **Approaching:** When approaching another rider, if you are trotting or cantering, slow to a walk and maintain your slow pace until you're well past the other horse.

» **Passing:** When passing another rider on the trail, do so at a walk. Many horses can become out of control when they hear or see a horse trotting or cantering up behind them. Make sure the rider ahead of you knows where you are and is okay with you passing, especially on narrow trails.

» **Spooking horses:** If you see another rider in trouble ahead of you on the trail, either offer to help (if you can) or stop and wait until that person has his or her horse under control before you proceed.

» **Be quiet:** When passing another rider, avoid yelling or doing anything that may spook the other horse.

» **Blind curves:** When riding on narrow trails in high brush, go slowly around blind curves. This rule is for your safety as well as the safety of others, because a hiker, a mountain biker, or another rider may be approaching from the opposite direction.

» **Dismounted riders:** Don't try to ride past someone who is attempting to mount a horse. Your horse's movement may prompt the other horse to start walking off while the rider is trying to get on. Stop and wait until the rider is safely in the saddle before proceeding.

IN THIS CHAPTER

» **Investigating the different disciplines**

» **Understanding breed shows**

» **Checking out trail events**

» **Getting the scoop on jumping competitions**

» **Looking at combined training**

» **Having fun with competitive driving**

Chapter **18**

Competing on Horseback

C ompeting with your horse as your partner is one of the most fun and rewarding things you can do. When you show your horse, you put your best feet forward (both your own and your horse's), telling the world "Hey, look what we can do!"

Equine sports run the gamut from simple stuff you can do with just about any horse to complex events that require teams of horses. Some are easy to participate in; others call for a considerable investment of money and time. To find the sport that's best for you — and your horse if you already have one — you need to do some research along with some soul-searching. You can begin your search for the right competition for you and your horse by reading the descriptions we provide in this chapter. The descriptions should give you a good idea of what's out there.

Keeping Traditions in Hunt Seat

Hunt seat is extremely popular in the United States and is the discipline you most often see when people are described as "riding English." These riders always use a hunt-seat saddle, with a seat that is inclined slightly forward (see Chapter 6 for details on the hunt-seat saddle and other hunt-seat gear).

The apparel worn in hunt-seat classes is based on British tradition, too. A hunt cap, hunt jacket, breeches, and high boots are the apparel judges expect to see in the show ring. This extremely traditional sport discourages individuality in appearance, so nearly all riders at a given show are dressed in almost exactly the same way.

Hunt seat is primarily an arena sport, offering both *jumping* and *flat* classes. The latter are classes that don't involve jumping. (Check out "Getting a Leg Up on Jumping Competitions" later in this chapter for details about events focusing just on jumping.) If you choose to compete in hunt seat, you'll compete in a variety of classes. *Equitation* is one of these classes, where your riding form is judged either "on the flat" or "over fences." In *hunters,* your horse's form and style over a course of fences is judged. The fences range anywhere from 2 to 4 feet in height, depending on the class. These classes are staged within different divisions, based on the age and expertise of either the horse or the rider.

REMEMBER

You can ride and compete on just about any breed in hunt-seat classes, although judges typically favor Thoroughbred and Thoroughbred-type horses, because these horses are the types traditionally used in the sport of fox hunting. That said, you will see many different breeds competing in hunt seat classes. Because jumping is an integral part of hunt-seat showing, you must become a proficient rider over fences.

Performing Precisely in Dressage

One of the oldest equine disciplines in the world, *dressage* dates back to training methods developed in ancient Greece. One of the Olympic disciplines, dressage has been a traditional favorite in Europe for centuries and has gained considerable popularity in the United States.

Dressage, an English discipline, consists of a series of subtle maneuvers that are meant to emphasize the horse's natural movement. Horse-and-rider teams perform in a rectangular-shaped arena marked with a series of letters. These letters act as targets for particular movements during the dressage test. Think of dressage movements as the compulsory exercises in figure skating, with the letters functioning as spatial indicators of correct positioning of horse and rider.

REMEMBER

Dressage riders at the lower levels of competition can wear the same type of clothing seen in the hunt-seat arena: a hunt cap, hunt jacket, breeches, and boots. In the upper levels, however, protocol dictates that dressage riders wear a black derby, white breeches, a black jacket, black high boots, and a white stock tie.

In dressage, horse-and-rider teams compete at different levels depending on their expertise. Judges score dressage participants on how close to perfect the horse-and-rider team performs precise movements. The scores of competing riders are compared at the end of each competition, and the riders with the highest scores in each level receive awards. Though riders technically are competing with each other in these events, most are more concerned with improving their own individual scores from one show to the next than they are about beating out the other riders.

REMEMBER

You can show horses of any breed in dressage, as long as they are physically and mentally capable of performing the required exercises. Thoroughbreds are popular in the sport, although warmbloods are most common in the higher levels of dressage competition because of their extraordinary athleticism.

Being Flashy in Saddle Seat

Saddle seat is one of the English disciplines, although the saddle for this type of riding is much different than hunt-seat or dressage saddles. Show saddles, as saddle-seat saddles are called, have a flatter seat than other English saddles. The saddle's construction forces the rider to sit far behind the horse's withers (the rise on the horse's back at the base of the neck), thus taking the rider's weight off the front part of the horse and encouraging the animal to show off the high action of his front legs.

Judging in saddle-seat classes typically is based on the horse's action or the rider's position in the saddle, depending on whether the class is a *pleasure class*, in which the horse is judged, or an *equitation class*, in which the rider is judged. The class you prefer to enter depends on a number of factors, including your and your horse's abilities. Many riders enter both types of classes.

For a horse to be successful in this discipline, he must be a flashy creature with animated gaits. In fact, horses in this event often have a perfect combination of charm, grace and energy.

REMEMBER

A saddle-seat horse usually is ridden with a double bridle (see Chapter 6 for a description of the double bridle) because it enables the rider to exert more control over the position of the horse's head. Saddle-seat riders are expected to wear derbies, jackets, and jodhpurs (special riding pants) in the show ring.

Competitions in the saddle-seat discipline most commonly are seen at breed shows at which competitors are riding gaited horses, such as the American Saddlebred, the Tennessee Walking Horse, and the Racking Horse. Some all-breed shows and single-breed shows also stage saddle-seat classes for Arabians, Morgans, and some other flashy breeds. You also see classes for saddle-seat riders at shows for gaited breeds, and at many single-breed and all-breed shows. A variety of different saddle-seat classes usually are offered, depending on the breed and type of show.

Working with Special Skills in Western

The western discipline developed more than a hundred years ago in America from the cowboy's need for a safe and comfortable way to ride horses among vast herds of cattle. This legacy is not lost in the modern world today: Many western events — specifically rodeos — feature classes designed to test the cattle skills of today's horses and riders. Even those classes that don't involve actual cows have a basis in working with cattle.

In most western classes, you see a very specific type of horse. You won't find many lanky Thoroughbreds or cobby Welsh Ponies here. The Quarter Horse dominates this discipline, although other western-type breeds like the Paint and Appaloosa also are common.

The following sections describe the most popular classes in western riding.

Pleasure classes

Western pleasure, along with its cousins western horsemanship and western equitation, are the most popular classes in western showing. In these events, riders demonstrate their own riding skills and the abilities of their horses. Horses in these events are expected to carry their riders quietly, comfortably, and obediently, all on a loose rein.

In western pleasure classes, horses are judged for their slow, steady movement and ability to carry their necks at the same level as their backs. The horse's conformation (the way he's physically constructed) weighs heavily in the judging because only horses built a certain way are capable of the movement required of a western pleasure horse. In western equitation classes, however, the emphasis is on the rider's riding skills and position in the saddle, rather than on the horse's conformation and movement. In horsemanship classes, riders must demonstrate that they can efficiently put their horses through a series of gaits and maneuvers. Horses in horsemanship classes must be obedient, responding quickly to their riders' cues.

Western riders must be good riders to be successful, and they must enjoy wearing a western hat! Both horse and rider apparel are important in these classes, especially in western pleasure. Expensive, silver-laden saddles and bridles are common, and riders are expected to wear a hat, fringed chaps, western boots, and a western vest or riding jacket.

Showmanship

Many of the riders who compete in pleasure and horsemanship classes also participate in western showmanship classes. In western showmanship, competitors don't actually ride the horse. Instead, they handle the horse from the ground and present him to the judge. The judge evaluates the handler's ability to show off the horse (make him look his best). The horse's conformation is not judged, although having an attractive and obedient horse certainly is helpful.

Any western-type horse can compete in western showmanship. Horses wear a special show halter, and handlers are expected to wear a western hat, a western vest or show jacket, long pants (jeans or special slacks made just for this class), and western boots.

Gymkhana

The faint of heart need not apply for the exciting, fast-paced sport of gymkhana (or gaming, as it's known in some parts of the United States). If you decide to compete in gymkhana, you'll find yourself galloping at top speed across arenas, making sharp turns while trying to beat the clock.

You typically see two gymkhana games at horse shows and rodeos, where gymkhana is especially popular: barrel racing and pole bending.

>> In *barrel racing classes,* metal or plastic barrels usually are set up in a clover pattern. The horse-and-rider team runs through the pattern at top speed, making a complete turn around each barrel as they pass it.

>> In *pole bending classes,* a series of poles are set up in a straight line, and the horse-and-rider team weaves in and out of the poles at a gallop.

Competitors ride the barrel racing and pole bending patterns one horse-and-rider team at a time. To pull off these feats, gymkhana horses are trained to make balanced turns and respond quickly to their riders, all the while going as fast as they possibly can.

REMEMBER

Gymkhana is a popular sport for good reason: Not only is it exciting to perform and to watch, but it's also accessible to many equestrians. Although it can be more dangerous than some of the other tamer western events, kids, especially, love gymkhana because it's so much fun. Gymkhana horses don't have to be expensive or highly trained to be successful at local events, and costly tack and attire are not necessary, because no dress code is enforced in the ring. Rider and horse simply need to be athletic and dedicated to the sport to succeed.

Western dressage

A fairly new discipline that is growing in popularity is western dressage, a sport that combines the principles of traditional dressage with western tack and apparel. Any breed or type of horse can compete in western dressage, and no fancy saddles or bridles are required. Good, clean, and functional western tack is all that's needed.

The elements of western dressage are similar to those of traditional dressage. Both disciplines look for balance in the horse along with a regular cadence and lightness in movement. The levels in western dressage are different from those in traditional dressage, however, and emphasize movement and maneuvers needed in a western working horse.

Just as in traditional dressage, horses competing in western dressage are scored according to how well they perform during a basic test. At the lower levels, competitors perform at a walk, jog, and lope. Higher-level competitors perform more complicated maneuvers also seen in traditional dressage tests.

Reining

The sport of *reining* is a western event that arose from the discipline's working legacy. Originally used as a way to maneuver horses around cattle, reining has become a challenging sport that requires substantial training for horse and rider. Reining horses are asked to perform spins, circles, and sliding stops at the slightest cue from the rider.

Reining horses are judged on their ability to execute the various reining maneuvers with ease and grace. In traditional reining classes, the horse-and-rider team performs maneuvers and patterns alone in an arena before a judge. A newer event called *freestyle reining* requires the horse-and-rider team to perform to music. A popular favorite among spectators, the horse-and-rider teams sometimes wear costumes that coincide with the rider's musical theme. In freestyle reining, spectators usually decide which team wins the class with the help of an applause meter.

Other than the costumes for freestyle reining, reining horses and their riders require no special attire. Neat, well-cared-for tack and western clothing is all that judges expect in the show ring.

Trail class

Good trail horses are willing to negotiate just about any obstacle you put in their way. This concept is the basis for the trail class that you find at many western shows. In this arena event, horses have to cope with a variety of objects that can possibly show up on the trail.

Trail class exhibitors compete one at a time in an arena that is set up with an obstacle course. Typical obstacles include a gate to open and close; a mailbox to open; and a tarp, a small bridge, and wooden poles laid on the ground to walk over.

REMEMBER

For a horse to be successful in trail classes, the animal must be very obedient, responsive, and willing to trust the rider's judgment. The horse must also be proficient at a maneuver called the *side pass,* which enables the horse to move in and around pole obstacles by walking sideways. Good trail horses also are skilled at backing up on command.

Trail classes require no special apparel, although successful horse-and-rider teams usually wear show tack and western show attire.

Cow classes

A number of different cow classes exist. Some require no direct contact with the cow, but others are rough-and-tumble events that cause the cow quite a bit of angst (and which get many animal rights activists up in arms) and sometimes result in broken bones for the rider. If you're interested in showing in cow classes, gauge each sport individually and pick the one that's best suited to you. Following is a review of the most popular cow classes that are commonly seen at horse shows and rodeos. Keep in mind that Quarter Horses, Paint Horses, and Appaloosas dominate these sports.

TIP

Because cow classes are based on the working cowboy tradition, fancy tack and clothing are not expected in the ring. All that cow classes require are good working gear and typical western clothing.

Cutting

Cutting is one of the gentlest of the cattle classes, requiring no direct contact with the cow. The sport has its roots in the 19th century, when the task of cutting individual cattle from the herd was part of a cowhand's job. In those days, cutting was a basic skill for every cowboy and his horse.

Today, cutting has been refined to a delicate art. The horse-and-rider team is placed in a pen with a small herd of cattle and asked to separate a cow from the group. Because cattle stick together at nearly any cost, separating one of them from a herd is a real challenge for the team. The horse and rider are judged on how fast and effectively they move the designated cow away from the group. Judges look for horses that are athletic and have innate *cow sense,* which is almost a psychic ability to know what the cow is going to do next.

What's interesting about this sport is that the rider's primary job in cutting is to not interfere with the horse. The rider simply tells the horse which cow to cut, and the rest is up to the horse. After the horse knows which cow needs working, the rider lets the horse do his job.

Team penning

Team penning is an exciting event that is rapidly growing in popularity. Unlike other western events, team penning calls for cooperation between several horse-and-rider teams. In team-penning classes, three teams must sort three designated cows from a small herd and pen them in a paddock located at the opposite end of the arena while making the fewest number of errors in the process. The penning is timed, and the fastest, most accurate team wins.

Much of the growing popularity of team penning is attributable to the fact that just about any horse can participate, as long as the horse is fast, obedient, and has good cow sense.

Calf roping

Calf roping is another cow class that sprung from the cowboy's job. In the Old West, cowboys used ropes to capture and restrain calves at branding time out on the range. These days, most calf roping goes on in the performance arena at rodeos, where it is a timed event.

Riders can choose from two types of roping: single roping and team roping.

>> In *single roping,* a horse-and-rider team chases down a calf in the arena until the rider gets a rope around the calf's neck. After the rope lands on the calf, the rider ties it to the saddle horn, the horse stops short, and the rider leaps off, runs to the calf, and ties three of her legs together. The object is to accomplish the task in the shortest amount of time possible.

Another version of single roping, called *breakaway roping*, doesn't require the rider to tie the calf. As soon as the rope becomes snug on the calf's neck, it breaks away from the saddle horn and the timer stops the watch.

>> Competitive *team roping* is performed by two horse-and-rider teams. One team is considered the *heeler*, the other the *header*. The heeler's job is to rope the calf's back legs, while the header gets the rope around the calf's neck.

Reined cow horse

Tradition is celebrated in *reined cow horse competitions*, where horses older than 3 are put to the test. In honor of the renowned California cow horse that served as the mount of the Vaqueros (Mexican cowboys) in the 1800s, reined cow horse contests illustrated the instincts and talents of today's western breeds.

Reined cow horse contests consist of three events, which must be performed by the same horse: herd work, rein work, and cow work.

>> *Herd work* consists of cutting (covered earlier in this chapter), where a single cow is removed from a herd and kept separate for a period of time.

>> *Rein work* involves performing a reining pattern and calls for deep training in this discipline (see the earlier section on reining for details).

>> *Cow work* is the part of the competition that requires the horse to control the movements of a single cow along a fence.

Cowboy mounted shooting

If you ever wanted to be a cowboy (or cowgirl), a sport called cowboy mounted shooting was made for you. This activity utilizes the tools of every well-respected cowboy and cowgirl: a good horse, a sure shot, and a penchant for excitement. Although cowboy mounted shooting is a competitive event, it is so much fun that it belongs in the category of pure enjoyment.

Cowboy mounted shooting is growing in popularity, in large part because the sport attempts to capture the excitement and spirit of the days of the Old West. Almost as fun to watch as it is to participate in, mounted shooting features skilled riders dressed in authentic 1800s cowboy apparel with their fast horses trained to run patterns at top speed. Riders use guns that are reminiscent of the type used by cowboys and cowgirls in the days of the Wild West. Just about any breed can be used in this sport.

Cowboy mounted shooting participants race against one another on horseback. The rider attempts to pop as many balloons as possible using a .45 caliber pistol loaded with blanks, while traversing a designated pattern on his steed at a dead run. Cowboy mounted shooters race each other two at a time, with the winner of each race advancing to compete with the winners of other match races until the two fastest and most accurate horse and rider teams battle it out for all the marbles.

Competitors participate in one of four divisions: men's, women's, seniors' (for folks ages 55 and older), and wrangler (for children 11 and younger). Children who participate in the sport use Hollywood-style cap pistols instead of real guns when they're on horseback, although they *are* allowed to fire .45 caliber pistols when shooting targets on foot and accompanied by a parent.

To be a part of cowboy mounted shooting, your biggest asset will be a penchant for speed, a desire to step back in time, comfort handling a gun, and good horsemanship.

Educating Yourself at Breed Shows

One of the benefits of owning a registered purebred horse is the opportunity that it gives you to compete in breed shows. Regional breed clubs, representing just about every popular breed, stage local shows at least once a year. These club shows are a great way to meet people in your area and educate yourself about your chosen breed (see Chapter 3 to find out more about different horse breeds).

The classes that breed shows offer depend quite a bit on the particular breed being exhibited. Clubs emphasize different aspects of their breed's history and style. Breed shows proffer a wide variety of classes, each of which is specific to the type of horse being shown.

Although we don't have room here to name every possible class you'll see at a show for a particular breed, a few popular classes are seen at a variety of different breed shows.

Halter classes

In *halter classes* — some of the most popular events at breed shows — horses are led into the ring wearing nothing but a fancy show halter. They are asked to stand and trot in front of the judge without a rider as the judge evaluates their conformation and movement.

Judges use a *breed standard* when evaluating horses in a halter class. The breed standard specifies the physical characteristics of a theoretically perfect example of the breed. We say theoretically perfect, because in real life, you won't find a perfect horse — every horse has faults. The judge has this standard committed to memory, and mentally compares each horse in the ring to this ideal.

Halter classes typically are broken down by age and gender. Horses as young as 4 months of age are shown in weanling classes that are divided by sex. Mares are judged together, as are stallions, and also geldings (see Chapter 4 for an explanation of these terms). Some shows even stage *Get of Sire* and *Get of Dam* classes, in which several offspring of a particular stallion or mare are brought into the ring for evaluation, with the award going to the parent horse.

Heritage classes

One of the most exciting breed classes for spectators and exhibitors alike is the heritage class. In *heritage classes*, horse and rider are decked out in dress that represents the breed's history.

Not all breeds have these classes, but the ones that do make the most of the event. At Morgan horse shows, riders wear apparel from colonial times, when the breed was first developed in Vermont. At Arabian breed shows, the heritage class features horses and riders wearing the spectacular native dress of the Bedouins. The cast of *Lawrence of Arabia* had nothing on the participants in these classes.

Some of the other breeds that feature heritage classes at their shows include Andalusian (Spanish tack and apparel), Paso Fino (South American or other Hispanic tack and costume), and Appaloosa (any costume representing the breed's history).

TIP

In heritage classes, the emphasis is on the authenticity and attractiveness of the tack and dress. People usually make their own apparel and horse clothing for these classes, because no stores sell ready-made heritage class garb (although some specialty catalogs can provide many of the bangles and fabrics you need).

Enjoying the Great Outdoors at Trail Competitions

Not all equine competitions happen in a show ring. In olden days, most horseback riding took place out in the wilderness, on trails that had been forged by mounted travelers or by migrating game. Riding on these trails was both exciting and challenging, and only the toughest horses and riders survived the harshest journeys.

Decades later, horse people who appreciate this legacy developed several events that celebrate trail riding while also adding a competitive factor: endurance riding, Ride and Tie, and competitive trail riding. This section looks at these sports, which do not require any formal apparel or specific tack.

Endurance riding

The sport of *endurance riding* has grown in popularity during the past 30 years. The sport's most noteworthy event, the Tevis Cup, takes place annually in Northern California and receives international coverage. Hundreds of smaller, local events are conducted around North America every year.

The object of endurance riding is to cover a given number of miles on horseback in the shortest amount of time. Endurance competitions often consist of 50- to 100-mile-per-day rides, or multiday rides that usually cover 50 miles per day over a period of from four to six days. The horse-and-rider team that gets to the finish line first is the winner. (Mandatory veterinary checks are given throughout the competition, and only horses that are considered physically fit are allowed to finish the event.)

REMEMBER

Endurance riding calls for a horse-and-rider team that is extremely fit and athletic. A team must undergo serious training in the form of conditioning over a period of months before it can compete in an endurance ride. This rigorous type of riding calls for a horse that is extremely well conditioned and comfortable on the trail. Riders must be fit, too. Imagine sitting in the saddle for 100 miles with only a few short breaks in between. Achieving that kind of muscle strength and stamina takes considerable work.

All lighter-weight horse breeds can participate in endurance competition, although Arabians dominate the sport because of their great capacity to travel long distances. Horses in endurance rides are dressed in any type of tack that the rider prefers, although most use specially made endurance saddles and halter/bridle combinations (see Chapter 6 for details on riding equipment).

Ride and Tie events

Ride and Tie events are an exciting sport that requires two humans and a horse to make up a team. An endurance race of sorts (see the previous section), Ride and Tie competition requires one person to be on horseback while the other is on foot. The human team members take turns riding and running across courses of 20- to 40-miles in length. Vet checks are conducted periodically to ensure the horse's safety.

In Ride and Tie, human team members must alternate riding and running, but the amount of time that one team member can spend riding is almost unlimited. As long as both riders spend a given amount of time on horseback, they can break up the running and riding however they prefer.

In Ride and Tie, the winning team is the one that finishes first with a sound horse. This sport requires considerable conditioning by horse and human.

Competitive trail riding

Another sport that takes place on the trail is an event called competitive trail riding. *Competitive trail riding* is for riders who enjoy conditioning their horses for trail riding and want to hone those skills to a fine art. Competitive trail events consist of approximately 12- to 50-mile-per-day rides through various terrains. Unlike endurance riding, competitive trail events are not races. Instead of using time as a determining factor, judges evaluate horses primarily on their physical condition, but their obedience to the rider along the trail also is a determining factor in many events. Speed is not important, as long as the horse and rider complete the ride within the minimum and maximum time limits. A veterinarian judge periodically examines the horses throughout the ride to determine their fitness as the day progresses.

Just about any breed can participate in competitive trail riding. The rider determines the type of tack he or she uses, but most riders use endurance saddles and halter/bridle combinations.

Getting a Leg Up on Jumping Competitions

Jumping on horseback is one of the most exciting ways to compete with your equine companion. A few events call for jumping, which requires considerable skill and training on the part of both the horse and the rider.

Cross-country jumping

The practice of jumping on horseback started centuries ago when horses were the only form of transportation, and tree-strewn trails were the only avenues of travel. Cross-country jumping most resembles the type of jumping riders practiced before automobiles and paved roadways became a part of everyday human existence.

In *cross-country jumping*, horse-and-rider teams are expected to travel over a given distance and negotiate a series of jump obstacles in a specified amount of time. The obstacles on cross-country courses can be daunting: Trenches filled with water, huge wooden fences, and combinations of the two are only some of the obstacles placed in the horse's way. The animal is expected to jump over whatever he encounters without the least bit of hesitation.

REMEMBER

Just about any breed of horse can compete in cross-country jumping, as long as the animal is athletic and possesses considerable jumping ability. No formal rider apparel is required for this sport.

Cross-country competitions can be staged on their own or in conjunction with combined training events, because cross-country actually is the second phase of combined training (covered later in this chapter).

Show jumping

Show jumping is an Olympic discipline for daredevils. Horse and rider have to be courageous to excel in this sport, because show jumping demands that horse and rider teams negotiate some pretty high fences.

In show jumping, horse-and-rider teams are expected to jump a series of fences — ranging anywhere from 3 feet 6 inches in the novice classes to 6 feet or more in more advanced classes — as fast as they possibly can. In show-jumping competition, the horse-and-rider team that can jump the highest fences with the fewest *errors* (knocking down a rail or refusing a jump) in the fastest time is the winner. (In the event of ties, horse-and-rider teams participate in exciting "jump-offs," which require negotiating a smaller, much harder course in the fastest time.)

Horses shown in show jumping are outfitted with close-contact jumping saddles (a version of the hunt-seat saddle). Riders wear hunt caps or helmets, hunt jackets, breeches, and high boots. The color and styles of apparel in this class are not important and tend to vary from rider to rider.

REMEMBER

Show jumping is an Olympic sport, and at the top levels, warmblood breeds (see Chapter 3 for more information about warmbloods) often compete with great success in this event. At smaller local or regional shows, you may see other breeds in show jumping, too. Basically, any horse that is athletic enough to take the jumps can compete in this sport, regardless of breed. As a rider, you must also be athletic and pretty darn fearless.

Checking Out Combined Training

Combined training, one of the Olympic disciplines, also is known as *eventing* and *three-day eventing.* By any name, this activity is a challenging marathon that requires horses and riders to display a variety of skills. Many in the horse world consider this exercise to be the most difficult of all equine sports.

Combined training events consist of three days of competition.

>> On the first day, horse and rider perform a dressage test.

>> On the second day, horse and rider negotiate a cross-country jumping course that consists of a series of obstacles laid out over a set distance through the countryside.

>> On the third day, the team confronts a show-jumping course.

Because each of these days of competition exacts a toll on the horse-and-rider team's skills and energy level, combined training requires considerable stamina and versatility from horse and rider. (We cover all these individual events earlier in this chapter.)

REMEMBER

To compete successfully in combined training, rider and horse must be well trained, well conditioned, and eager to compete. A variety of good jumping breeds, like the Thoroughbred and warmblood breeds, are most often seen in combined training events.

The type of clothing that riders wear depends on the phase. The dressage and show jumping phases call for dress typical for these sports, although the cross-country phase allows riders to utilize tack and apparel that suits the individual team. (Safety helmets always are worn in the cross-country and show jumping portions of this sport.)

Steering Yourself Toward Competitive Driving

For equestrians who prefer to be behind the horse instead of on top of him, driving is an attractive sport. Older riders and physically challenged equestrians are especially drawn to competitive driving because it requires less athleticism than the riding disciplines. Driving competitions call for one or more horses to pull a two- or four-wheel rig. Most driving competitions in the United States call for one or two horses to a rig, but draft breeds often show in six- to eight-horse hitches (see Chapter 3 for information on draft breeds).

Many breed clubs encourage driving, and usually offer driving classes in their shows. The Morgan, American Saddlebred, Miniature Horse, and Arabian are some of the light breeds that can be shown in breed-specific driving classes, while all the draft breeds are routinely shown with heavy hitches.

The judging of driving, or harness, classes occurs in a variety of ways, depending on the type of rig and breed of horse. Arena classes usually are made up of flashy, animated horses. This type of driving generally features horses with high-stepping movements.

Driving marathons, which are the harness equivalents of cross-country jumping without the jumping (see "Cross-country jumping" earlier in this chapter) demand that horse teams pull rigs through a countryside course dotted with obstacles they must negotiate. Driving marathon teams must be extremely well conditioned.

Combined driving — another driving event — is an Olympic discipline that consists of three phases much like the combined training sport (see "Checking Out Combined Training" earlier in this chapter). In combined driving, a team of two to four driven horses performs the following:

>> Presentation and arena dressage on the first day, which consists of walking and trotting patterns

>> *Marathon driving* on the second day, which consists of traversing a six-mile course

>> Negotiating an arena obstacle course on the final day, which consists of cones set up in various patterns

WARNING

To compete in driving classes, horses must be specially trained to pull a rig. If you are serious about showing in this discipline, you must invest a good amount of money in a quality harness and rig in which to present your horse.

HITTING THE ROAD TO THE SHOW IN A TRAILER

Before you can compete, you have to physically take your horse where he needs to go, which means hauling your horse in a horse trailer. Some horse owners would never dream of not owning a trailer. Others get by just fine by paying other horse owners or professional towers for the service whenever they need it. Either way, here are some important factors to know about trailering. (See Chapter 6 for details on buying a horse trailer.)

- **Trailer safety.** Whether you're using your own trailer or renting someone else's, make sure that the trailer is in good condition. Make sure that floorboards are not rotted, that divider and door latches are working properly, and that the ramp springs are in good condition. Likewise, be sure that the trailer is big enough for your horse to travel in comfort and that it provides plenty of ventilation. And just in case of an emergency on the road, be sure to bring extra hay, water, buckets, a tire jack and lug nut bar, wheel blocks, a spare tire, and a longe line.

- **Learning to trailer.** Trailering a horse requires its own set of skills. Find a trainer or experienced person to help you learn to load and unload your horse, and hitch the trailer. You'll want someone to teach you to drive with a horse trailer, including how to back up. Practice before show day.

- **Loading the horse.** Not every horse is amenable to getting inside a trailer. Fear and/or poor training are at the root of most loading difficulties. No matter how badly you want your horse to get into a trailer, you cannot physically force him to load. The only way that a half-ton beast is going to get into that tin can is if he is properly trained to do so.

  Practice loading your horse in and out of the trailer long before show day. If your horse refuses to load, get the help of a horse trainer. Don't try handling the situation on your own or letting someone get involved who isn't knowledgeable. Poor handling of a horse that refuses to load only makes the situation worse. If you're unable to restrain him or need to load him in an emergency, call a veterinarian to sedate the horse.

- **Towing realities.** You need a powerful vehicle to pull a horse trailer. A loaded two-horse trailer weighs around 5,000 pounds or more. Don't try to pull this kind of weight with a standard SUV or small pickup truck. If you do, you're at serious risk for an accident. You'll need a1/2- or 3/4-ton pickup truck or SUV to tow safely.

- **Careful driving.** When you're pulling a trailer with a horse in back, keep in mind that the horse is struggling to keep his balance. Drive as carefully as you can, making your turns wide, slow, and gradual. Avoid short stops and quick accelerations.

- **Horse safety.** Horses can easily injure themselves when riding in a trailer. If you'll be going on a long haul, dress your horse with shipping boots (padded wraps that go around a horse's legs) and a head bumper (a padded helmet of sorts). If you are traveling in cold weather, considering covering him with a light blanket.

Chapter **19**

Riding for the Fun of It

The greatest thing about horses is how much you can do with them. The horse world is filled with all kinds of activities for those who ride — and even for those who don't like to climb on board but just enjoy being around horses.

In this chapter, we introduce you to several of the most popular and enjoyable noncompetitive equine activities. These activities are meant to let you spend time in your horse's company and have plenty of fun doing it. (For details on competitive activities, see Chapter 18.)

Riding the Trails

The number-one activity among horse owners throughout North America is trail riding, a hobby that takes both horse and rider into the wide-open spaces simply for the sheer joy of it. Whether you live in the urban wilds of New York City or the untamed wilderness of the Pacific Northwestern forests, trail riding is something you and your horse can enjoy together.

What trail riding is

Trail riding is a very old activity. Before the days of automobiles, riding a horse on the trail was usually the only way to get from point A to point B. Today, people trail ride just for the fun of it. Few activities are as relaxing and therapeutic as riding a horse out in the open. Horses have a way of helping humans feel connected to nature, and never is this truer than when you are riding on a shady, wooded trail or through a sweet-smelling meadow.

You can trail ride locally on your own or with a friend, or trailer your horse out to trail ride. You can also participate in group trail rides, which are organized events usually sponsored by a riding club.

How you ride on trails

Trail riding is a pretty simple activity. You just locate a trail, saddle up your horse, mount up, and start riding. Trail rides can be as short as an hour or as long as an entire day. Some trail rides even stretch out over a week or more. You just have to decide how much trail riding you want to do.

Short rides don't call for much preparation. Your tacked-up horse and an idea of where you are going is all you require. Assuming that trails are available in close proximity to where you keep your horse, you can probably ride to the trail head (the place where the trail starts). Otherwise, you need to trailer your horse to get there.

Don't forget your horse's comfort on the trail. Unless you're riding in extreme cold or desert heat, horse-eating insects are a problem in the wide-open spaces. Spray your horse with equine insect repellent before you go on your ride. If gnats are a problem in your area, you may even want to invest in a simple knitted or mesh bonnet that protects your horse's ears from these biting insects (available from tack stores, online, and in equine product catalogs).

TIP

If you plan to take longer rides, be sure that you and your horse are properly conditioned. The worst thing to do to a horse is let him stand in his stall all week and then get on him on a Saturday and ride him for four hours on the trail. He'll be sore and miserable the next day, and will be less than enthused the next time you come to take him out. Instead, starting at least one month ahead of time, gradually increase the time you spend riding by about 15 minutes each ride until you're doing at least two-thirds of the time and distance you plan to do on a long ride.

REMEMBER

On longer trail rides, make sure your horse will have access to water (particularly important if the weather is hot) and that you know where you're going in advance. Of course, you can always just go exploring, but make sure that you have an idea of how to get back to where you started. (A GPS trail app can be helpful to keep you from getting lost; Endomondo and Gaia are two.) Contrary to myth, horses don't always know the way back home, especially if you're on a trail the horse has never seen before. If you are going alone, be sure to tell someone where you're going and when you'll return, just as you would if you went hiking by yourself.

What you need

One of the nicest things about trail riding is you don't need a bunch of fancy stuff to do it. Here are the basic trail riding requirements:

» **A horse:** The most obvious thing you need to trail ride is a horse. You don't have to have a fancy animal that costs as much as a Mercedes. All you need is a quiet, obedient mount that is comfortable being ridden out on the trail. If you plan to go on long rides, your mount must also be physically fit.

» **Tack:** You shouldn't ride your horse on the trail without a saddle and bridle. You can use any kind of saddle for trail riding, although western saddles and endurance saddles are the most comfortable for longer rides and the tack of choice for those who do nothing but trail ride. The kind of bridle you use depends on what discipline you typically ride. Many trail riders use combination bridle/halters with attached lead ropes so they can safely tie their horses up during breaks on the trail. (See Chapter 6 for details on tack.)

REMEMBER

Make sure that whatever kind of tack you use is in good repair before you head out on a trail ride.

» **Clothes:** A park ranger may object if you try to trail ride in your skivvies, so clothes are a must. You'll need comfortable riding clothes if you plan to enjoy yourself. If you're riding in hot weather, wear a cool shirt that protects you from the sun but lets your skin breathe at the same time. In cold weather, wear layers of clothing to stay warm. Wear appropriate riding pants and high boots or paddock boots for safety. And don't forget your helmet. Taking a spill while riding on the trail is a constant concern, so protection for your head is a must. Helmets also come in handy when you ride underneath low-lying branches. (Check out Chapter 6 for more about riding clothes.)

» **Accessories:** All kinds of fun accessories are available to trail riders. The basic ones you need for longer rides are a saddlebag, a water bottle and holder, a hoof pick, and a small first-aid kit (see Chapter 11 for information on what a first-aid kit should contain). Your saddlebag can hold the hoof pick, the first-aid kit, your lunch, insect repellent, lip balm, a compass (if you know how to read one), and whatever other items you want to bring with you. The hoof pick is to remove any rocks that lodge in your horse's hooves. The water bottle and holder are for your hydrating needs, and the first-aid kit is to deal with any minor injuries (yours or your horse's) that occur on the trail.

TIP

Always bring a fully charged mobile phone with you on trail rides, and keep it attached to your body (not to the horse). In an emergency situation on the trail, a mobile phone can be a lifesaver.

>> **A buddy or two:** Riding alone on the trail can be relaxing and enjoyable, but going with a friend is always best, especially when you're first starting out as a trail rider. If an emergency arises — such as your horse becoming seriously injured or you falling and becoming immobile — having another person with you can make a big difference in the eventual outcome. Also, most horses are more relaxed on trail when riding with another horse.

Companionship is another reason to ride with a buddy. Trailing riding is a great way for horsy friends to enjoy each other's company.

Camping with Your Horse

If you love regular camping, then you will *really* love horse camping. Few things are as wonderful as waking up on a dewy morning in your tent and hearing your horse munching his hay just outside.

Horse camping is not a new activity. Before the days of cars, plenty of people on long journeys were *forced* to horse camp! Today, horse camping is a recreational activity and quite enjoyable at that.

What horse camping is

Horse camping is, simply, camping with horses. It has all the same elements as regular camping, except that your horse comes with you and you get to ride him on your camping trip. Horse camping can be done the same way as car camping, where you drive up to your campsite, or the same way as backpacking, where you hike — or in this case ride — to your campsite.

Many people go horse camping in tents, with their horses tied or corralled nearby. Others bring RVs along so they can have a bit of luxury in the great outdoors. Many people think that the best horse camping comes when you sleep in a tent, though. When you tent camp, you stand a better chance of hearing your horse moving around through the night. Not only are you able to keep watch on your horse, but you also get neat, regular reminders that he's out there. Sure, if you're a light sleeper, you won't get a really good night's rest this way, but we think that knowing your horse is okay is better than sleeping like a rock. Save that for when you get home!

The biggest reason people take their horses camping is so they can go trail riding with them. Although most campers hike on camping trips, horse campers *ride*. Coming out of your tent in the morning, feeding the horses, cooking up your breakfast, and then heading out on the trail is a great feeling.

How you camp out

Camping with horses is a little more complicated than camping without them. You need to trailer the horse to the campsite and then secure the horse so he doesn't wander off in the middle of the night.

Horse campers use a few different ways to keep their horses close to camp:

- » **Campground corrals:** Campgrounds that are specially designated for horses often have permanent corrals made of pipe or other strong material. These corrals usually are secure, and they're your best bet when horse camping. When your horse is in a permanent corral, you tend to rest a little easier. You rarely see campground corrals in the backcountry, so keep that in mind if the security of a corral is important to you.

- » **Portable corrals:** A number of different portable corrals are on the market. They're designed to keep camped-out horses from leaving the campsite of their own accord. These portable corrals fold up; you can store them in a truck or horse trailer — or even in a horse pack (a backpack that goes on a horse whose job is to carry only equipment) — and then put them together when you set up camp. Some of them come with electricity so the horse gets a mild shock if he tries to bust out.

WARNING

The benefits of portable corrals are that they allow the horse freedom to move about and lie down. The problem, however, is that they serve mostly as a mental barrier rather than a physical one. If a horse really wants to get out of a portable corral, he will — and that includes the electric ones.

- » **Tie-outs:** Many horse campers opt to tie their horses to a tie-out, or picket line, strung between two trees or staked to the ground. For a horse to be safely tied out or staked out, the animal must be used to this kind of restraint. Otherwise, the horse may get himself tangled up, panic, and incur serious injuries. (See Chapter 13 for details on tying a horse properly.)

WARNING

The benefit of tying out a horse when camping is that it gives you the freedom to camp wherever you like, knowing your horse is secure. The downside is that the horse is at risk for getting tangled in the line.

- » **Trailer tying:** Some horse campers tie their horses to the rings on the side of a horse trailer with a long lead rope. This method is good for keeping the horses nearby and under close watch, but the problem is that the horse may get his lead rope tangled in the trailer wheel wells or on the trailer door latch. You need to use wheel well covers as well as towels and tape to cover any area where the lead rope can get hooked. If you tie the horse short so that his rope won't get tangled, you'll make it so that he can't lie down, something he needs to do to get valuable REM sleep. (See Chapter 20 for information on how horses sleep.) One solution is to use a high-tie, which is an arm that extends outward from the top of the trailer.

It's important to know how to tie a horse long with a lead rope and to use a high tie so that the horse remains safe. Ask an experienced horse camper to show you how to tie your horse using these methods.

What you need

To really enjoy your horse–camping expedition, you need the following:

>> **A plan:** Embark on your camping trip with a solid idea of where you're going and how to get there. Make reservations for your campsite, if possible, and be sure to choose a campground that has drinkable water, which is available to your horse at all times. Horses need plenty of fresh water to stay healthy, especially in hot weather.

>> **An experienced horse:** Horses that never leave the stable are not good candidates for horse camping. A horse needs to be used to traveling and riding on unfamiliar trails before you take him on an overnight trip. Your horse also needs to be relatively calm. Horses that frighten at the drop of a hat can be a hazard on a camping trip. The horse must load easily into a trailer, too, unless you want to begin and end your camping trip with a battle!

>> **A horse trailer:** Unless you plan to ride from the stable to the campground, you need a horse trailer to pull your steed behind you. Make sure that your trailer is in good shape before you head out on a camping trip (see Chapters 6 and 18 for more about horse trailers).

>> **Camping experience:** Don't make your horse-camping experience your very first camping experience. Successful camping — especially tent camping — takes some practice. Learn how to do it on your own before adding your horse to the mix.

>> **Camping buddies:** Plan your horse-camping trip to include a friend or two. Camping with friends is not only safer, but it's much more fun, too!

>> **Camping gear for humans and horses:** Don't throw all your gear together at the last minute. Make a list a week before your trip so you won't forget to bring something important.

Besides your usual camping equipment, your horse needs you to bring some stuff for him too: a halter and lead rope, saddle, bridle, saddle pad, grooming tools, a first–aid kit for the road, a water bucket, a supply of your horse's usual food, and insect repellent.

Strutting Your Stuff in Parades

If you've always wanted to participate in a parade but you couldn't walk and play the sousaphone at the same time, then a horse may be just the answer. Maybe you can ride and play the sousaphone, instead! Then again, maybe not, but have you ever seen a parade without horses in it? Probably not. Horses and parades go hand in hand. And as an equestrian, you automatically qualify to move from parade watcher to parade participant.

Riding in a parade can be tremendous fun. You and your horse are in the spotlight (along with your mounted comrades), and all you have to do is look good and wave.

What a parade equestrian unit is

The equestrian units that you see in big parades are part of organized riding groups. The riders may be members of a youth riding club, representatives of a breed organization, or part of a horseback drill-team group (see "Joining a Drill Team" later in this chapter for details on this type of group). The group's theme in the parade usually represents whatever the riding club is all about. For example, if the club is a military-style riding group for youngsters, the kids wear their uniforms and most likely carry flags. If the riders represent a local palomino horse club, all the horses are palominos tacked up in their finest garb.

How you participate in a parade

To become a participant in a big parade, you must be a member of an organized riding group, unless, of course, you are a celebrity or can justify participating on your individual merits. (If you have to think about whether you're a celebrity, chances are good that you're not.) In many smaller towns and cities, however, the parades are small and informal enough that individual riders can also sign up.

If riding in big parades is for you, your first step is to join a local riding group. Of all the different kinds of riding groups, pick the one that best suits your age group and riding interests. Your parks and recreation department should be able to provide you with some names and numbers of riding groups in your area.

REMEMBER

If you're joining an organized group primarily to ride in parades, make sure that parades are a regular part of the group's activities before you sign up.

Parade rides usually start early in the morning and last for several hours. The equestrian entries tend to be spaced apart in between other parade participants, and all participants start the parade route at a specific time. The equestrian entries are expected to ride through the entire parade route to the end with no breaks. You're on stage, after all, and parades don't have intermissions!

What you need

The basics of what you need to ride in a parade vary, depending on your riding group. However, some basics are the same for all parade riders:

>> **A good parade horse:** Parade riding is a blast for humans, but for some horses it can be nothing more than a series of nerve-wracking horrors. Marching bands, weird-looking floats, cheering crowds — all these things can drive certain horses to distraction. To have a good time riding in a parade, you need a horse that has a quiet personality and some experience with crowds and loud noises. Your riding group can help you mentally condition your horse for parades, but you need to start with an animal that is relatively calm to begin with.

If you want to ride in parades, you also need a horse that loads into a horse trailer easily. The I'm-not-going-in-that-trailer attitude just won't cut it on the morning you're rushing to get to the parade grounds on time.

TIP

You don't have to own a horse trailer to participate in parades. Other people in your riding club will own trailers, and your horse usually can double up with one of theirs when you need to take them to the parade grounds.

>> **Nice tack:** If you want to ride in larger parades on a regular basis, you probably need to invest in a nice show saddle, complete with silver trimmings. Most — but not all — equestrians in parades ride in western show saddles. Check with your riding group to find out what type of tack your fellow members use for parades.

>> **Fancy clothes:** Again, what you wear depends on who you are riding with. If your group has a western theme, then some attractive western show clothes are in order. If you belong to a breed club, the group may prefer to dress in clothing that emphasizes the breed's heritage. And guess what you wear if your riding club is a military unit? If you said anything other than your uniform, drop and give us 50!

Joining a Drill Team

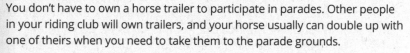

If your favorite part of Hollywood westerns is when the cavalry charges the enemy, then drill-team riding may be for you. Drilling on horseback is tons of fun and gives riders an opportunity to meet and socialize with others who enjoy the same activity.

What drilling is

Drilling on horseback is an old activity, one that goes back all the way to the Roman legions and possibly before. In the old days, when horses were the primary vehicles of war, drilling was used to train mounted soldiers to follow commands with precision and obedience.

Today, drill-team work is done mostly for fun. Riders who enjoy drilling get together and form clubs that practice at least once a week and sometimes more. They perform their precision drill work in parades, at county fairs, and during horse shows. Some local horsemen's associations have their own drill teams or can refer you to one in your area.

How you drill

Most drill teams consist of ten to twelve horse-and-rider duos, sometimes more. A drill caller gives drill commands that horse-and-rider teams follow. Each command requires a specific movement; when several horse-and-rider teams perform these moves in conjunction, the group ends up moving as a unit.

REMEMBER

Because of its military foundation, drill-team work calls for discipline on the part of the riders and obedience on the part of their horses. You need to memorize each maneuver and have your horse execute it at the moment you hear the command. You rehearse exhibition drills, and after a few practices with your group, you know exactly what is coming from the drill caller. The drills you perform at exhibitions and horse shows are the same drills that you and your team have performed at home many times over.

What you need

One of the perks of drill-team work is that you don't need to invest a whole lot of money to participate in the activity. The following is all you need:

>> **A cooperative horse:** Just about any horse can do drill-team work, as long as the animal is obedient and well mannered. Some horses really enjoy drill-team work and look forward to it (you can tell by their happy, relaxed attitude when they're working — see Chapter 2 for tips on reading equine body language). They like the excitement of working right next to other horses and the quick movements and sharp turns that drill-team work requires.

WARNING

Horses that don't like being in close proximity with other horses don't do well at drill-team work and can even pose a danger to others if they have a tendency to kick or bite other equine participants.

>> **Good tack:** You don't need fancy tack to ride in a drill team unless the riding group you belong to demands it. At least for practice, anyway, you can simply ride in a comfortable, well-fitted western saddle. (Some groups use English saddles or the old-style military McClellan saddles to more closely replicate the tack used by the cavalry.)

>> **An outfit:** Drill teams usually are color-coordinated, so your group probably will tell you what you need to wear when the drill team is performing for the public. You'll definitely need some kind of hat (most likely a western one), plus a shirt and pants in specific colors or even designs. This outfit is unlikely to cost you much money. You may even be able to pull it together from stuff you already have in your wardrobe.

Reliving the Past in Reenactments

Like to watch period films, particularly those set in Civil War times or during the Indian Wars? Then you've no doubt seen reenactors in action. Although the vast budgets of today's motion pictures may lead you to believe all those soldiers and cowboys you see on the silver screen are actors, in reality, they're usually mounted reenactors, or riders who dress up in period garb and ride their horses in mock battles on a regular basis — whether cameras are present or not.

What a reenactment is

Reenacting famous battles has been the hobby of thousands of horsemen for decades. For that matter, non-horsemen play the part of foot soldiers in mock warfare. Reenactors live in all parts of the country and recreate battles from a variety of different wars and periods. Civil War reenactments are the most well-known, although reenactments of Indian and U.S. cavalry fights, Revolutionary and British battles, and scuffles from the Mexican-American War are among the many other events that are commemorated year-round in the United States by people who seem possessed by the spirits of those who have preceded them throughout history.

How you reenact

TIP

Getting involved with reenacting first means joining one of the many reenactment groups. They aren't hard to find if you have access to the Internet. Entering "reenactment" and "horse" and the name of your state in a search engine should give you a list of groups near you.

After you find out about reenactment groups in your area, contact one or more of them and tell them that you're new to this activity and would like to find out how their particular group works. After you get to know the group and what it does, you can decide what type of person from the past you want to portray. If the Civil War intrigues you, you'll need to decide if you want to be on the Union side or the Confederate side. If you like the idea of reenacting U.S. Cavalry battles, you'll have to decide which part you'd like to play in these events.

After joining a group, you'll discover all about how reenactments work and how you can incorporate your horse into them.

What you need

You need a love of history and a burning desire to relive the past to be a reenactor. You also need a sense of adventure and a bit of courage, because some of the battles that take place during reenactments can really get the adrenaline flowing.

The type of equipment and apparel you need depends on the reenactment group you join. Here are the basics:

>> **The right horse.** You'll need a horse that looks the part. If you want to represent a U.S. cavalry soldier, you need to have a horse that is bay, chestnut, or black. The U.S. Cavalry did not use Appaloosas and Paints, so those breeds won't fit in with the group. If, however, you want to help reenact shootouts between outlaws and sheriffs, the color of your horse won't be that important.

   Your horse needs to be calm and steady because reenactments often involve the sound of gunshots, galloping out in the open, and even battling on horseback. Special training will likely be needed so your horse can participate.

>> **The right equipment.** Your horse also needs tack that is appropriate to his position within the reenactment. If he's a cavalry horse, he needs a regulation cavalry saddle and bridle. You'll also need the appropriate gear for yourself, such as a sword, rifle, and any other accoutrements carried by cavalry soldiers. The reenactment group that you join will help educate you about the kind of tack you need.

>> **The right apparel.** Clothing is an important part of reenacting, and you'll be expected to purchase a uniform or other apparel to look the part. The reenactment group that you join will help educate you about the kind of apparel you need.

Having a Horsy Vacation

Can't get enough of your equine companion? Want to take that horse with you next time you go on vacation? Don't laugh — many people do just that, and have a great time, too! The practice of taking a horse along on vacation is becoming more and more popular every year. People are discovering that having their horse along on a trip — when they can do more than weekend riding — is just plain fun.

If your usual vacation spot is a beach in the Bahamas, you'll need to alter your plans a bit to accommodate your horse, but not by much. The number of neat places you can go with your horse in tow is amazing.

You can take your horse on vacation with you in one of two ways:

>> You can go camping with your horse in specially designated horse-camping campgrounds or in the backcountry (where the paved roads don't go). (See the section on horse camping in this chapter.)

>> You can trailer your critter to a horseback vacation resort that allows you to bring your own horse.

Even if you can't bring your own horse with you, you can still enjoy a great horsy vacation. Check out all your options in the following sections.

Towing your horse to a resort

Horse resorts are resorts with facilities and activities that are horse friendly. They usually are located in wilderness areas and feature homey, country-style themes. Many offer organized trail rides, riding lessons, and other horse activities. Many also offer a number of wonderful luxuries for non-horsy human guests.

Before you pick a horse resort for your vacation, do some research. First, figure out how far you want to drive to get there (remember, your horse will be in tow!). Then, start scoping out the horse resorts within that driving distance. The Internet is a great resource for this research. By putting "horse" and "vacation" plus the state of your destination in a search engine, you'll get a list of horse resorts to choose from.

WARNING

You can consider shipping your horse ahead of you by using a horse transportation company, and then flying to the resort yourself. This option will cost you a bit of dough, though, so be prepared.

Before you make reservations at any horse resort, ask these questions.

>> Can I bring my horse?

>> What health certificates are required?

>> Can you refer me to written information on the facility, including rates?

>> Can you provide me with some guest references?

>> Do you have what I want in a vacation?

Taking a trip without your own horse

If you can't take your horse with you, or would rather not go through the hassle of transporting your equine buddy, you can still have a horsy vacation. In fact, if you want to combine horses with your holiday, you have a plethora of options to choose from. Just put "horse" and "vacation" in any Internet search engine, and you'll see what we mean.

Horseback vacations come in many different styles. Some take place at resorts, where riding is one of several activities in which you and your family can participate. Others are intensive adventures where you ride for days on end while you see the countryside. International horse vacations are becoming very popular, and you can choose from trips like a weeklong ride through Mongolia, a horseback visit to Machu Picchu in Peru, or a horsy pub crawl through the Irish countryside.

REMEMBER

Spending time on a horseback vacation is a great way to learn to ride, provided you choose the right kind of vacation. A weeklong, training-intensive vacation can provide an incredible opportunity to learn while you get away from it all. If you just want to enjoy some new scenery on horseback, you can go to a dude ranch or other riding vacation facility where daily trail rides are the main activity.

Whatever horseback vacation you choose, be sure to research it first. Ask plenty questions and get referrals from other guests to make sure the vacation is everything that it's hyped up to be. Then pack your boots and your helmet and go have some fun!

5

The Part of Tens

Chapter **20**

Ten Horse Myths

Given how long horses have been a part of human culture, the fact that oodles of equine misinformation abound isn't surprising. Although the horse may not be as maligned as Sasquatch, the poor equine has suffered his share of unfortunate myths. As horse lovers, we're here to set the record straight regarding horses, their behavior, and various other stuff about them.

Horses Are Dumb

Horses are not the only nonhuman animals to suffer under this assumption. In fact, dogs seem to be the only species that isn't regularly thought of by humans as lacking in brainpower.

The myth that horses are stupid is a result of human misunderstanding of equine behavior. Humans tend to judge other animals by themselves, or at the very least, by man's best friend, the dog. After watching and interacting with horses for a short time, you realize that these animals are smart — often smarter than we would like them to be.

Horses are neither predators like dogs nor cognitive thinkers like humans. They are a prey species that has been designed by nature to function in a completely different way. The main purpose of nearly all of equine behavior is to survive in a potentially hostile environment. So, although horses may not be capable of sniffing out bombs like beagles or understanding the exact meaning of human language, their behaviors all add up to brilliance at the job of survival. See Chapter 2 for more information about equine instincts and behavior.

Horses Will Run Toward a Fire

We're not sure where this myth came from because we've never heard of a horse that ran toward a fire instead of away from it. Now it's possible that going back to the barn could make sense from the horse's perspective in certain circumstances because horses that have lived their entire lives in box stalls (an unnatural way to keep a horse, by the way) associate those stalls with safety. The instinct to return to a place of safety during a frightening moment dominates a horse's thinking. A horse doesn't have the reasoning power to understand that the barn is no longer safe because fire will soon consume it.

Horses Don't Sleep Lying Down

Because they're prey animals and need to make a quick getaway in times of emergency, horses have an amazing ability to doze on their feet. However, contrary to myth, they *do* lie down for heavy-duty shut-eye. For a horse to get the few hours of valuable REM sleep each day that is necessary for good health, he must either lie flat on his side or in a recumbent position with his nose resting on the ground.

Most Horses Are Mean

If you've ever ridden a horse that has treated you unkindly, you're probably surprised to see meanness listed in this book as a myth. Unfortunately, a great many people have had unpleasant first-time experiences with horses. Then again, most people have their first riding experiences at poorly run, rent-by-the-hour stables (something we vehemently recommend against in this book). Not realizing that the horses at many of these establishments are poorly trained and badly treated, these first-time riders get up on the animal expecting to have a pleasant experience and end up traumatized because the horse tries to rub them off on a tree, run away with them, or get down on his knees and roll while they're in the saddle.

Horses that behave this way are reflecting the unkind and callous way they've been treated by the people responsible for their care and by no means are the norm in the horse world. The great majority of horses are gentle, friendly, and willing to do anything asked of them, provided they're extended kindness and respect in return.

Horses Are Aloof

Human beings have a tendency to judge all other animals by the dog. Most dogs are happy, friendly, and demonstrative. When a dog likes you, you know it. That wagging tail and kissy tongue are hard to miss.

Horses, on the other hand, are different. Dogs are easy when it comes to love. With a horse, you have to earn it. And after you do earn that love and trust (and gaining such feeling from a horse is an honor and an accomplishment on your part), it will be expressed to you in subtle ways: a head gently pressed against your chest, a soft whinny, or a nuzzle with a velvet nose. Horses aren't aloof; they're simply more discerning and more subtle in demonstrating affection than your average canine.

Horses Vocalize a Lot, Just Like in the Movies

Next time you see a western, play close attention. You'll discover that the horses in the movie whinny every time they appear on screen. You won't see their mouths move, or witness any logical reason for their vocalizations. Instead, they'll just gallop into scenes, accompanied by the sound. Sometimes you'll hear the whinny as the horse comes to a sudden stop; other times, as the horse takes off at a mad gallop. Sometimes you'll hear the whinny when the horse is just standing there in the background, doing absolutely nothing.

In case you haven't figured it out by now, the horses in movies are not actually whinnying. Their neighs are equine sound effects that have been added by the filmmakers for effect. As you become more and more familiar with equine behavior, this constant cinematic whinnying will start to drive you crazy. You'll come to realize that horses whinny for only certain reasons: when they anticipate being fed; when they're greeting a friend; or when they're engaged in courtship or parenthood. They don't whinny when their actor-rider needs to make a grand entrance; they don't whinny when the director wants to make sure that the audience knows they're watching a western; and they sure as heck don't whinny with their mouths closed!

Horses Are Always Healthy

Horses, as a species, are plagued with all kinds of health problems, many of which have been exacerbated by domestication. The average horse needs to be seen by a vet every so often for minor problems, but plenty of horses come down with at least one major illness in their lifetimes. The term "healthy as a horse" to indicate someone in good health must have been coined by someone who never owned a horse! See Chapters 10 and 11 to find out more about equine health problems and how to prevent them.

They Shoot Horses, Don't They?

Well, they used to. A gunshot wound to the head at one time was the traditional method of putting a horse out of its misery. In some very rural places, shooting still is the method of choice for destroying a horse. But for the most part, an injection administered by a veterinarian is the most widely used — and most humane — form of euthanasia for suffering equines these days. See Chapter 11 for more about equine euthanasia.

Old Horses Go Off to the Glue Factory

This myth is a hundred years old or more, yet it still persists. In the old days, horses too old to work were sent to the glue factory for slaughter so their parts could be used to make glue. Today, natural glue is made mostly from the skin, bones, and hooves of cattle, which are by-products of the food-animal industry. Instead of going to the glue factory, unwanted horses these days are sent off to slaughter, where their meat is used mostly for human consumption in parts of Europe and Japan. Unlike the days of the glue factory, when only old horses were used for their parts, today's slaughterhouses receive horses of any age and condition. See Chapter 12 for more information about equine slaughter.

A Broken Leg Equals a Death Sentence for a Horse

Horses used to be routinely destroyed when they broke a leg because mending a fractured leg was notoriously difficult. The fact that equine legs are too big for casting and the unavailability of general anesthesia, sterile conditions, equipment large enough to handle a horse, and surgeons capable of performing the delicate surgery made the procedure fail most of the time. Attempts to fix broken bones often resulted in infection in the affected leg or severe founder in the opposite hoof, a result of bearing all the weight of the horse while the broken leg was healing.

Nowadays, through much work and determination in the veterinary profession, a good number of veterinarians are skilled enough to perform the necessary surgery. Equipment and metal leg implants also large enough for a horse needing care for a fracture are readily available. The problem is that this can all be very expensive, and many horse owners opt to have the horse euthanized instead.

Chapter **21**

Ten Great Movies about Horses

The combination of beauty, grace, and power in horses lends itself to the silver screen. Flowing manes and tails, galloping hooves, and big, expressive eyes make for great cinematography. This reality has not been lost on filmmakers who have been making movies about horses since motion pictures began.

You've no doubt seen many horses in the movies through the years. They're a staple in just about any adventure film that takes place before the turn of the 20th century, providing transportation for cowboys, crusaders, and ancient Greeks. In these films, horses provide a backdrop to lend credibility to the story. After all, you can't shoot a movie about an ancient battle without having horses in the picture.

Although the majority of movies containing horses aren't about the horses themselves, some movies have focused primarily on equine characters. Not merely vehicles on which to perch actors, the horses in these films are the stars. The stories center on their speed, courage, and huge capacity for love, and in the process, capture the essence of what horses are all about.

The film industry has produced scores of wonderful horse movies over the years. Here are ten of the best, in our opinion.

Black Beauty

The classic book *Black Beauty,* written by Anna Sewell in the late 1800s, has been made into films no less than six times since the first *Black Beauty* was released in 1917. The most recent version of the story came out in 1994 and is a great tribute to Sewell's brilliant novel.

Told from the point of view of Black Beauty, a black stallion living in Victorian England, the movie gives a sympathetic and realistic view of what it's like to be a horse. We watch as Beauty changes hands many times, never knowing what his fate will be and finding himself at the mercy of sometimes kind, sometimes cruel owners. The end of the film brings tears to even the most stoic horse lover.

The Black Stallion

Based on the first book in *The Black Stallion* series by Walter Farley, *The Black Stallion* the film, released in 1979 and produced by legendary film director Frances Ford Coppola, is a truly classic horse movie. Beautifully shot, the story centers on a boy named Alec and a jet-black Arabian stallion he calls The Black.

Alec and The Black find themselves shipwrecked on a desert island after the ship they're traveling on sinks in stormy seas. The two build a profound bond as they await rescue and return to civilization, where The Black becomes a racehorse like no other.

The Black Stallion Returns

Because of the huge commercial and critical success of *The Black Stallion,* Farley's second book in the series, *The Black Stallion Returns,* was made into a film in 1983.

In this movie, Alec and The Black are reunited. When The Black's original owners from the Middle East come to America to retrieve him, Alec stows away on a ship to Morocco to find his horse. The result is an adventure through the picturesque Sahara and a desert race between Arabian horses that is a definite must-see.

Hidalgo

If you love action, adventure, and horses, then you'll appreciate the 2004 film *Hidalgo*, starring Viggo Mortensen. It's the tale of a pinto mustang stallion named Hidalgo and his master, Frank, who travel to the Middle East to compete in a grueling race. The story starts out in the American West and ends in the sands of the Sahara.

Although billed as a true story by Disney, *Hidalgo* is actually a controversial film among some in the horse industry. Taken from the journals of Frank Hopkins, a horseman who lived in the 1800s, the events shown in the film cannot be corroborated, according to some researchers. Supporters of the film say Hopkins' journals are accurate, and a stallion named Hidalgo did travel to the Middle East in the late 1800s to compete against hundreds of Arabian horses in a 3,000-mile endurance race.

Regardless of whether you believe the story, *Hidalgo* is a great film for horse lovers. It features exciting racing scenes and beautiful horses.

The Horse Whisperer

Actor and horseman Robert Redford turned the best-selling novel *The Horse Whisperer* into a film in 1998. Starring Redford, Kristin Scott Thomas, and a young Scarlett Johansson, the movie centers around a girl and her horse as they struggle to recover from a horrific riding accident.

Horse people love *The Horse Whisperer*, in large part because of Redford's efforts in equine accuracy. Unlike many other films about horses, *The Horse Whisperer* is right on in its portrayal of horse actions and behaviors.

The Man from Snowy River

It's hard to find a horse person who hasn't seen and loved the 1982 version of *The Man from Snowy River*, an Australian film about a young boy named Jim Craig who's trying to save his family's farm in the picturesque outback. An old rancher, played by Jack Thompson, takes the boy under his wing and helps him become a skilled horseman.

The beautiful Australian scenery combined with some hair-raising chase scenes with wild horses leave a lasting impression of this film on all who see it.

National Velvet

One of the most famous horse movies of all time is *National Velvet*. Released in 1945 and starring Elizabeth Taylor and Mickey Rooney, *National Velvet* tells the story of a girl named Velvet who defies the odds and tackles the daring sport of steeplechasing on an amazing horse named Pie.

When Pie and Velvet enter the Grand National steeplechase, their skills at hurtling terrifying obstacles while galloping at full speed are put to the test. The two prove to be a dynamic team that gives the male riders and their horses a run for their money.

Seabiscuit

In the 1930s, when the United States was struggling with the Great Depression, a hero rose up from the West and gave everyone hope. This champion was a small chestnut stallion named Seabiscuit.

Based on the bestselling book by Laura Hillebrand, the movie *Seabiscuit*, starring Jeff Bridges, was released in 2003 and did an amazing job of capturing the mood of pre–World War II America. Although some of the horse details in the movie are a bit inaccurate, the film still does a great job of illustrating how the courage and heart of one horse can help raise the spirit of a nation.

Spirit: Stallion of the Cimarron

This beautifully animated film by Dreamworks Animation takes place in the Old West and centers on a young Kiger Mustang stallion named Spirit. Spirit lives a great life in the wild as leader of a band of mares until he is captured and made to work for the U.S. Cavalry. Because of his wild nature, Spirit butts heads with a colonel, who wants him shot for his bad behavior. Just as he's about to be executed, Spirit is rescued by an imprisoned Lakota boy named Little Creek who has escaped his bonds.

Spirit, written by mustang advocate John Fusco, is an acclaimed film that is praised by many horse people because of its accurate portrayal of equine behaviors. In fact, the animated image of Spirit is actually based on a real-life Kiger Mustang stallion also named Spirit, who is living out his life at the Return to Freedom American Wild Horse Sanctuary in Lompoc, California.

War Horse

When Steven Spielberg directs a movie, people pay attention. *War Horse,* released in 2011, is no exception. The story of a British boy named Albert and his beloved horse Joey who are separated during World War I, this highly acclaimed film features some incredible equine acting and edge-of-your-seat moments.

Based on a children's novel published in 1982, *War Horse* was nominated for six Academy Awards. Elaborate puppet horses were used in the making of the film to help keep the real equine actors safe. Spielberg became enamored of the living horses in the film, telling *Variety* magazine, "By the end of this experience, everybody had a new respect for the intelligence and the sensitivity of horses."

Index

About the Authors

Audrey Pavia is the former editor of *Horse Illustrated* magazine and an award-winning freelance writer specializing in equine subjects. She has authored articles on various equine topics in a number of horse publications, including *Thoroughbred Times, Horse & Rider, Appaloosa Journal, Paint Horse Journal, Veterinary Practice News, American Farriers Journal* and *USDF Connection* magazines. She has written six horse books besides *Horses For Dummies*, including *Horseback Riding For Dummies, Horse Health & Nutrition For Dummies*, and *Trail Riding: A Complete Guide.*

In addition to her experience as an equine writer, she is also a former managing editor of *Dog Fancy* magazine and a former senior editor of the *American Kennel Club Gazette*. She has authored more than 1,000 articles on the subject of animals and has written several books on various kinds of pets.

Audrey has been involved with horses since the age of 9. She has owned and cared for horses throughout her life, and has trained in both western and English disciplines. She currently resides in Norco, California, with her two Spanish Mustangs, Milagro and Rio.

Janice Posnikoff, DVM, is a highly respected veterinarian with over 20 years experience. She is a graduate of the Western College of Veterinarian Medicine, University of Saskatchewan, Canada. She was owner of OC Equine Vet Services in Orange County, California, practicing high-end sport horse medicine for 15 years. Returning to her home in Manitoba, she is now an associate at the province's top referral center, Elders Equine Veterinary Services, enjoying sporthorse practice, helping in surgeries, and adding leading-edge dentistry to her expertise. She continues to work as a contributing author to *Horse Illustrated* and other publications. To her many clients, she is known as "Dr. P."

Dedication

Audrey: To my parents, John and Haydee, for always encouraging my love for horses.

Authors' Acknowledgments

Audrey: Thank you to my editors Tim Gallan, Ashley Barth, Georgette Beatty, Tracy Boggier, Neil Johnson, and Kyle Looper; brilliant writer and friend Gina Spadafori; my husband, Randy Mastronicola; my attorney, Patricia Crown; technical editor Laurie Reese; my dear friend and constant support, Betsy Sikora Siino;

and my sister, Heidi Pavia, DVM. Heartfelt gratitude goes out to Gemma Giannini; Moira Harris; Lora Duckett; Jim Bennett of J. Bennett Farms; Lisa Scebbi of Diamond Elite Training; Sue Kellogg of Kellogg Equestrian Academy; Jeanne Smith and Paddy Korb of Amber Ridge Farms; Doug Kraus, Matt Rayl, and everyone at Serrano Creek Equestrian Center; Jenny Walker, Cathy Blakesley, Susan Cox, Elizabeth McCall, Buddy Zech, and Joe Allen of the Equestrian Therapeutic Horsemanship Center; Wendy Kaufmann of Rancho Extravaganzia Paso Finos; Carroll Brown Arnold of *America's Cutter* and *America's Barrel Racer* magazines; Diana Deterding of the Dymar Agency; Leslie Thompson of Leslie Thompson Training; Stacie Moriarity, Cindy Perez, and Janet Roberts; Pam Shannon of the Arabian Horse Registry of America; Tina Ashford of the American Saddlebred Association; Susan Bavaria of the International Arabian Horse Association; the staff at the American Morgan Horse Association, and the American Horse Council.

I must also thank the horses that have taught me so much throughout my life: Milagro, Rio, Red, Rosie, Peggy, Snickers, Bailey, Val, Bailey, Lucy, Spec, Chyann, Oash, Molly, Monday, Tommy, Inflation, Tejano, Amorita, Miguelena, Gitano Jevon, Charlie, Autumn, Coke, Pal, Flash, Magic, Abby, Evita, Teddy, Delilah, and Pepper. I don't know who I'd be without them.

Janice: Thanks to Henry Dodd, Dr. Rex Leach, and most of all, my mom and dad. You have all made me the vet I am today.

Publisher's Acknowledgments

Acquisitions Editor: Ashley Barth

Project Editor: Tim Gallan

Technical Reviewer:
  Laurie Reese (previous edition)

Production Editor: Magesh Elangovan

Special Art: Pam Tanzey

Cover Image: © Ilya Marchenko/Shutterstock

Leverage the power

Dummies is the global leader in the reference category and one of the most trusted and highly regarded brands in the world. No longer just focused on books, customers now have access to the dummies content they need in the format they want. Together we'll craft a solution that engages your customers, stands out from the competition, and helps you meet your goals.

Advertising & Sponsorships

Connect with an engaged audience on a powerful multimedia site, and position your message alongside expert how-to content. Dummies.com is a one-stop shop for free, online information and know-how curated by a team of experts.

- Targeted ads
- Video
- Email Marketing
- Microsites
- Sweepstakes sponsorship

20 MILLION PAGE VIEWS EVERY SINGLE MONTH

15 MILLION UNIQUE VISITORS PER MONTH

43% OF ALL VISITORS ACCESS THE SITE VIA THEIR MOBILE DEVICES

700,000 NEWSLETTER SUBSCRIPTIONS TO THE INBOXES OF

300,000 UNIQUE INDIVIDUALS EVERY WEEK

# of dummies

Custom Publishing

Reach a global audience in any language by creating a solution that will differentiate you from competitors, amplify your message, and encourage customers to make a buying decision.

- Apps
- Books
- eBooks
- Video
- Audio
- Webinars

Brand Licensing & Content

Leverage the strength of the world's most popular reference brand to reach new audiences and channels of distribution.

For more information, visit dummies.com/biz

PERSONAL ENRICHMENT

Staying Sharp
9781119187790
USA $26.00
CAN $31.99
UK £19.99

Facebook
9781119179030
USA $21.99
CAN $25.99
UK £16.99

Guitar
9781119293354
USA $24.99
CAN $29.99
UK £17.99

Investing
9781119293347
USA $22.99
CAN $27.99
UK £16.99

Beekeeping
9781119310068
USA $22.99
CAN $27.99
UK £16.99

Digital Photography
9781119235606
USA $24.99
CAN $29.99
UK £17.99

Meditation
9781119251163
USA $24.99
CAN $29.99
UK £17.99

Pregnancy
9781119235491
USA $26.99
CAN $31.99
UK £19.99

Samsung Galaxy S7
9781119279952
USA $24.99
CAN $29.99
UK £17.99

iPhone
9781119283133
USA $24.99
CAN $29.99
UK £17.99

Crocheting
9781119287117
USA $24.99
CAN $29.99
UK £16.99

Nutrition
9781119130246
USA $22.99
CAN $27.99
UK £16.99

PROFESSIONAL DEVELOPMENT

Windows 10
9781119311041
USA $24.99
CAN $29.99
UK £17.99

AutoCAD
9781119255796
USA $39.99
CAN $47.99
UK £27.99

Excel 2016
9781119293439
USA $26.99
CAN $31.99
UK £19.99

QuickBooks 2017
9781119281467
USA $26.99
CAN $31.99
UK £19.99

macOS Sierra
9781119280651
USA $29.99
CAN $35.99
UK £21.99

LinkedIn
9781119251132
USA $24.99
CAN $29.99
UK £17.99

Windows 10 All-in-One
9781119310563
USA $34.00
CAN $41.99
UK £24.99

SharePoint 2016
9781119181705
USA $29.99
CAN $35.99
UK £21.99

Fundamental Analysis
9781119263593
USA $26.99
CAN $31.99
UK £19.99

Networking
9781119257769
USA $29.99
CAN $35.99
UK £21.99

Office 2016
9781119293477
USA $26.99
CAN $31.99
UK £19.99

Office 365
9781119265313
USA $24.99
CAN $29.99
UK £17.99

Salesforce.com
9781119239314
USA $29.99
CAN $35.99
UK £21.99

Coding
9781119293323
USA $29.99
CAN $35.99
UK £21.99

Learning Made Easy

ACADEMIC

9781119293576
USA $19.99
CAN $23.99
UK £15.99

9781119293637
USA $19.99
CAN $23.99
UK £15.99

9781119293491
USA $19.99
CAN $23.99
UK £15.99

9781119293460
USA $19.99
CAN $23.99
UK £15.99

9781119293590
USA $19.99
CAN $23.99
UK £15.99

9781119215844
USA $26.99
CAN $31.99
UK £19.99

9781119293378
USA $22.99
CAN $27.99
UK £16.99

9781119293521
USA $19.99
CAN $23.99
UK £15.99

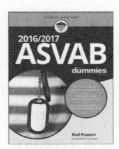

9781119239178
USA $18.99
CAN $22.99
UK £14.99

9781119263883
USA $26.99
CAN $31.99
UK £19.99

Available Everywhere Books Are Sold

dummies.com

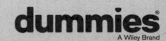

A Wiley Brand

Small books for big imaginations

9781119177173
USA $9.99
CAN $9.99
UK £8.99

9781119177272
USA $9.99
CAN $9.99
UK £8.99

9781119177241
USA $9.99
CAN $9.99
UK £8.99

9781119177210
USA $9.99
CAN $9.99
UK £8.99

9781119262657
USA $9.99
CAN $9.99
UK £6.99

9781119291336
USA $9.99
CAN $9.99
UK £6.99

9781119233527
USA $9.99
CAN $9.99
UK £6.99

9781119291220
USA $9.99
CAN $9.99
UK £6.99

9781119177302
USA $9.99
CAN $9.99
UK £8.99

Unleash Their Creativity

dummies.com